Digital Photography

A practical course for beginners

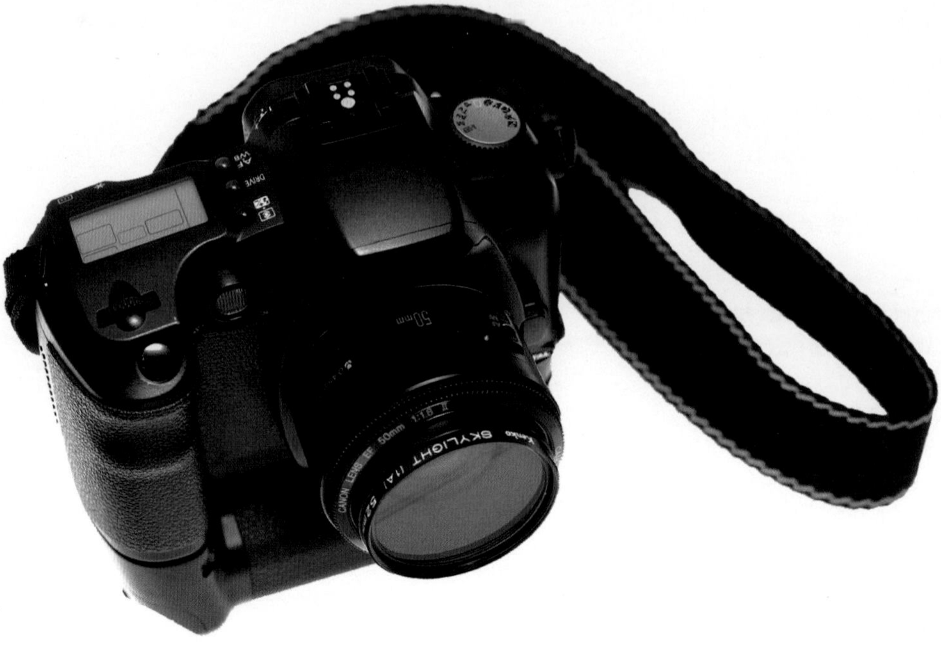

REBO
PUBLISHERS

Editor:
Jordi Vigué

Photo edition:
Santiago Garcés

Graphic Desing:
Paloma Nestares

Layout:
María Hernádez

Photo archive:
Gorg Blanc

English translation:
Abandon Agency, Prague, The Czech Republic

Typesetting and pre-press services:
A. R. Garamond, Prague, The Czech Republic

Proofreading:
Sarah Dunham

ISBN 90 366 1904 1

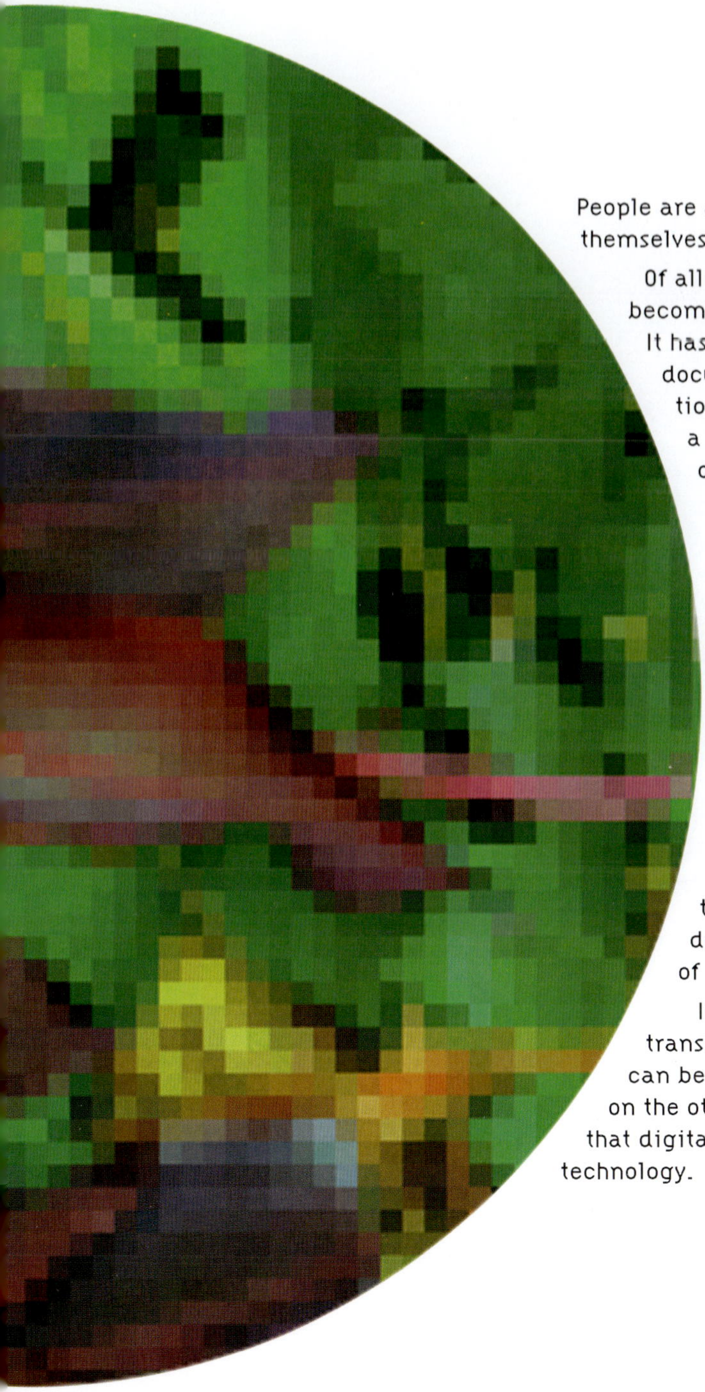

People are always in need of new ways to express themselves and communicate with others.

Of all the artistic means, photography has become the most popular with the general public. It has always been used for artistic expression, documentation, and the exchange of information. A camera catches a moment in time, a glimpse of a space, and the characteristics of an age with the movement of a finger.

Photography successfully supplements millennia of means of communication such as words, letters, and paintings, and in many cases replaces them.

Today the world of audiovisual communication exceeds our previous expectations. All of this development has been enabled thanks to the digitization of practically everything around us.

It is this global digitization that allows us to watch television, surf the Internet, or walk through streets virtually. And photography has also been engulfed in this development. By some accounts, 92 percent of all cameras sold are now digital.

If we bear in mind that a mobile phone can transmit photographs, and that these pictures can be viewed seconds after they were taken on the other side of the world, it becomes clear that digital photography is more than a nascent technology.

Digital photography: Basic concepts

What is digital photography?

The basic difference between digital cameras and refillable film cameras is that the picture is not recorded thanks to a photosensitive chemical layer, i.e., film, but through photosensitive sensors called CCDs (Charge-Coupled Devices) that transpose light charges to digital information.

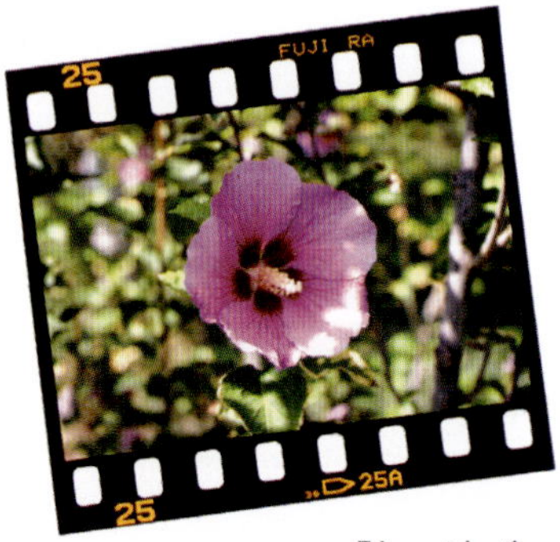

▲ Film with silver halide layer

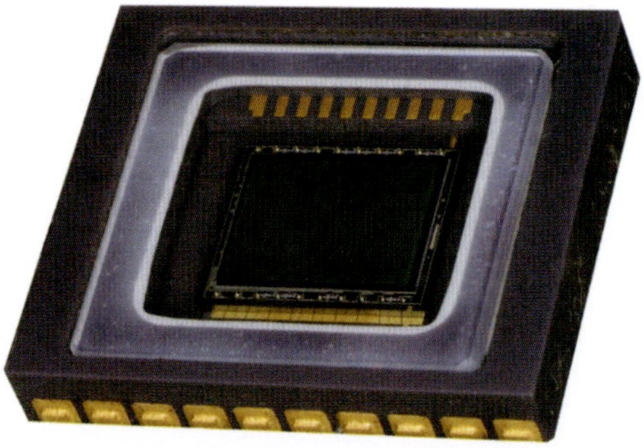

▲ CCD (Charge-Coupled Device)

Level of gray

A CCD is a chip made up of millions of small squares called pixels, whose function is to record light. Each of these pixels is covered by a color filter that can be red, green, or blue. The system that allows the pixels to convert gray shades to colors is called RGB (Red, Green, Blue). The filters allow the pixels to distinguish among colors. Without them the pixels would be able to receive the intensity of light in the range between white and black, in 256 shades of gray.

In the case of a very bright photograph, if the pixels did not have filters the result would be a picture in which white predominated. Conversely, a poorly illuminated scene would result in a picture in which dark gray and black predominated.

For this reason each pixel must be covered by one of three color filters - red, green, or blue - in order to be able to record the color of the relevant filter and not just a range of shades of gray.

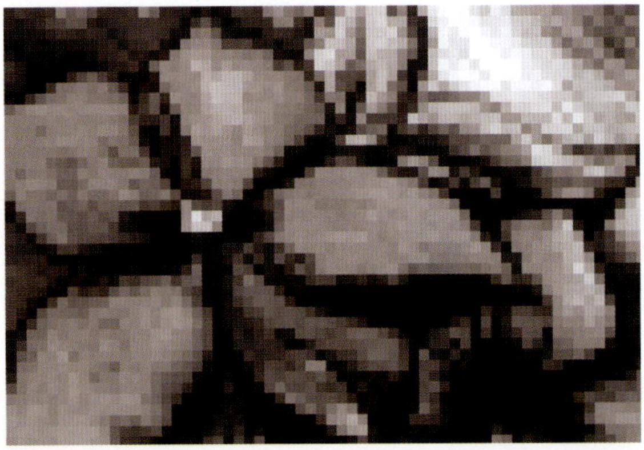

◂ CCD without RGB filter

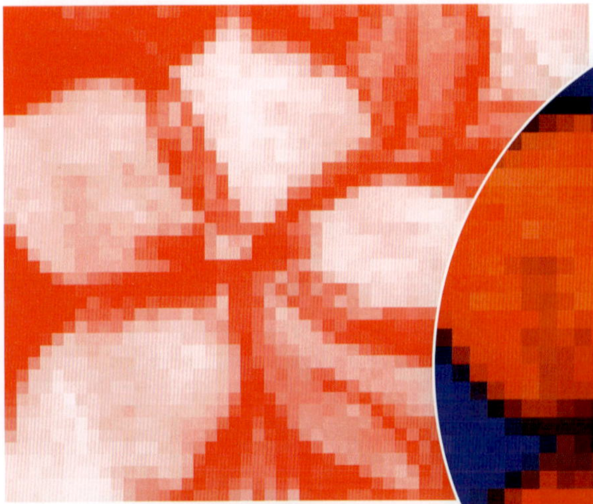

▲ Recording of pixels with red filter

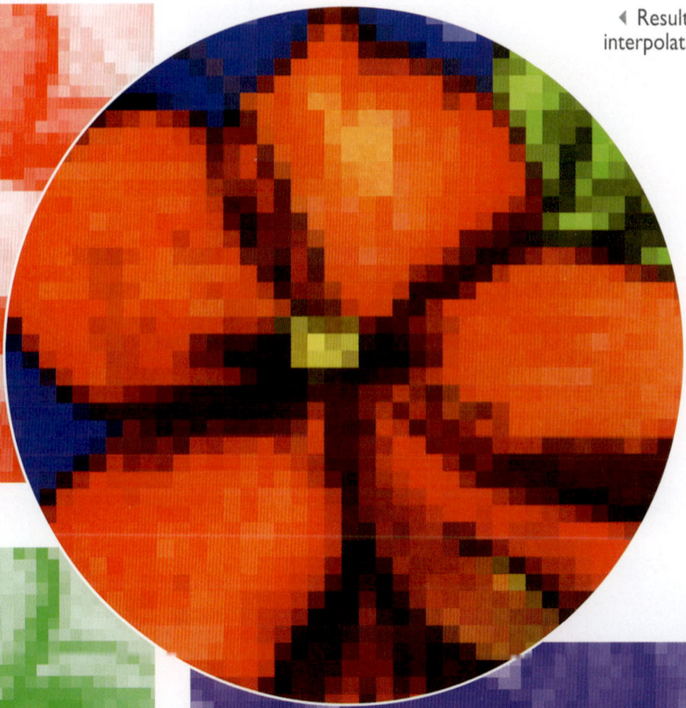

◀ Result of interpolation

▲ Recording of pixels with green filter

▶ Recording of pixels with blue filter

When each pixel has registered a color, a process called color "interpolation" begins, which makes it possible to take a photograph in the full range of color shades in such a way that the final result is not made up of only red, green, and blue.

This process is realized on the principle of the median value of the color created from the colors of the neighboring pixels that surround it.

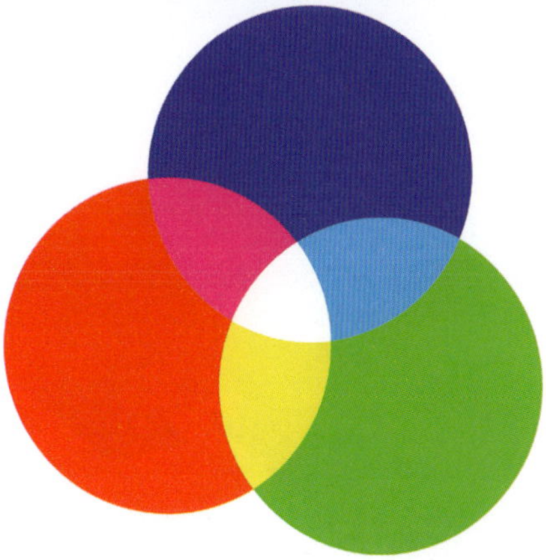

Photographed object

When the camera completes the interpolation process - so that the photograph can be made visible - it records the picture through a series of digital values that are transferred either to the camera's display or through a computer to a printer.

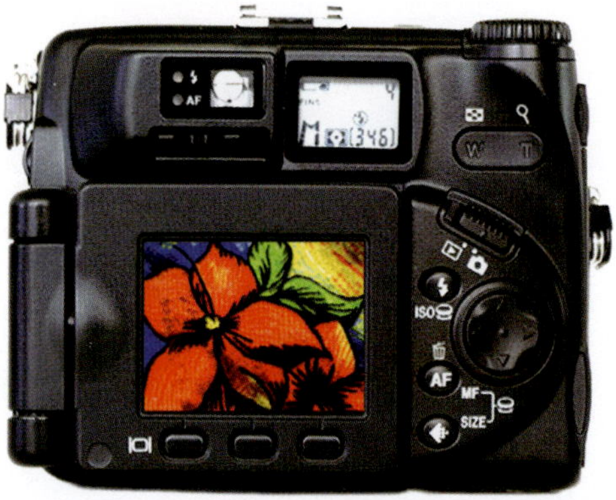

Imaging on the camera's display

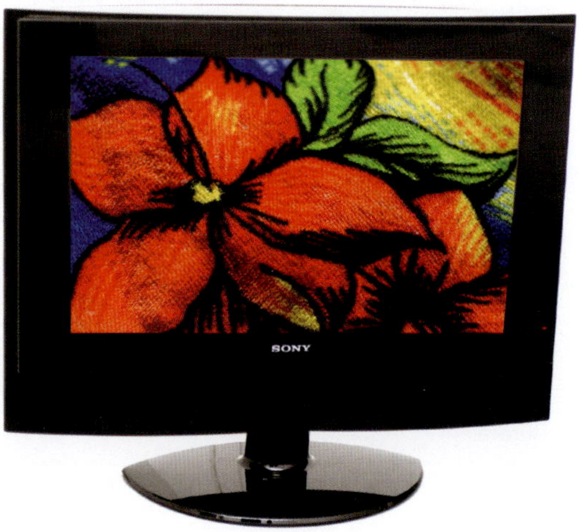

Imaging on the computer monitor

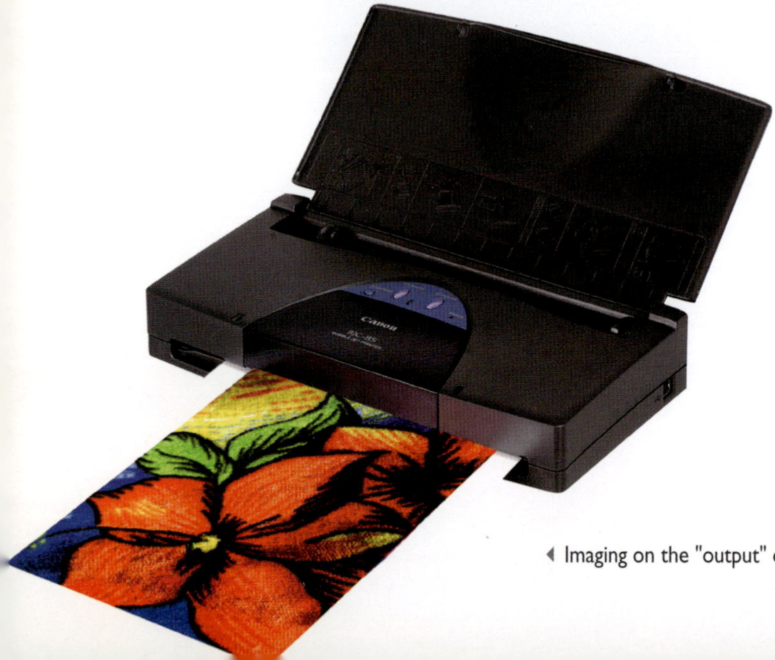

Imaging on the "output" of the printer

The difference between digital and classic photography based on silver halide

To a great extent digital photography owes its success to the fact that thanks to the display on the camera it is possible to make the picture visible just a few seconds after it has been taken. Conversely, classic photography has lost its popularity because of the long process that must be followed before a picture can be looked at.

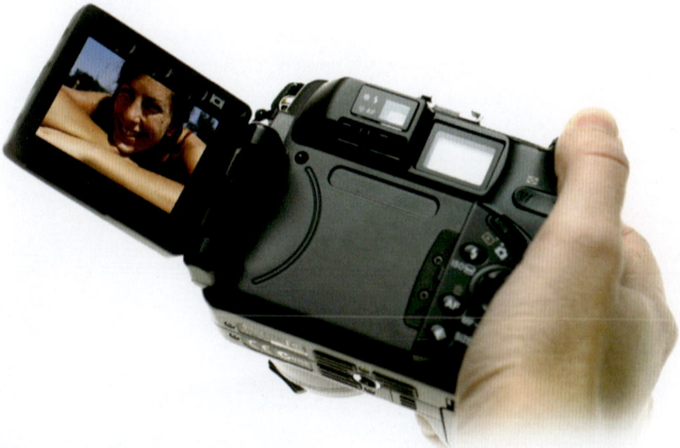

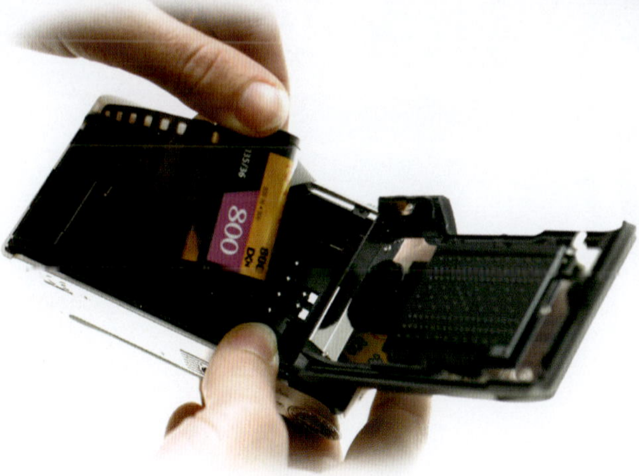

When a classic camera is used it is necessary to remove the exposed film and develop it, and only then can one judge whether the photograph has come out or not.

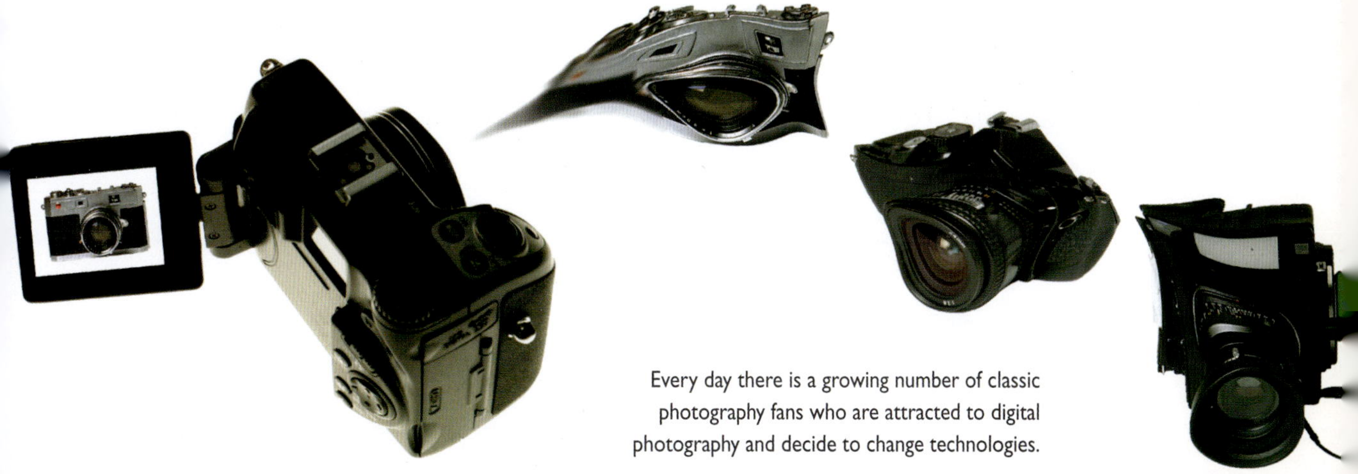

Every day there is a growing number of classic photography fans who are attracted to digital photography and decide to change technologies.

Although digital cameras are still more expensive than classic cameras, once you have bought one you don't need to buy any film or pay for the development of unsuccessful photographs.

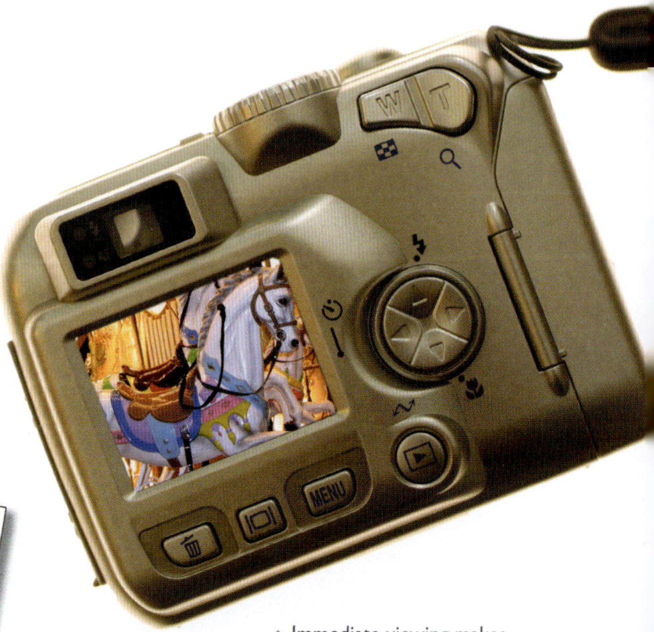

Immediate viewing makes it possible to correct mistakes without delay.

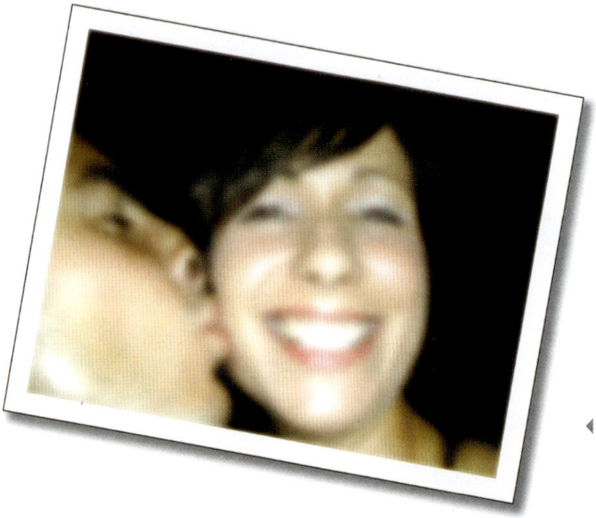

If you have to wait for the picture to be developed and printed you can be unpleasantly surprised.

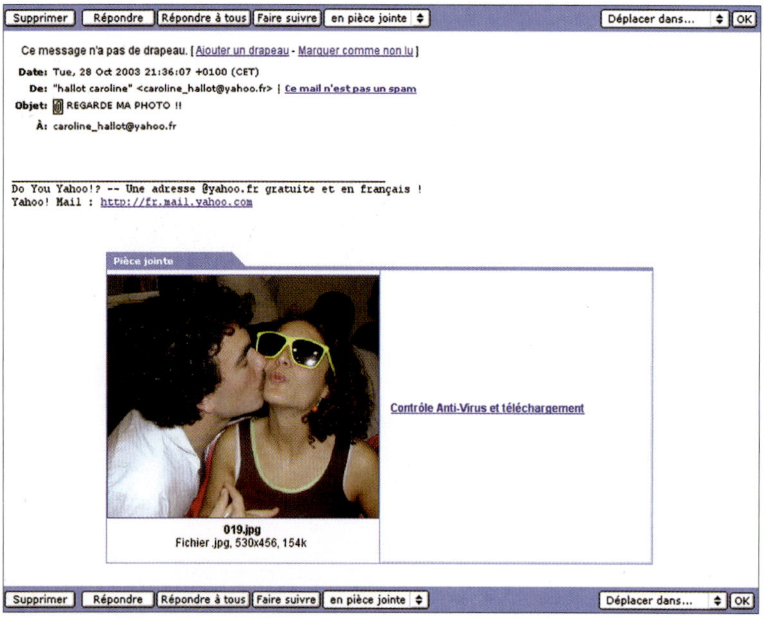

It is now possible to conveniently send pictures by e-mail.

Today access to a PC and the Internet is possible nearly anywhere in the world. For digital photographs various types of files can be used that make possible both professional publication and simple perusing of memories within family circles or among friends.

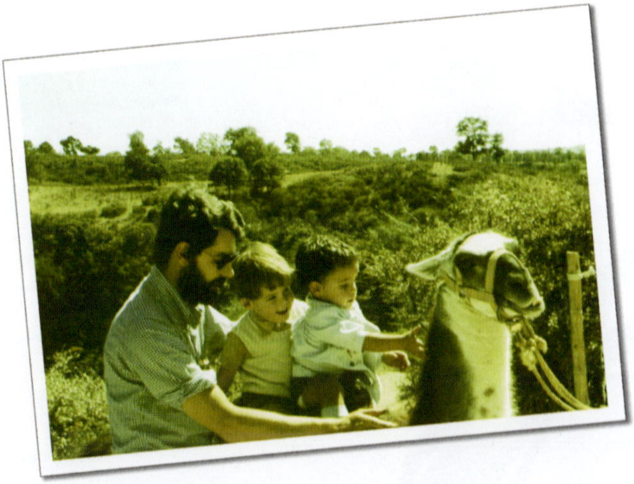

Despite all the development of classic photography materials with silver halides, after a long time these materials have a tendency to lose quality. This is unavoidable due to their chemical properties.

▲ Over the years the quality of photographs based on silver halides worsens.

▼ However, digital photographs maintain their original properties with respect to color.

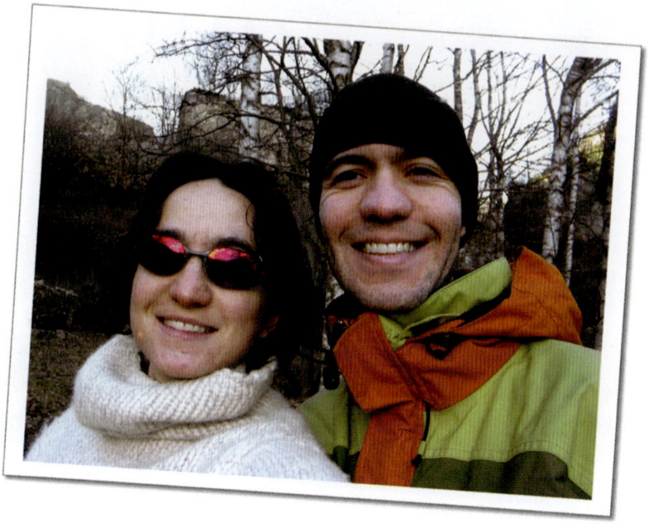

Conversely, digital photographs don't lose their quality, because they are archived in a way that they remain unchanged by time or the effects of climatic conditions. So it is possible to obtain a printed copy from an archived file after many years without any change in quality.

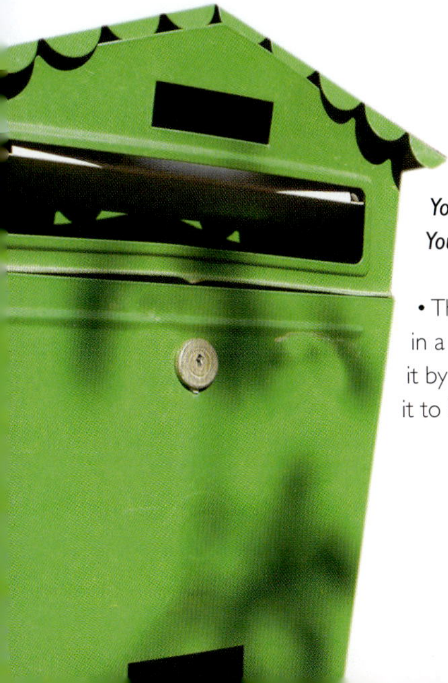

You want to send a classic photograph to a friend in another country. You have two options:

• The first is to have a copy made in a laboratory and then send it by mail, and finally ... wait for it to be delivered.

• The second option is to have a scanner at home or have the photograph digitized in a laboratory so that you can send it to your friend by e-mail.

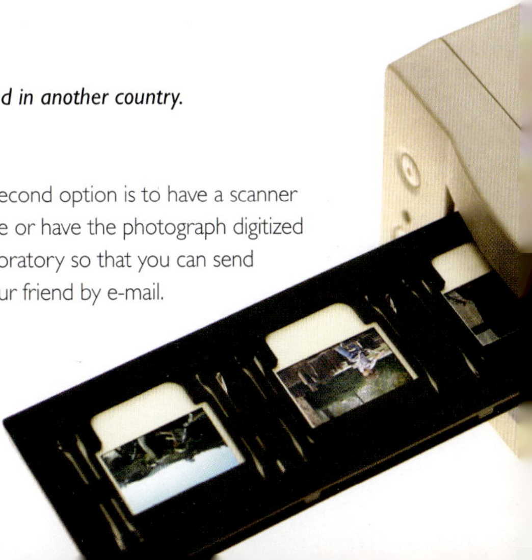

Why go through all that when all you need to do is simply take a picture with a digital camera, transfer it to a computer, and send it by e-mail?

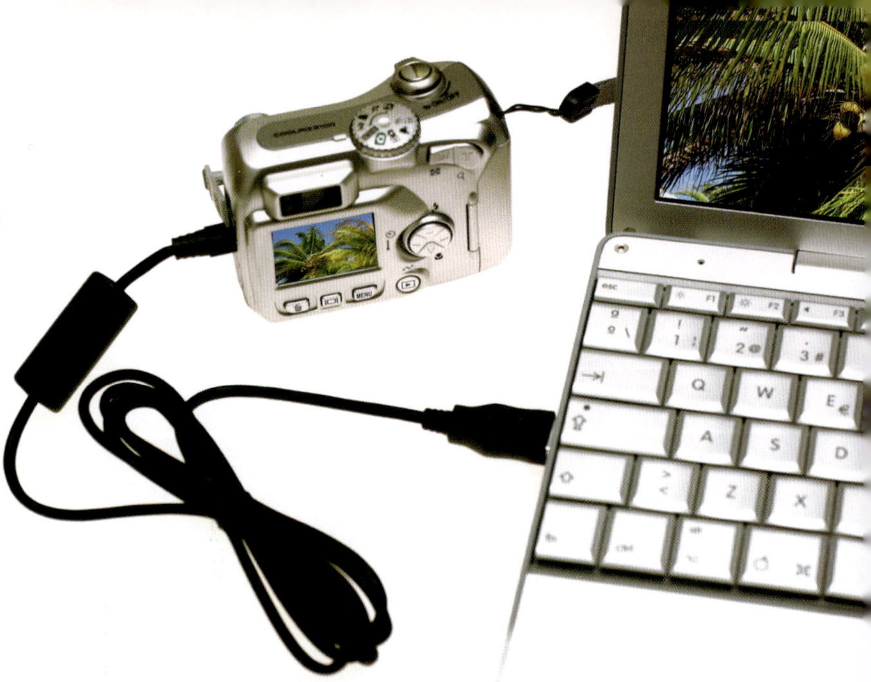

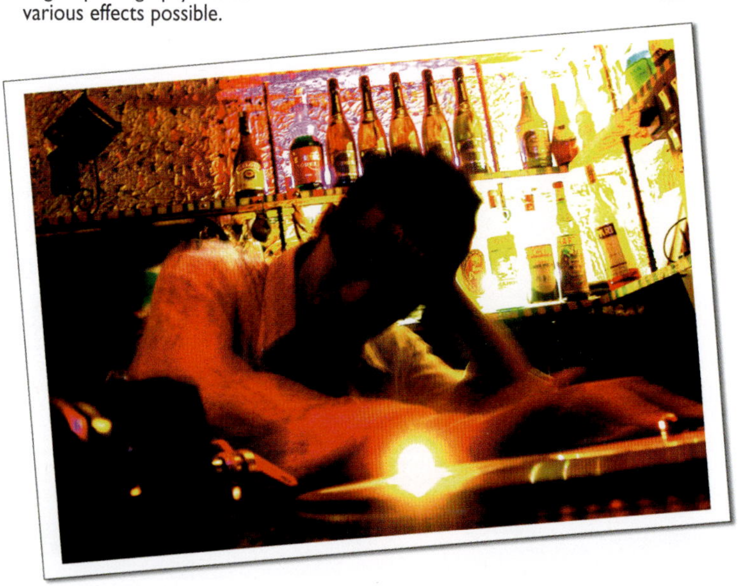

Digital photography makes various effects possible.

Otherwise, one of the great advantages of digital photography is freedom in imagination and creativity. It is possible to take the most original pictures in all sorts of situations and then modify them without worrying about ruining the film (and thus losing money). If you don't like a picture there's nothing simpler than deleting it and taking more pictures.

Even though there are reasons for staying with classic photography, one can come to the conclusion that it's good to use digital photography along with classic photography and to alternate the two technologies as needed, as most professionals now do.

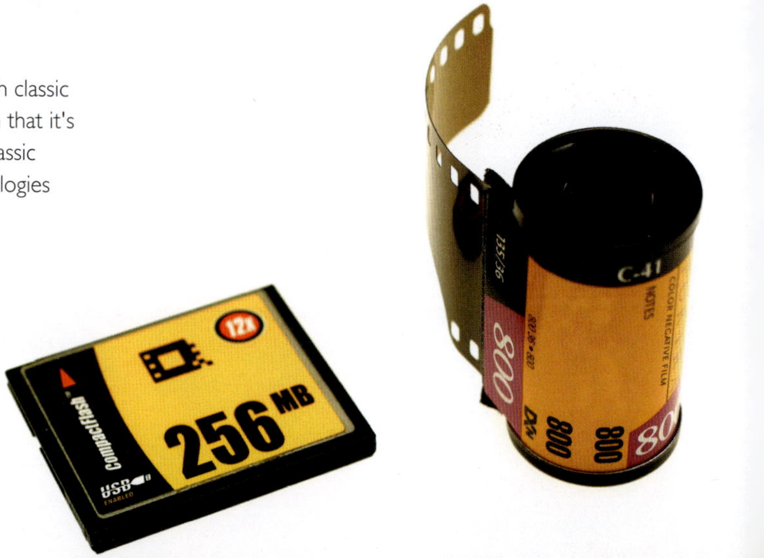

Digital and classic photography complement each other very well.

Basic terms

In order to easily penetrate the world of digital photography, knowledge of several terms is crucial.

Attachment
An electronic file (photograph, video, text...) sent by electronic mail together with a message.

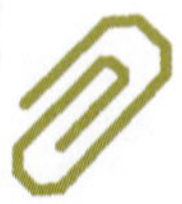

Bit
The smallest information unit.

Byte
An information quantity unit (1 byte = 8 bits)

Copy
See "Remote transmission".

CCD
(Charge-Coupled Device) A photosensitive chip that converts light rays to digital information that is further processed

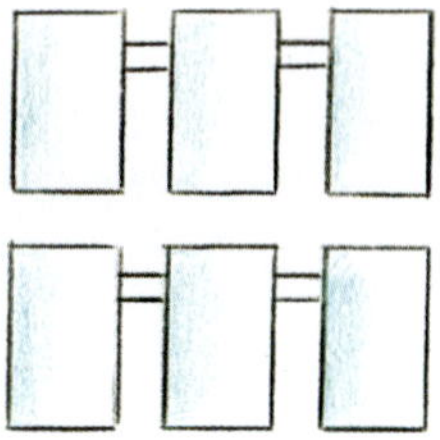

CCD

by the camera to acquire an image.

CMOS
(Complementary Metal Oxide Semiconductor) A photosensitive chip that is ever more frequently used in the most powerful cameras. For now it is less common than the CCD.

CMOS

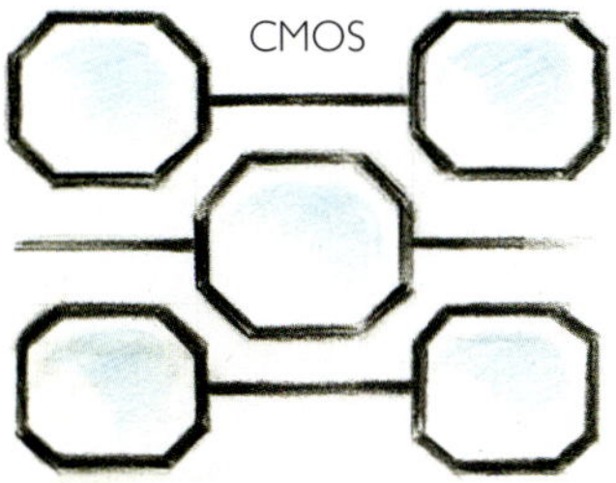

Compact Flash
One of the possible memory cards.

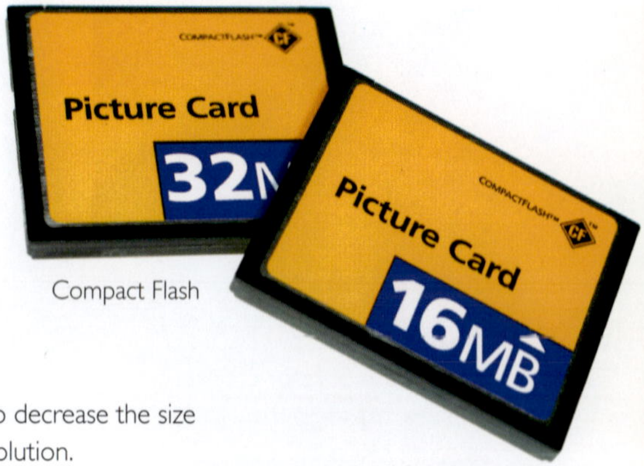

Compact Flash

Compression
An activity that makes it possible to decrease the size of an image without limiting its resolution.

Compression

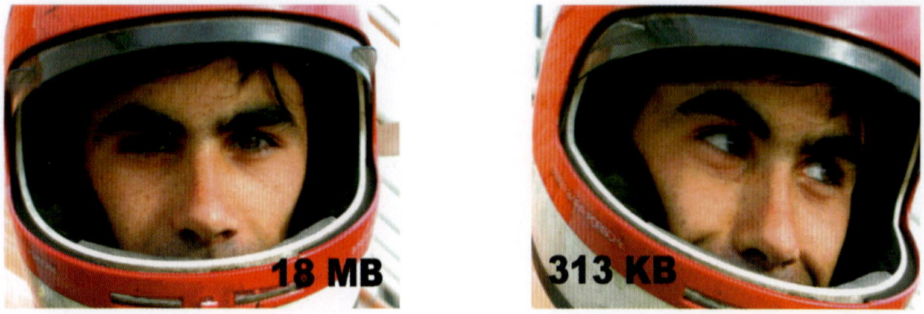

Without compression → compressed picture

CMYK
(Cyan, Magenta, Yellow, Black)
This is the set of colors that is usually used for professional color printing.

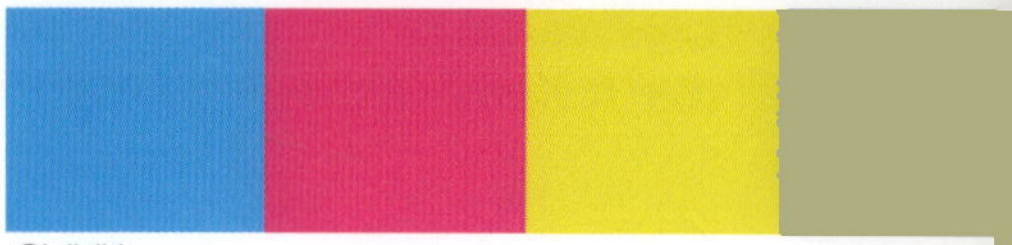

CMYK

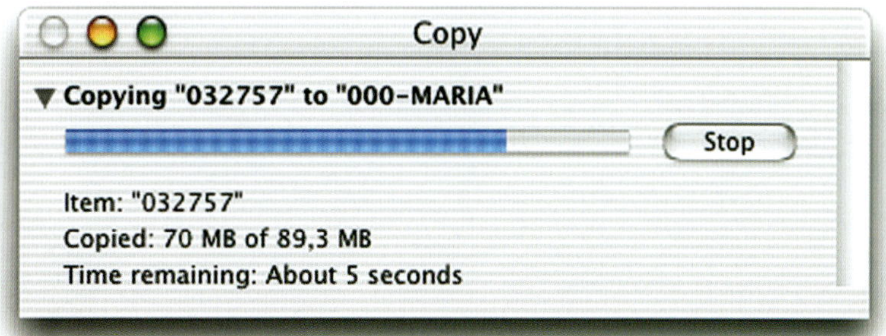

Download

Transfer *(remote transfer or copying)*
The transfer of a file to a computer from an outside source.

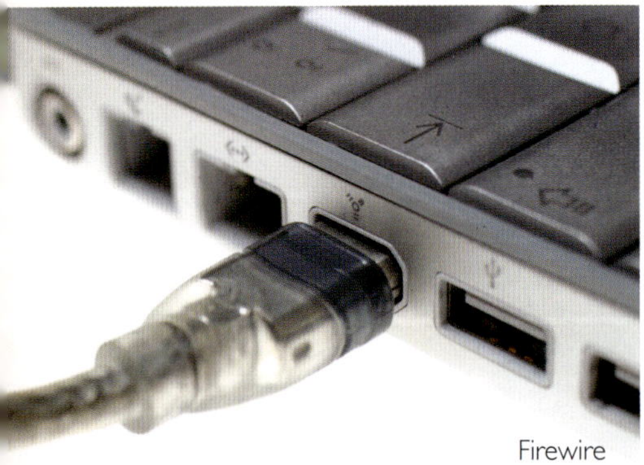

Firewire

Firewire

(IEEE 1394) A port for connections to Apple computers that allows the transmission of a large quantity of information in a short time.

GIF

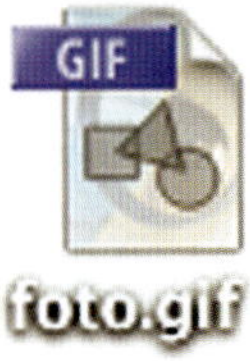

(Graphic Interchange Format) An image file generally used in Internet graphics. However, it isn't recommended for photography, because it can carry only 256 color shades.

Gigabyte

(Gb) A memory unit of 2^{30} bytes.

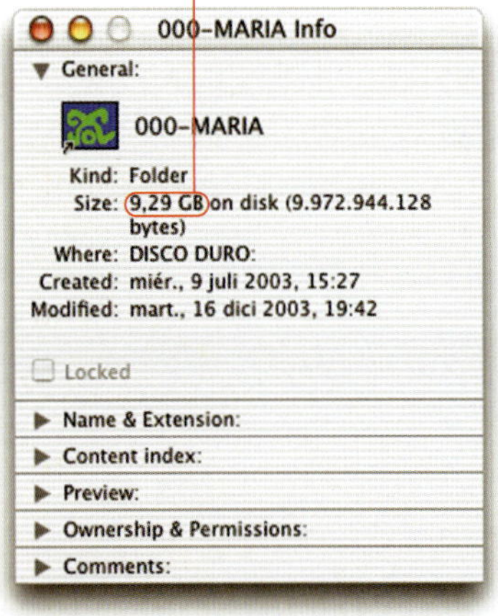

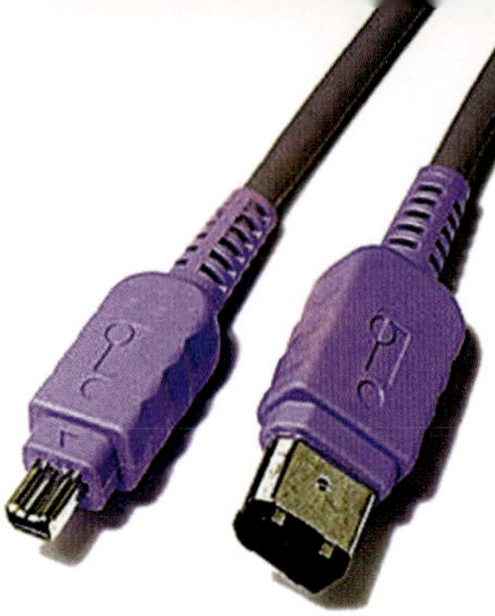

i.Link

i.Link

The term used by Sony for transmitting data through an IEEE 1394 port.

JPEG

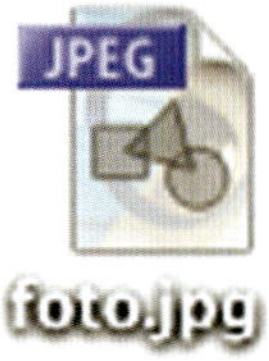

(Joint Photographic Experts Group) The most commonly used compression format for digital photography.

Kilobyte

(Kb) An information measurement unit that equals 2^{10} bytes.

LCD

(Liquid Crystal Display) A small screen on a digital camera that allows pictures to be seen immediately after they have been taken.

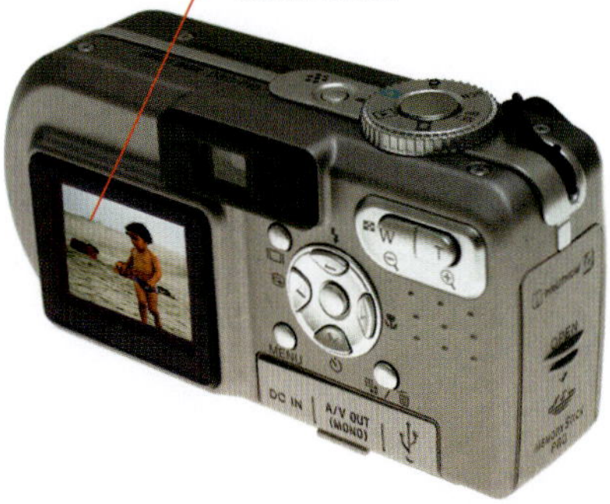

Li-ion

(Lithium-ion battery) A battery that offers up to twice the capacity as compared with NiMH batteries of the same size. They are expensive and require a special charger.

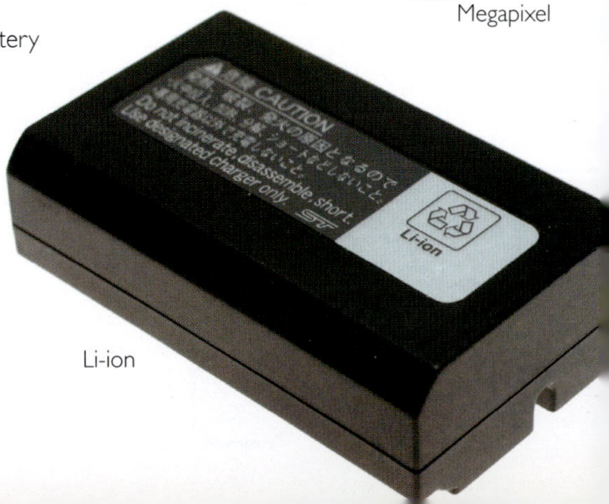

Li-ion

Megabyte

(MB). A unit of memory corresponding to 2^{20} bytes. Don't confuse this with the term megabit (Mb); 1 byte = 8 bits.

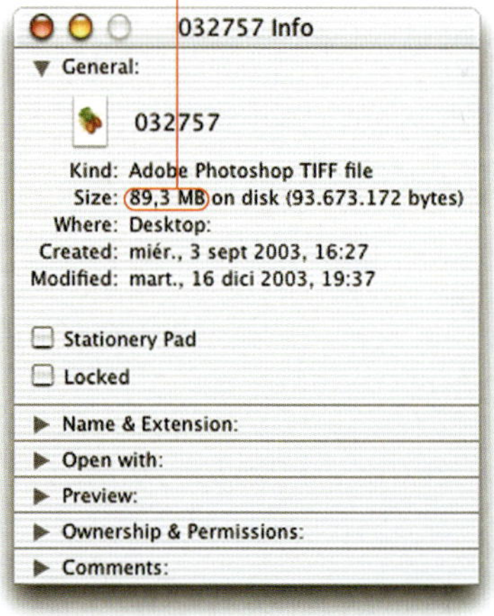

Megapixel

The capacity of an image sensor or CCD in millions of pixels. The more megapixels a camera has the higher the quality of the photograph, as it saves more details.

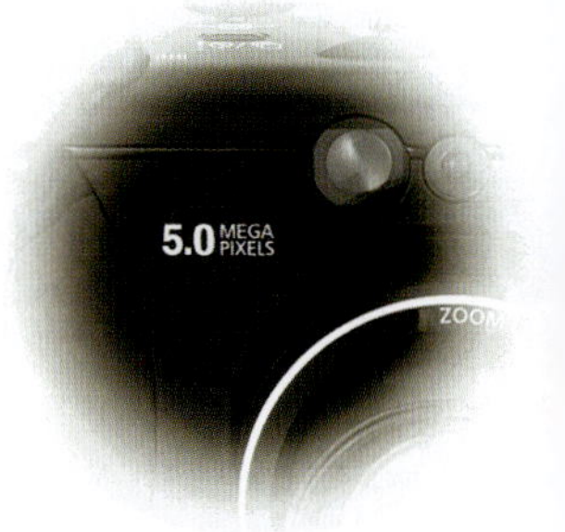

Megapixel

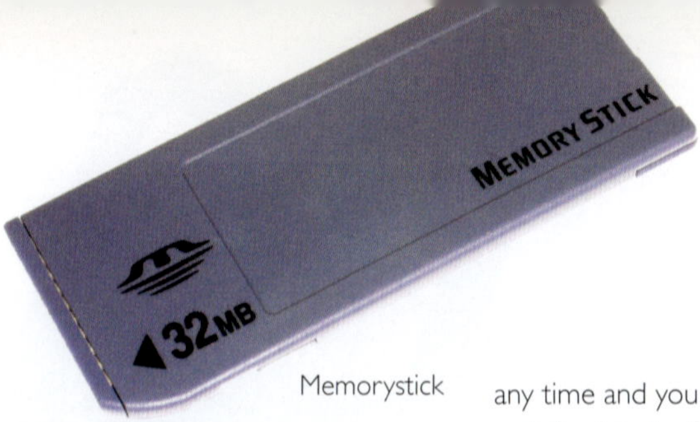

Memorystick

Memory stick
A Sony brand memory card.

MPEG
(Moving Picture Experts Group)
Compression format for digital video.

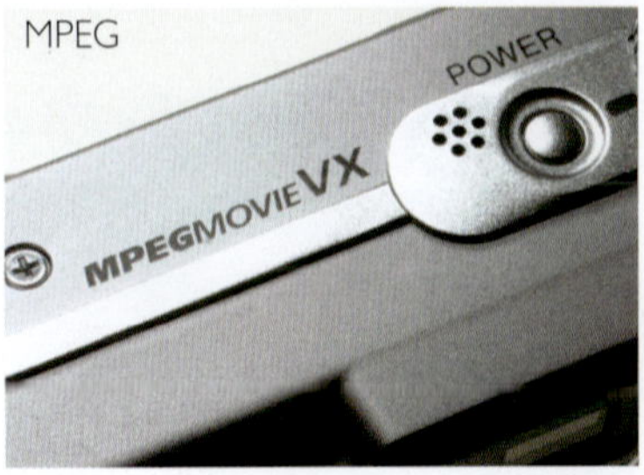

MPEG

NiCd
(Nickel Cadmium) The most robust and generally most wide-spread rechargeable (can be charged up to 700 times) battery. Its main drawback is that it must be completely discharged before it is charged; it is thus best used only as a backup.

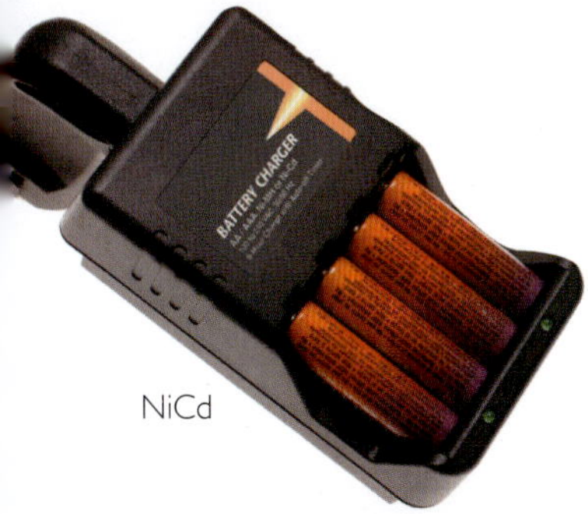

NiCd

NiMH
(Nickel Metal Hybrid) A hybrid battery that uses nickel and another metal. It offers 40% more capacity than a NiCd battery. It can be charged at any time and you don't have to wait for it to be fully charged; it loses no more than 5% of its charge in a day.

Noise
A digital image pixel did not record the light with sufficient precision.

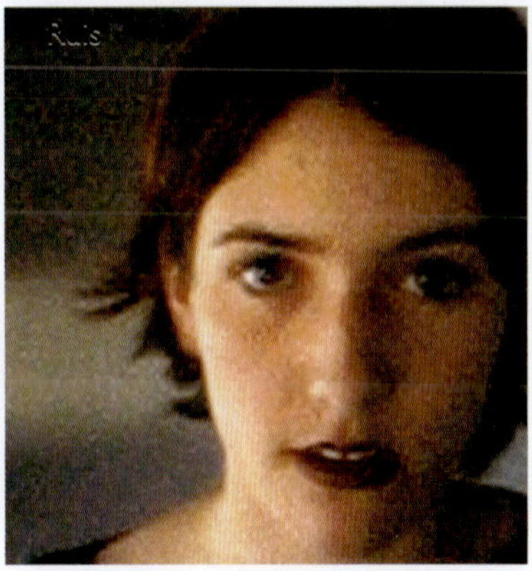

NTSC
The American video format.

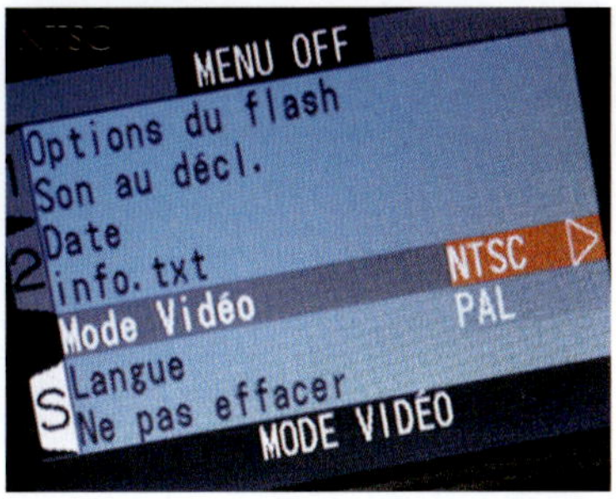

PAL
The European video format.

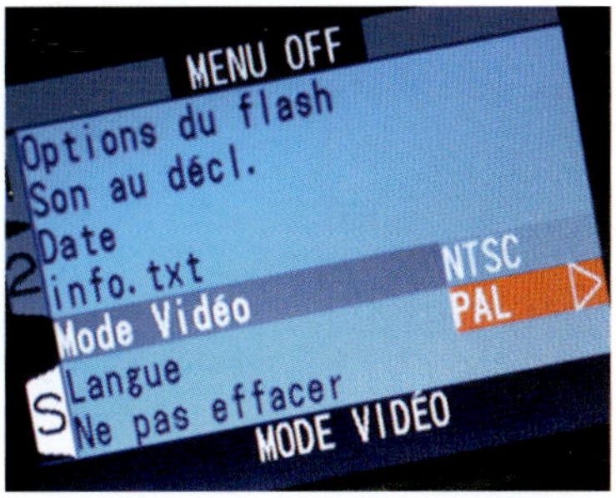

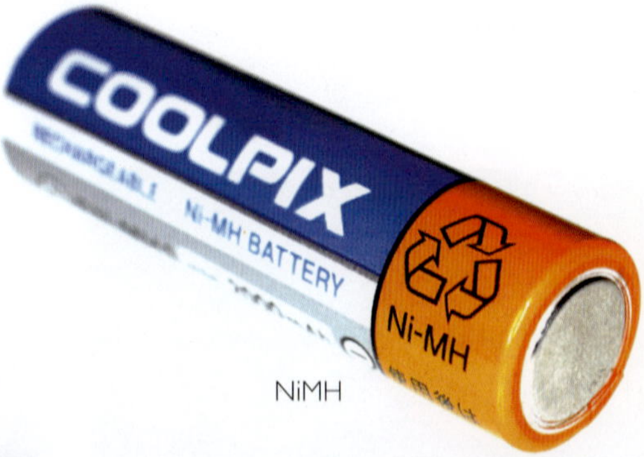

NiMH

PC Card
An adapter that makes it possible to insert a memory card into a portable computer.

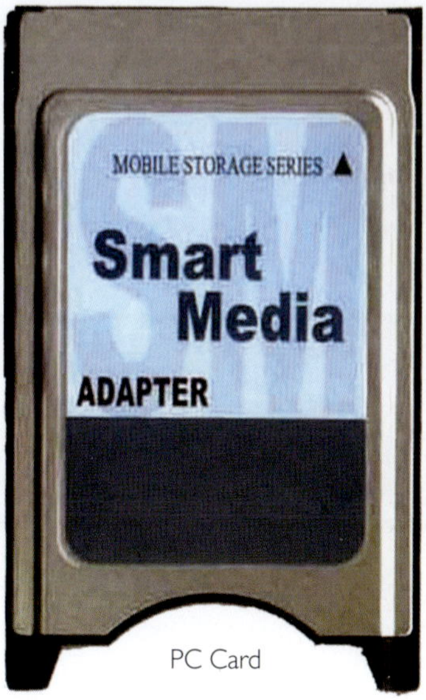

PC Card

Pixel
Pixels are the individual photosensitive elements of a CCD, or points that create the image on the sensor.

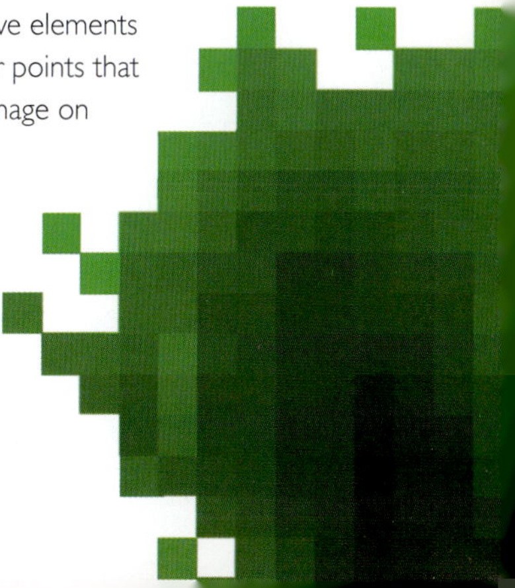

RAW
Unprocessed and uncompressed image file format.

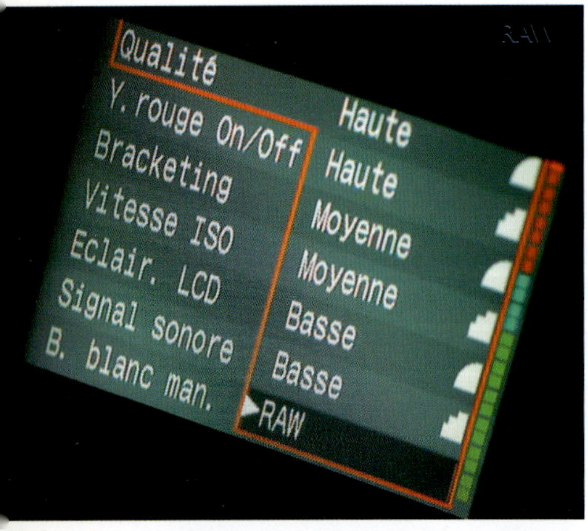

Resolution
The level of quality based on the number of pixels that create an image. The more pixels there are, the better the image resolution is.

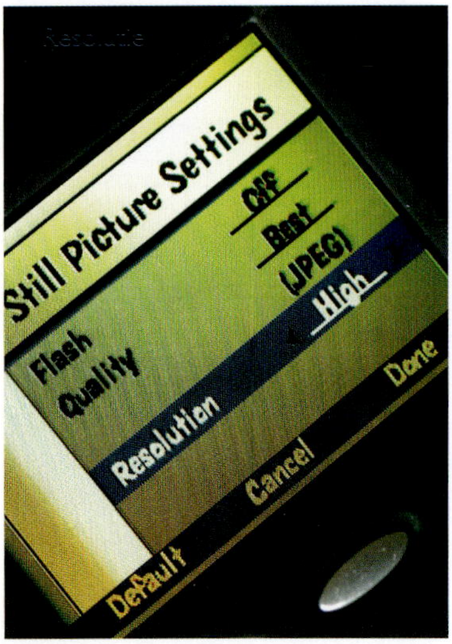

RGB
(Red, Green, Blue) The system used in most digital cameras; combinations of these three basic colors create a color image.

Smartmedia
A common type of memory card.

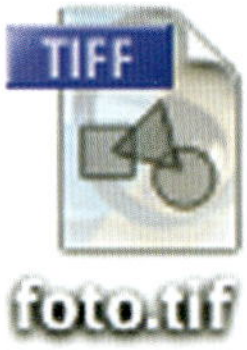

TIFF
(Tagged Image File Format) The most widely used uncompressed image file format.

USB
(Universal Serial Bus) A port for a very fast connection.

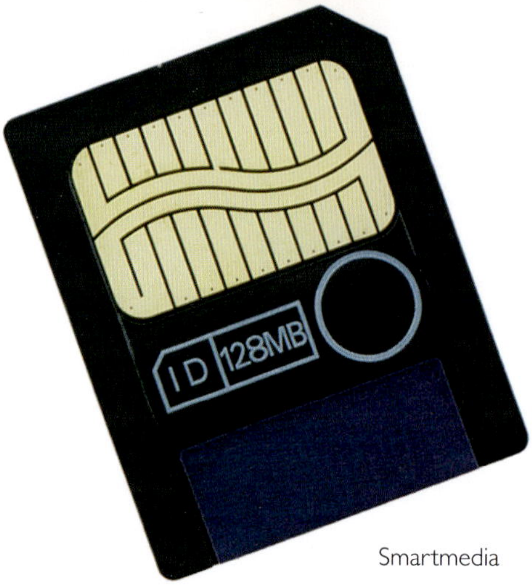

Smartmedia

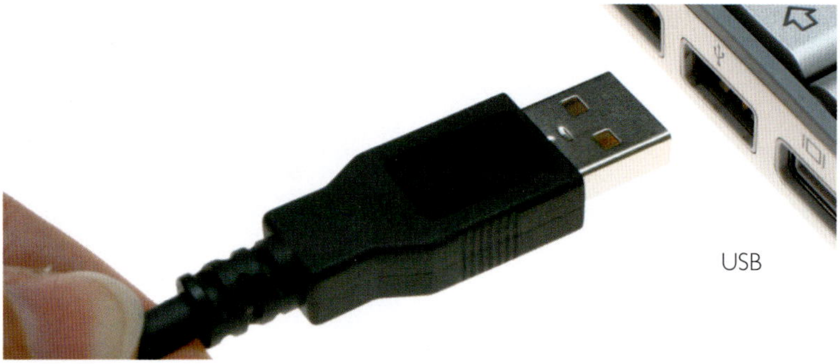
USB

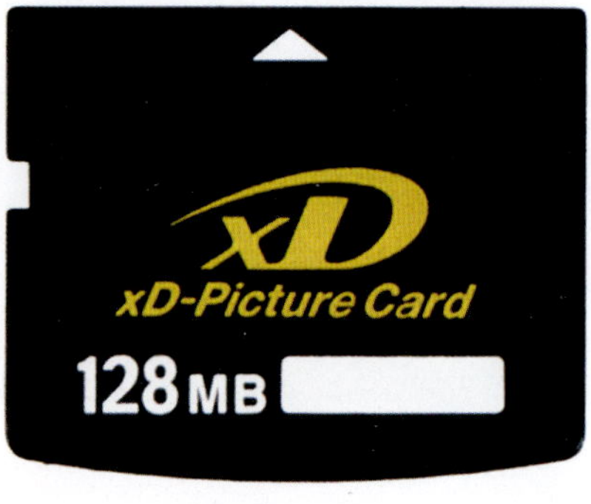

XD-Picture Card

XD-Picture Card
The smallest memory card, generally used in Olympus brand digital cameras.

RGB

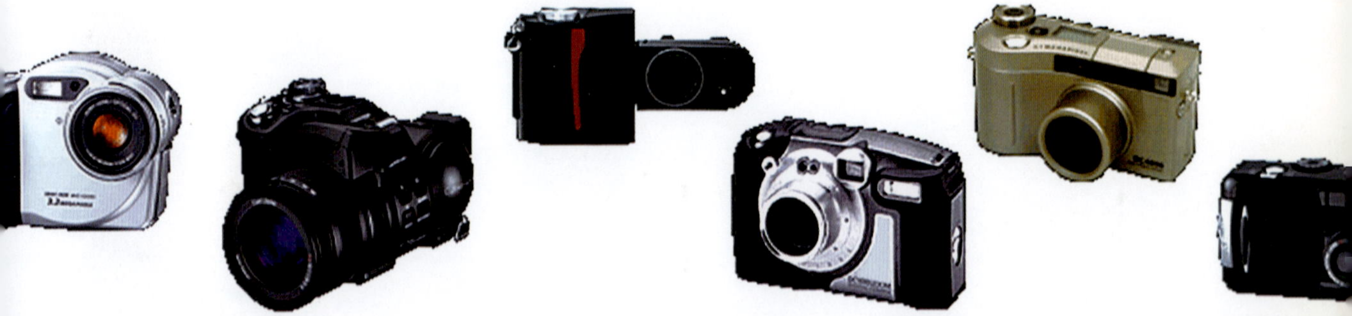

The basic parts of a digital camera

Due to the astounding development of the technology, it's possible that some of the cameras presented on these pages are already obsolete. Nevertheless, all digital cameras work essentially the same way and are made up of the same basic parts.
To make optimal use of any digital camera it's important to know its individual parts, including how they function.

Here we will use a compact, amply equipped Nikon Coolpix 5000 camera.
Its parts are indicated in two summarized overviews.
The first section explains in detail the basic parts without which a digital camera cannot function. The second shows other elements that various cameras may feature.

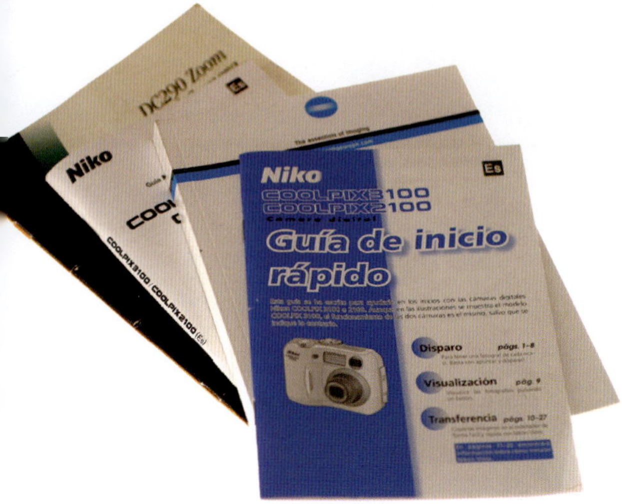

The best way to acquaint yourself with the various parts of a digital camera is to carefully read the user's guide.

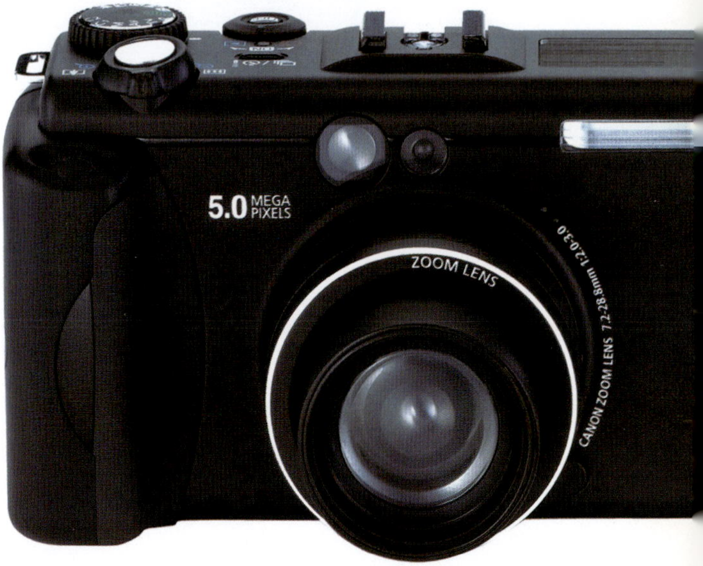

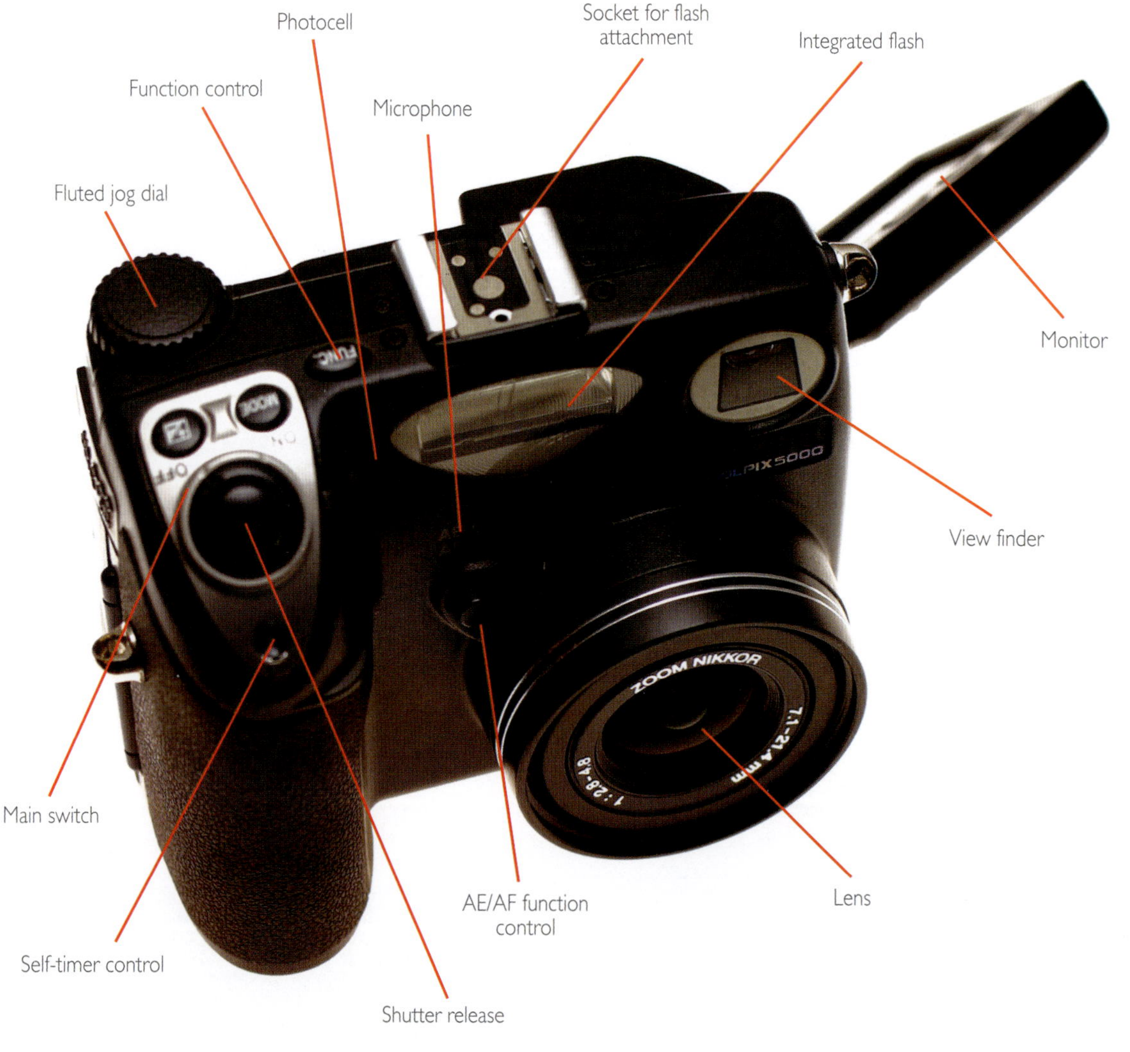

Basic parts

Photocell Its function is to evaluate the mean value of the illumination of the surrounding environment for correct exposure.

Main switch For turning the camera on or off.

Battery compartment cover This covers the space intended for the battery (batteries).

Shutter release The button you push to take a picture. It usually also serves for focusing.

Integrated flash Depending on the camera type this offers a flash for a various number of functions programmed for different conditions.

Slot for Compact Flash card (in this case). This is where the memory card is.

Monitor A screen for displaying the picture and the camera's menu.

Lens The optical set for transferring the image to the CCD.

USB connection port (in this case) The camera's port for connecting a cable to transfer data from the camera to a computer.

Charging input port (in this case) This is for connecting the camera directly to the charging source so you don't have to draw on the battery. On several models this charges the battery directly as it cannot be removed from the camera.

View finder This window is for selecting the shot before you take the picture. Most digital cameras have one. If not, you can use the monitor to check.

Other camera parts

AF/MF button (Auto Focus/Manual Focus) modes This allows you to choose the focus mode and in the playback mode to delete images.

AE/AF (Auto Exposure/Auto Focus) button This is for blocking the camera's auto focus or exposure functions.

Image size For controlling the picture's quality and size.

Multi selector Lets you navigate through the menu as it is displayed on the monitor.

Monitor switch For turning the monitor on or off and for checking data displayed thereon.

Zoom control For zooming in or out. Only some cameras have functional optical zoom.

Flash/ISO button For selecting flash mode and, in conjunction with the jog dial, for setting the sensitivity value.

Function button Use this together with the jog dial to change many of the camera's functions without having to access the menu via the monitor.

Exposure button For selecting the exposure mode using the jog dial.

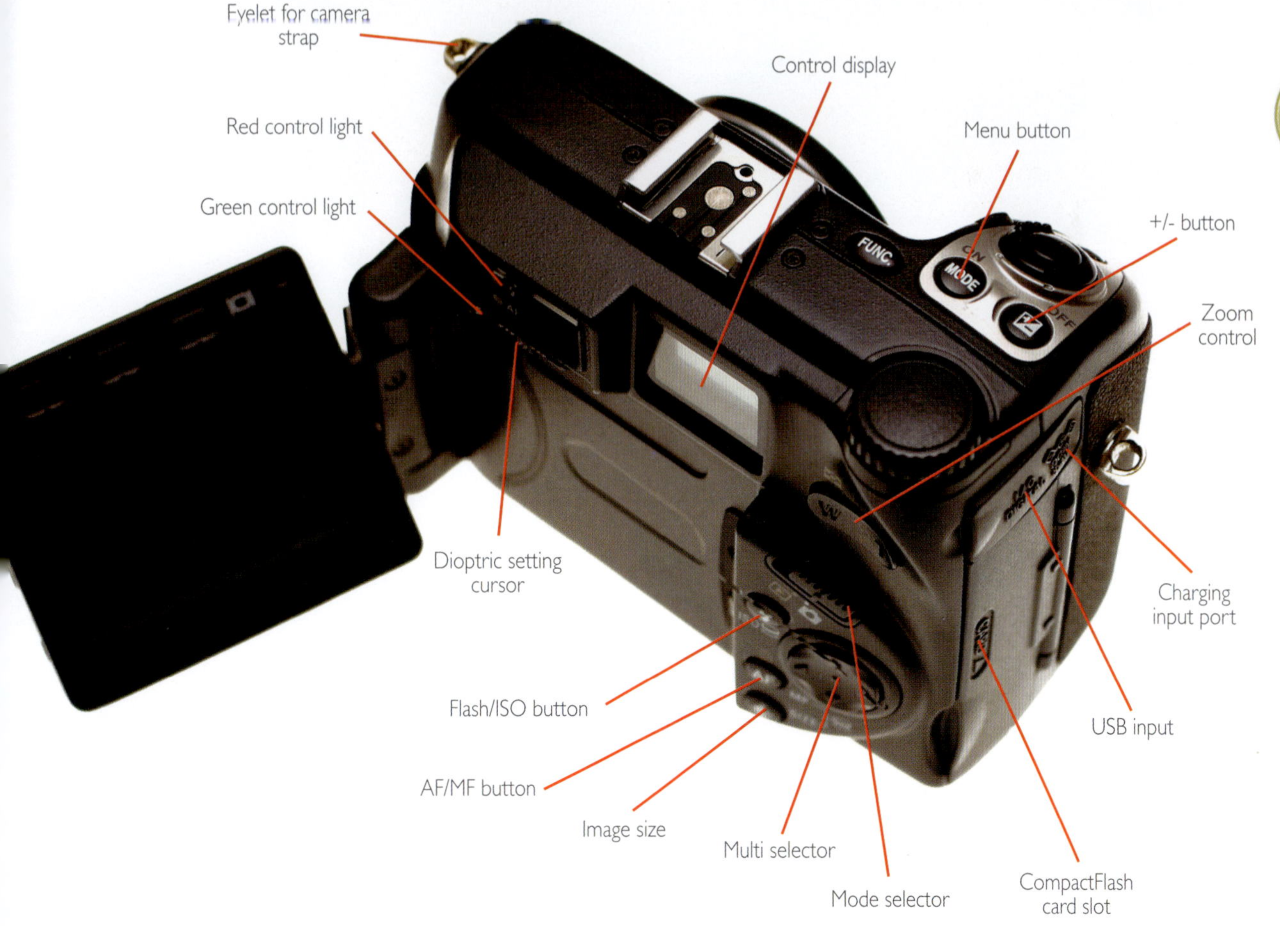

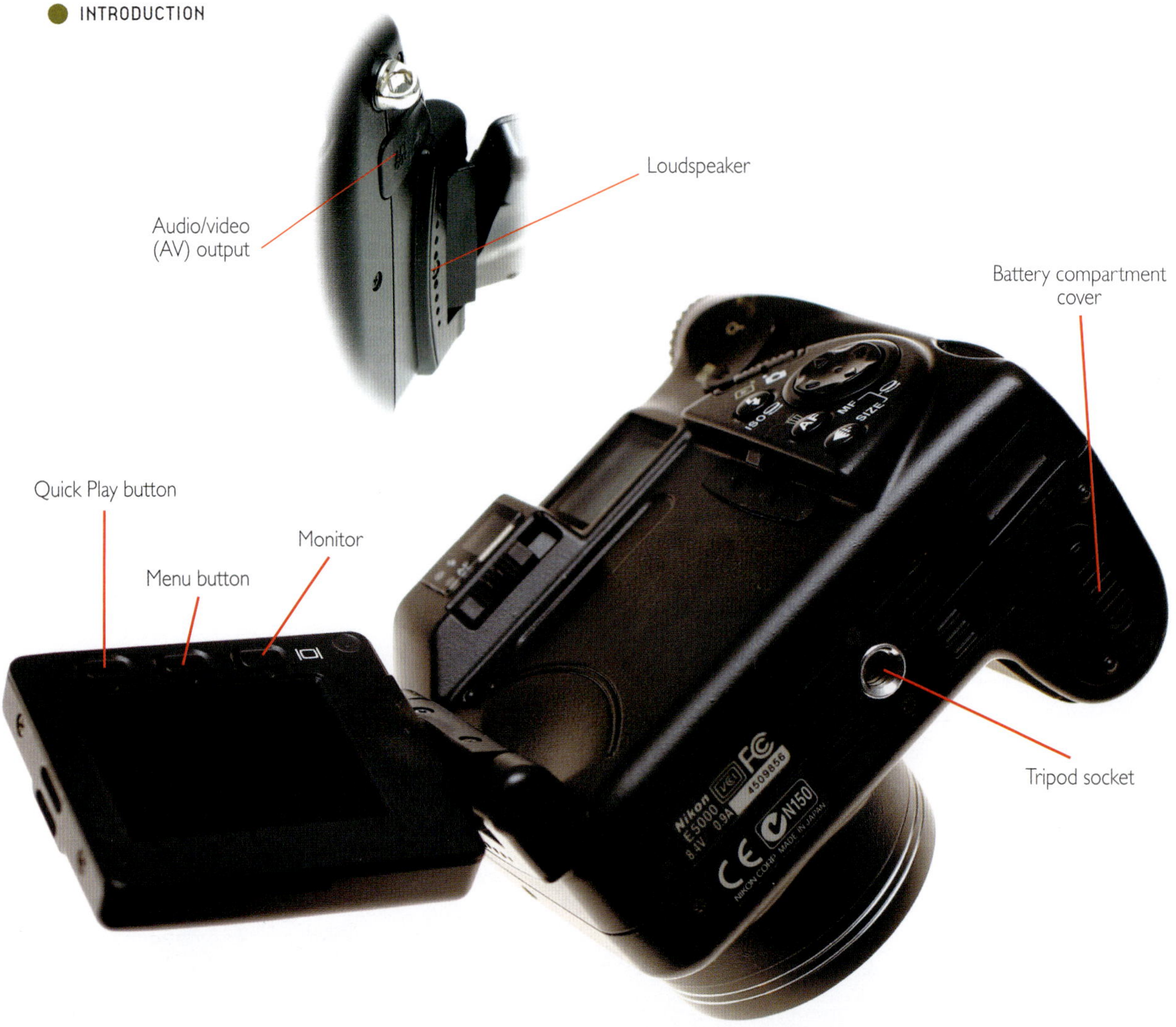

+/- Used with the jog dial for compensating exposure values (toward either underexposure of overexposure). See the EV discussion on page 36.

Quick Play button Allows you to quickly save a picture to memory before taking the next picture.

Dioptric setting cursor A cursor for setting the dioptric value as needed.

Control display A small screen on which you can read the menu without having to use the monitor, thus sparing your battery. Available only on selected cameras.

Flash attachment socket For attaching a flash or other accessory.

Speaker Allows reproduction of sound accompanying a video or recorded audio files, if the camera is so equipped.

Fluted jog dial Its uses include selecting the menu, calling up recorded information on a picture, or entering information.

Eyelet for camera strap A loop for affixing the strap to the camera.

Mode selector For setting the camera to either take pictures or play them back on the monitor.

Multi selector For navigating through the menu, for switching from picture taking to playing back and sorting pictures.

Audio/video (A/V) output For connecting the camera to a TV with cables.

Self-timer lamp A blinking light that counts down to a self-timed exposure.

Red flash-ready light Indicates battery status and readiness for use.

Green autofocus light Provides information on focusing.

Types of pictures and their uses

In order to get the most out of your camera it's important to really know not only the camera but also all the accessories, starting with the memory card.
There are various levels of digital photograph quality. Depending on how you take pictures they can be used for various purposes. The two main things you should always keep in mind are the quality and the resolution of the pictures.

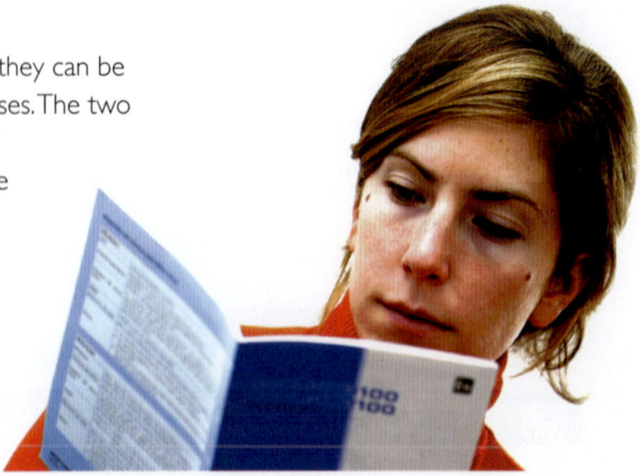

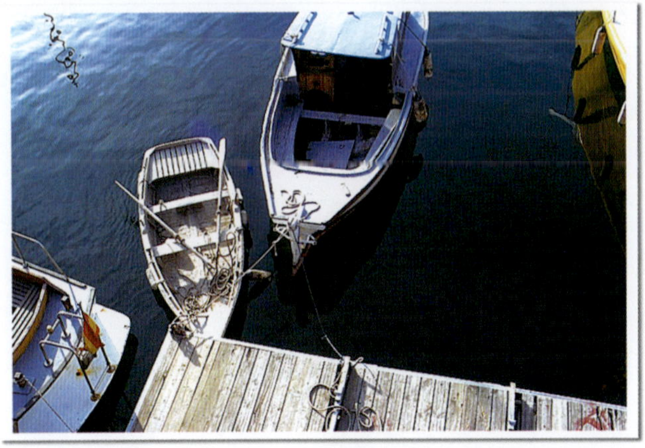

◂ A-4 format

Photographs of very high quality (and thus little compressed) and large size (or high resolution) can be printed in large format.

▾ 12 x 8 cm format

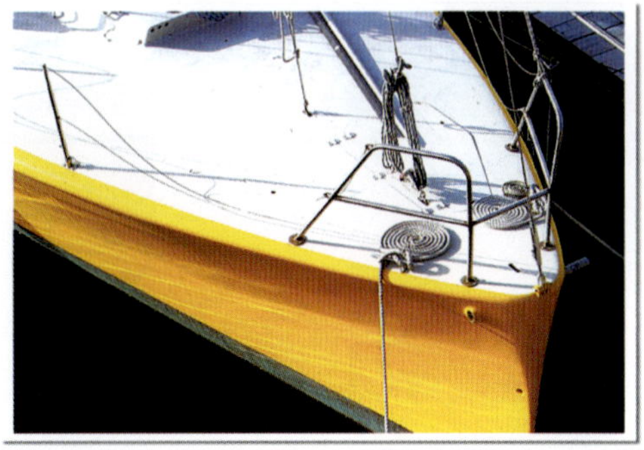

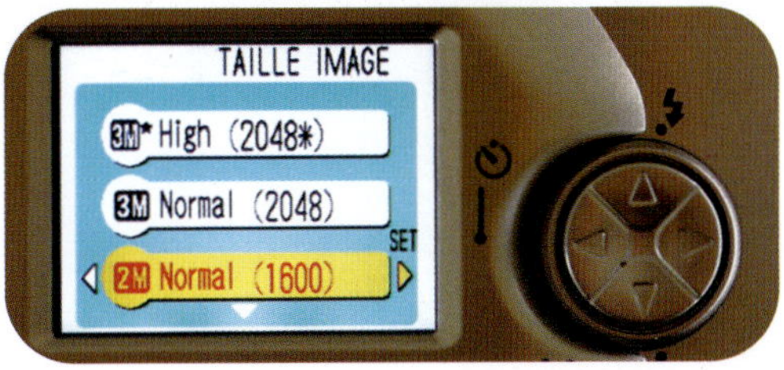

Digital cameras allow you to choose the quality levels of your photographs. Your choice depends on what you are going to use a picture for. For example, it's better to choose high quality for printing - 2048 x 1536 pixels. If you're going to send the picture by e-mail it's better to stay at 1600 x 1200 pixels, as the resulting quality is good enough for e-mailing.

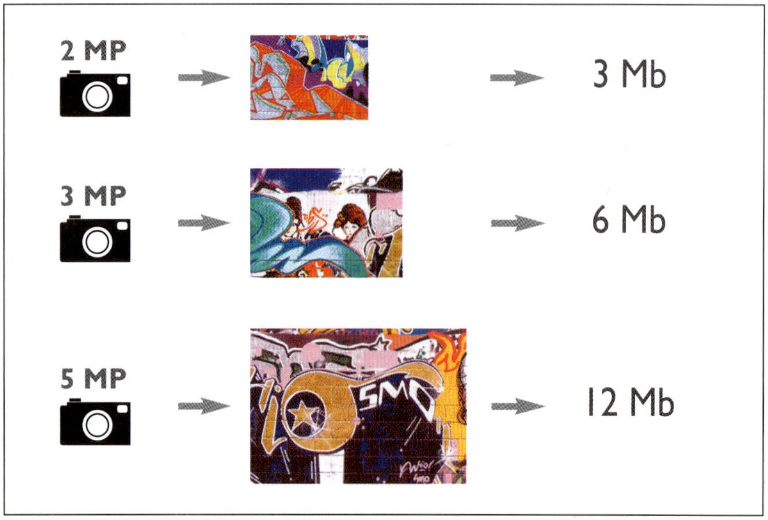

This table shows the connections between the number of pixels contained in the image, the size of the image, and the amount of space needed in the internal memory or the memory card.

◂ The size and resolution of a digital image depend on the number of pixels. The more pixels there are the greater the size and resolution of the image, as of course is the amount of space taken up in the internal memory or the memory card.

The quality of an image depends further on the type of compression you choose. In general, digital cameras offer several levels of compression for taking pictures: very high, high, medium, lower, and low compression.

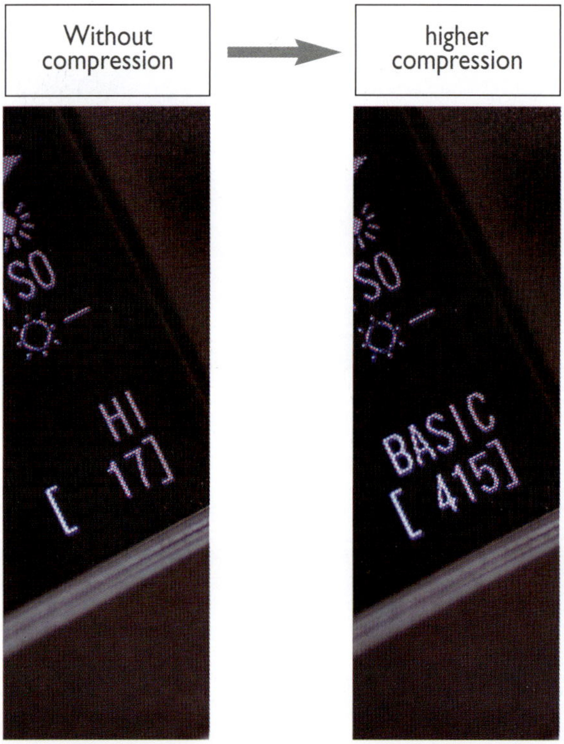

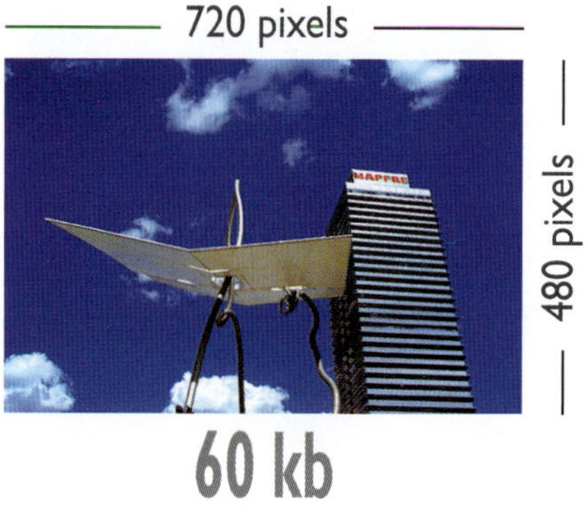

It is thus possible to achieve pictures of the same size but of differing quality, i.e., varying levels of compression. In such cases the amount of space taken up in the internal memory or the memory card varies as well.

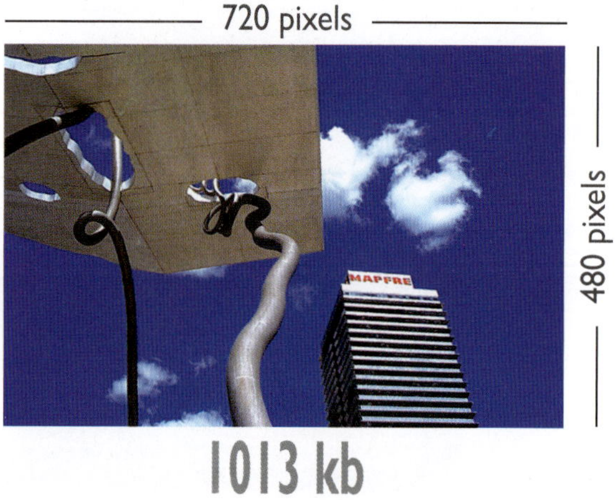

The reason for various levels of compression is simple. Without compression you would never have enough space in the memory card, and the images would contain too much data for use over the Internet or in a computer. In order to use the correct compression level you must bear in mind that the higher the compression is the more pictures you can store on the memory card.

A great disadvantage of compression is the accompanying loss of data, which can affect the colors and details in the picture. So it is important to consider your future use of the picture in advance to avoid spoiling it.

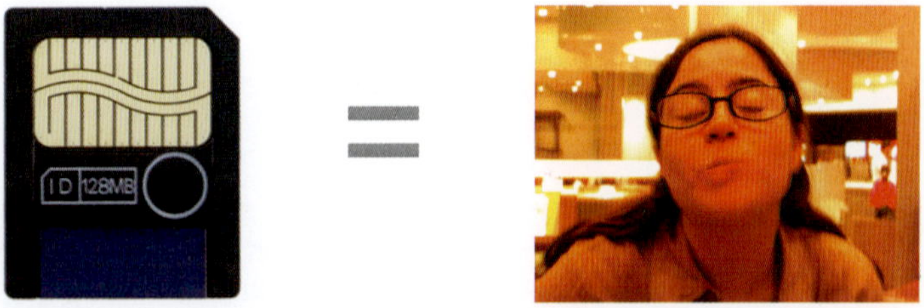

Without compression

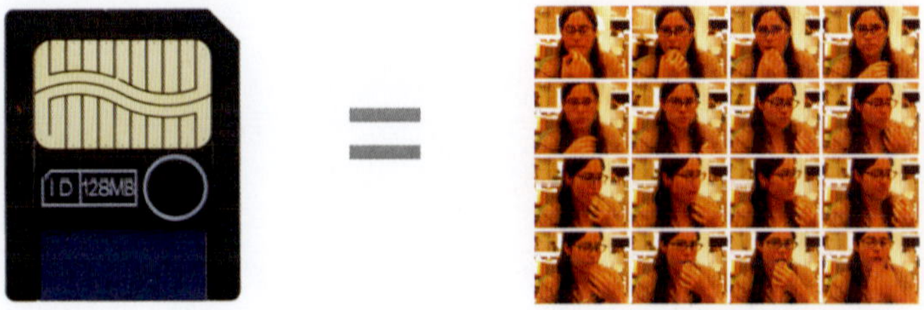

With compression

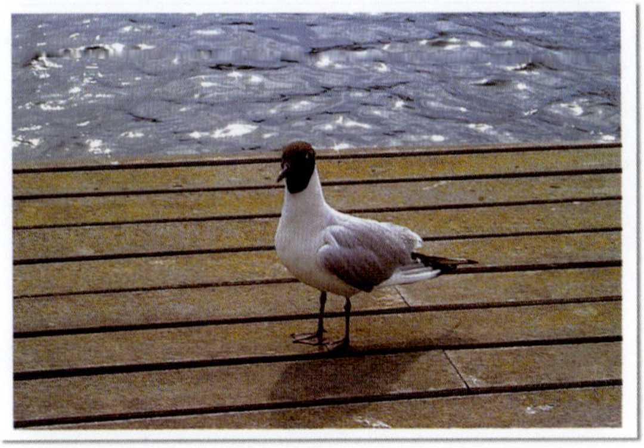

▲ Notice the very good quality of this picture, printed from an uncompressed file.

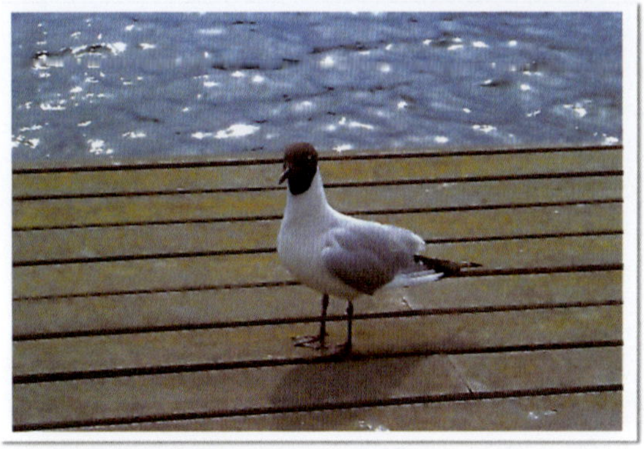

▲ This picture, printed from a compressed file, is of lower quality.

If the photographs are intended only for e-mail the quality achieved through higher or medium compression should suffice. If you want to print the pictures it's better to choose uncompressed pictures or only slightly compressed pictures in order to ensure satisfying quality.

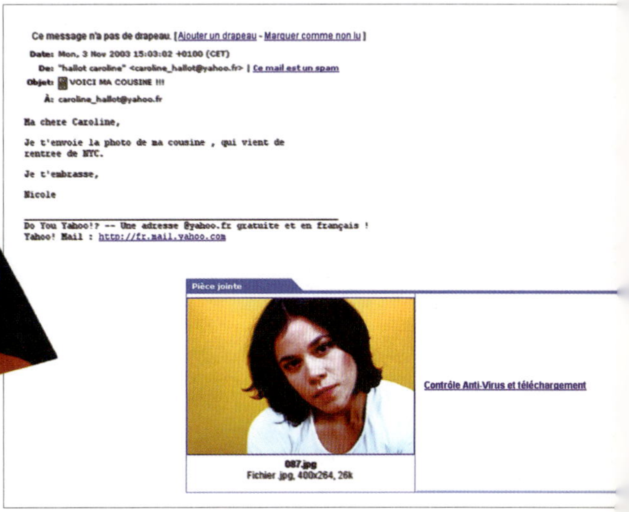

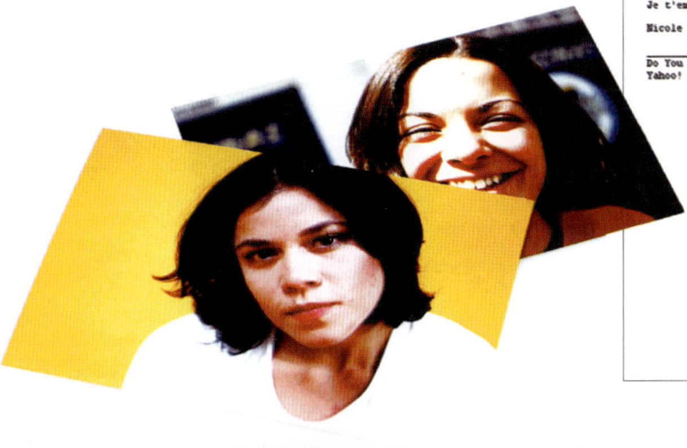

JPEG A very common compression format

TIFF A common format that usually does not offer compression, so the images do not lose their high quality.

RAW A format without compression that is not integrally processed by the camera; it must be finished in a computer. Its great advantage is that it offers files that are 60% smaller than in TIFF format.

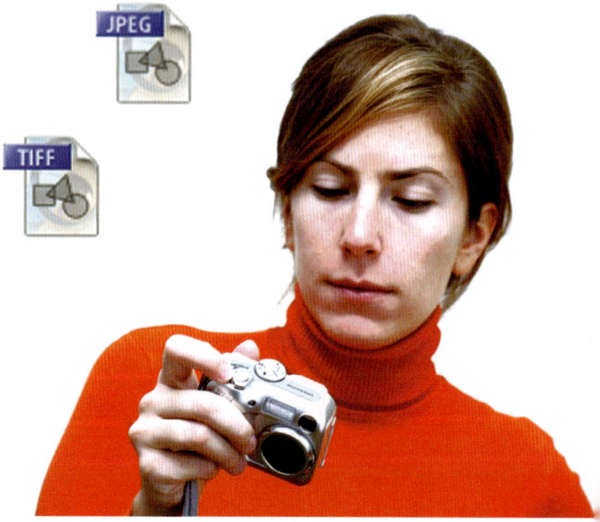

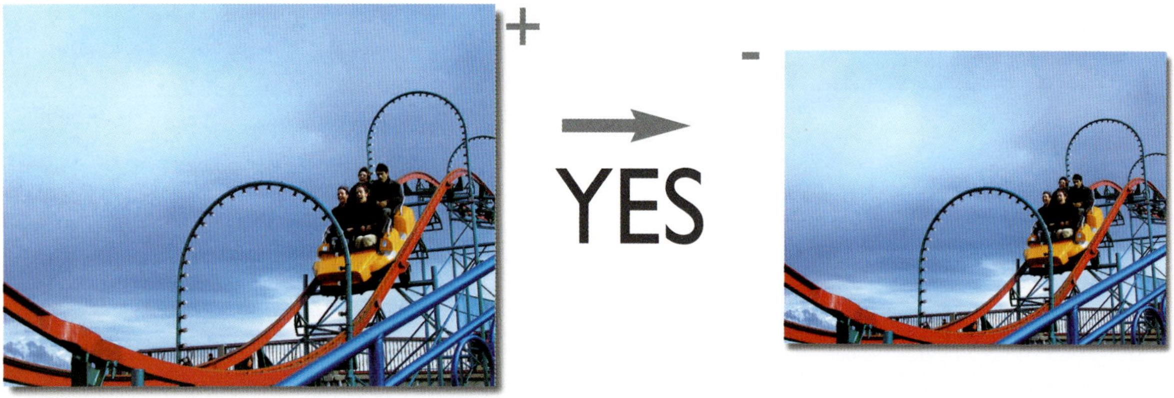

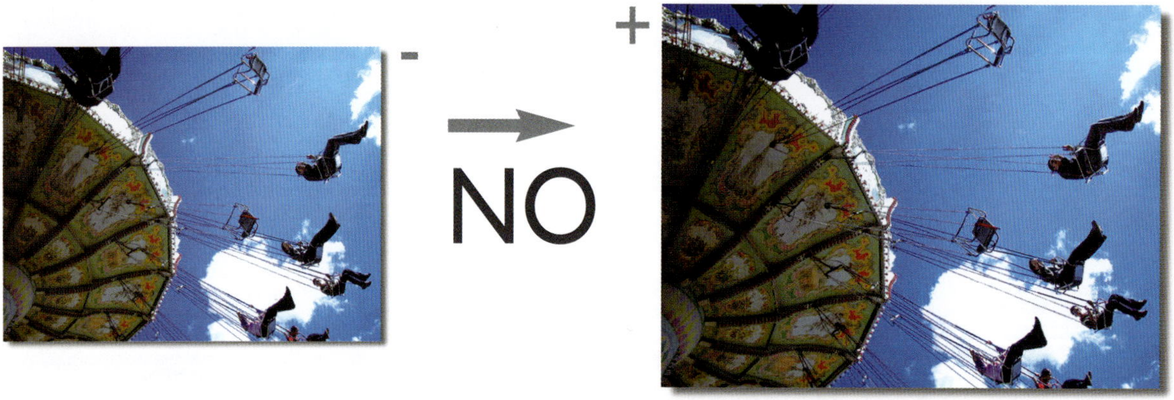

We recommend not compressing images unless it is truly necessary. A large image can be additionally reduced without loss of quality. Conversely, a small image, if enlarged, will lose quality markedly.

Reducing or increasing the size of photographs can be set directly in some cameras. But changes in size are more frequently made in a computer with the help of various programs for editing pictures.

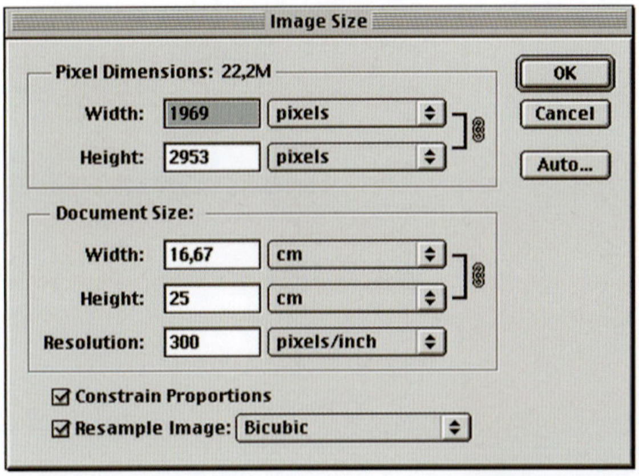

Here are a few examples of the resolution required for printing high-quality photographs.

If you intend to send your pictures via e-mail, don't forget that the smaller their files are the easier they are to send. For example, pictures with resolution of about 640 x 480 pixels with maximum compression can not only be very easily sent by e-mail but can also be used to illustrate documents written in Word.

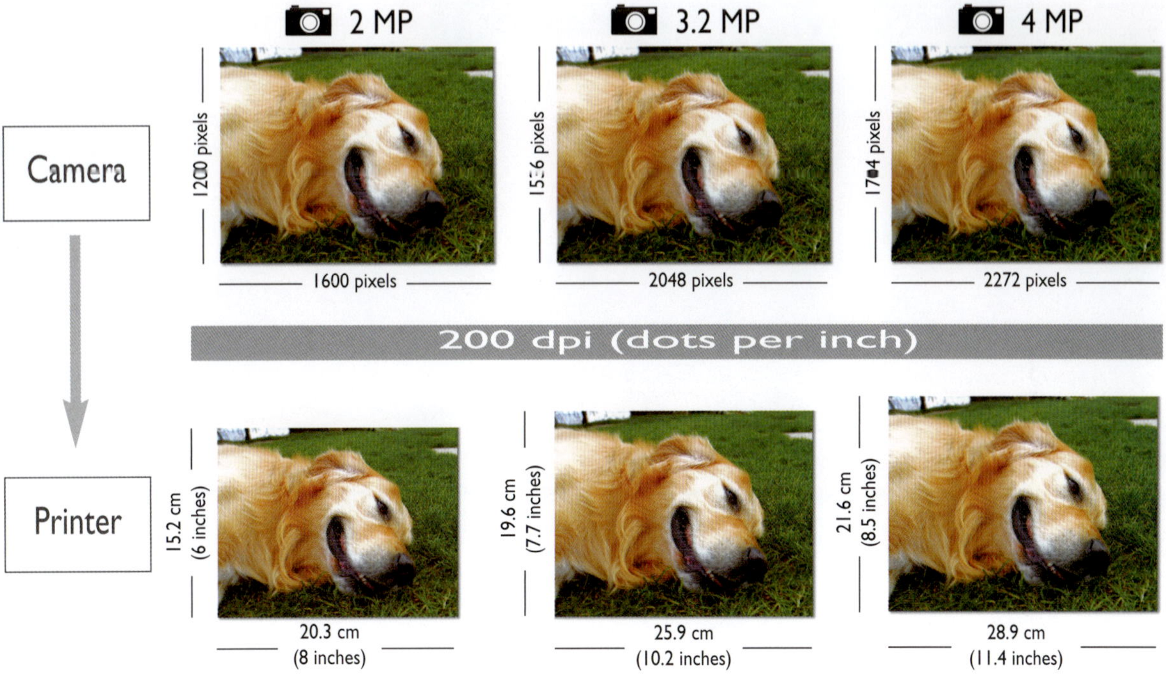

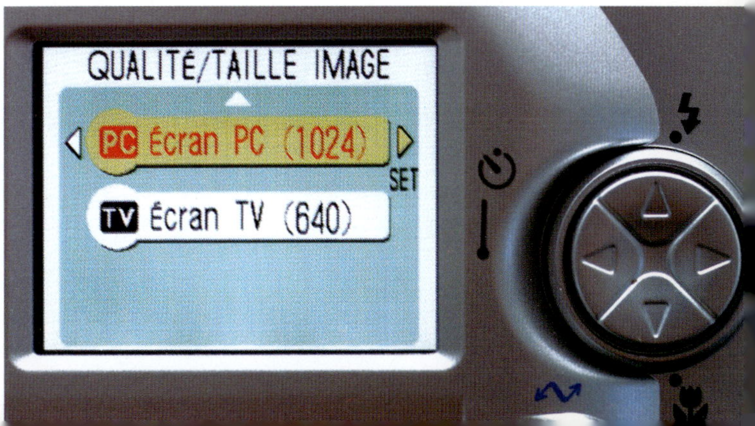

Some cameras also offer a direct file size setting for "electronic mail," which automatically sets the resolution at around 640 x 480 pixels.

Types of digital cameras

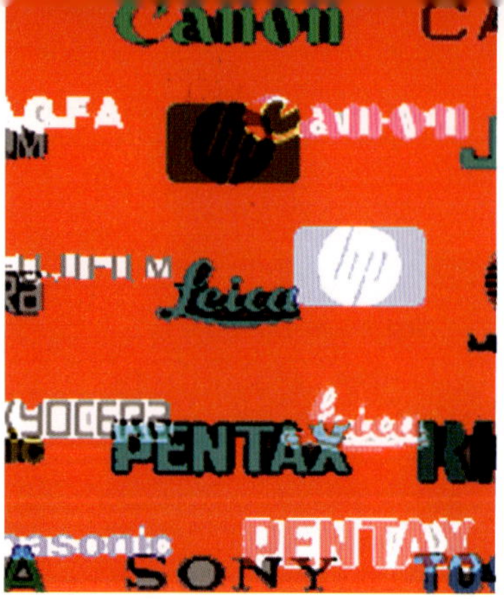

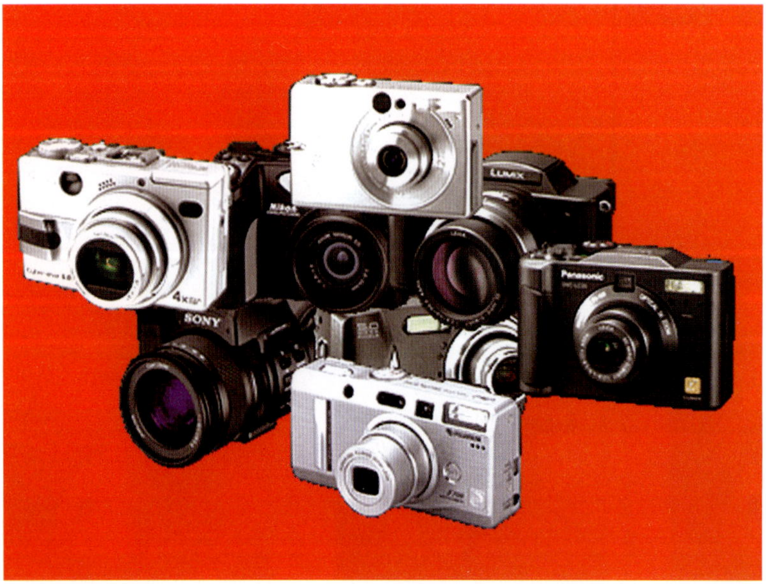

It is generally known that there are a large number of camera manufacturers. Understandably, this is also reflected in the enormous variety of cameras that are offered on the market.
Here are various types of digital cameras and their most significant characteristics, and we will make several recommendations to pay attention to when making your purchase.

Compacts

We'll start with **compact digital cameras**, which look somewhat like classic compact cameras. They are small, and their lenses are usually fixed or equipped with only a low-power zoom. Their resolution can reach as high as 5 megapixels, which allows the printing of pictures from postcard size to A4 format.
Their main advantage is that they are very easy to operate, and they are also reliable and sell for reasonable prices.

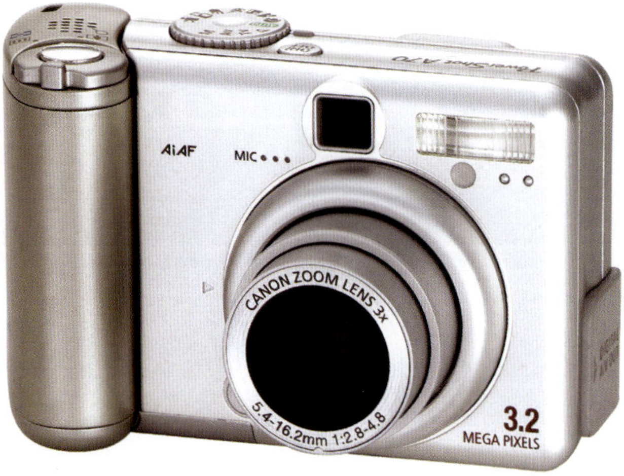

Semiprofessional cameras

Let's now look at **semi-professional digital cameras**, which differ from compact cameras in several ways. Their exteriors reveal the basic difference. They are somewhat larger and are made of tougher materials. Thanks to their greater resolution, which exceeds 5 megapixels, semi-professional cameras allow enlargements exceeding A4 format size.
They have more functions than compact cameras and they often allow more manual settings. These models are excellent for users who

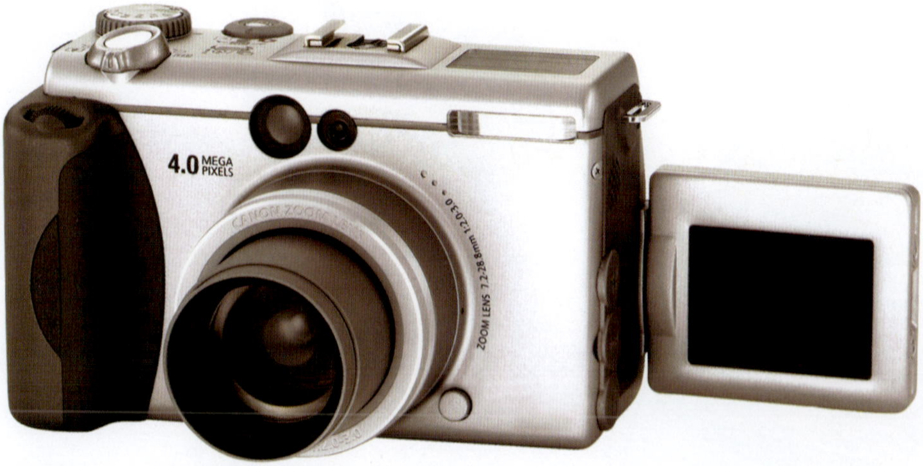

like to take control of their cameras. Some cameras can be equipped with external accessories like flashes or supplementary lenses. With semi-professional cameras it is necessary to emphasize their resolution and great flexibility. In some cases they can cost twice as much as compact cameras.

Professional digital cameras

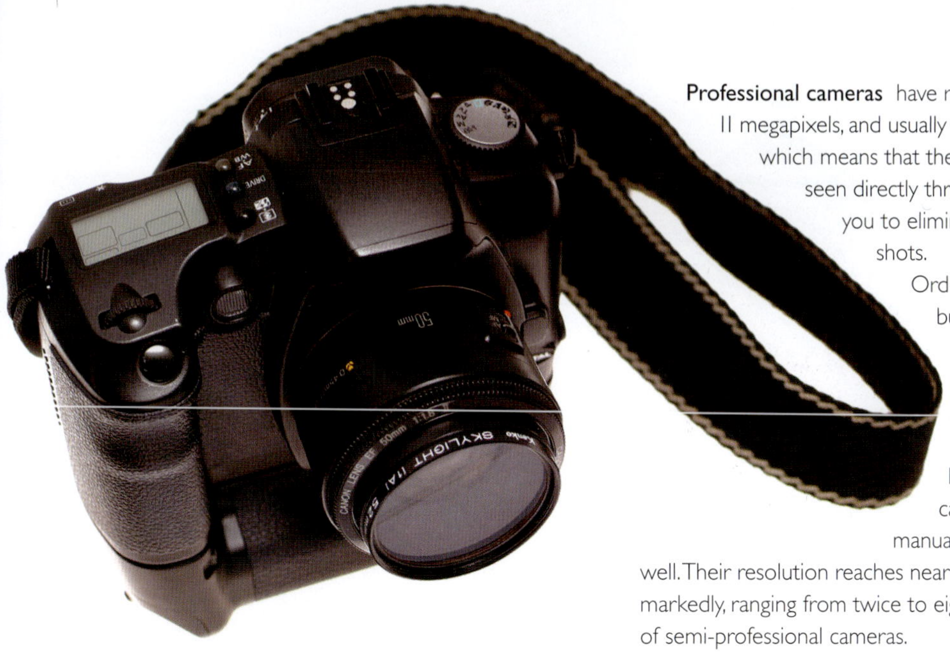

Professional cameras have resolutions of up to 11 megapixels, and usually have SLR type mirrors, which means that the photographed object is seen directly through the lens, which allows you to eliminate any errors in framing shots.

Ordinarily, these cameras are built like classic cameras so that all of the lenses and other accessories offered by the manufacturers can be used.

Professional cameras can be controlled not only manually, but automatically as well. Their resolution reaches nearly A3 format. Prices vary markedly, ranging from twice to eight times the prices of semi-professional cameras.

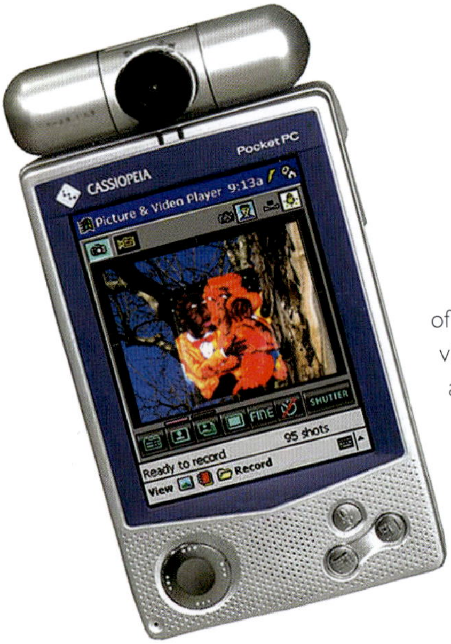

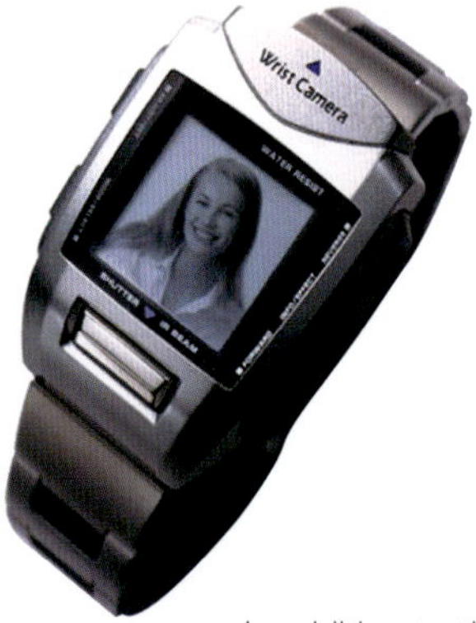

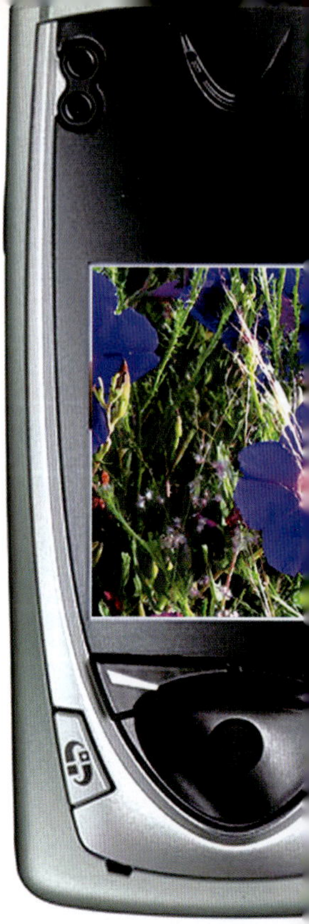

In addition to these three groups of digital cameras there is a broad range of other products that can take digital photographs: digital video cameras, cell phones, watches, digital personal assistants, and so on.

However, the quality of pictures taken using them is generally not comparable to those taken with digital cameras, as their resolution is very low.

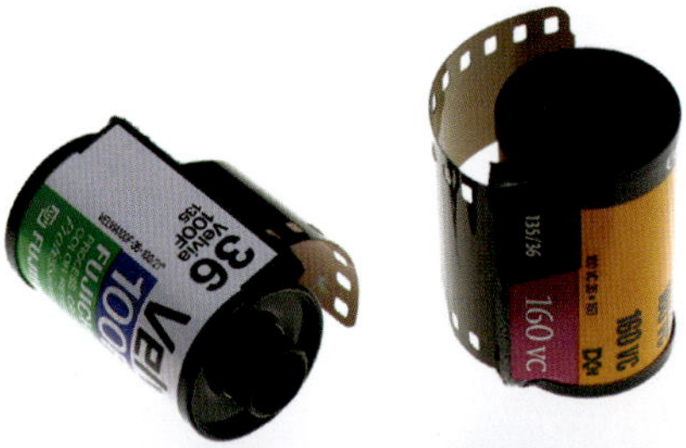

Additionally, digital cameras need other accessories for taking pictures and operating, in particular memory cards and batteries. Various memory cards for digital cameras are analogous to film for classic cameras. Without memory cards cameras wouldn't be able to save any information, that is, to take pictures.

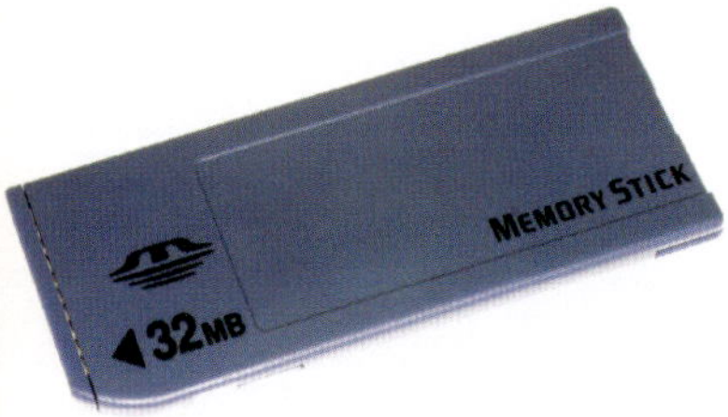

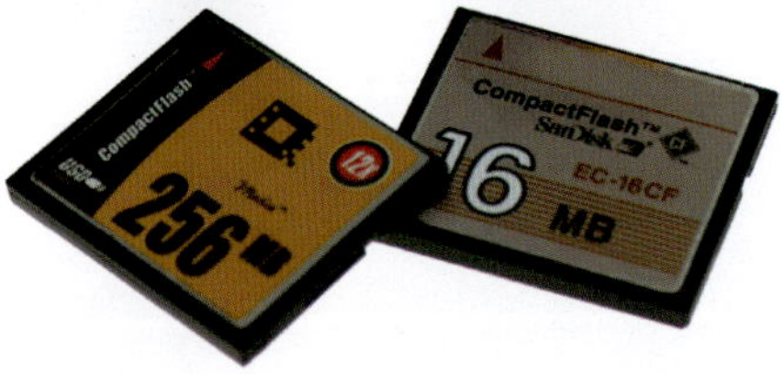

When the first digital camera models appeared on the market some of them had a certain type of hard drive that couldn't be removed. When a disk was full it had to be cleared before the camera could be used again. Today nearly all digital cameras use some type of removable memory (memory cards).

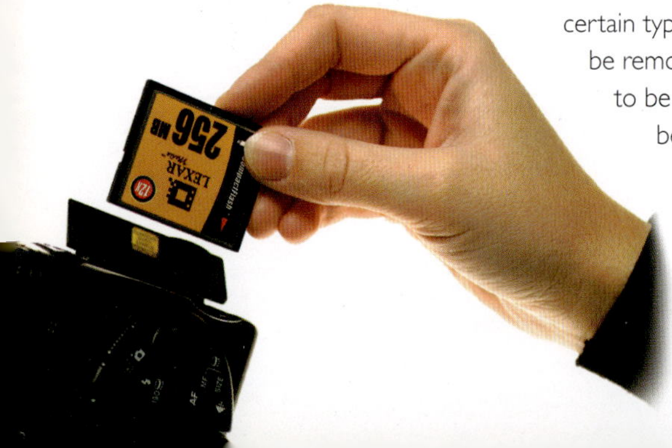

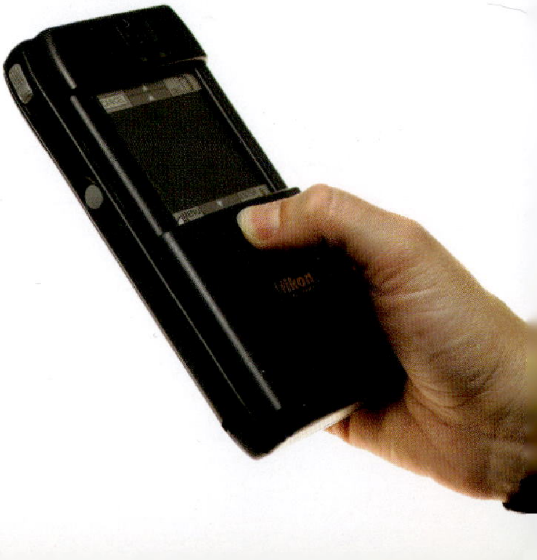

The following cards are currently in use:

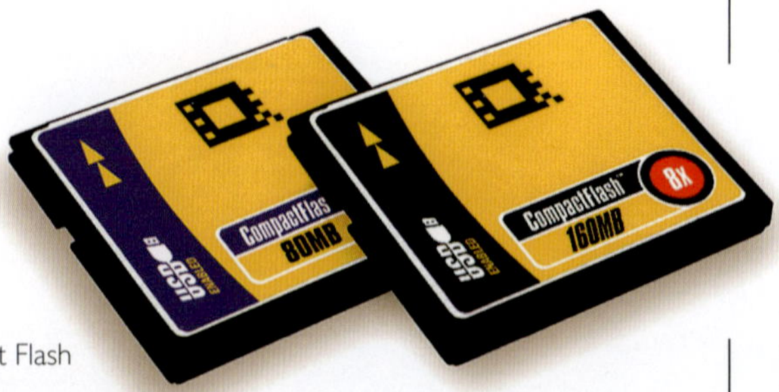

Compact Flash

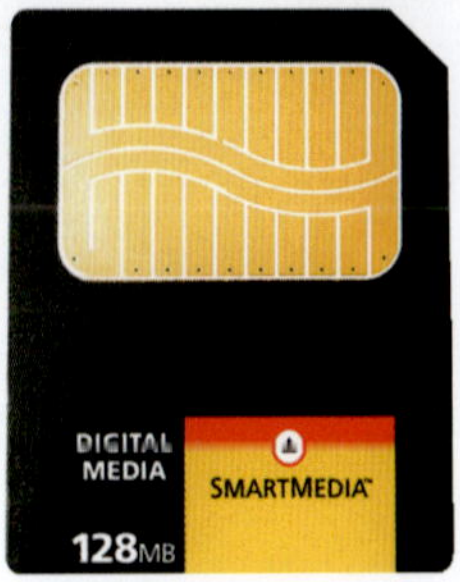

Smartmedia

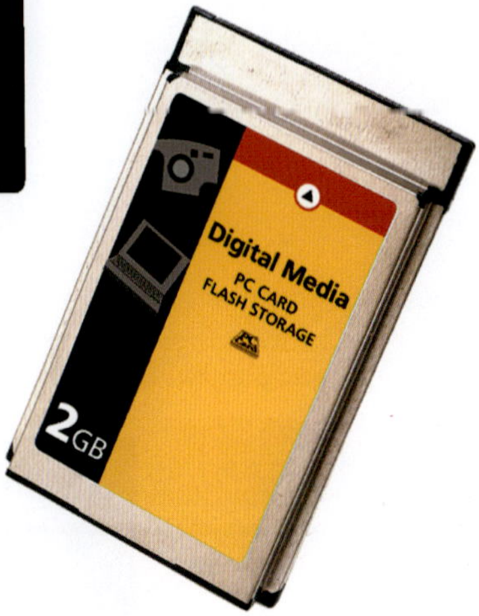

PC Card

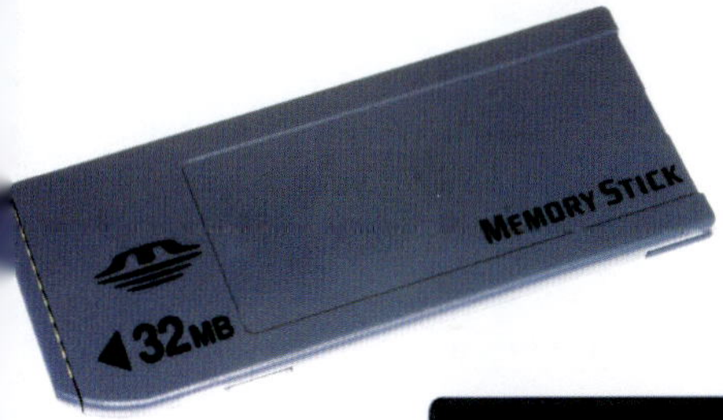

Memory Stick

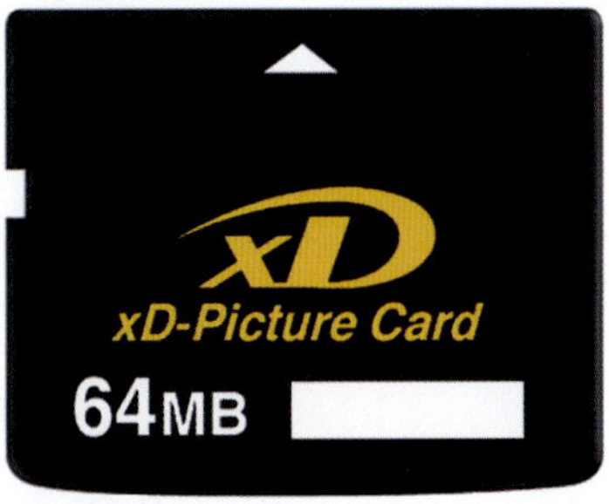

XD Image Card

In general, the only characteristics by which individual memory cards differ are size and the speed at which information is recorded. Differences among memory cards are like the variety of automobile models there are on the market. Manufacturers simply make products that will sell best and can be patented so they won't be copied. So each brand develops its own technologies and therefore, as with cars, there are cards with slower or faster recording and various memory sizes. When choosing a memory card one must first analyze two aspects - capacity (the larger the better) and the speed at which the card records information (faster recording is better, because it allows you to take the next picture sooner). We recommend that these cards always be kept in protective cases or in the camera itself. If you have several memory cards make sure that cards not currently in use are protected against dust, moisture, and extreme temperatures.

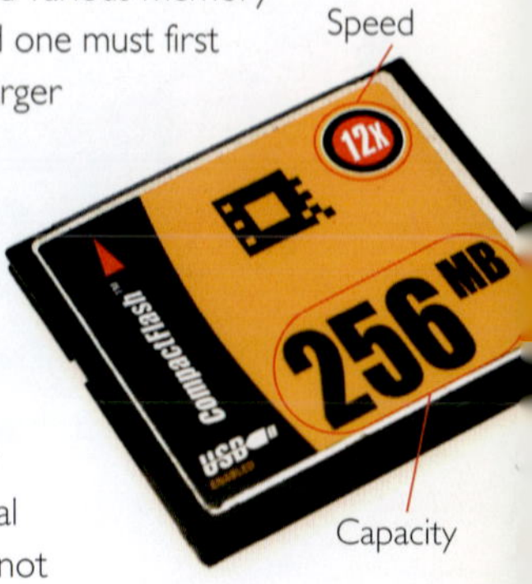

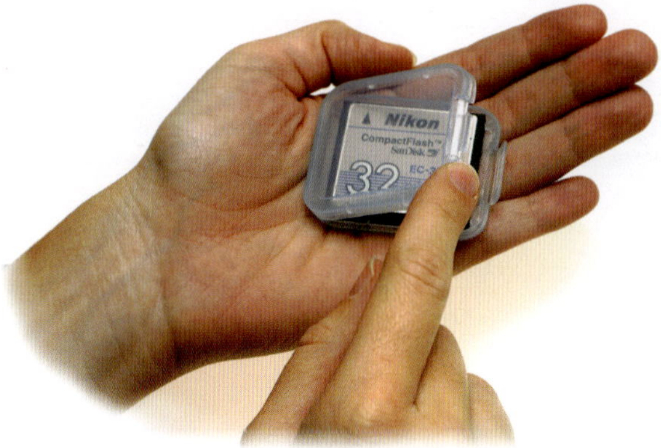

Batteries are extremely important. Although they all serve the same purpose, individual types vary - some last longer than others. This is an essential element. Without a battery you can't take pictures!

Monitors and flashes are very draining on batteries.

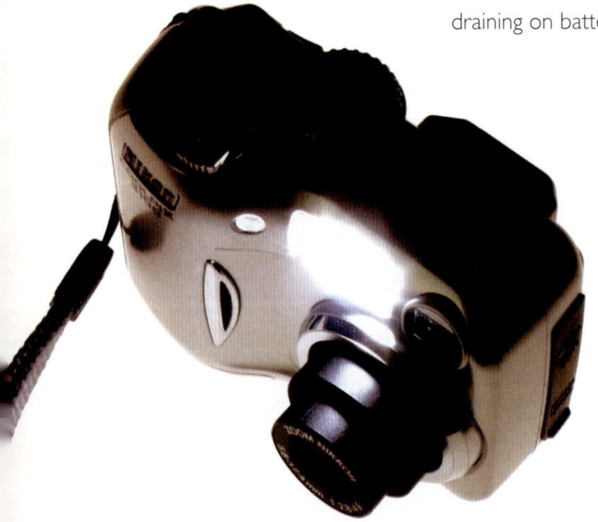

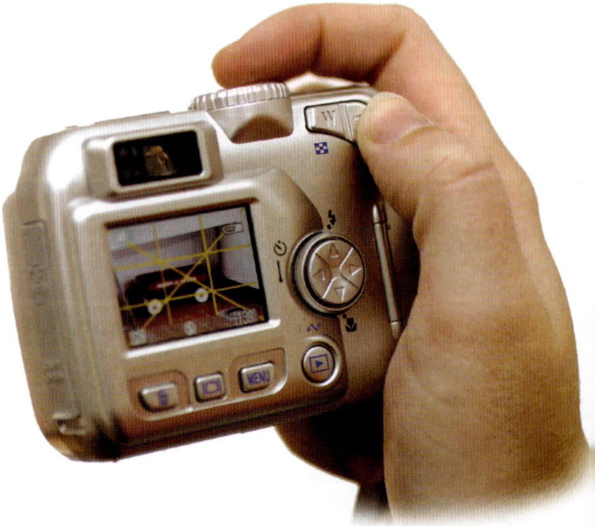

Various types of batteries can be used in digital cameras.

Li-ion

(Lithium-ion) These batteries have great capacity that allows them to be used for the longest time. They're expensive, but they're usually included with cameras. Various firms offer batteries under various brands. Among them there are also standard-type batteries that cannot be charged, such as AA batteries. Li-ion batteries can be charged.

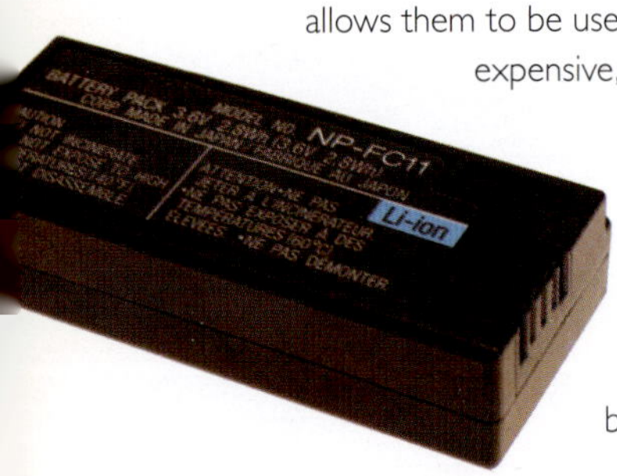

NiCd

(Nickel Cadmium) These batteries have smaller capacities and are therefore often replaced by NiMH batteries. The advantages of NiCd batteries are that they are charged very quickly and cost less.

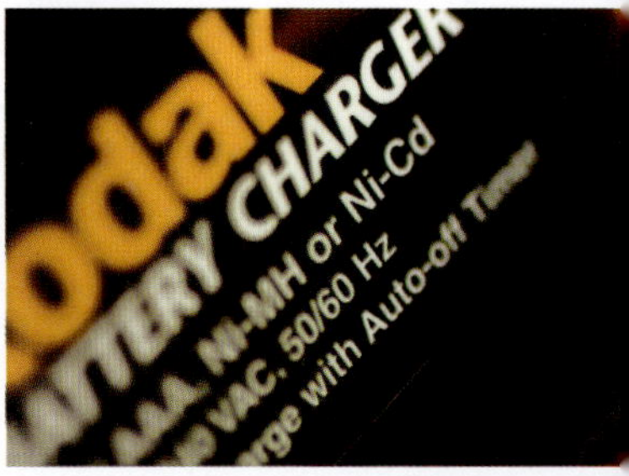

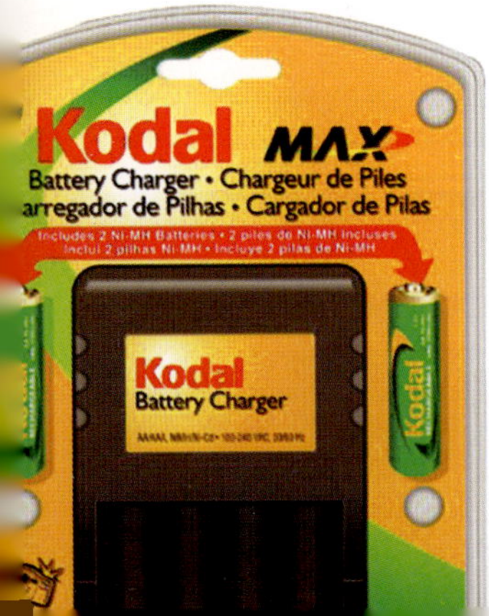

NiMH

(Nickel Metal Hydride) These standard batteries are often used in cameras for which AA batteries are also intended. NiMH batteries can be charged, and their price is reasonable.

Alkalai batteries

These are the most common batteries. They are found nearly everywhere, but they are used less in digital cameras because of their smaller capacities. There are also alkalai batteries that can be recharged, but users spend more time charging them than using them.

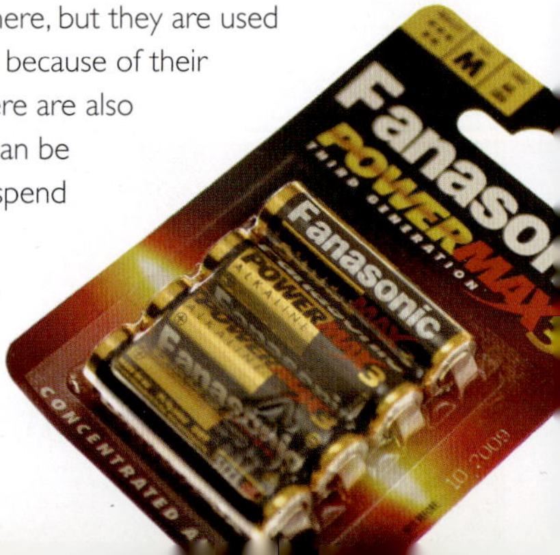

DIGITAL CAMERA MENU

Now that we have presented the basic parts of a digital camera the time has come to acquaint you with what these cameras' menus offer you.
Each brand has its own characteristics, but all firms seek out and develop many functions or preset options with the goal of making the camera practical and easy to use.

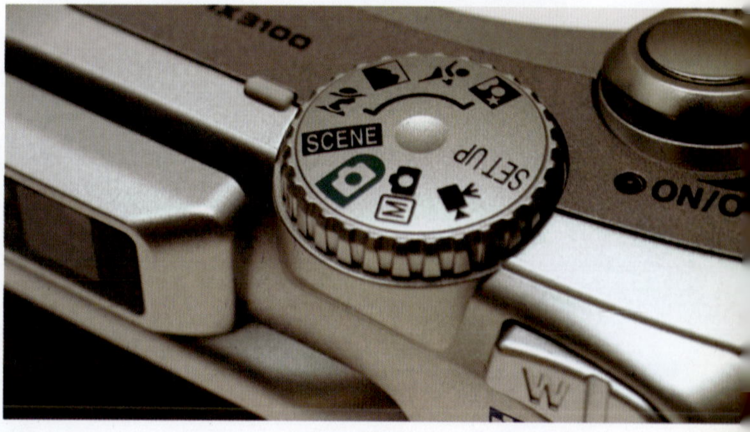

▸ This camera's multi-selector offers preprogrammed functions: portrait, landscape, and motion.

There are thousands of digital camera models, but we will present functions here that are general and common and crucial for users.

Sensitivity

Like classic cameras, digital cameras have several sensitivity settings (in ISO units) for taking pictures in various lighting conditions.
As with film, the higher the sensitivity the less important lighting is for the photograph.

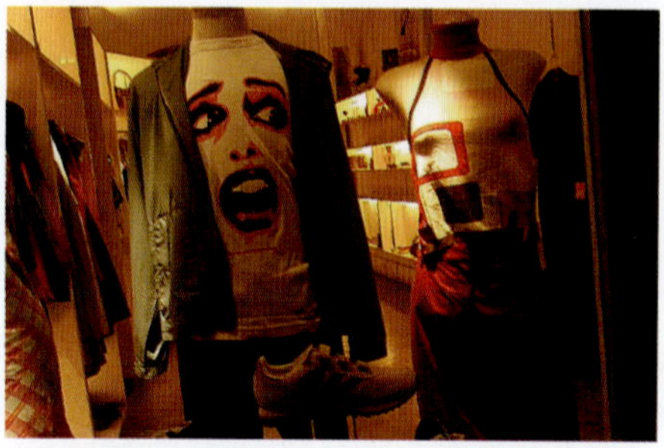

▲ This photograph of a display window was taken at night with limited lighting; therefore, heightened sensitivity was used.

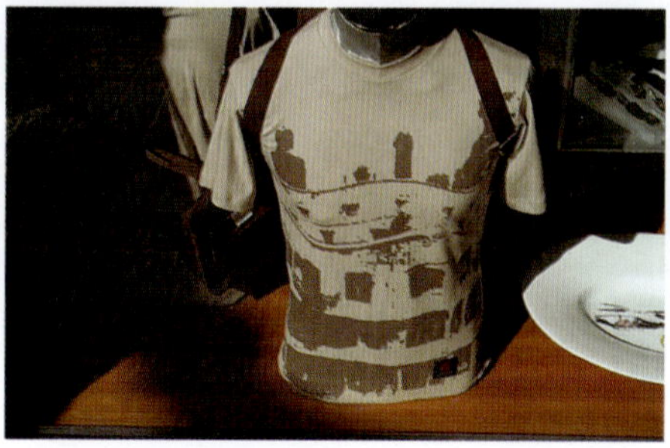

▲ This photograph of a display window was taken in full daylight at low sensitivity.

Some digital cameras allow you to adjust the sensitivity (ISO) manually, while others adjust it automatically with the help of previously programmed functions.
On a sunny day with great light intensity a low sensitivity setting (ISO 50 or 100) is generally used. This applies provided that the lighting can be regulated (influenced) – this setting can be used at night with the use of a tripod.

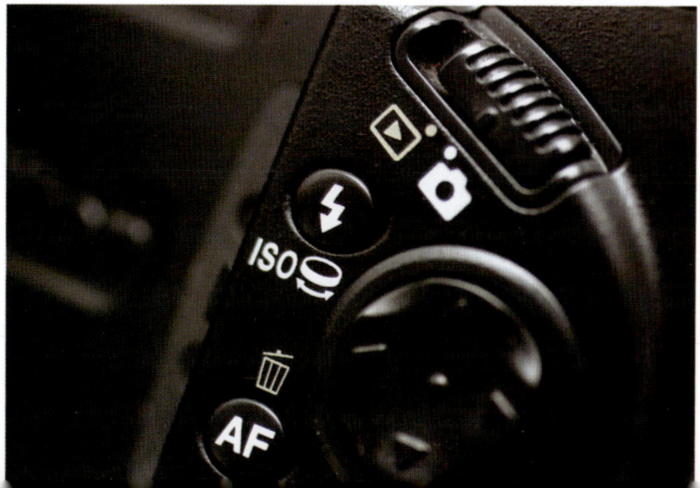

◂ This control allows you to set the camera's sensitivity (ISO).

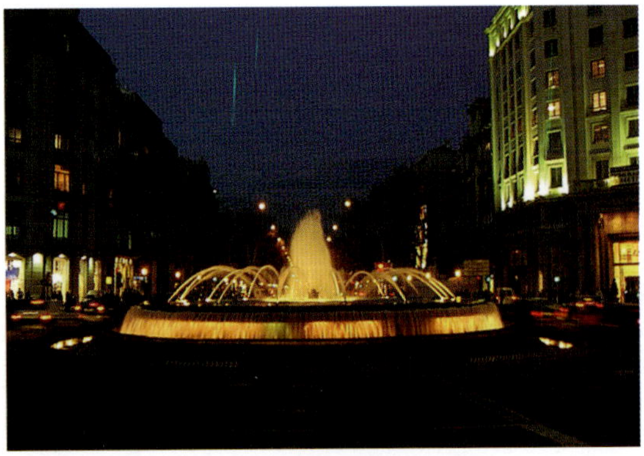

▲ For this picture the sensitivity was set at ISO 100 and a tripod and the self timer were used.

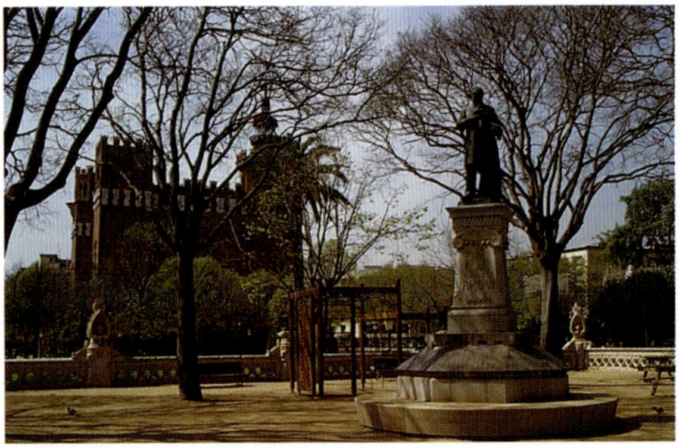

▲ With bright light the camera automatically set the sensitivity to a low value.

Increased sensitivity (ISO 400 or 800) must be used in situations with weak lighting, when no tripod is available, or, under good lighting conditions, when you need to catch motion.

▶ For this picture the camera automatically selected increased sensitivity.

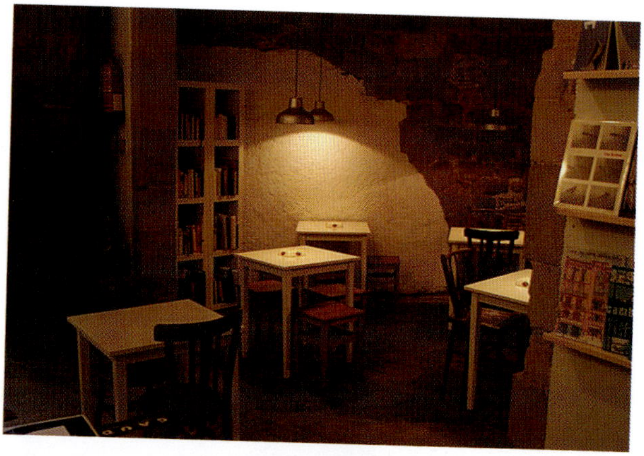

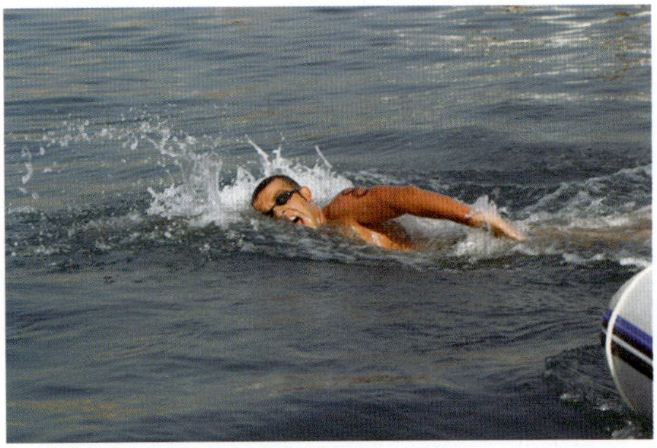

◀ Even though the lighting was bright, increased sensitivity was used in order to catch motion. So in the picture we can see drops of water splashing off the swimmer's body.

One disadvantage of this technique is that the more high sensitivity is used, the more "noise" (graininess with classic film) shows up in the picture.

▼ This picture was taken with low sensitivity and the use of a tripod.

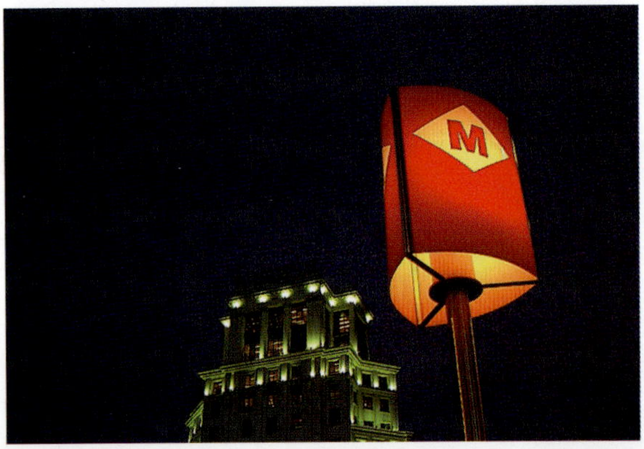

▼ This picture was taken under the same lighting conditions as the preceding one, but with higher sensitivity.

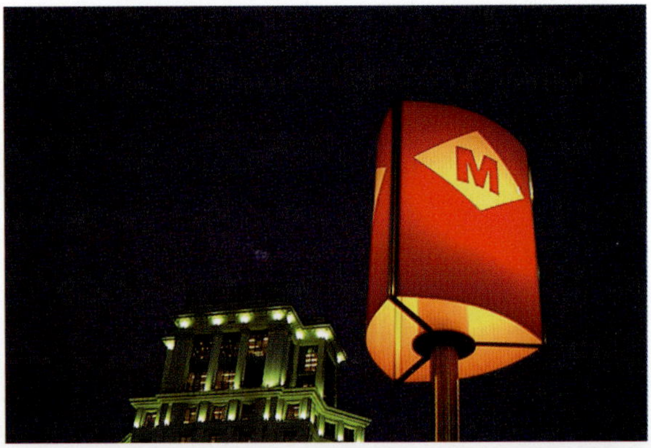

The following exercise will allow you to better recognize the camera's sensitivity setting. If you can set the sensitivity manually on your camera, you can verify this experience in practice.

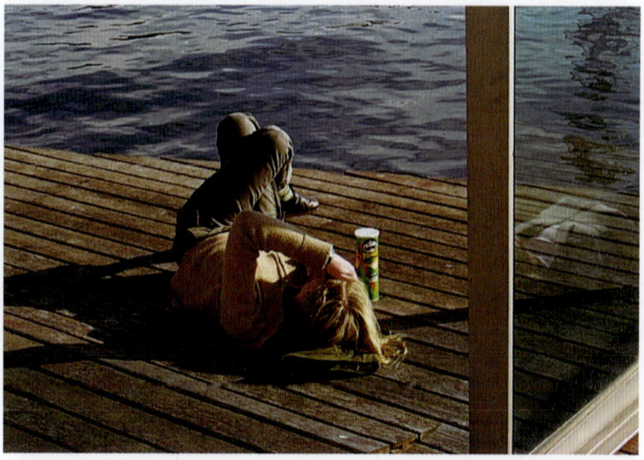

1. With the ISO setting at the lowest value, take a photograph at high noon (the photograph will be clear).

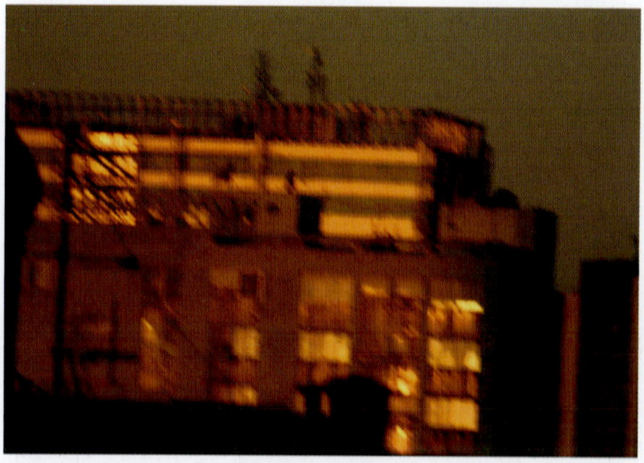

2. With the same low ISO setting as in the preceding picture take a picture in the evening (the photograph may be blurred by movement).

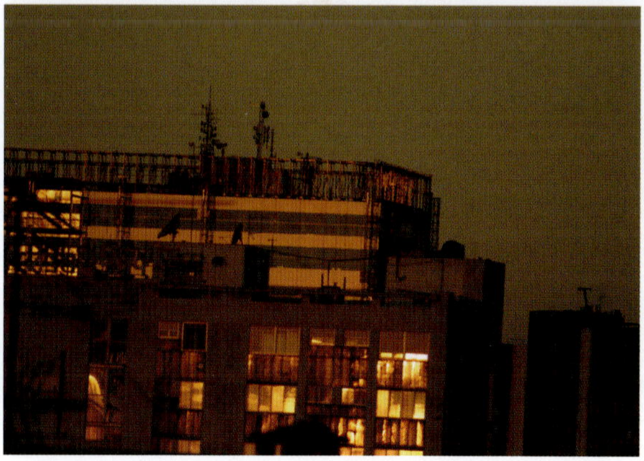

3. With the same lighting as in example 2 and the same sensitivity setting, affix the camera to a tripod and use the self timer (the picture will be clear).

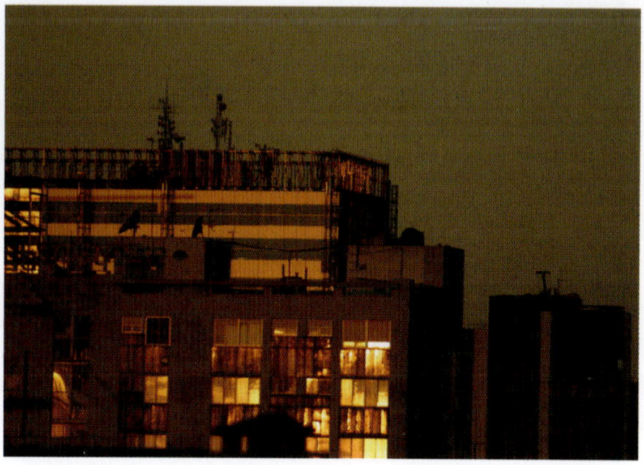

4. Under the same lighting conditions as the two preceding pictures use a higher sensitivity (ISO 400 or 800) and take the picture without using a tripod (the picture will be clear, but it will be noticeably grainy, or noisy).

Other examples of photographs with the sensitivities used when taking them:

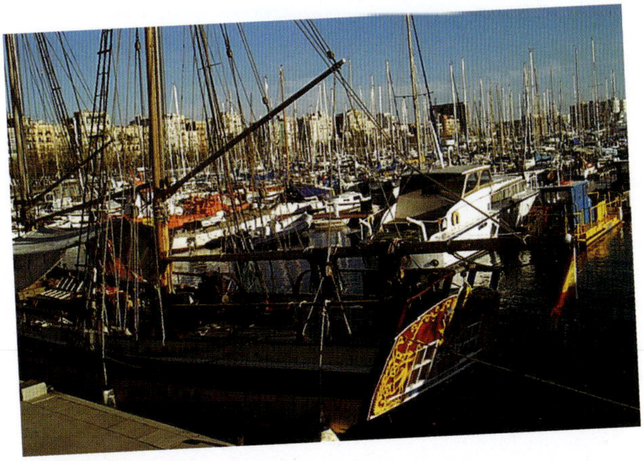

The ISO 50 setting was used here.

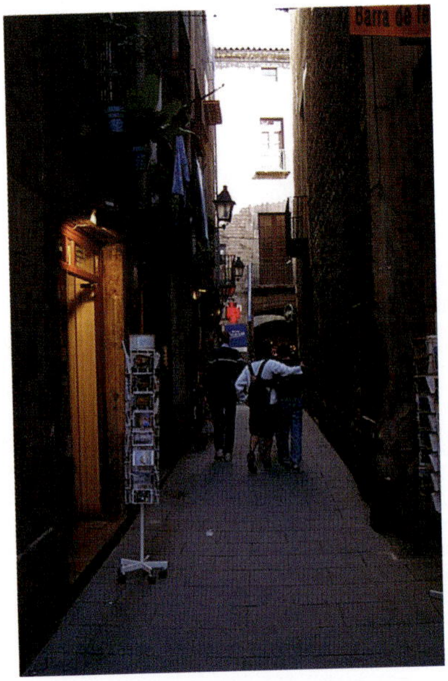

As can be seen from the upper part of the picture, this was taken on a sunny day, but the lane was too narrow to allow the sun's rays to penetrate to the extent required for using the ISO 100 setting. The ISO 200 setting was used here.

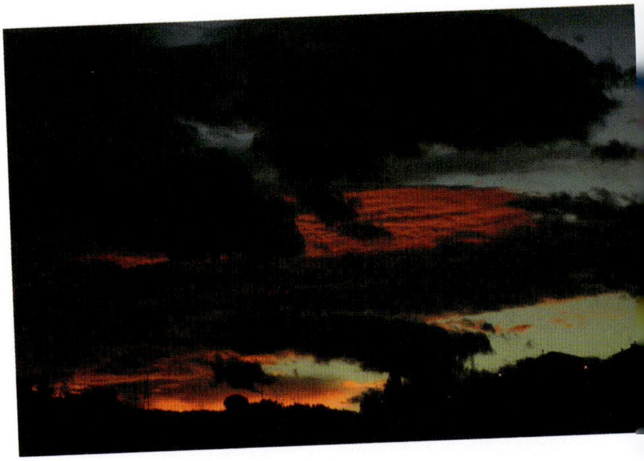

This photograph was taken from a moving car, so a tripod could not be used. ISO 800 sensitivity was used.

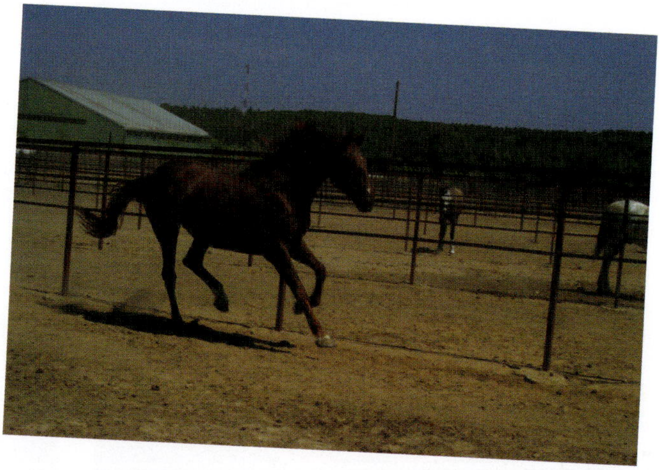

For this picture, even though it was taken on a sunny day, the ISO 400 setting was used in order to catch the motion of the horse.

White balance

This function allows you to adjust the camera to individual types of light, making it possible to preserve yellowish indoor light without switching to daylight (white) and vice versa. We'll return to this problem on page 41 (types of light).

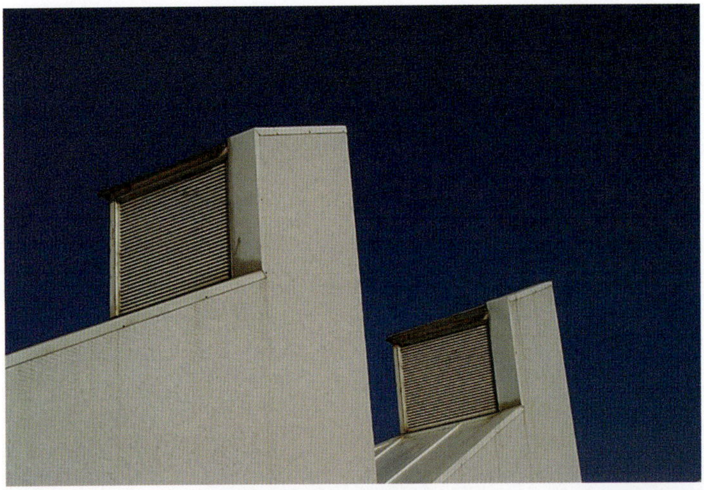

Daylight

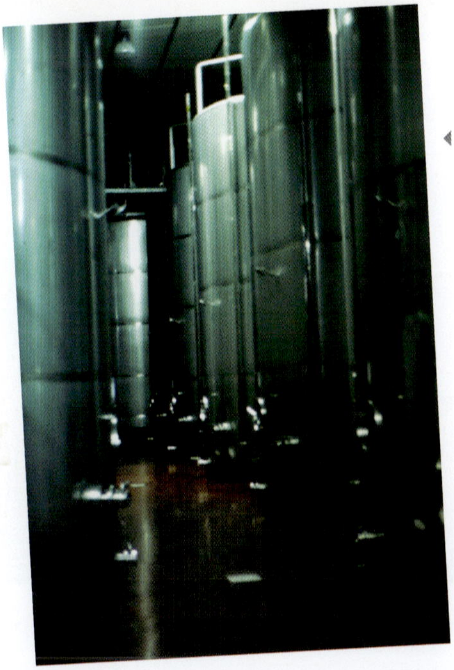

◀ Fluorescent lighting

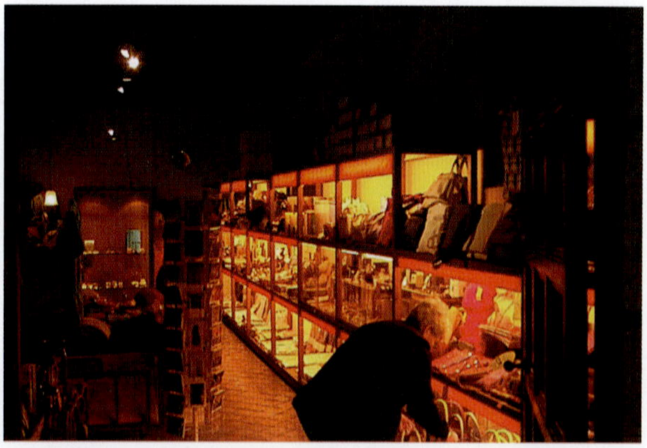

▶ Classic incandescent lighting

Exposure compensation

Photographs are often too light or too dark, because the camera doesn't always correctly measure the brightness of the object, especially with back lighting or when the shot has too much contrast.

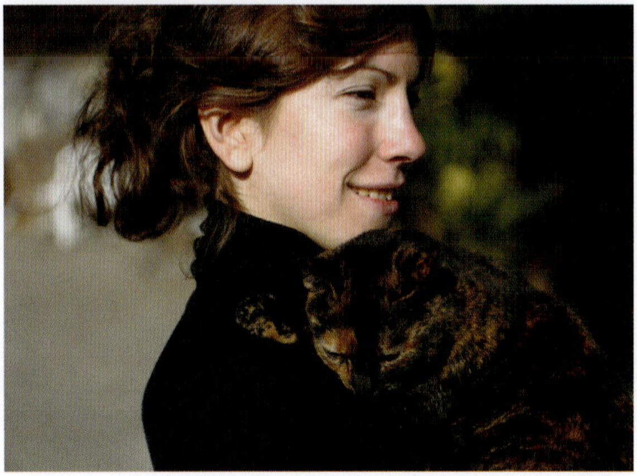

▲ These two pictures were taken at two different exposure settings, the result being that one of them is less colorful and has less contrast.

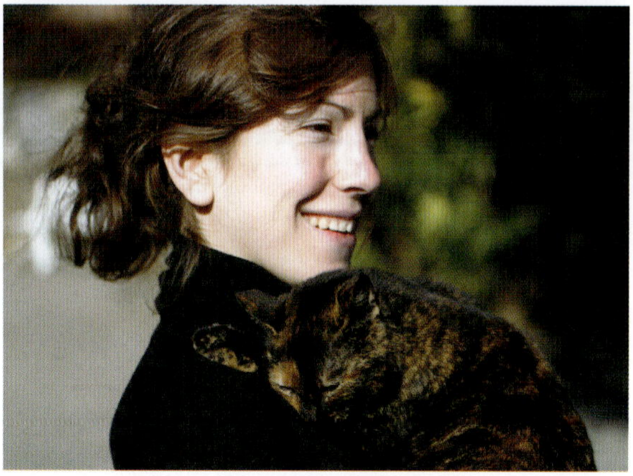

This possibility is used to compensate automatic exposures so the picture has the right exposure. Digital cameras usually offer the possibility of exposure compensation from +2 to -2 EV for overexposure or underexposure.

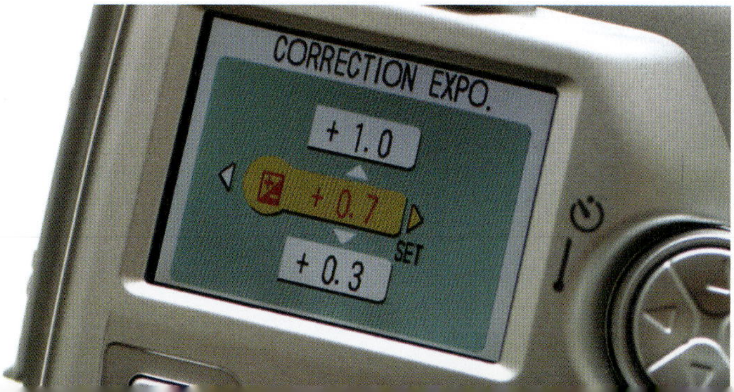

The following exercise will allow you to understand this function well.

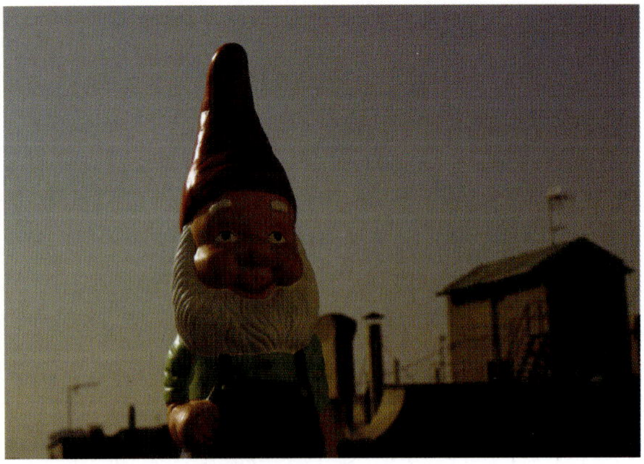

1. We take a portrait shot of the figure with the sky or another bright background (the photographed object appears too dark).

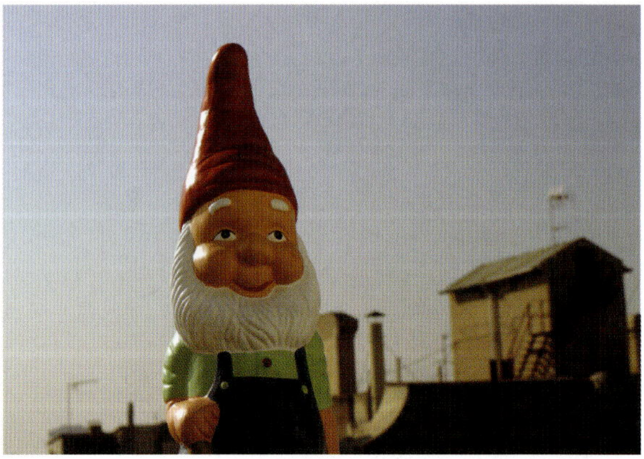

2. This portrait was taken with 1 EV overexposure (+1 EV).

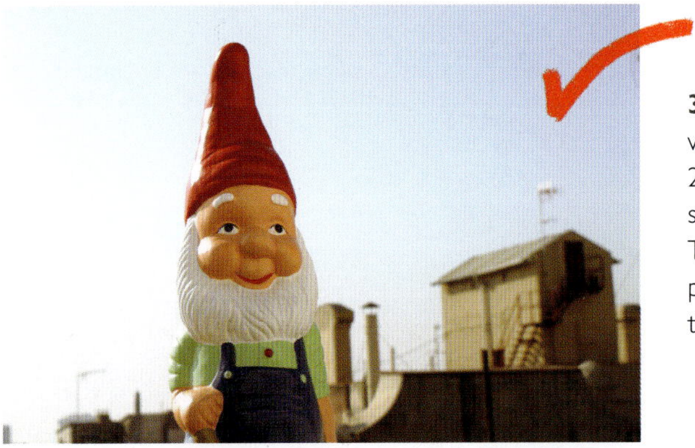

3. This portrait was taken with 2 EV overexposure (+2 EV). This is the best picture of the three.

As we can see, the camera doesn't always correctly evaluate the light that's available. So it's necessary to adjust the camera by using exposure compensation.

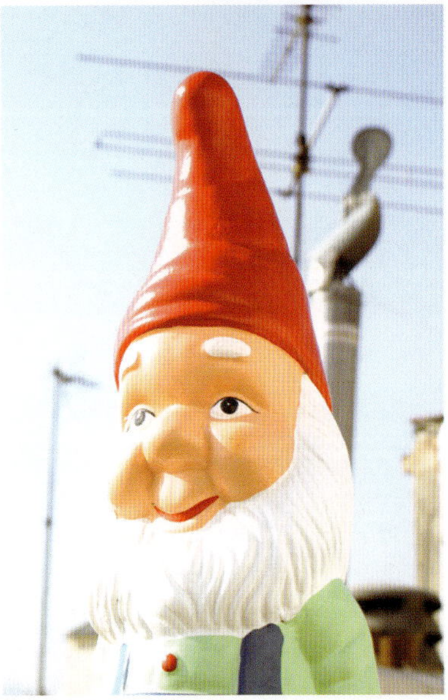

4. Portrait of the object illuminated by direct sunlight.

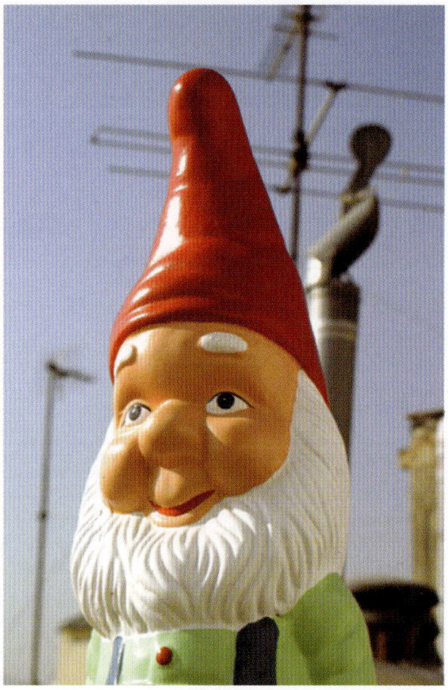

5. The object photographed under the same conditions with 1 EV underexposure (-1 EV).

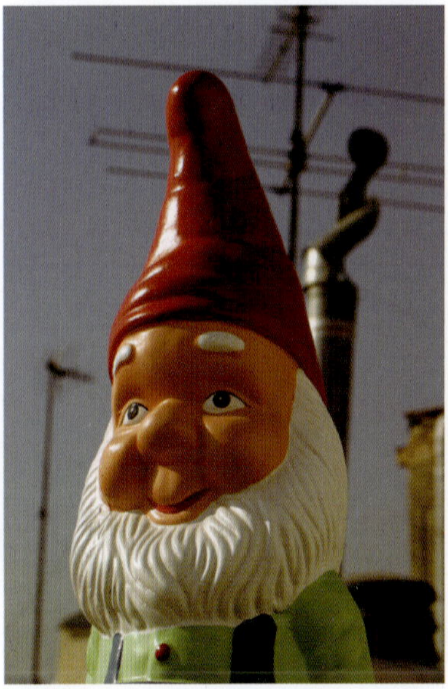

6. One more time, but with 2 EV underexposure (-2 EV).

These three shots show us that the camera isn't able to set the correct exposure by itself.

7. We select the brightest exposure.

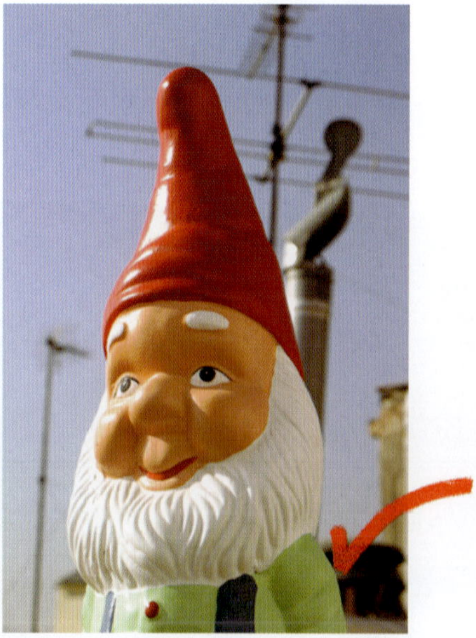

Flash types

Digital cameras usually have five programmed options for using the flash in various situations, whether portraits or just illuminating the darkest places. The five functions are as follows:

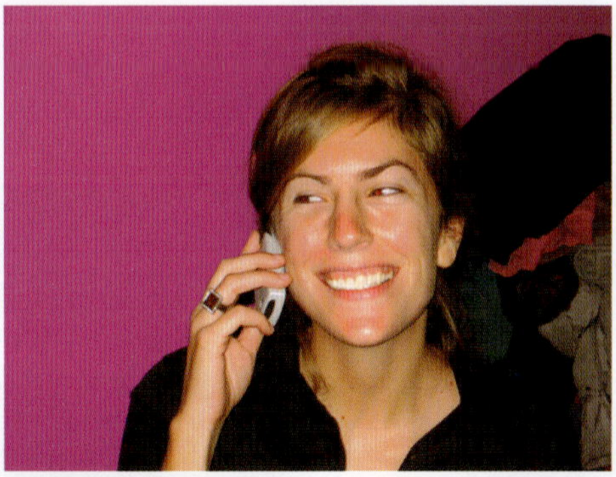

AUTO Automatic. In this mode the flash is used automatically whenever the camera deems it necessary. In this case the camera used the flash because of insufficient lighting. But we have to be careful in cases where the photographed object is a person, because the eyes can appear red in the picture.

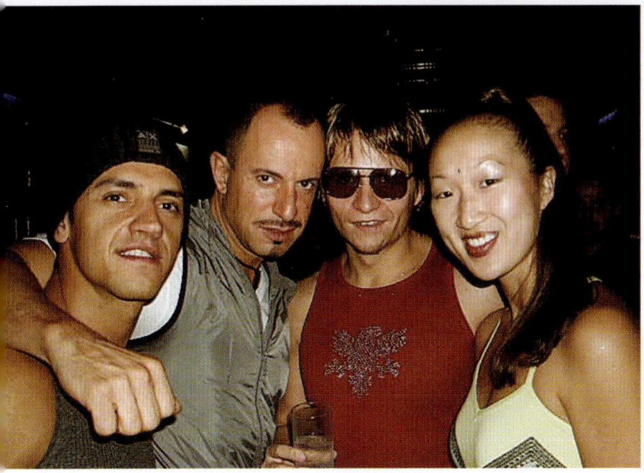

Red eye reduction. Before the camera takes the picture with the full flash it emits several lower-intensity flashes that cause the pupils to contract, thus reducing the red eye effect.

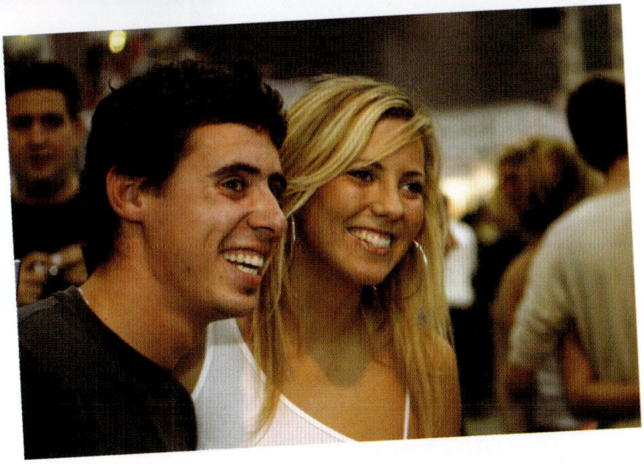

Permanent flash. The flash goes off every time regardless of the light intensity. This mode serves to illuminate dark places. Here there was sufficient light and the flash was used only to eliminate shadows around the eyes and to give more brightness to the couple.

Without flash. This option is useful for taking pictures in places where no flashes are allowed (e.g., in museums). Additionally, in this photograph of a display window the light would have been reflected back from the glass if the flash had been used.

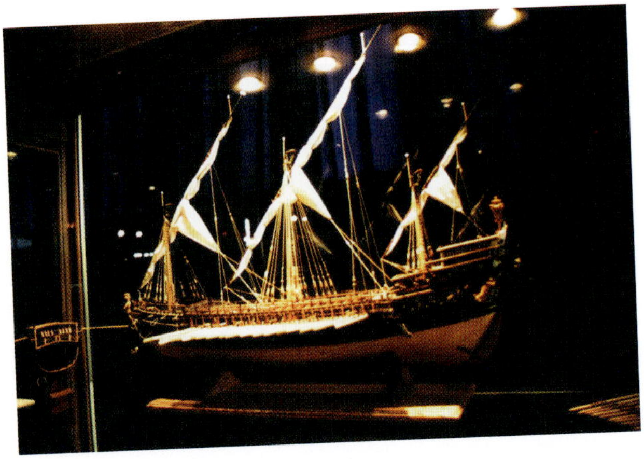

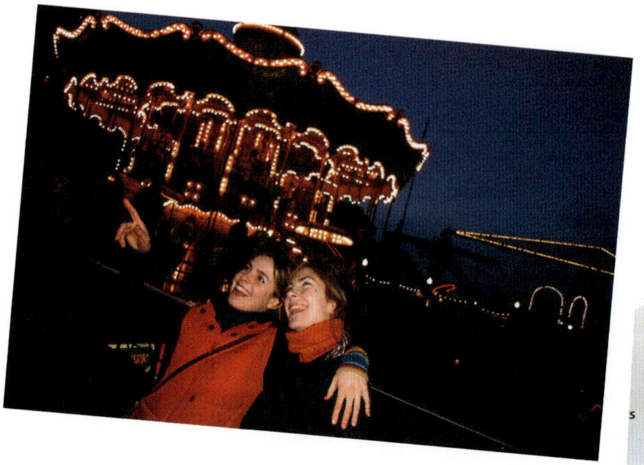

Extended synchronization. The camera takes a long exposure that is a combination of the flash-illuminated people in the foreground and the remaining extended part that brightens the dark background. If you're taking a picture of people you have to ask them not to move for a while so they aren't blurred in the picture. In this case, thanks to the long exposure the circus lights are clearly seen.

The following exercise will help you fully understand the results when using the various flash functions.

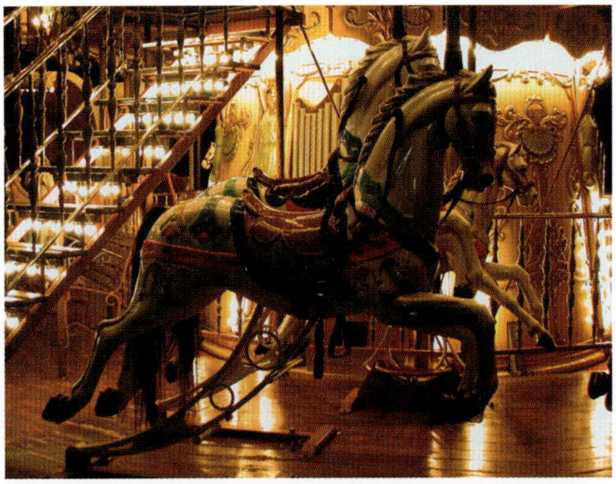

1. Choose an object that isn't as well lighted as the background. Take a picture of it with the flash off.

2. Take the same picture with the permanent flash.

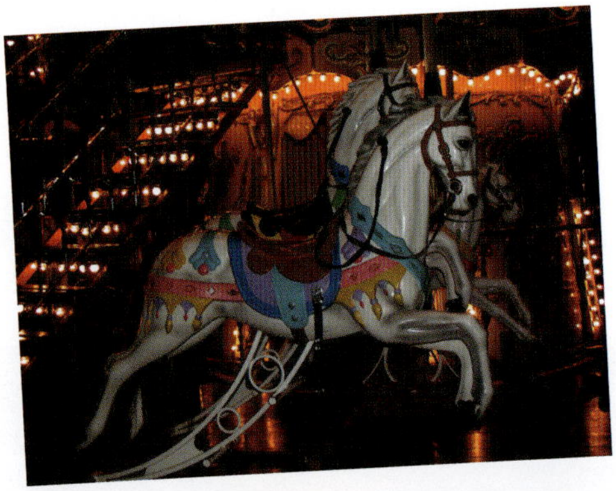

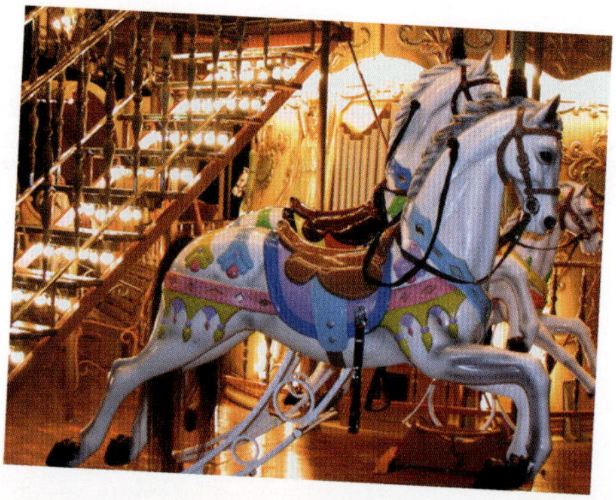

3. Take the same picture with the extended synchronization option on.

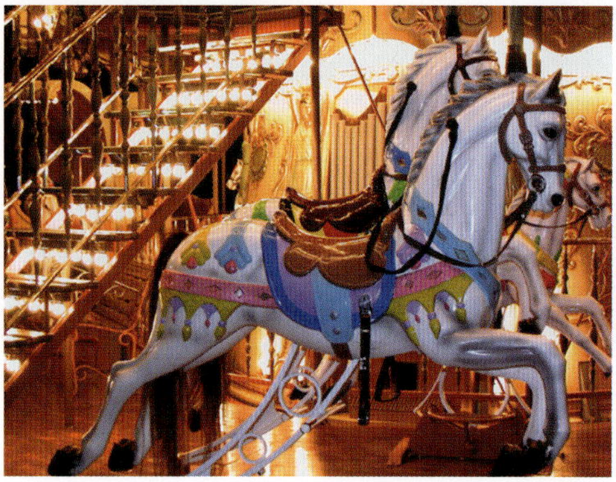

4. Judge for yourself which picture is the most interesting.

Recommended equipment for a beginner

It's hard to recommend a digital camera model because tastes and requirements differ. Moreover, new models are being developed with dizzying speed. We can only go through what a camera should come with when you buy it in order for you to be able to use it right off. It's good to buy a set of extra batteries, an extra memory card, and a small tripod.

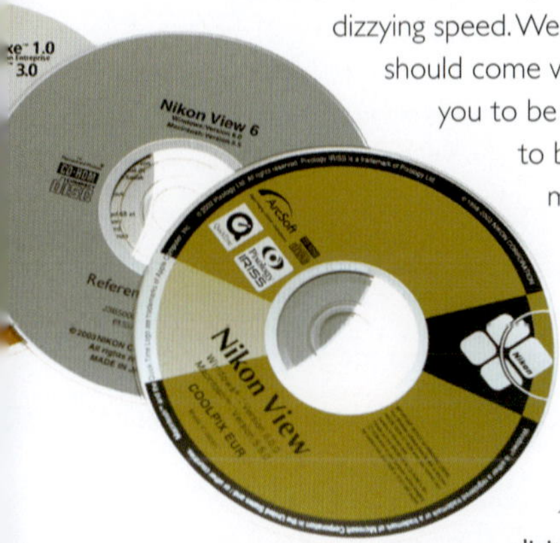

▲ In general, digital cameras come with installation CDs for moving pictures to computers (basic equipment) and sometimes with other CDs for modifying, processing, and archiving photographs; the CDs also contain manuals in PDF format.

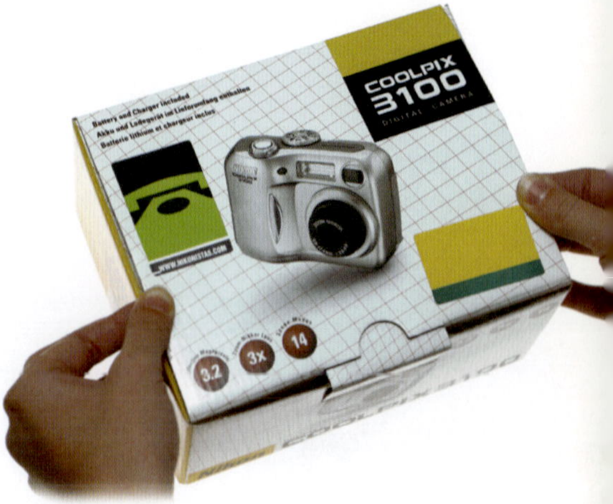

▲ When you buy a camera check to make sure the package is intact and that there are not any signs of it having been jolted.

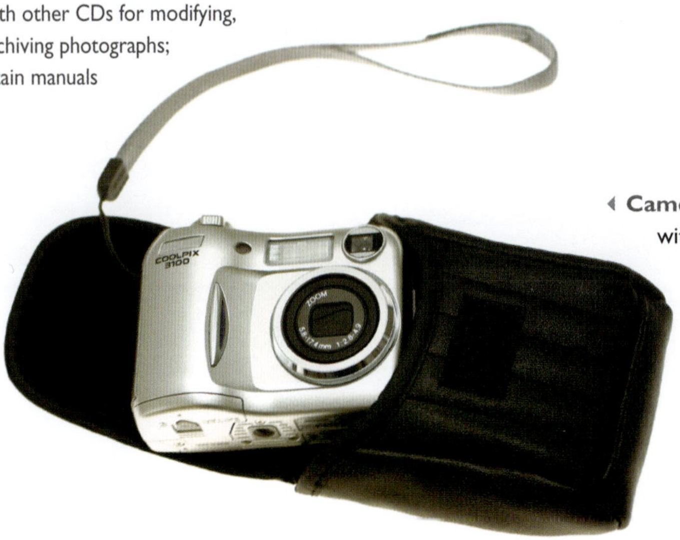

◀ **Camera.** Cameras don't always come with a case, so you should also buy one in order to protect the camera well.

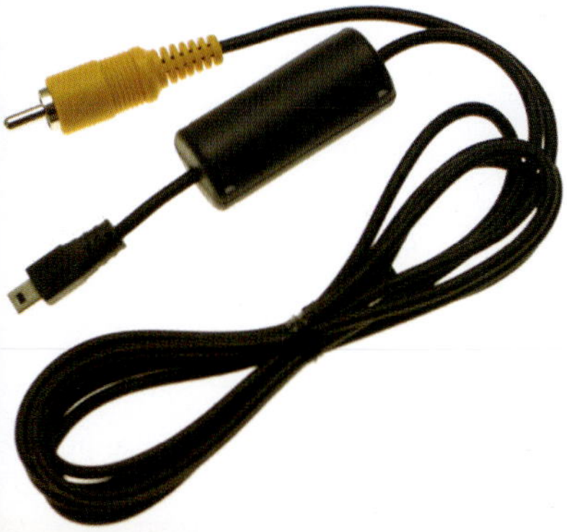

◀ **Video cable.** This allows you to view your pictures right on a television screen.

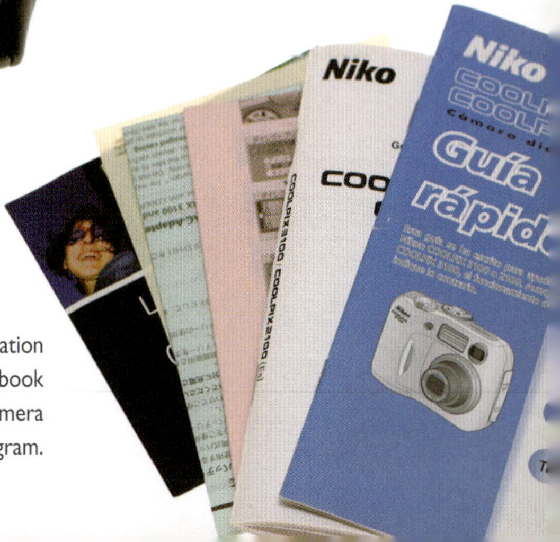

▶ It's necessary to have all the information brochures available, along with a handbook with instructions for operating the camera and the installation program.

Cable interface The ways to connect this cable can differ (USB, Firewire, I.Link, etc.).

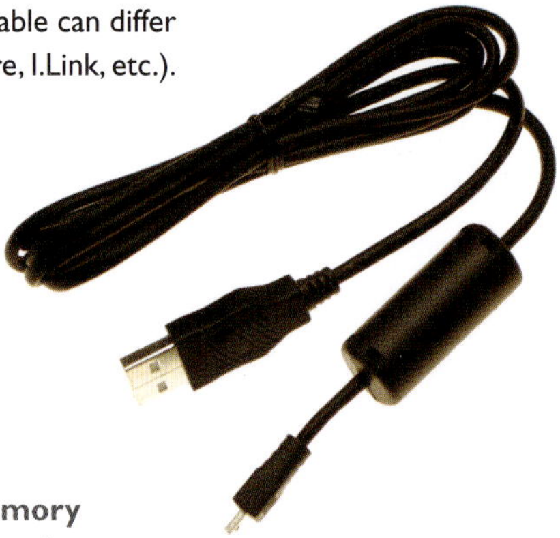

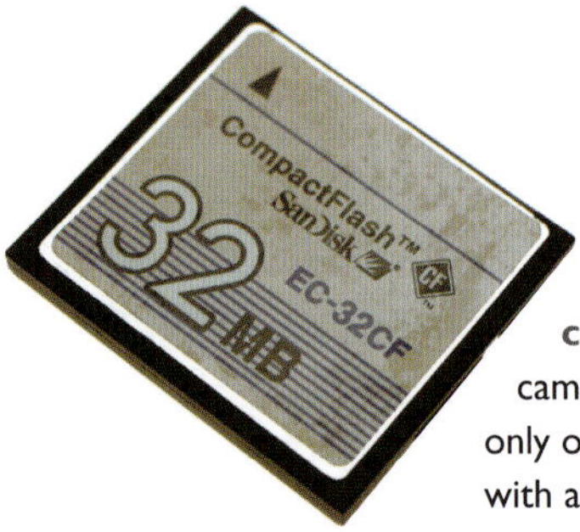

Memory card Most often cameras are sold with only one memory card with a clearly marked capacity.

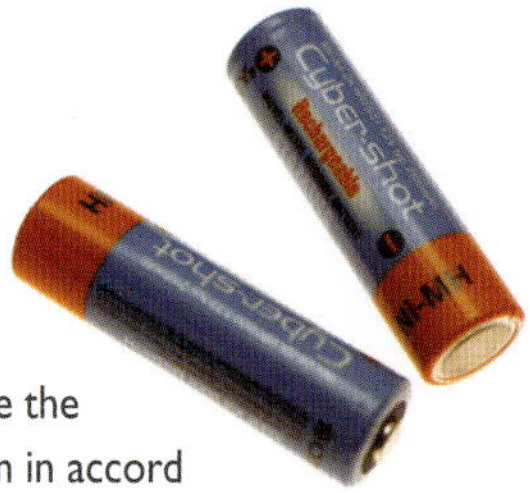

Batteries usually come without any charge on them, so before the first use you must charge them in accord with instructions in the user's guide. Try to avoid touching the battery's contacts (poles).

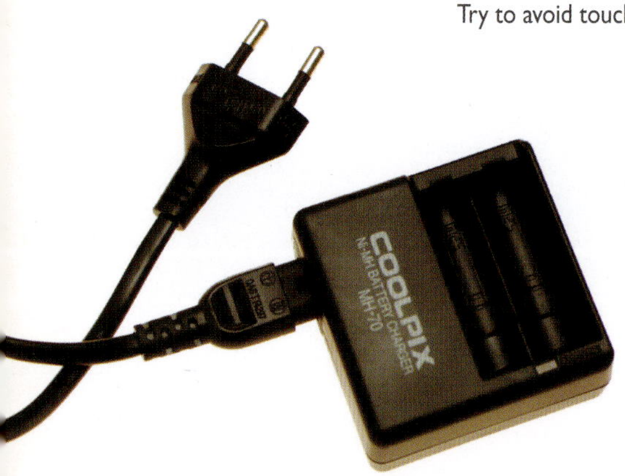

Battery charger The charger must correspond to the voltage in the mains. Most modern chargers can use the entire range of voltages from 100 to 240 V.

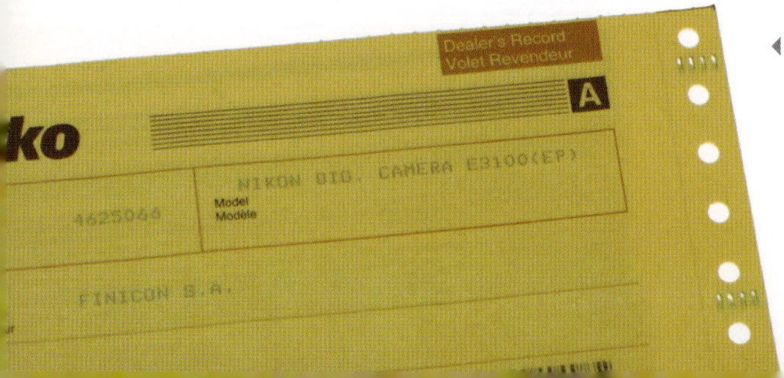

It is absolutely necessary to keep the guarantee certificate so you can have your camera repaired or replaced if there is any defect.

Types of light

There are various factors at play when you take a photograph: the photographed object, the camera, the photographer, and many others. But the most important factor, without which a picture cannot be taken, is always light.

There's no way to take a picture without light.

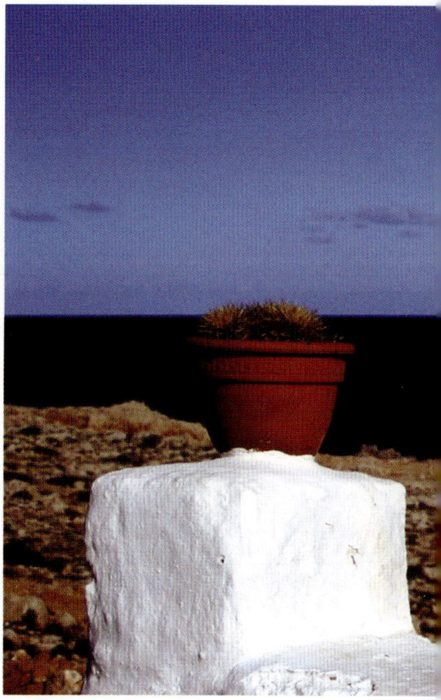

This is a true picture of what the photographer saw.

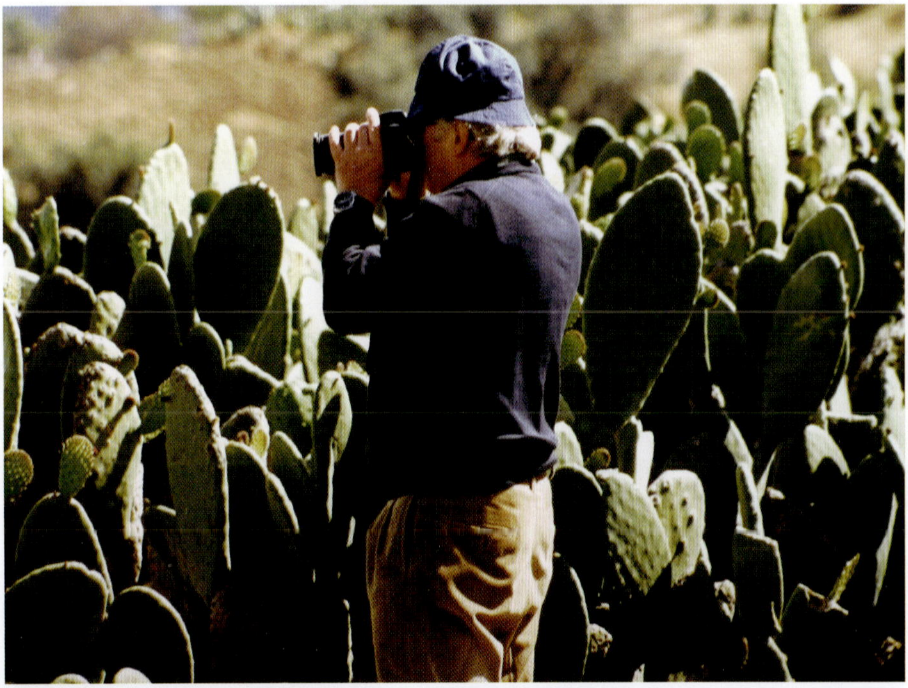

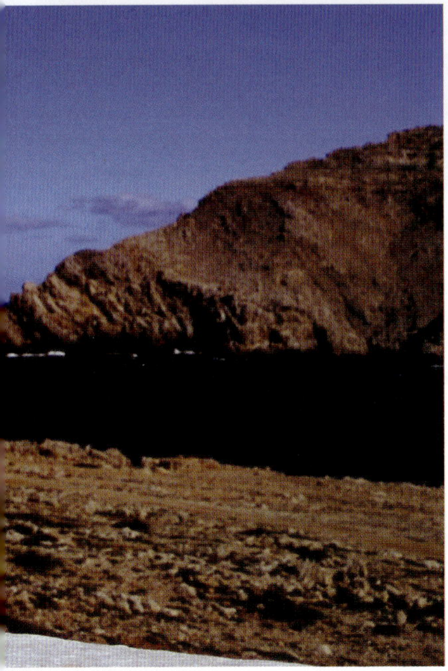

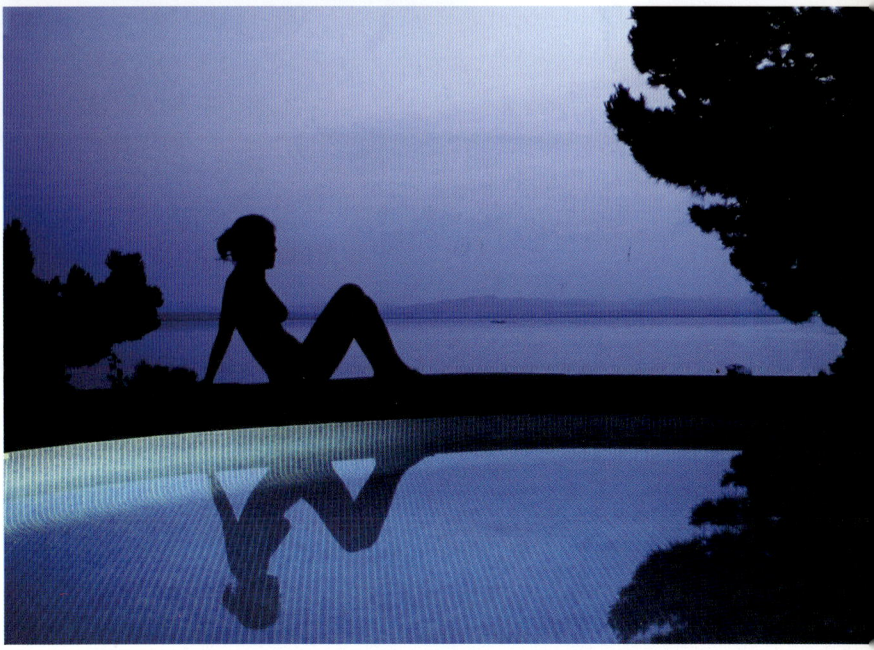

▲ In this shot the colors at the end of a summer day were modified through one of the camera's functions. The printed picture is much cooler, but it's still great.

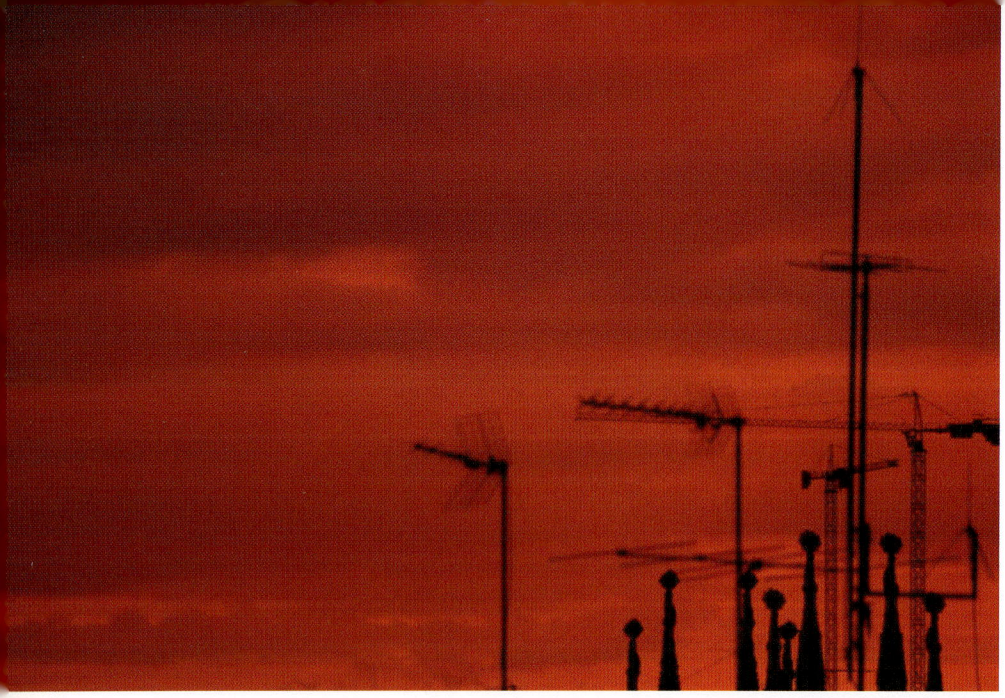

We often hear someone say, "What a camera! It must take terrific pictures!" It's true that a good camera can assist you in taking great pictures. But the key to success is that you have to understand and use light properly.

If you thoroughly understand the kind of light you're dealing with you'll take great pictures.

Even though sunlight may always seem the same, that is very far from the truth. Light comes from various angles and at different temperatures, and we then see it in an even more differently due to natural influences (rain, clouds, fog, etc.) Nearly all climatic factors, even the slightest, can directly affect the light.

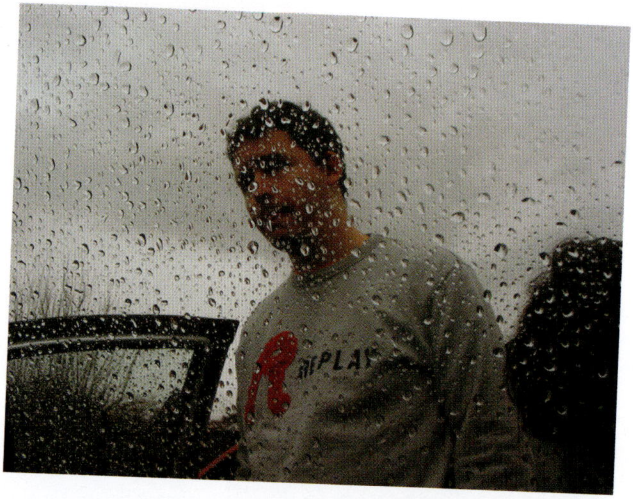

Pictures taken in cloudy or rainy weather aren't usually very high-contrast.

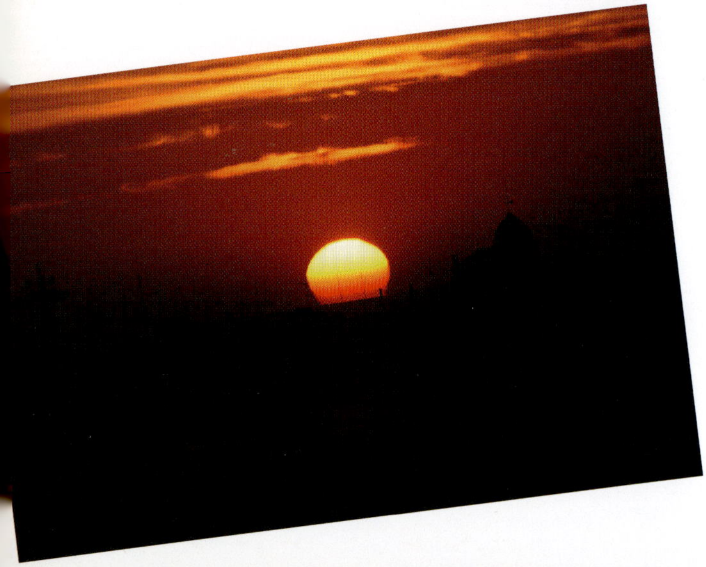

In some cases clouds can be used to diffuse sunlight. Such lighting is good for taking portraits.

The lower the sun is the less color warmth its light has, because it must pass through a greater distance of atmosphere.

▸ Even though the sunlight is dazzling, it's toned down by the tree canopy, affecting the picture's resulting green coloration,

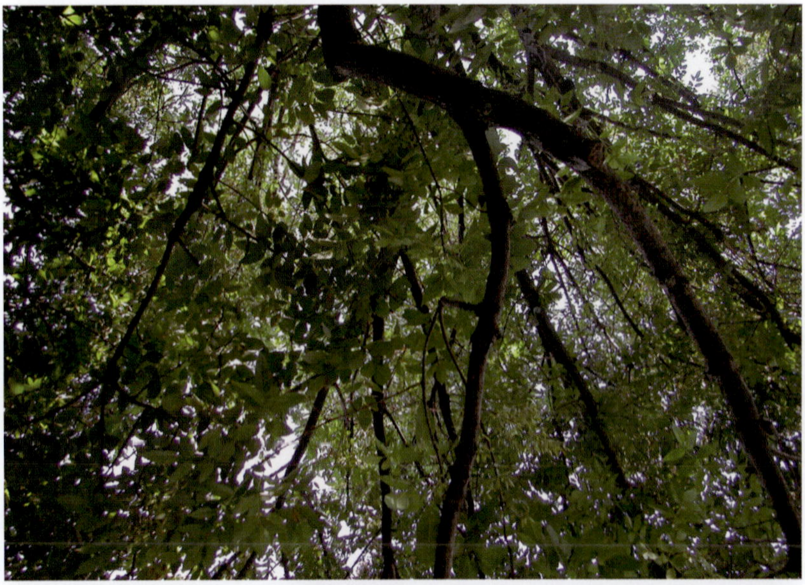

▾ Here the shadow points to the side thanks to the position of the sun.

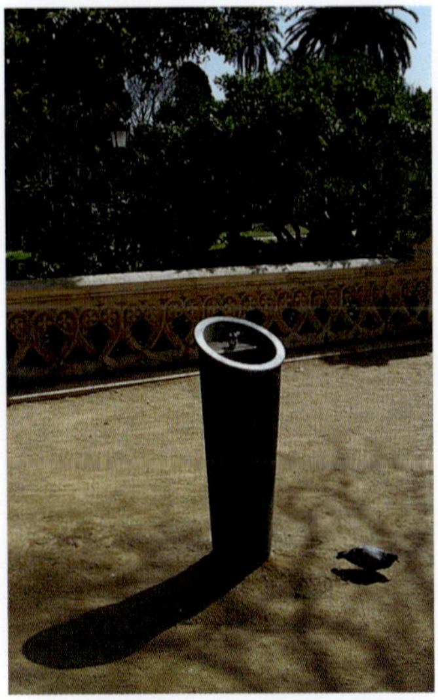

▸ In this shot the light is hitting the circus's emblem head-on, resulting in very highly contrasting colors.

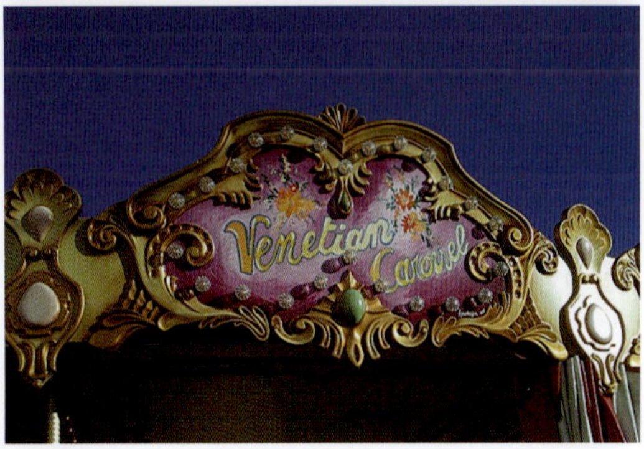

We speak of the "direction" of lighting when addressing the angle or position of the sun or artificial light source - e.g., head-on, back, or side lighting - or it can refer to taking photographs against the light source.

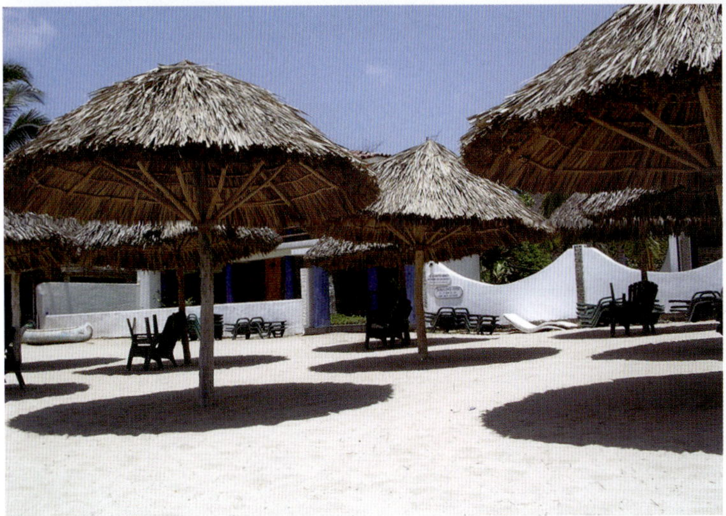

▴ When the sun is at its zenith shadows are not extended, so they lie directly under the objects that cast them.

▾ In this case the light source is directly in front of the camera and we can see the shadows projected in the photographer's direction.

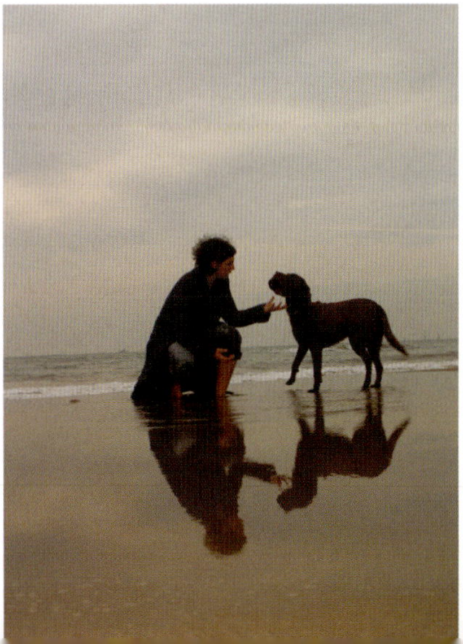

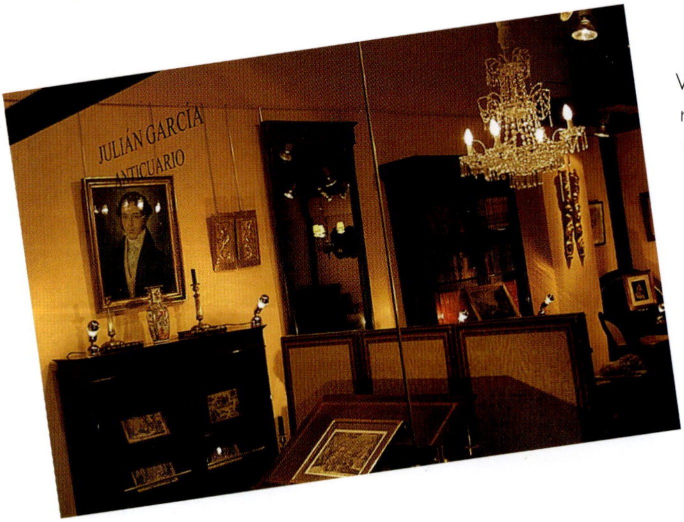

When we refer to the color "warmth" of light it is with respect to varying ratios of the basic colors (red, green, and blue, sometimes just RGB) in the given light. The color warmth of light is measured in degrees Kelvin (K). This color scale runs from red and yellow predominating (light from a classic incandescent bulb) to blue and white predominating (daylight or flash).

◀ A typical example of the warm light you have when you use classic tungsten-filament bulbs for taking pictures; it contains a large share of yellow and red shades.

▶ In this picture, which was taken in daylight, the white tones remained unaffected.

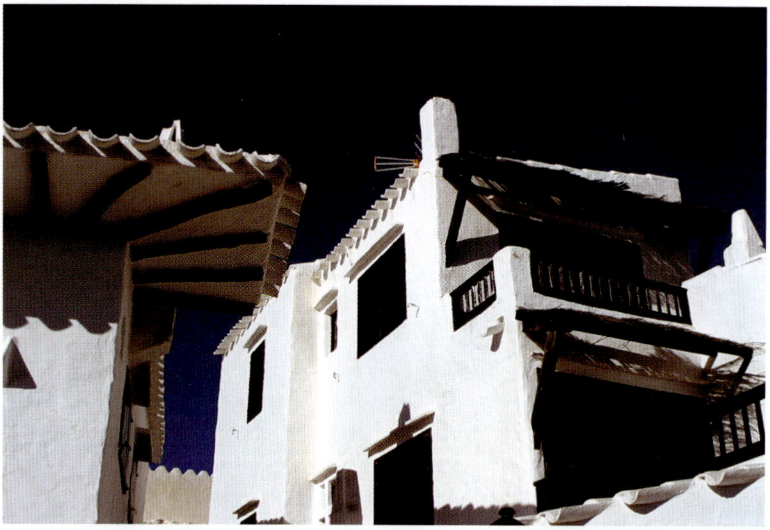

Natural and artificial light alike are rich in their range of color warmth . Indoors we usually find light in its "purer" form, unlike outdoors, where the purity of the color character is lost because various types of artificial lighting sometimes blend together, or, as the case may be, artificial light and daylight.

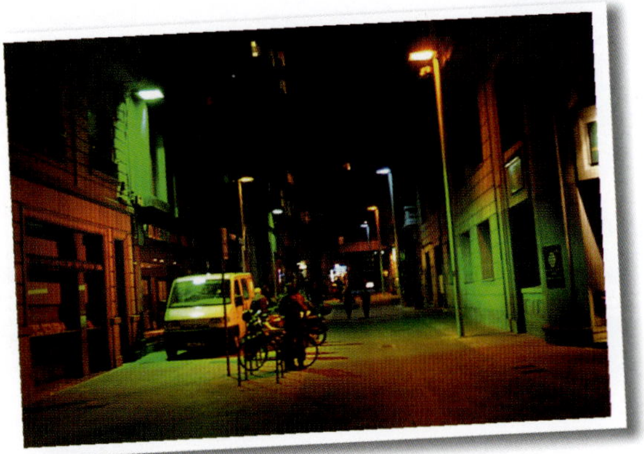

▲ We often encounter situations where light from various sources commingle.

If you take pictures using artificial lighting, the pictures will take on color tones that depend on the type of light source (incandescent bulbs give off light that is heavily yellow or orange, while fluorescent lights give off light that is predominantly green or bluish).

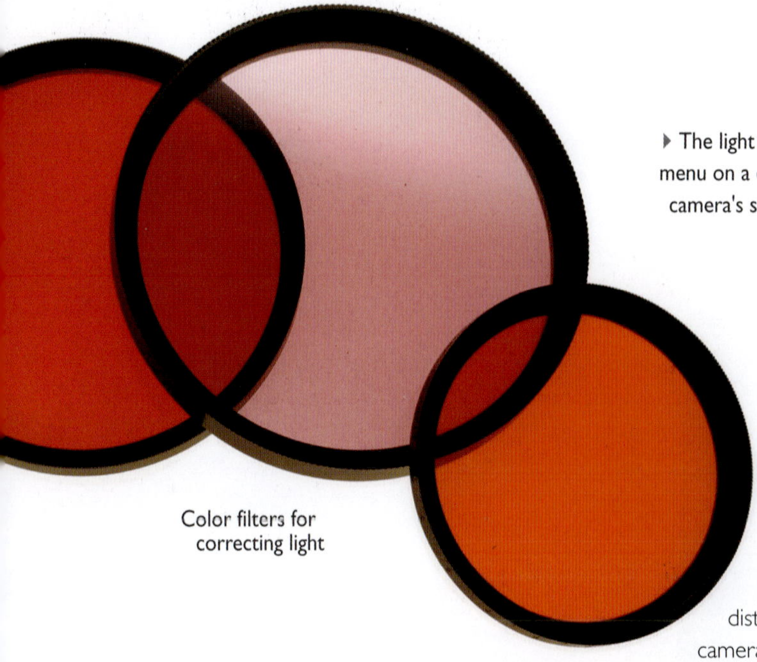

Color filters for correcting light

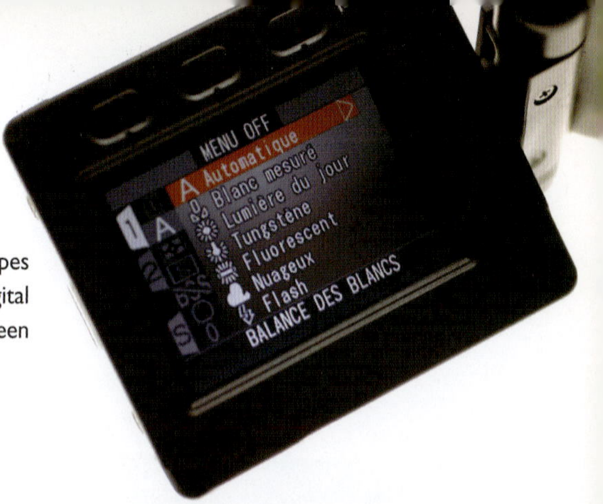

▸ The light types menu on a digital camera's screen

In order to make the best use of this feature you must always have a clear idea of the light that is illuminating the scene you want to photograph. For example, you have to ask yourself whether you have daylight, artificial light, or mixed light. You have to know how to distinguish everything that the manufacturer of your camera offers you and what is on the camera's screen to easily and quickly find your way to the depicted icon. If you make the correct choice the light correction your camera makes will be perfect.

Taking pictures with film with a halide layer requires great attention to the type of light illuminating the scene and also to the type of film to be used. Once film is loaded into the camera it offers no other way to compensate for the light than to use color filters. Digital cameras are totally different in this way, as they have mechanisms that can compensate for light either automatically or manually.

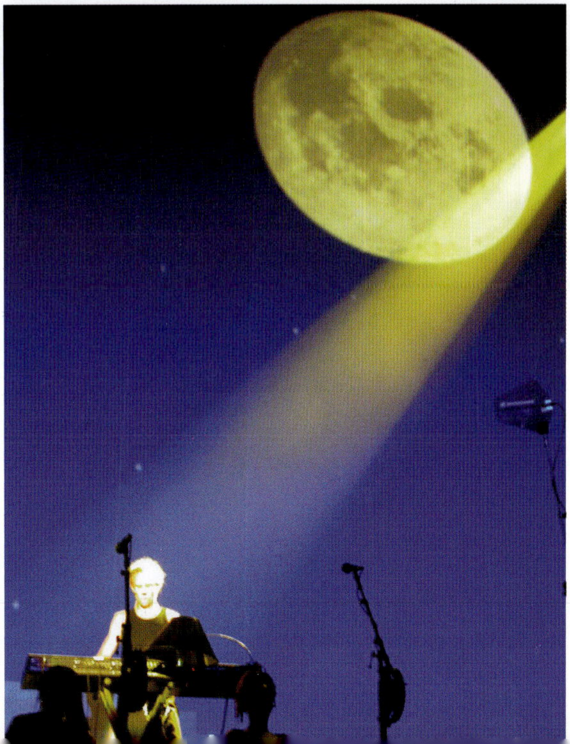

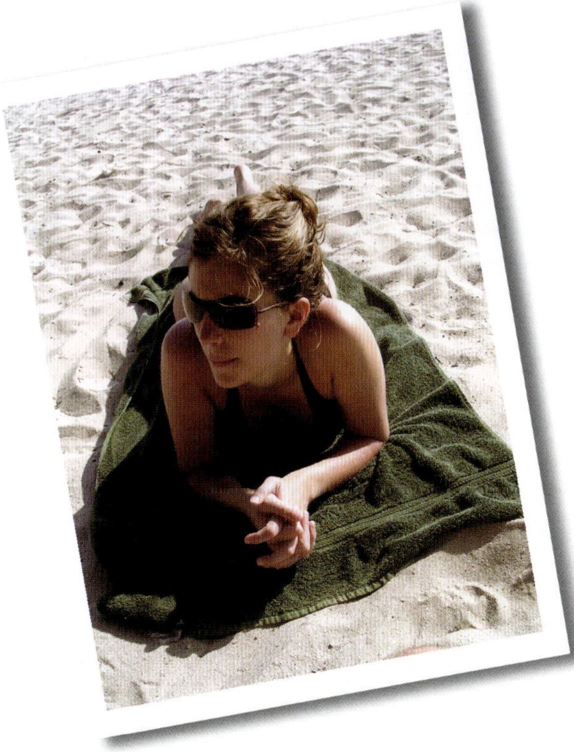

▲ Here the daylight is very clear, which makes using the Daylight setting the right choice.

It's impossible to create a function that could make corrections for all possible types of light, as there is a limitless number of combinations.

Therefore, most digital camera manufacturers offer seven different ways to allow you to adapt to practically all commonly arising situations.

Here are several of them:

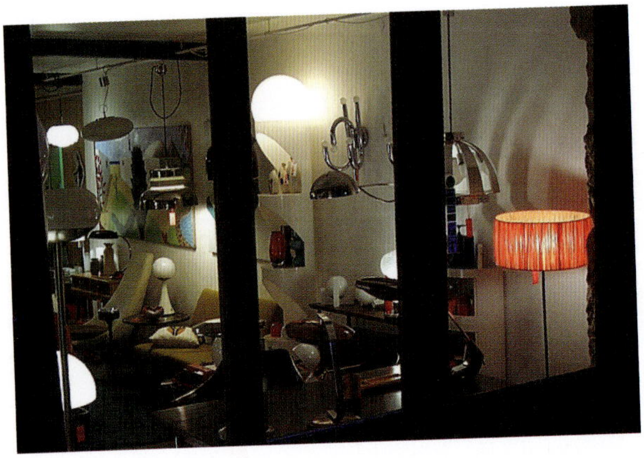

AWB AWB

AWB is an automatic mode that allows you to adapt to nearly all situations, sience it covers a color warmth range from 3,000 to 7,000 K.

This lighting fixture boutique is dominated by yellowish light, but it was automatically corrected for by the camera.

Sun

This setting is good for a clear day, usually around noon, with very bright outdoor light with a color warmth of about 5,500 K.

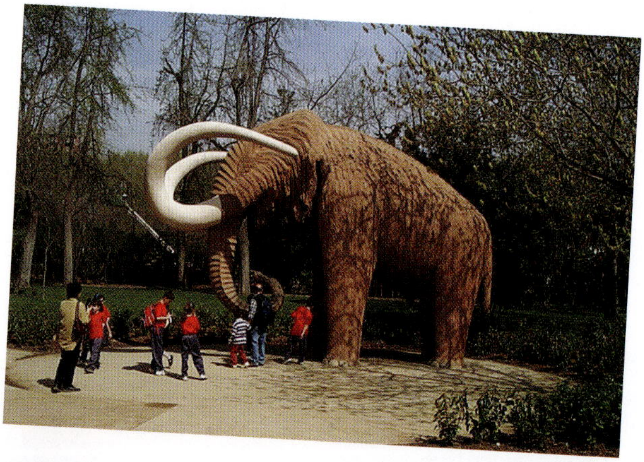

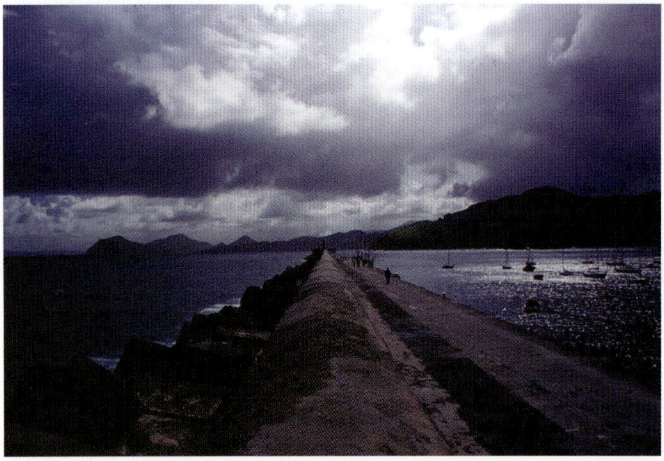

Clouds

This setting is for when the sky is full of clouds, when the color warmth is around 6,000 K.

Some examples of adapting to artificial lighting:

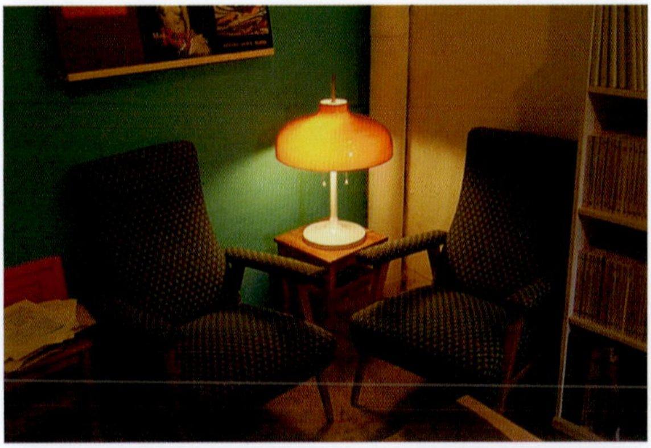

Tungsten bulb

Adapting to light from an incandescent filament (classic light bulb). This is the most common indoor lighting, and its color warmth is about 3,200 K.

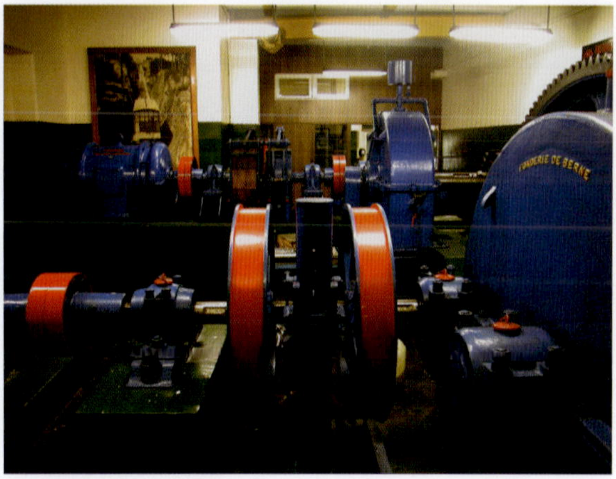

Fluorescent

In this case the mode adapts to white fluorescent lighting which is often found indoors and has a color warmth of 4,000 K.

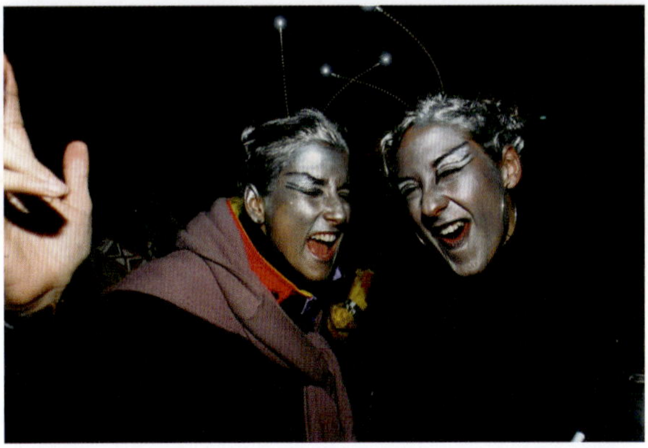

Flash

This function is used for lighting provided only by the flash, and its color warmth is close to 6,000 K. (Because this color warmth is very similar to the color warmth of daylight, the flash mode can also be used in some situations with clear daylight.)

▼ These dog food morsels are in a kitchen illuminated by incandescent bulbs whose light was transformed here to daylight through the use of the White Balance function.

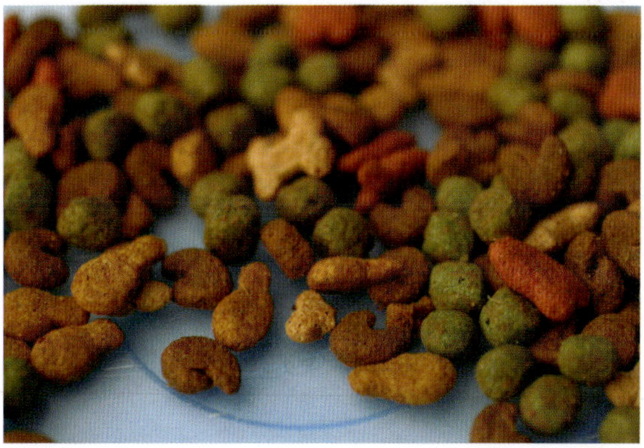

WB (White Balance)

Sometimes it's good to calibrate the lighting. This is most often the case with mixed lighting. In such a case all you have to do is take a picture of a pure-white object and save the picture in the WB mode, whereby the given lighting is shifted to white. With this mode you can cover the range of color warmths from 2,000 to 10,000 K.

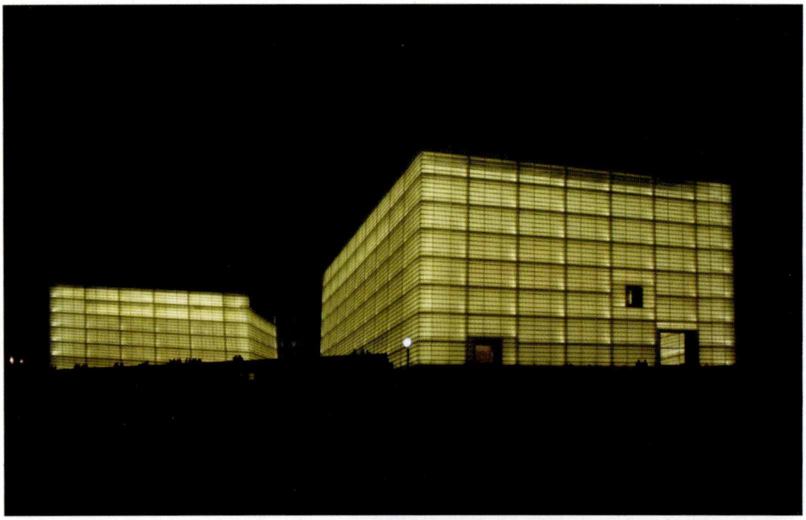

The best way to get to know various lighting types and the places where they are found is to conduct some tests and compare the results on the basis of the selected mode with respect to lighting type.

Here the camera was set to the incandescent lighting mode.

Here the camera was set to the daylight mode.

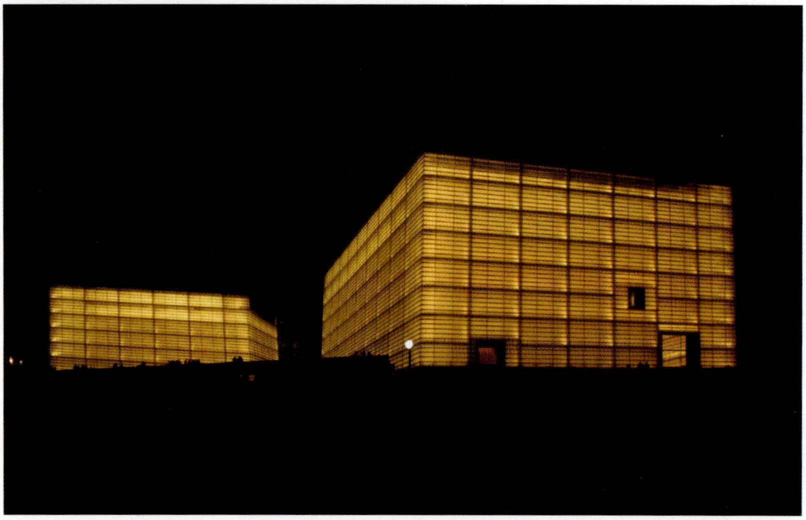

You can also try the following exercise: choose a situation with a certain type of lighting and try the various modes for taking pictures.

AWB

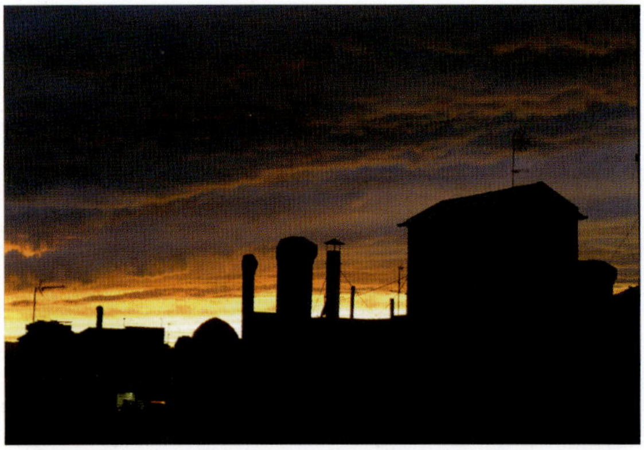

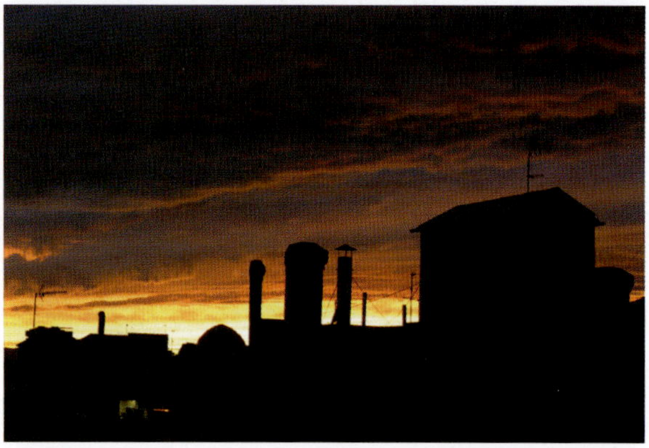

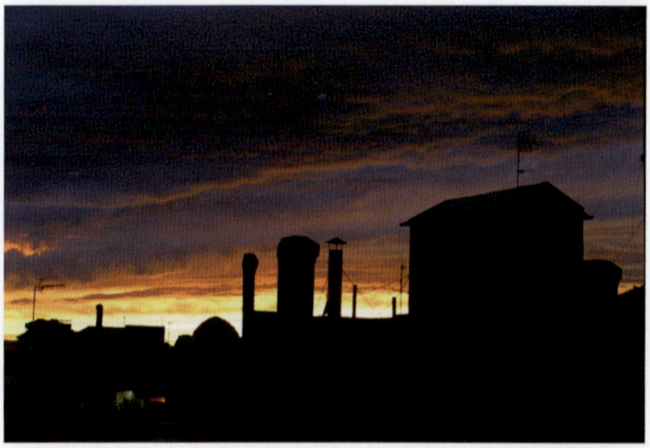

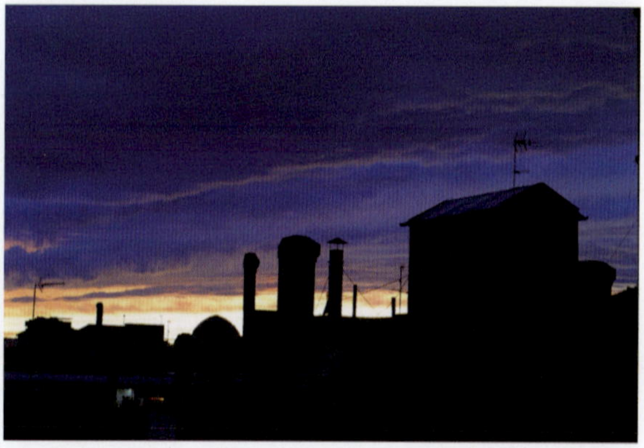

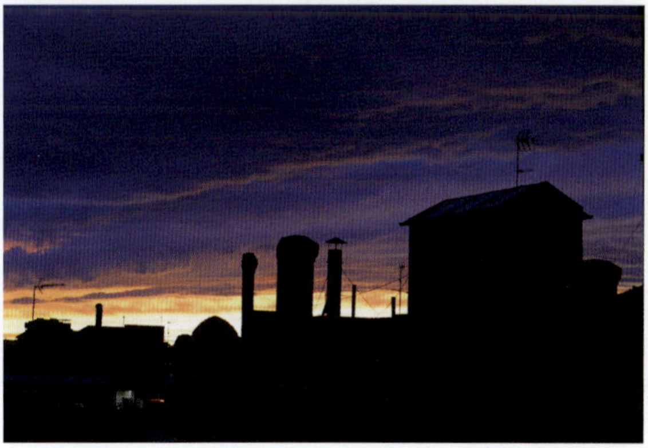

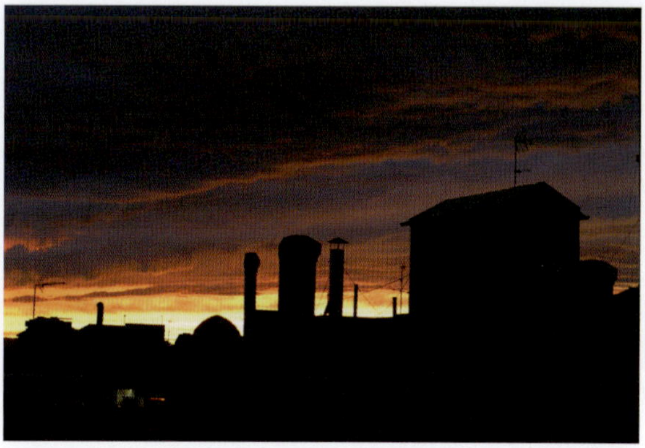

WB

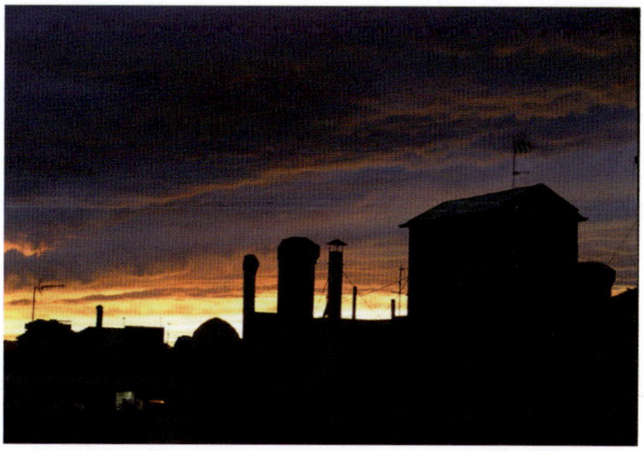

The colors in this sunset scene contrast very highly. It's important to do this test with various functions for the scene lighting method. You can then use the results to estimate situations and for making the right choice for future pictures.

After you look at these results you will find that a randomly used mode need not always provide the best results. Consider that digital photography has the great advantage that you can experiment freely and try all the possible functions, which, although they might seem absurd at first glance, can result in surprising pictures.

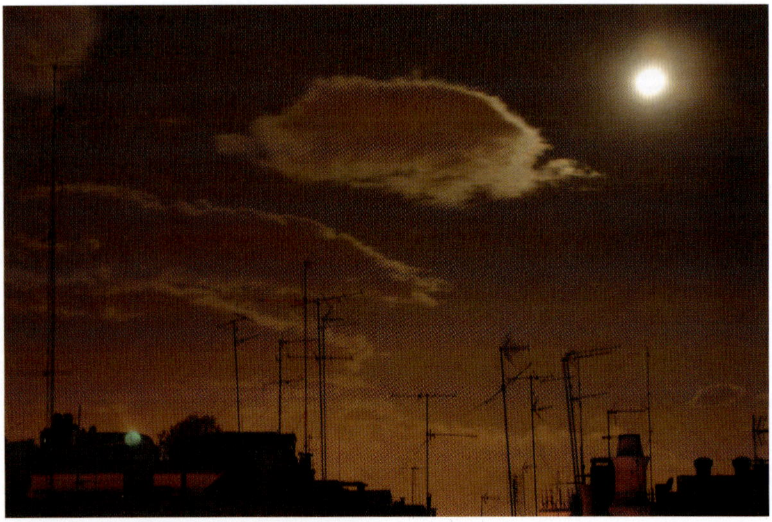

During such a night, under the light of a full moon, with the use of a tripod it would be logical to use the Daylight setting, since the moon reflects daylight. Nevertheless, the result isn't as you might expect, since it is affected by the reflection of city lights.

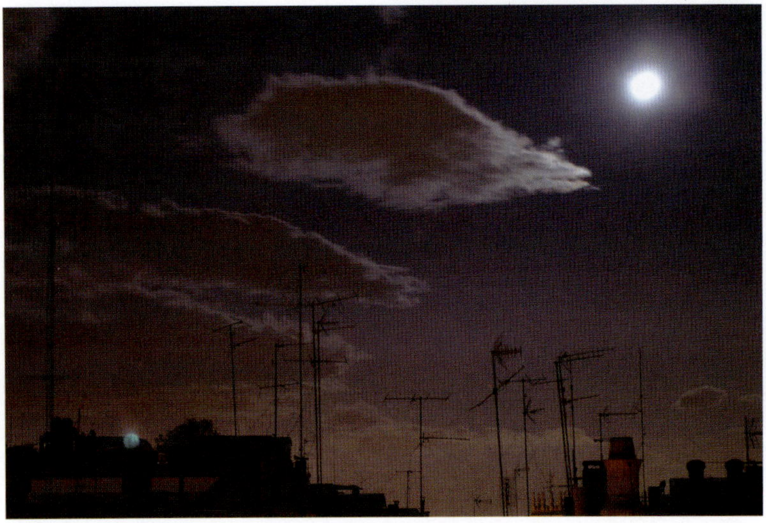

To get a picture that gives you a feeling of true night-time lighting it was necessary to choose the incandescent lighting mode.

TOPIC 2 TAKING PICTURES

Photography can be broken down into various categories. We know that there is something called microphotography, and when reading the press we find reporting photography. It's very difficult to break photography down according to topics. So here are some examples of analyzed pictures broken down into ten groups according to what is in the pictures:

▾ Outdoor portrait

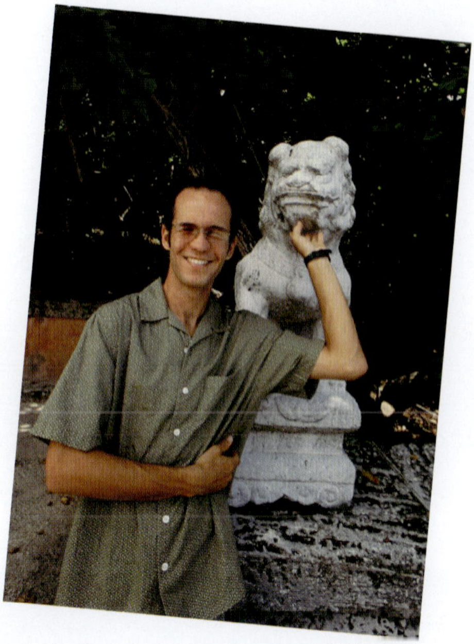

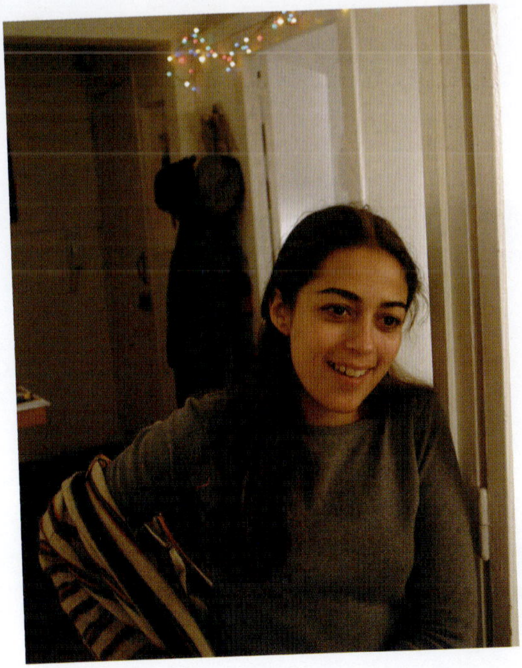

◂ Indoor portrait

▾ Animal pictures

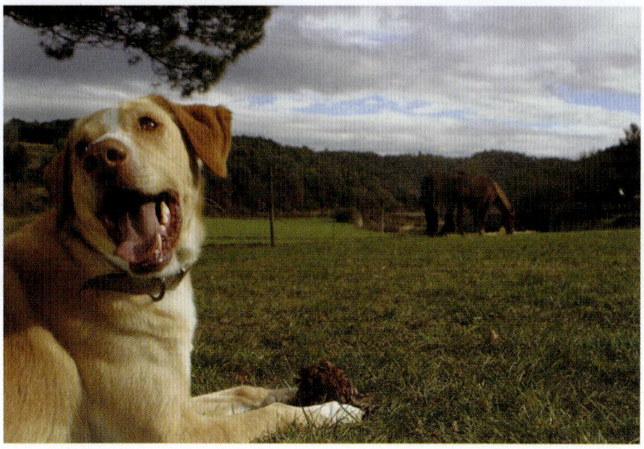

▾ Group portrait

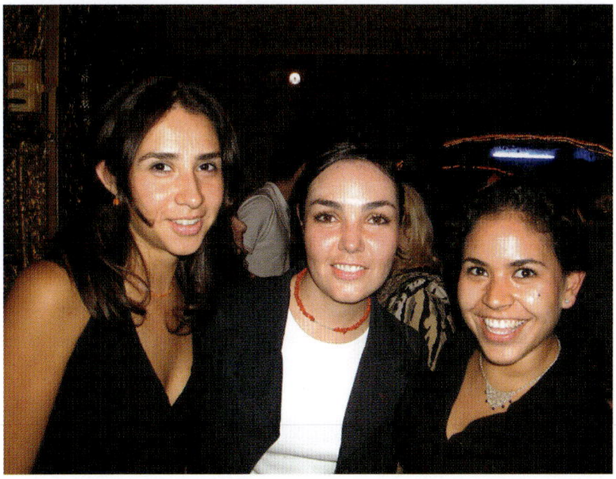

▾ Cityscape

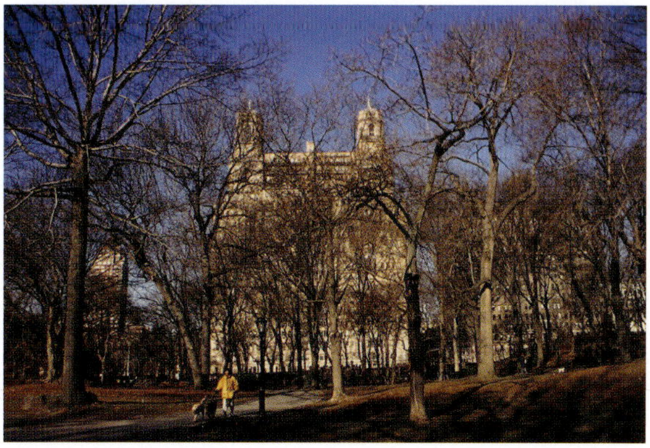

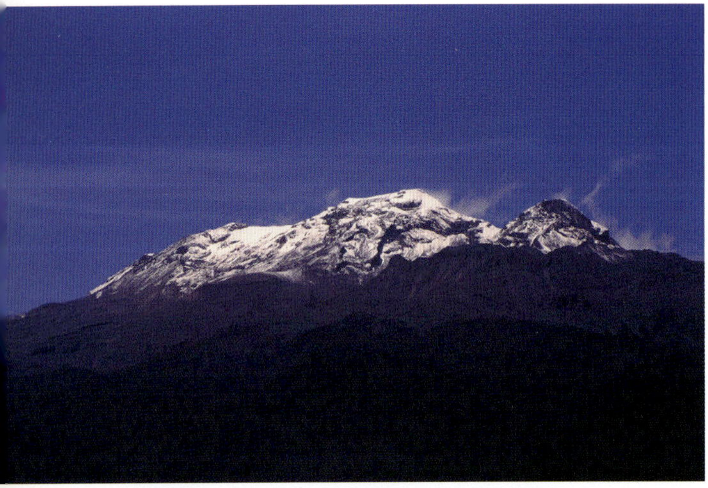

◂ Mountainscape

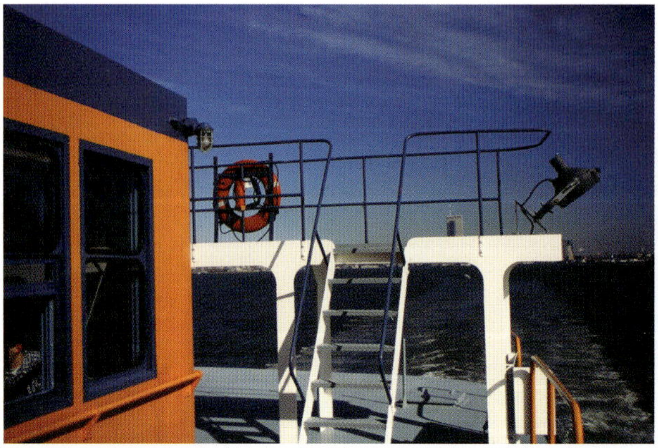

▴ Seascape

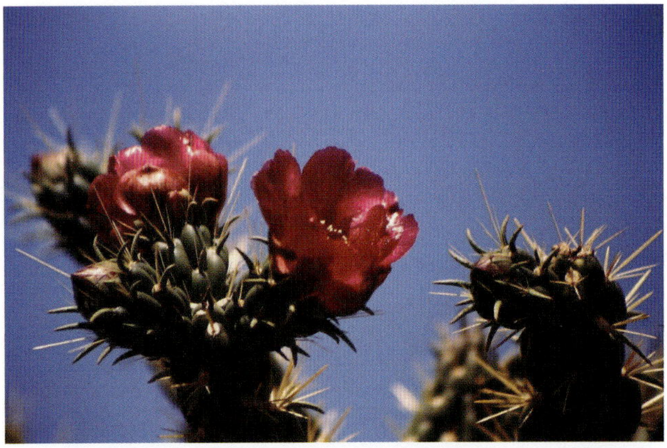

▴ Macrophotography

▾ Night-time picture

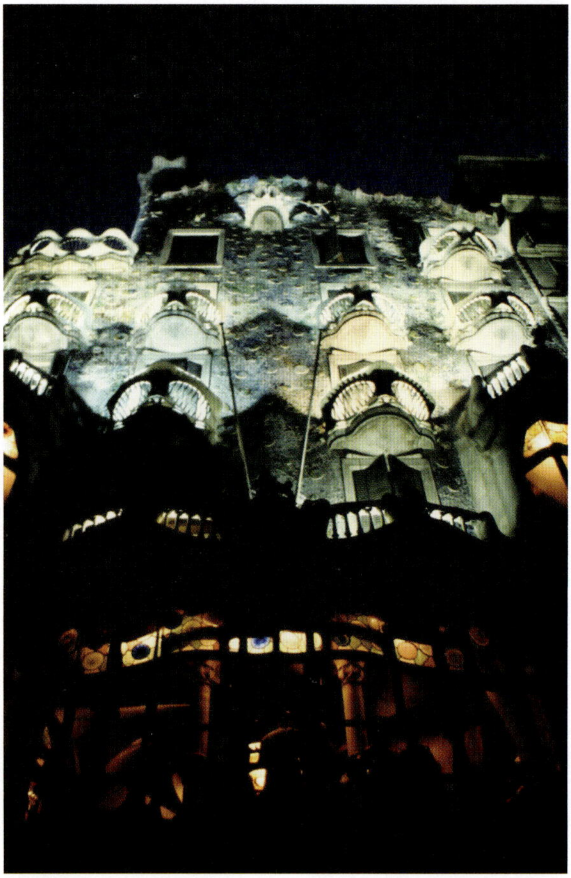

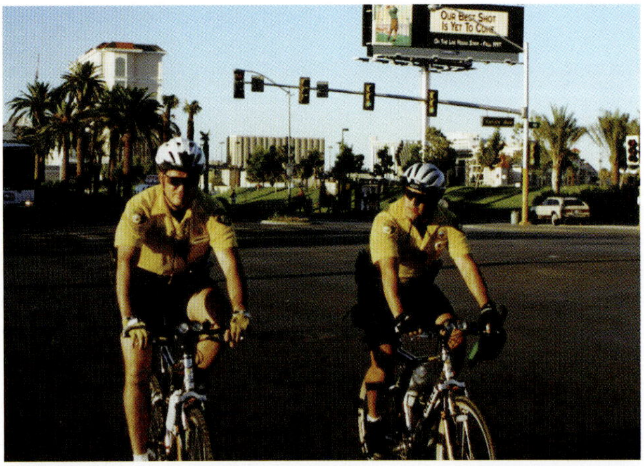

◂ Motion picture

Throughout this chapter we'll comment on shot selection, use of modes, and the photographer's position. In order to facilitate the reading and understanding of options, we use icons that define the selected lighting mode type and the method for using the flash. Before we get to taking pictures, here are a few useful bits of advice. It will be best to start with the right way to hold a camera, to which sufficient importance isn't always assigned.
This pictogram delineates the position of the camera with respect to the photographed object.

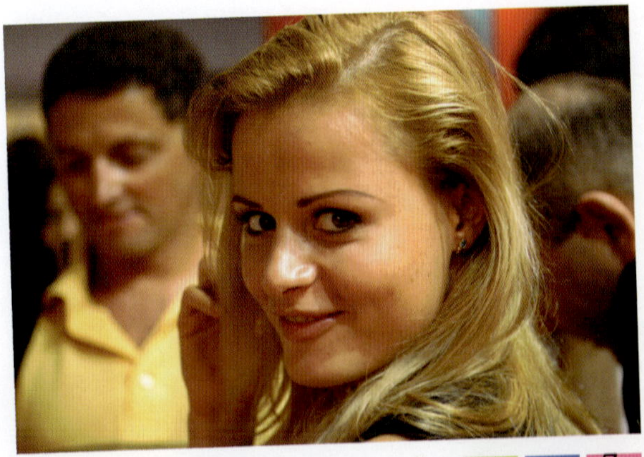

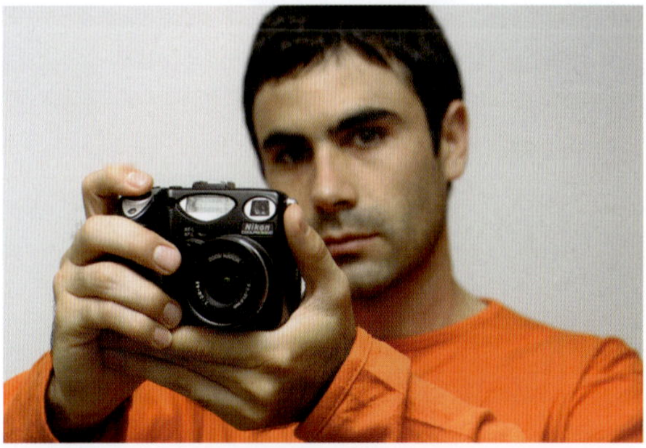

If you hold the camera correctly you won't encumber the functioning of any of its parts. When you hold the camera like this you get greater stability and none of the parts of the camera like the flash or the lens are covered.

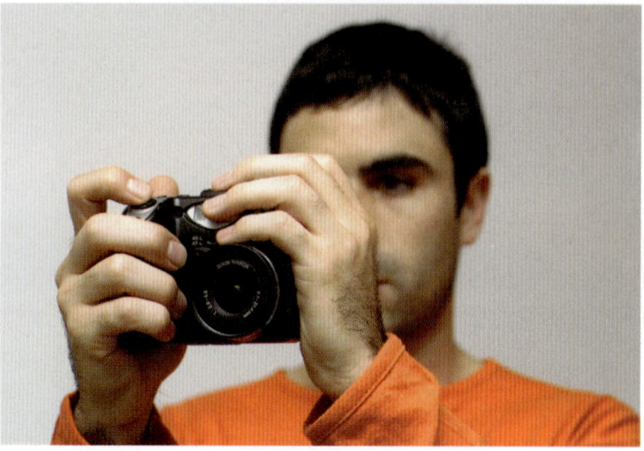

Erroneous ways to hold a camera

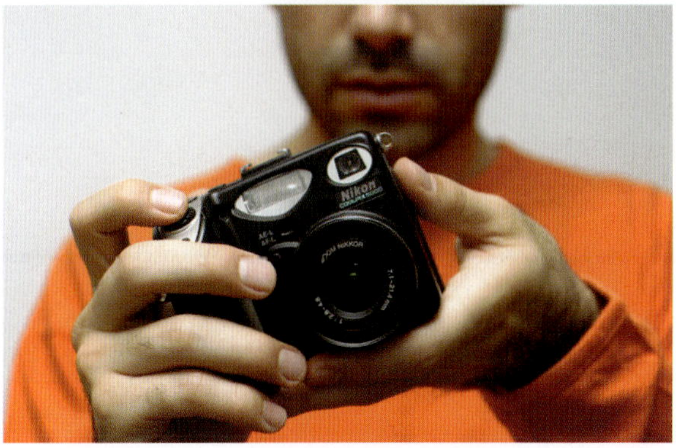

When you are getting ready to take a picture it's good to hold the camera freely and level. You can then change this position as needed. If you get used to always holding the camera level you can avoid various unpleasant surprises like crooked pictures or bad shots.

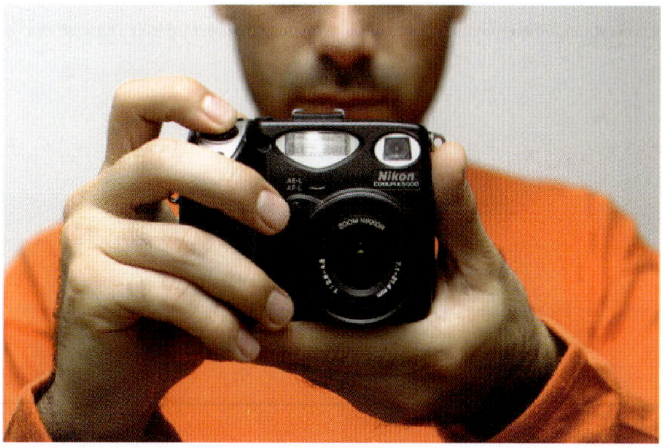

When the rays of the sun or the light source strike the camera's lens

You can keep the sun's rays from striking the lens by shading it with your free hand. But you have to make sure your hand doesn't appear in the picture. This way you can avoid undesirable reflections in the picture.

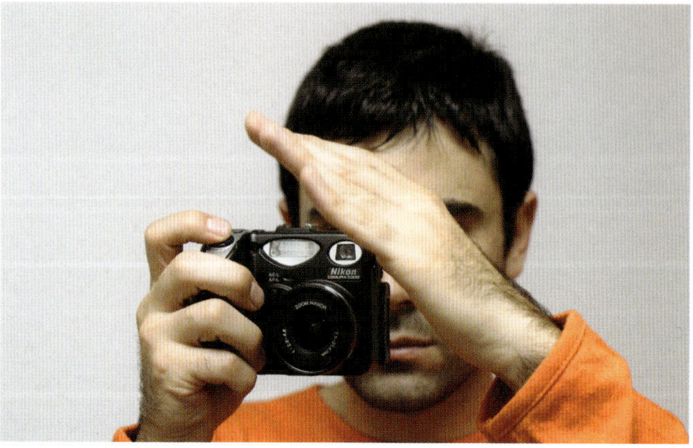

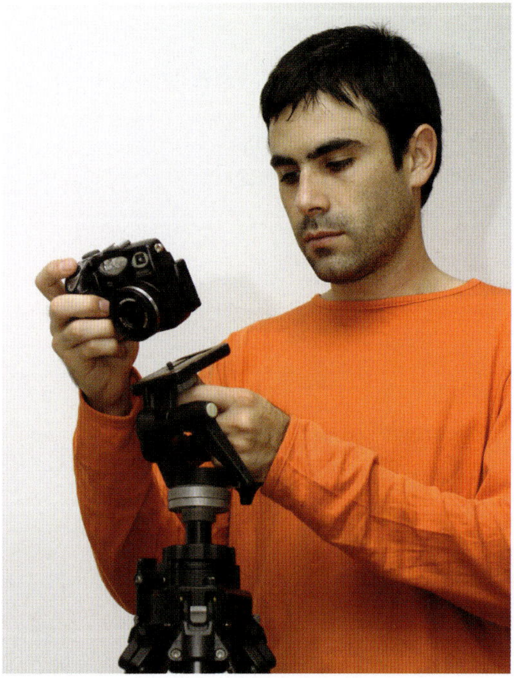

When the light is weak there is the risk that the camera could move during the exposure.

This situation calls for the use of a tripod and the self timer. This eliminates the danger of moving the camera when pressing the shutter release. Your pictures will be flawlessly clean.

> But always keep in mind that if the camera isn't anchored firmly or absolutely level the pictures could be blurred or slanted.

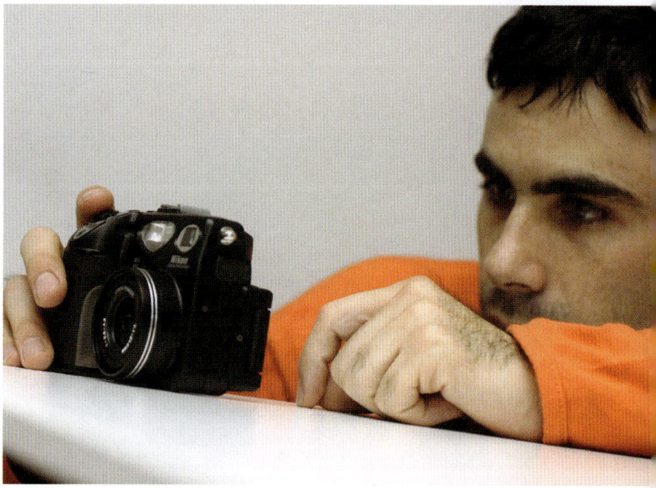

When you need a tripod but don't have one

Look for a horizontal surface to put the camera on and use the self timer, which also allows you to get into the shot if you wish.

Lighting modes					
AWB					
automatic	sunlight	clouds	incandescent light	fluorescent light	flashFlits

Flash modes				
AUTO				
automatic	red eye reduction	flash	no flash	night

Outdoor portraits

For outdoor portraits the main thing to always keep in mind is the direction from which the light is coming. The light's direction is the decisive factor when you're looking for the shot you'll like best. However, if your choice of shots doesn't correspond well to the angle of the light then you'll need to choose a good combination of the modes that your camera offers.

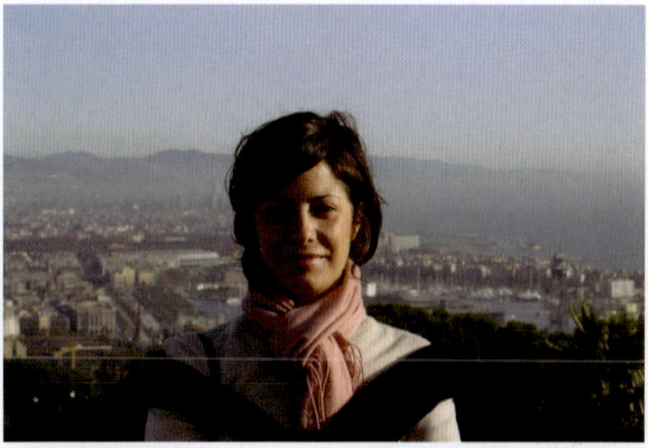

▲ This young woman is standing in a position where the light strikes her from the side and thus illuminates only half of her face.

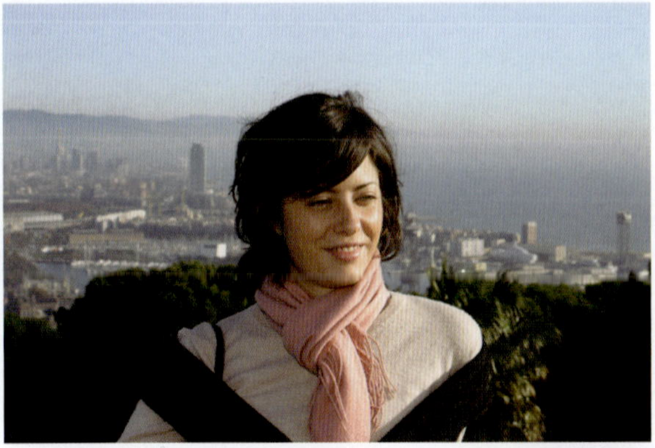

▲ This is the same exact situation, but the flash was used to compensate for the zones with insufficient light.

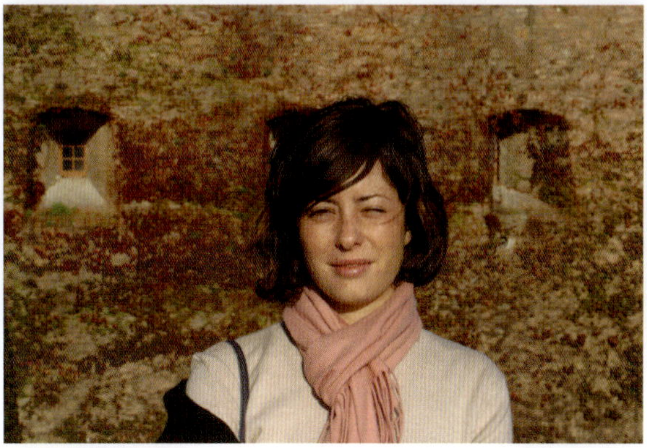

▲ In this picture the light is falling straight into the woman's face and illuminates it sufficiently. The drawback is that the light is too bright, and it's hard for the subject to avoid squinting.

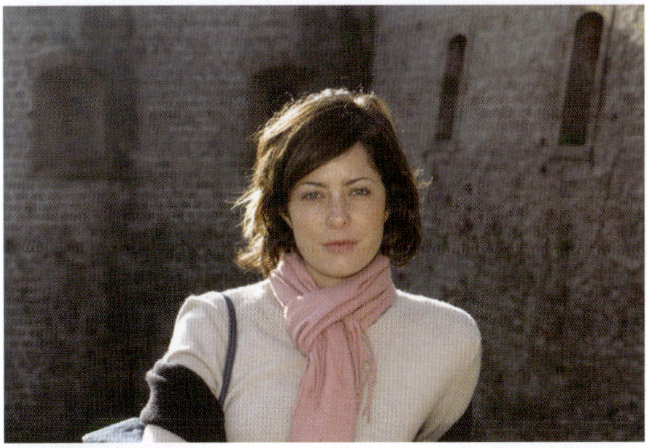

▲ Here the subject has her back to the sun, so she appears to be set apart from the dark background. Because the light was coming from behind her it was necessary to use the flash, without which the subject would have been completely underexposed. It was also necessary to shade the lens against the direct impact of the sun's rays.

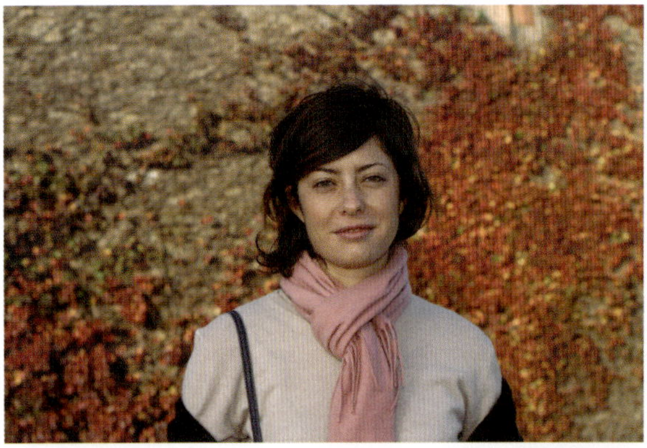

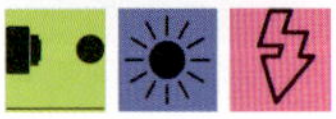

▲ In this picture the model is in the shade, in front of a light background. The flash was used to ensure that she was fully illuminated and wasn't in contrast to the light background. This mode allowed the picture to be perfectly balanced without excessive contrast and without the model's face being directly exposed to the sun.

Another consideration is how to frame the picture to emphasize and enhance the main subject. You can use the zoom that is built into the camera for this. Of course you can also change the distance between the camera and the subject, too.

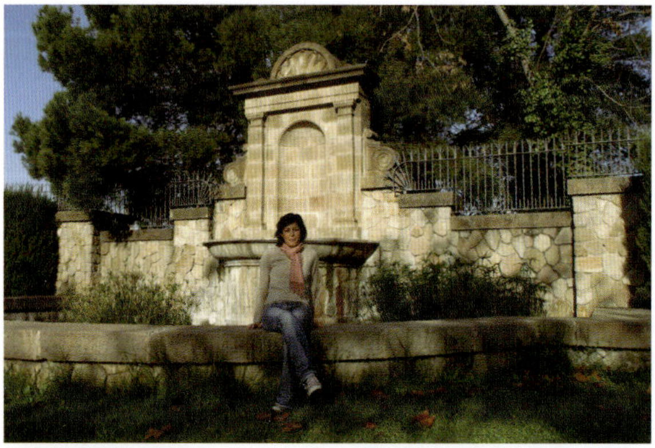

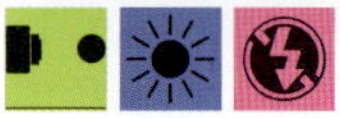

▲ Here the subject was photographed as a part of the environment. The width of the shot makes clear the place where the picture was taken, creating a balance between the subject and the setting.

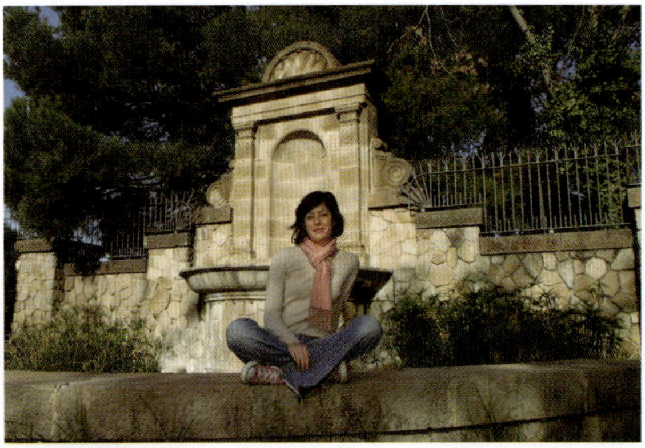

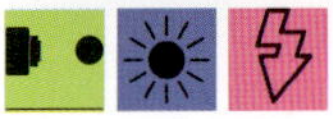

◀ In this somewhat smaller frame the subject gains greater importance without losing too much of the background, which is still easily recognizable.

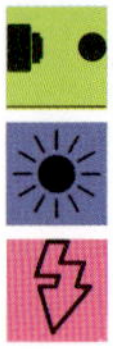

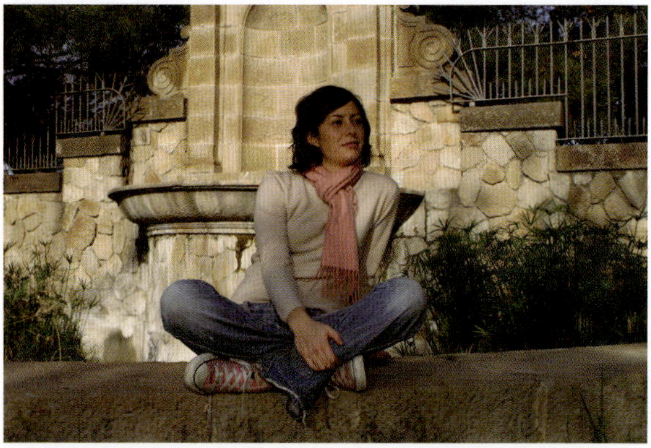

▶ If we frame the picture very tightly the subject gains too much emphasis as opposed to the background. We recommend framing a shot like this if the background is only for creating an atmosphere.

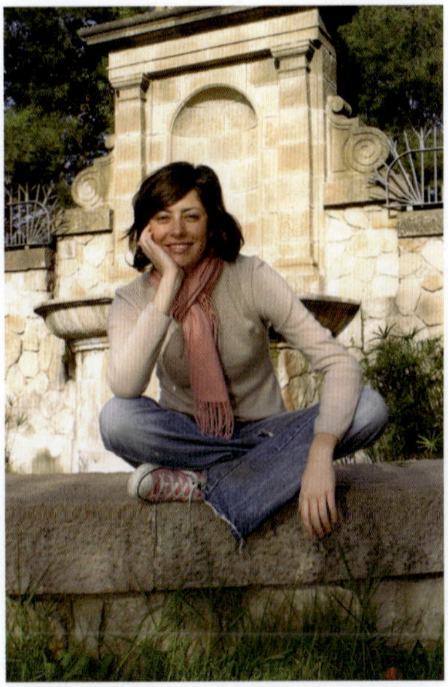

The camera can be held vertically any time. Sometimes very tight framing causes a loss of background in a horizontal picture (see the preceding shot). For such situations we recommend that you hold the camera vertically.

A third consideration is the angle from which you take the picture. Trying various angles for viewing the subject allows you to emphasize details of the setting in the composition.

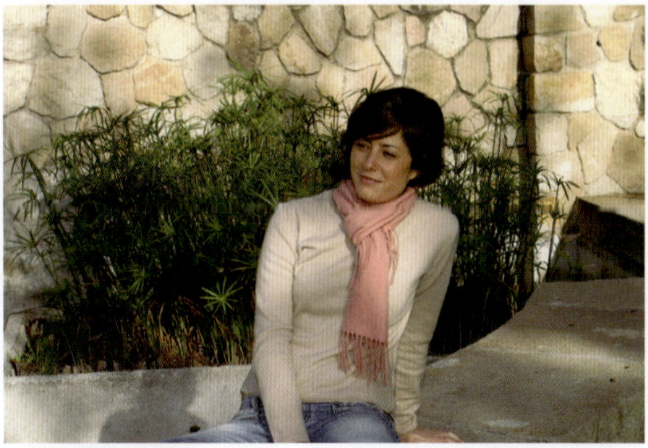

This picture was taken from a somewhat elevated position (aiming down), thus emphasizing the plants in the background.

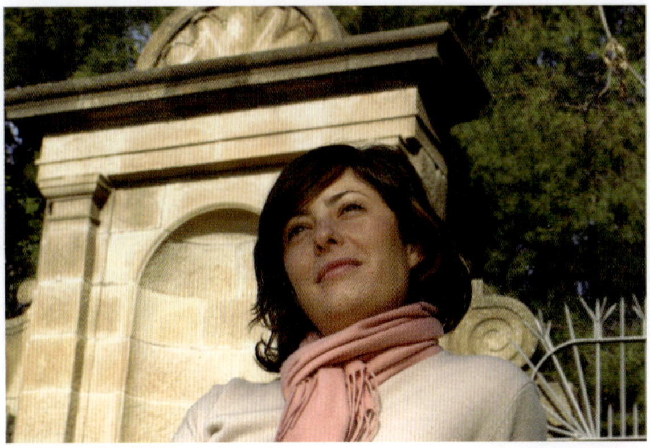

Here the picture was taken from a somewhat lower position (aiming up), thus highlighting the woman's face and the wall of the fountain.

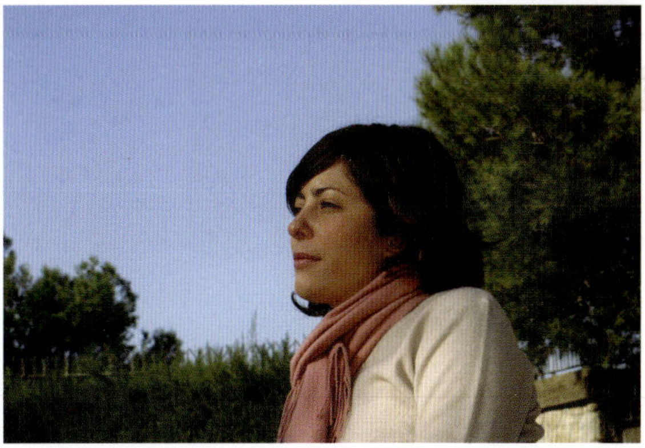

In this picture the camera isn't positioned as low as in the preceding shot, and by moving to the side it was possible to emphasize the blue sky, thus producing a "lightened" picture.

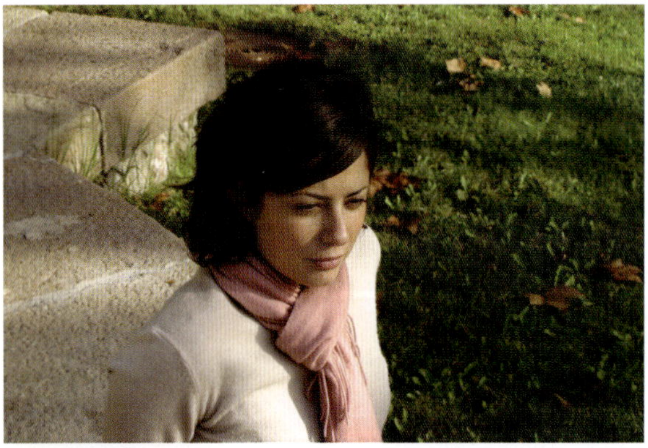

▲ Here again the shot was from slightly above, this time in order to "seat" the subject against the green lawn.

▼ In this picture the camera was right in front of the model's face. But the shot was intentionally taken from a bit to one side to include the shrubs in the neutral background.

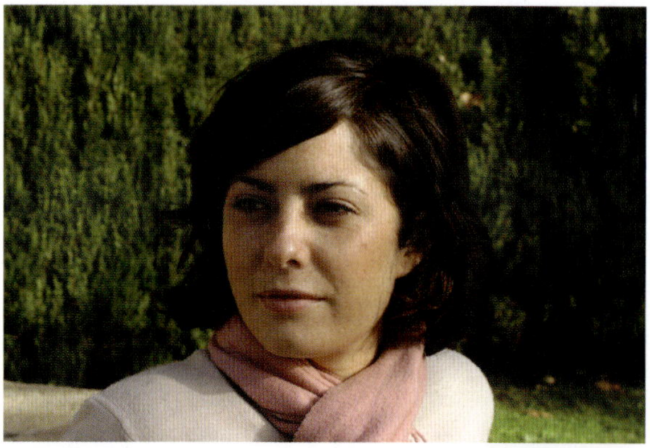

Finally, the fourth important consideration you should keep in mind is the position and behavior of the subject, which create a natural quality in the picture.

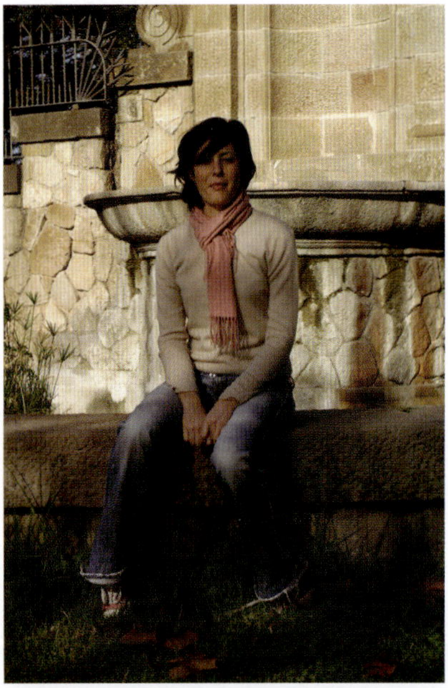

◀ The woman's unnatural position gives the impression that she is posing unwillingly.

▶ In this shot the woman's position is more natural. All it took was a slight movement or change of position.

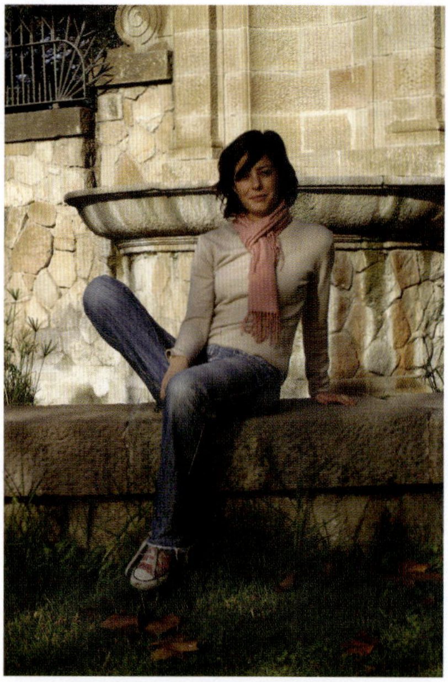

Taking good pictures requires that you have a good relationship with the model and that you communicate well with each other.

Here are some examples of pictures taken outdoors under various conditions and at different times of the day.

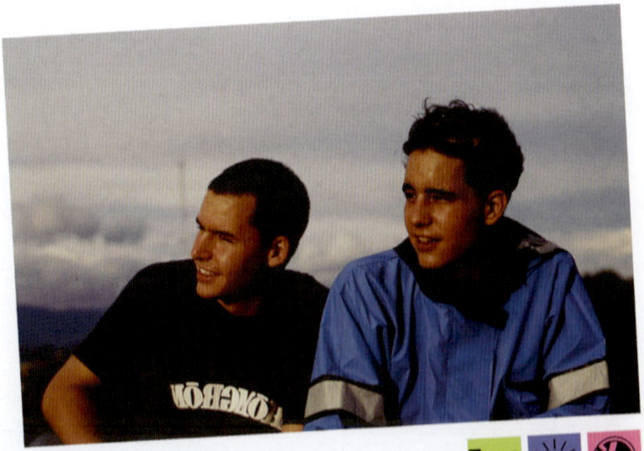

This picture was taken in the late afternoon, when the sunlight offers warmer shades, which explains the red tinge of the faces. The flash wasn't used, and although their faces are turned towards the sun the lighting isn't sufficient.

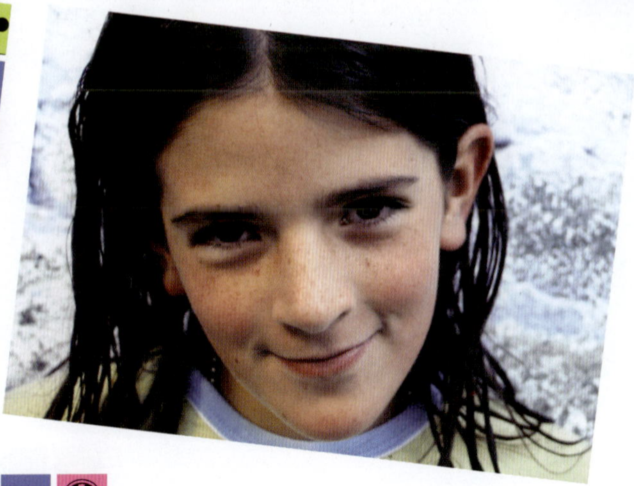

Here the shade of the skin is cooler; the picture was taken at noon with indirect light.

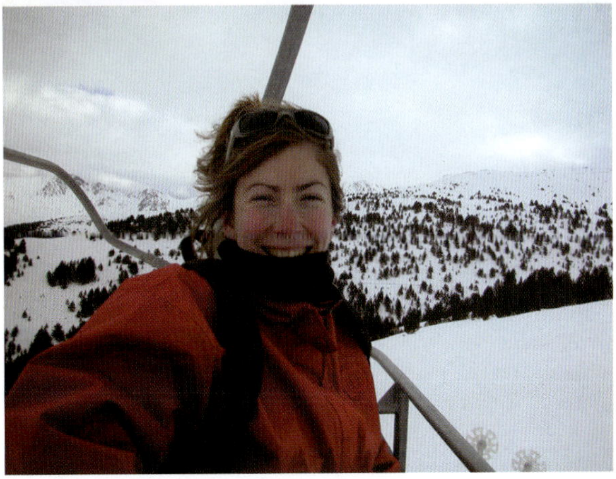

In this "winter" portrait the clouds and the snow disperse the light and make it uniform. There are no shadows to be seen and the shading is cool.

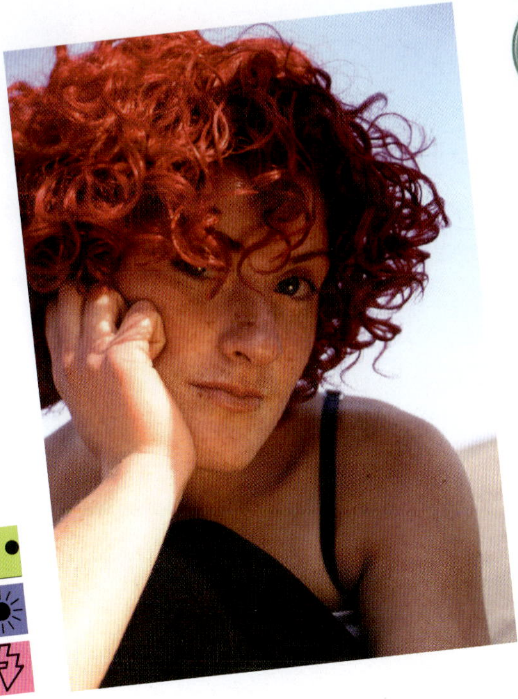

This portrait was taken at noon, which explains the light on the top of her hair and forearm. The flash was used only in order to make her face stand out and give her eyes luster.

INDOOR PORTRAITS

The first thing that is necessary for indoor photography is an analysis of the type of lighting we're exposed to; is the light produced by incandescent bulbs, fluorescent lights, or mixed sources? Is there enough daylight to illuminate the person we want to photograph?

Then it's good to determine whether the flash should be used. Before we proceed to actually taking a picture, it's always a good idea to conduct a couple of tests, because the light from a flash combined with the light in the room can lead to an unconvincing result.

In the end, the digital format allows for such tests, which makes it easier to achieve the best results.
The third and final decision is the choice and angle of framing, which allows us to include the person in the setting or isolate him or her from it.

▸ The first example is an indoor portrait with the use of daylight. The subject is facing away from the window, through which daylight is entering. Note that a small reflective surface is used (held by the subject), which somewhat illuminates the lower part of her face but leaves her eyes in shadow - the scene takes on a special expression. If you don't have a professional reflective surface you can use cardboard covered with aluminum foil.

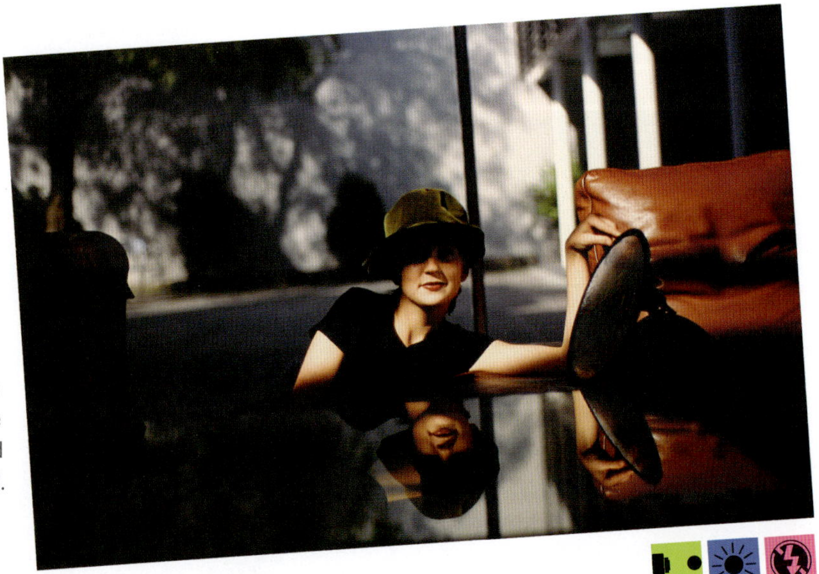

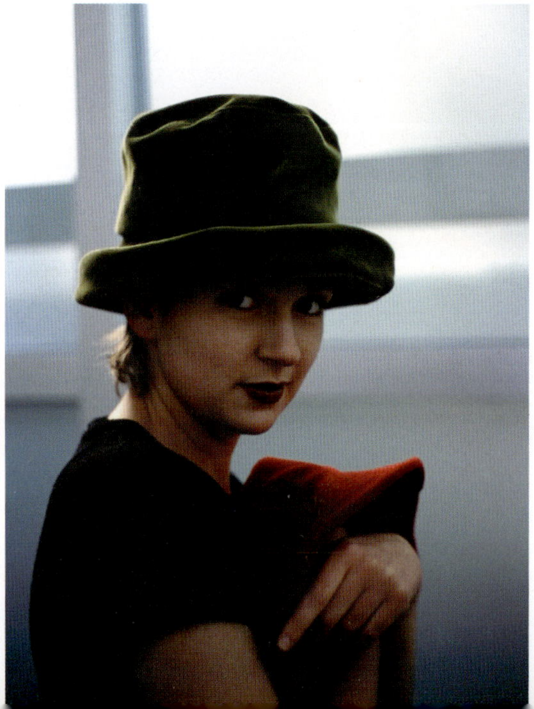

AWB

◂ In this case, again using daylight, the subject is posing in front of a frosted glass window. We chose this vertical format to catch some of the diffused light (this type of glass makes this possible) in order to exclude the marked shadows in the preceding picture.

If you're taking a portrait using daylight there's no harm in conducting tests in the automatic mode. It sometimes happens that the window pane changes the light that passes through it and that the automatic mode allows a correction for this change.

Under the same lighting conditions as in the preceding picture, this time we chose a horizontal format and the subject was moved to a place where two frosted glass windows merge, in order to make better use of the entire environment's lighting. The shot was framed in such a way that the camera was close to one of the windows, which gives the picture perspective.

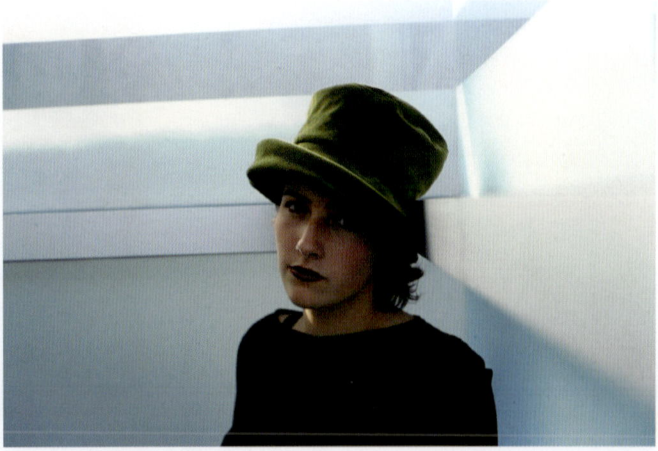

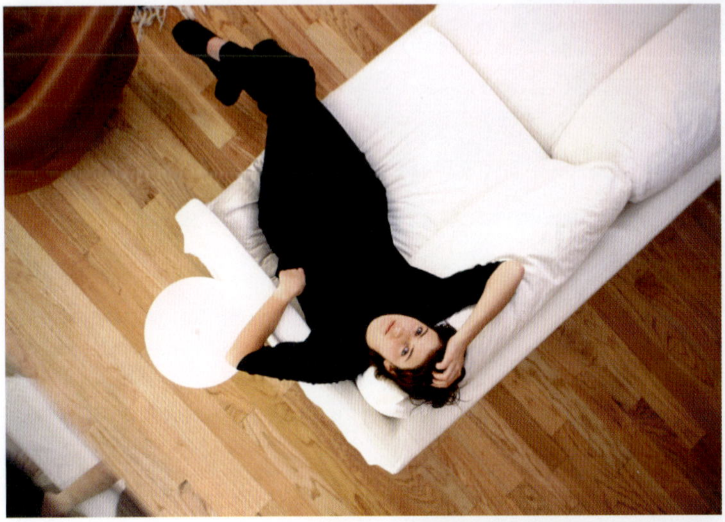

In this case the unusual but interesting shooting angle was achieved by shooting from above under incandescent light, which is sufficiently diffused and uniform.

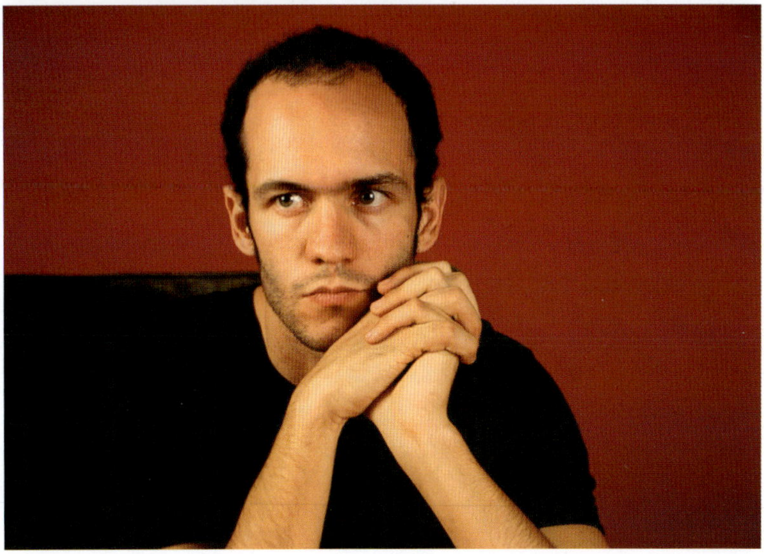

Here the subject is located between two office lights. From one side the subject is illuminated through a white diffuser (reflector cover) and from the other side by a classic incandescent light. The left side is closer to its light source so it is more brightly illuminated.

Under the same conditions as the preceding picture, this one was taken in vertical format and a greater distance between the camera and the subject was chosen so that the picture would also include the chair on which the subject is sitting.

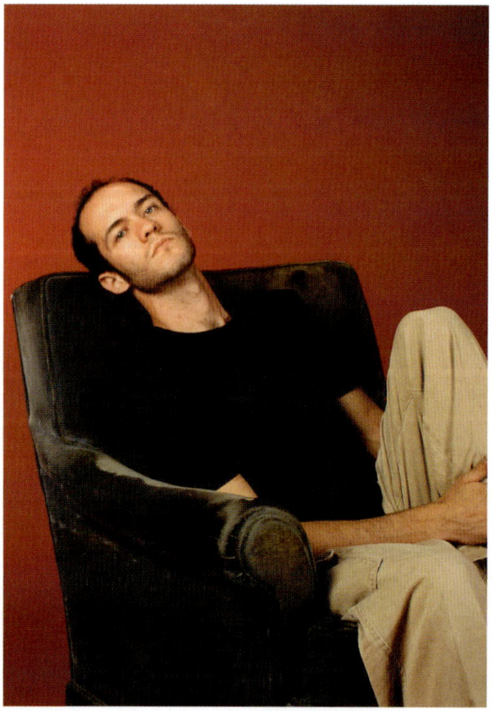

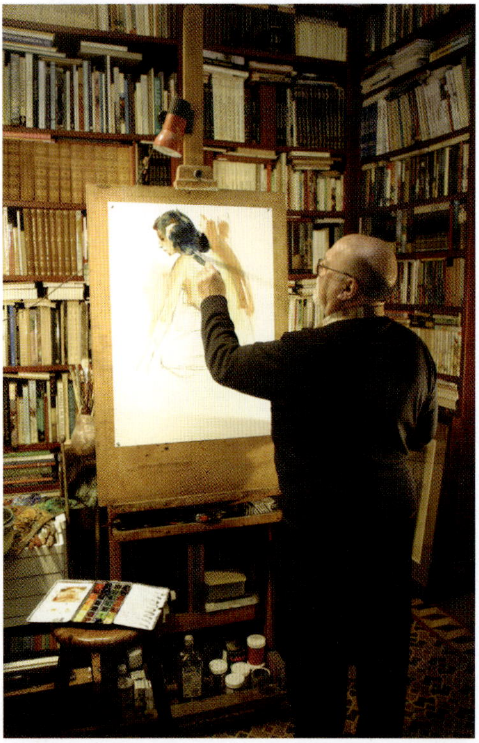

Sometimes you want to catch a subject at work. You can illuminate such scenes perfectly with three classic incandescent light sources. The first light, on the ceiling, provides overall, well dispersed lighting. The second source is to the artist's left and casts light on the canvas. The third light source is to the artist's right and slightly behind him in order to provide supplementary lighting and better highlight the painter's silhouette.

In another shot that was taken under the same conditions as the one before, the view is no langer from behind but rather from the side. The light sources are the same, but now the subject is illuminated; the light that was illuminating the paintter from behind is now shining almost directly in his face. The light on the ceiling still lights up the scene as a whole and softens the shadows.

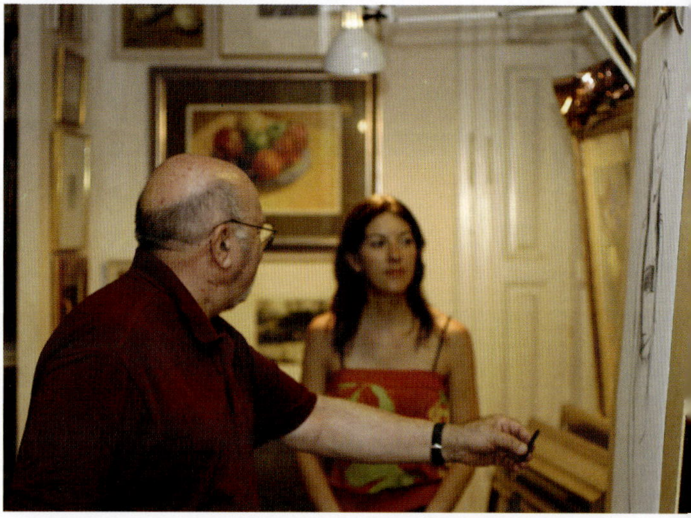

The lighting in this scene is from fluorescent lights along the entire space. We chose the automatic mode because in this case it gives better results than the fluorescent lighting mode; the curtains in the background affect the color of the light.

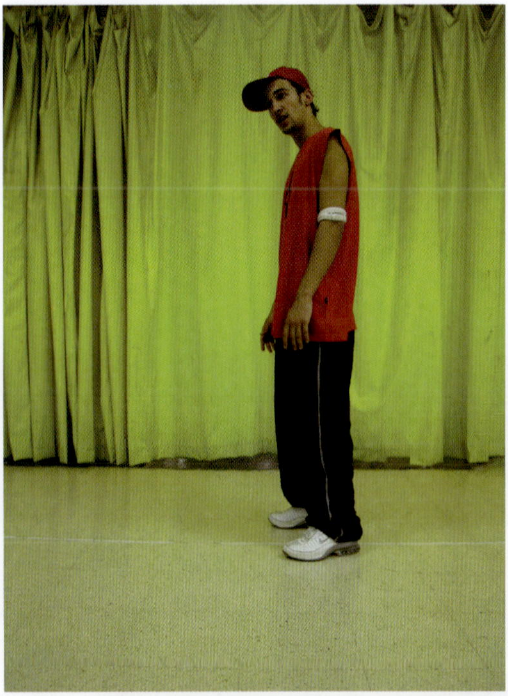

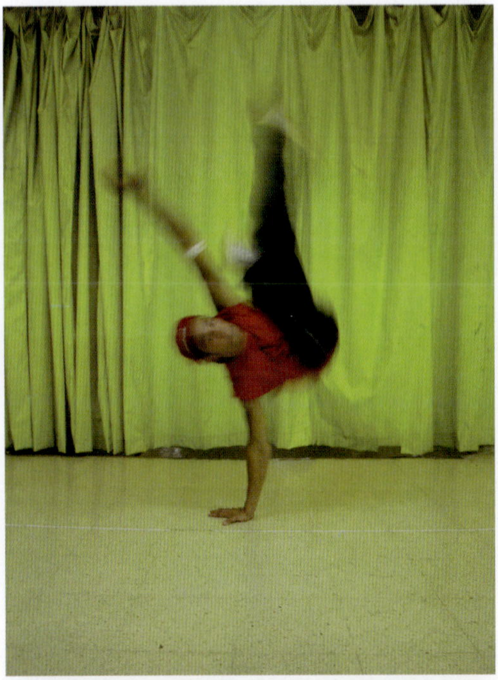

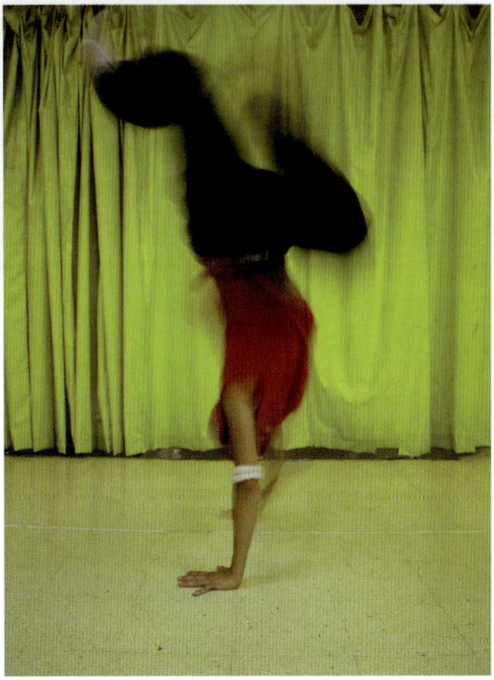

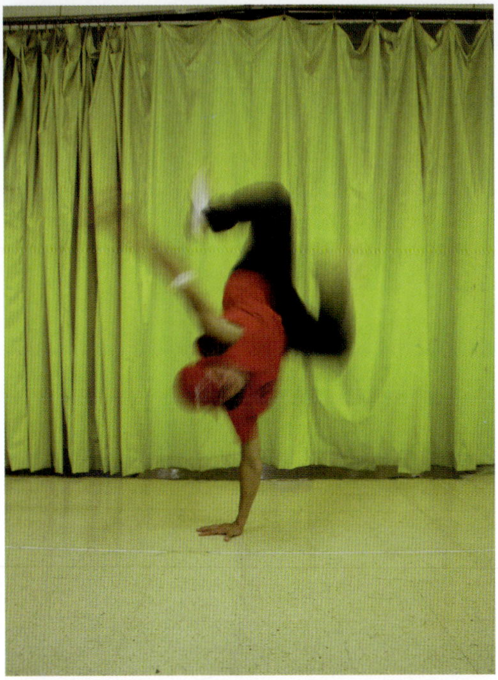

Even though the lighting is dispersed and uniform it's not necessarily strong enough. So in the first shot the dancer was asked not to move. In the following pictures the images are always a bit blurred, but this gives a better idea of his movements.

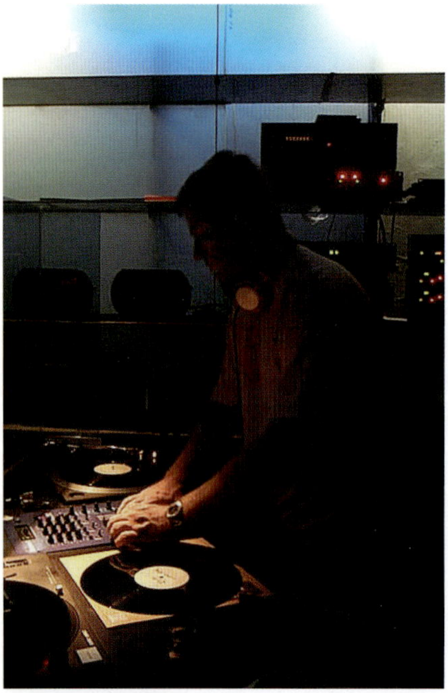

In this portrait the intention was to place greater emphasis on the activity than on the model. First the photographer focused his camera on the counter with the records and depressed the shutter release half-way, thus fixing the camera's focus. Then, without letting the partially depressed button go he re-aimed the camera and completed the exposure.

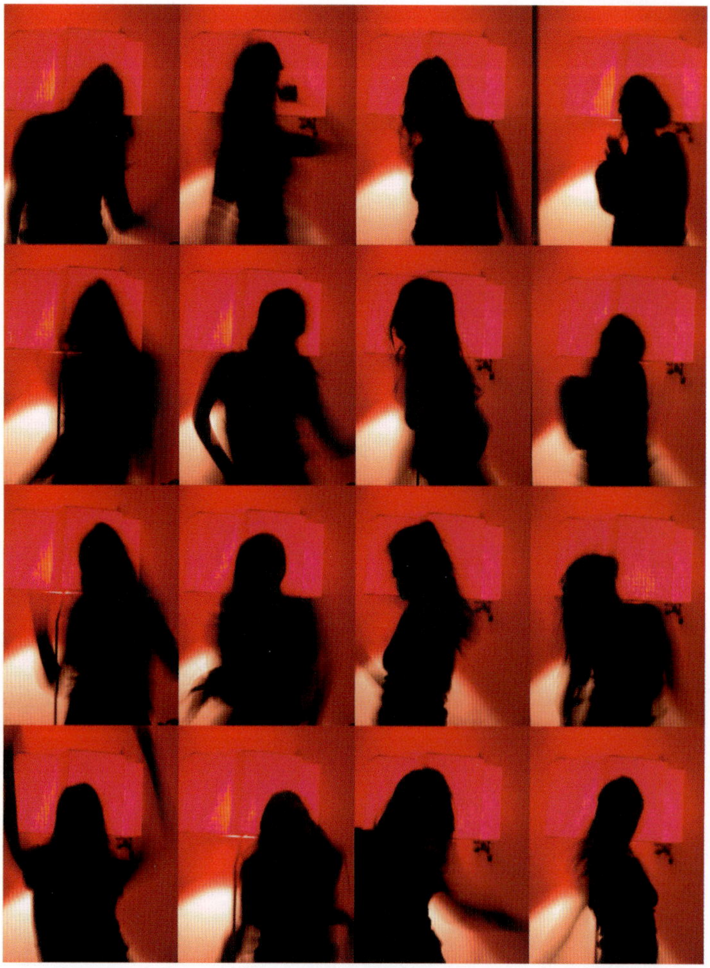

Thanks to current artificial light sources there is great variability in the possibilities we can encounter with interior lighting. In this sequence the photographed subject was opposite a lamp with a classic incandescent bulb fitted with a red cover. As you can see yourself, the result is surprising, to say the least.

Group portraits

Pictures are very often taken of groups of people. Whether it's a holiday celebration or a family get-together there's always someone with a camera. There are two considerations you should always keep in mind when taking such pictures.

Because you're going to take a picture of several people, make sure that they are all in the right places, that no one's left out of the shot or blocked out. The other important consideration is the flash. When taking group shots you usually have to back up in order to include everyone in the shot. If you need to use the flash because of insufficient light the scene might not be sufficiently illuminated because it's too far away.

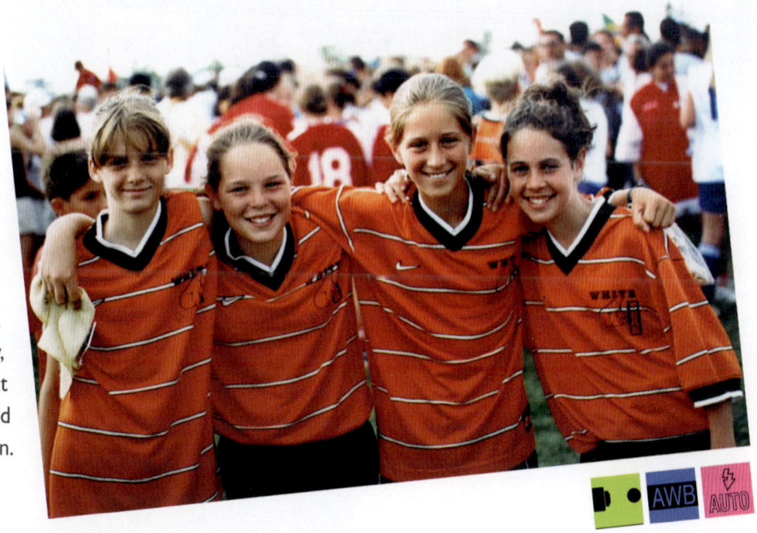

This group photograph is a classic example of a well illuminated outdoor scene. The flash wasn't necessary, nor did shadows that sometimes appear around eyes need compensation.

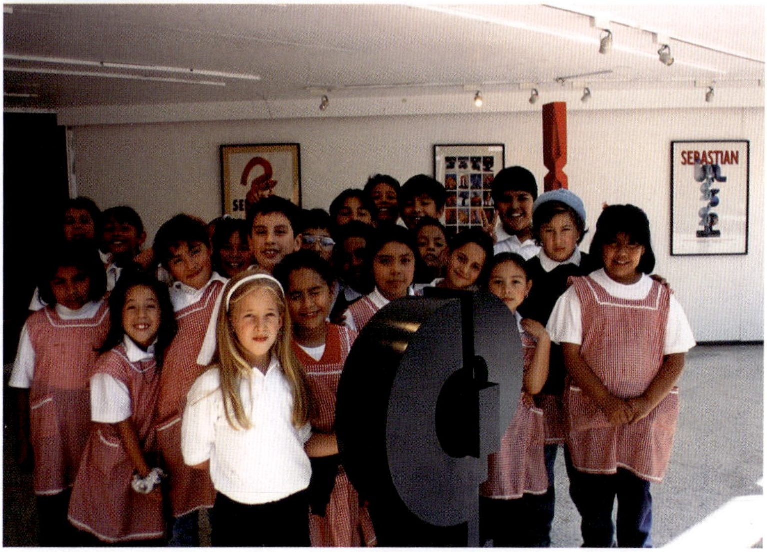

In this picture the children are in a hall that is illuminated by outdoor light. The children were visiting an exhibition, so a sculpture that was chosen for its proximity to the light source served as the foreground. The children were positioned to be out of the direct rays of the sun, which indirectly provided even lighting for the scene.

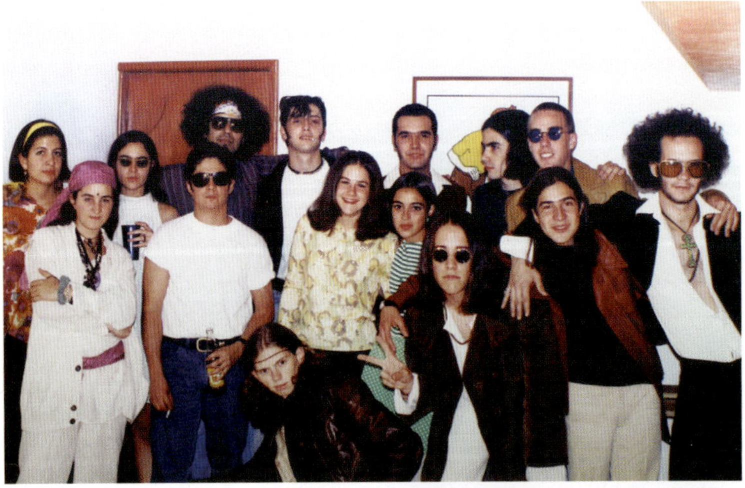

This picture from a family celebration was taken in a small room with white walls. The light was from an incandescent bulb on the ceiling, which was also white. It was easy to convert the color tone of the light by choosing the camera's appropriate function.

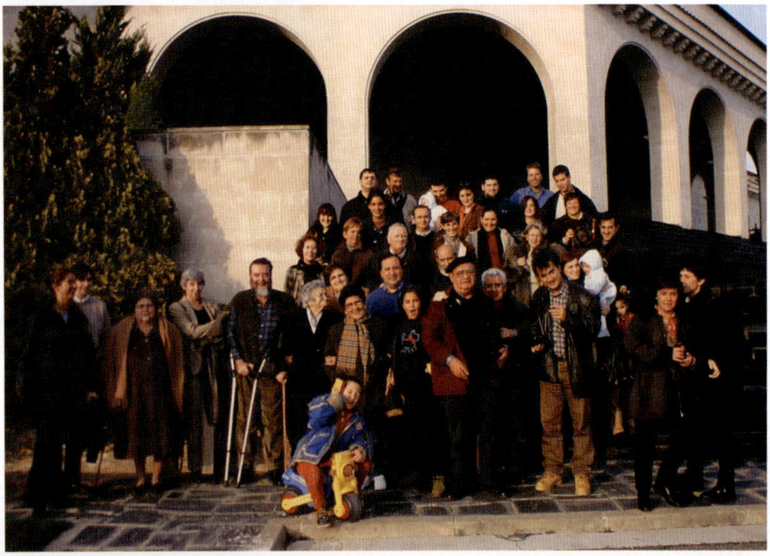

This is a good example of a large group where it wasn't possible to use the flash to compensate for facial shadows because of the great distance. In such cases you have to find the lighting angle that illuminates the faces the best.

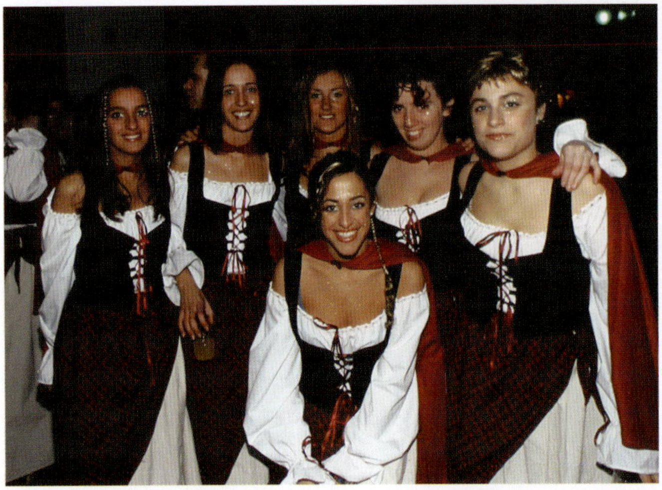

A classic example of a group picture usually taken during the course of a wedding reception or other similar occasions.

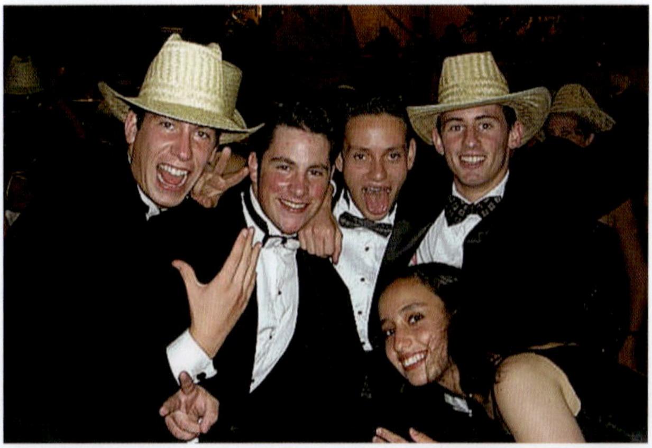

A typical situation - the guests have had dinner and are beginning to dance and form small groups. In general no one will wait - you have to take a picture quickly, because new people are constantly joining the group and the scene gets larger, which can complicate taking the picture. The photographer has to work quickly, all the while paying attention to the composition.

The photographer decided to take two pictures to commemorate this group of friends - one with the flash, the other without. We think the shot without the flash (below) has a more natural effect, as it better captures the cafe's light, even though the people aren't as bright as in the shot with the flash (right).

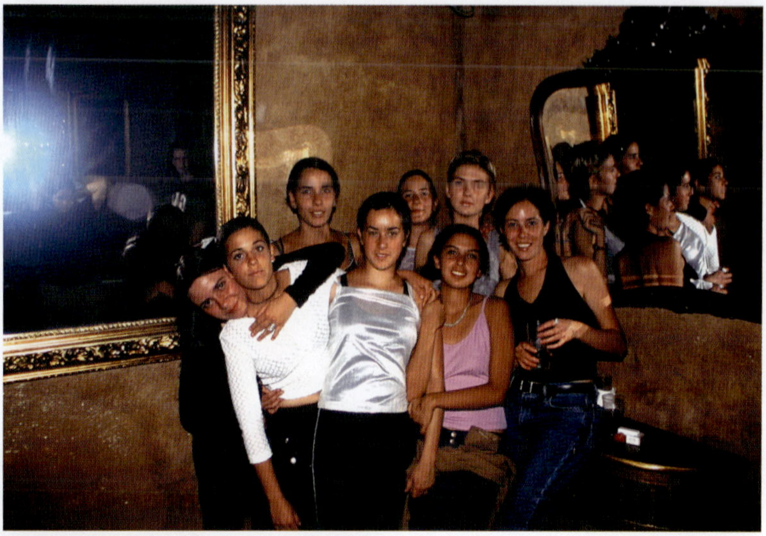

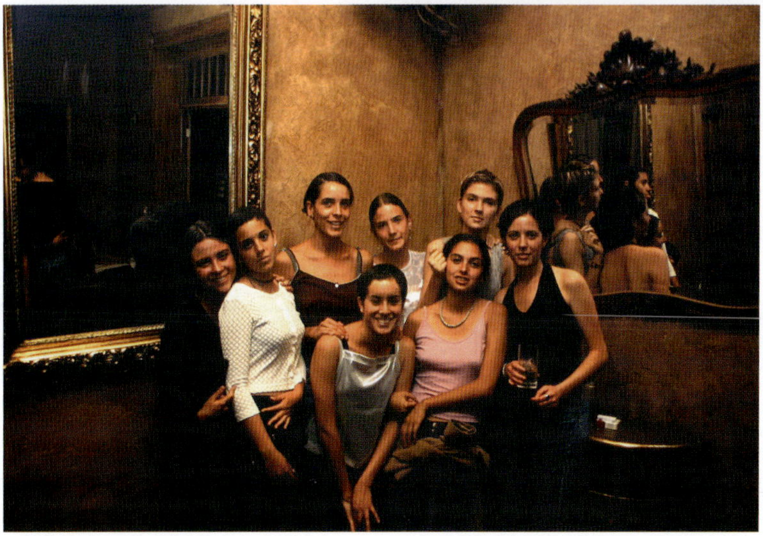

If you want to emphasize the lighting of the surroundings, first make sure that there's enough light to sufficiently illuminate the people. If there isn't enough light, you can still use the Night mode.

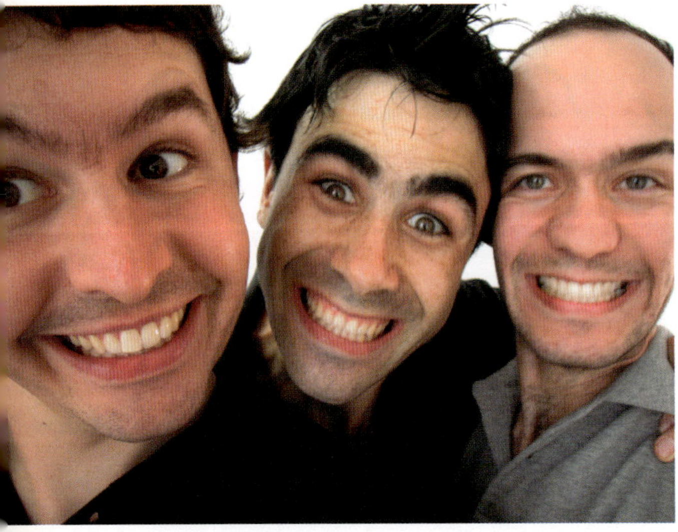

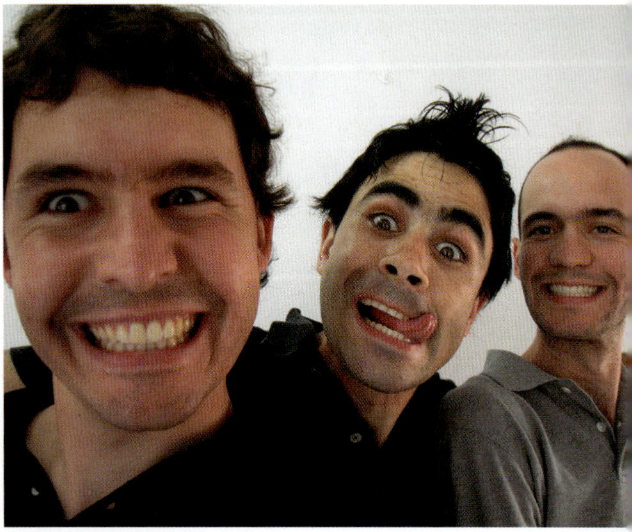

For these four pictures an environment that provided sufficient light was chosen - a room with four white walls, one large window and four skylights; the young men were well illuminated. The camera's flash wasn't used because the room was bright enough for taking clear pictures of stationary subjects. Unfortunately, in their attempts to be funny the guys were constantly moving.

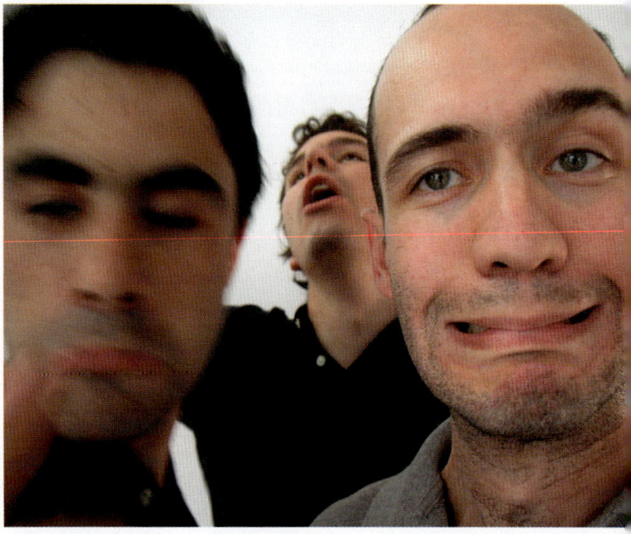

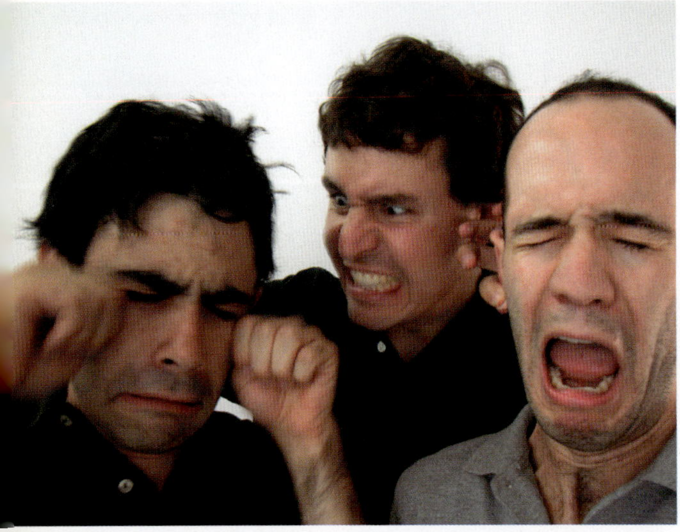

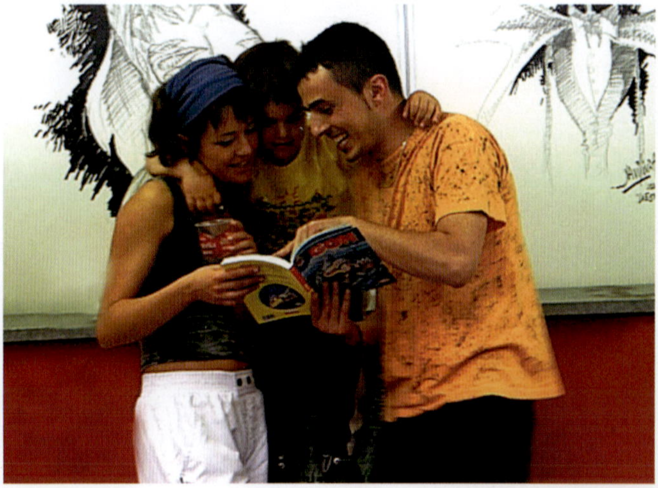

Whether the members of a group aren't trying to pose - we get a photograph that is much more natural, as on the left - or the shot is arranged (below), the most important thing is to always apply a certain measure of fantasy, and as we've said before, to constantly experiment.

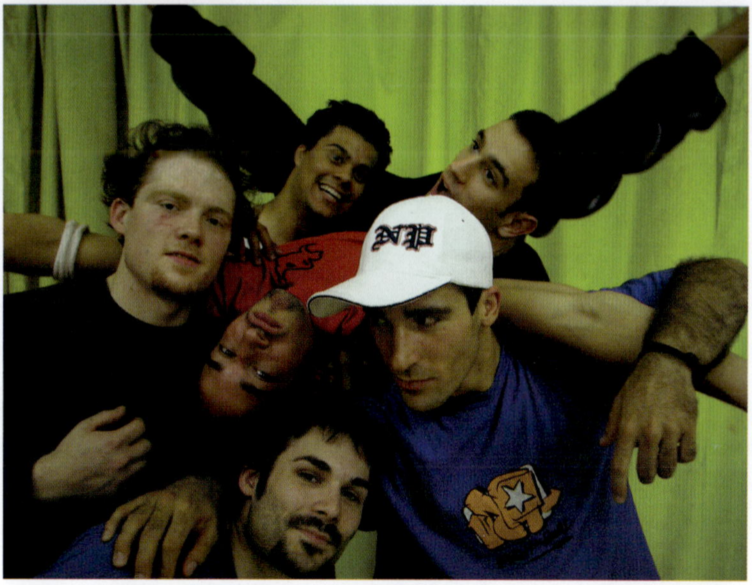

If you are taking a picture of a moving group or a situation that requires quick action, make sure you don't leave any people out of the shot. It's better to take a wider shot, as you can always trim the picture later with an editing program.

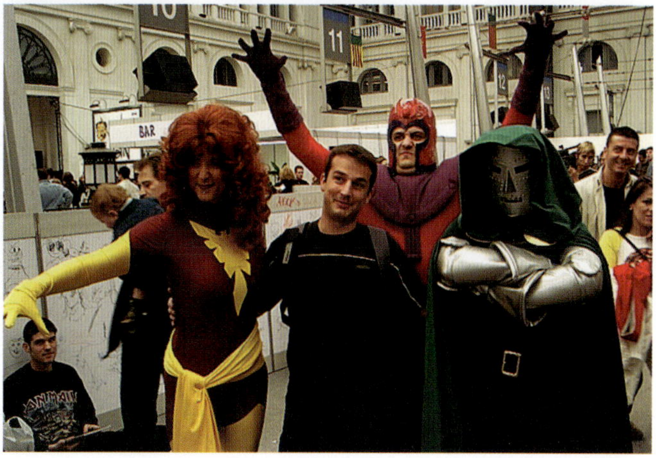

The last factor we must keep in mind is obstacles that could obstruct the picture. When getting ready to take a picture, don't hesitate to adjust your shooting angle to suit the environment, whether you need to lie on the floor, stand on a chair in front of the subject, or arrange the positions of the subjects.

TAKING PICTURES OF ANIMALS

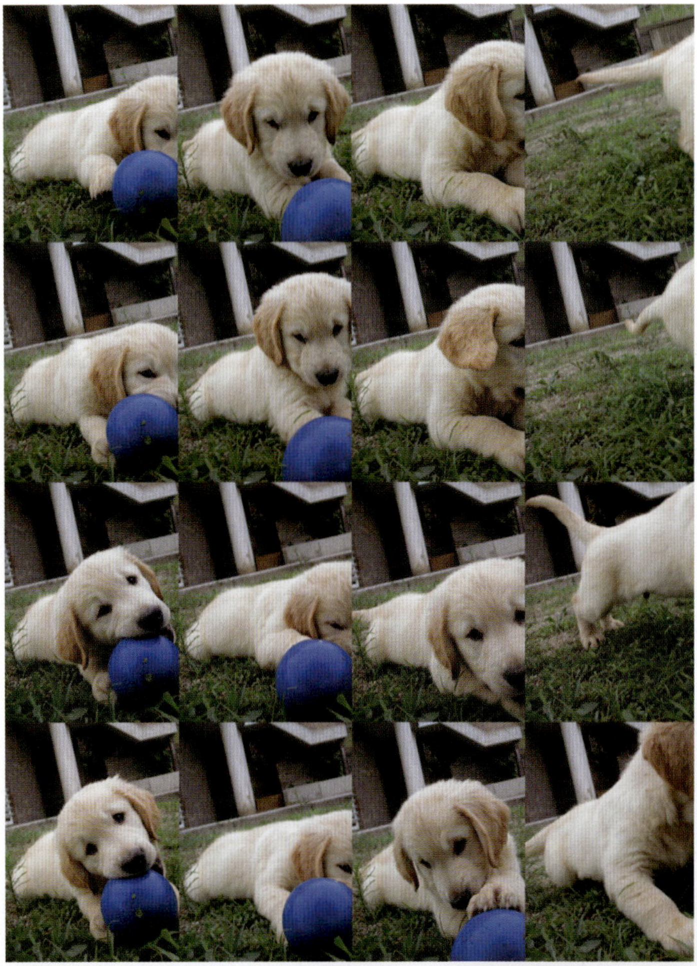

Taking pictures of animals requires a lot more patience and attention to catching the right moment. We're very aware that animals are unpredictable and that we can expect all sorts of surprises from them. This type of shot is very popular with pet owners.

In this sequence we can see that the puppy changed its position several times in just a few seconds. The individual shots couldn't keep up with these movements, so some of the shots are "cut." When taking pictures of animals the photographer has to be extraordinarily prepared and not try to catch the action with a single shot. It makes more sense to take several pictures and then choose the best one.

AWB AUTO

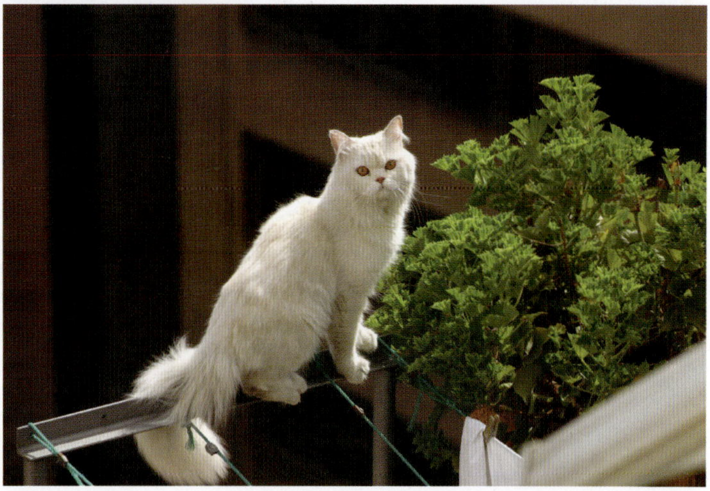

Cats are best at posing in front of the camera's lens, as they always turn towards the photographer - the camera picques the cat's curiosity. This makes cats relatively good subjects for pictures.

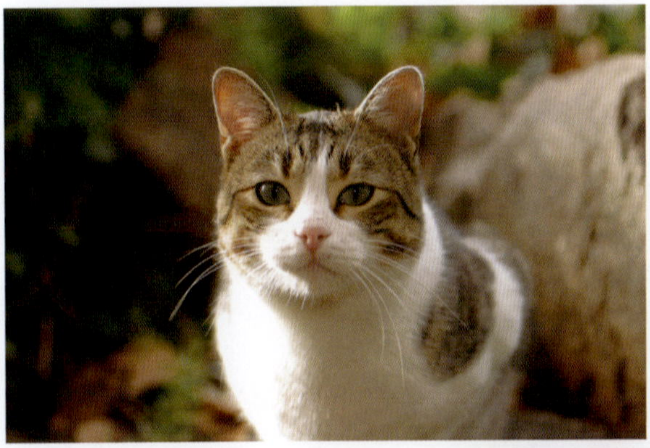

In this shot the cat was standing on a window sill in the sun. All it took was a quick movement to catch its attention. The flash was used to compensate for the light from the window and to add a bit of luster to its eyes.

It's a bit harder to photograph dogs, especially if they're young. Use a dog's favorite toy to distract it in order to get better pictures.

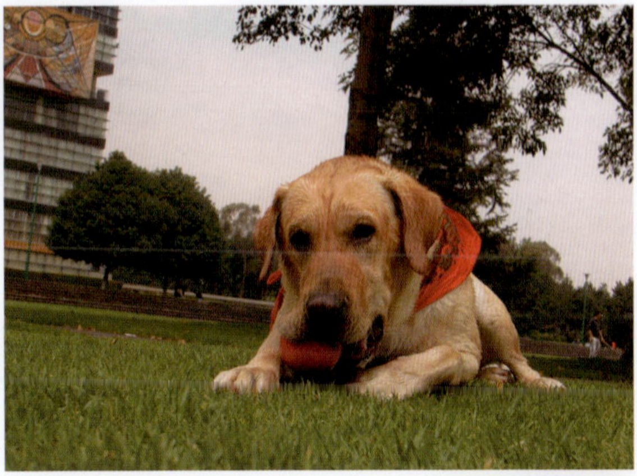

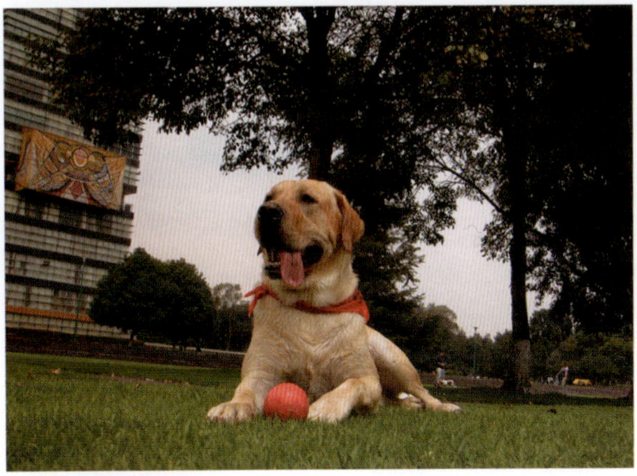

It's ideal to take a picture from the animal's level, which makes it the central subject and diminishes the background. For example, this picture was taken from ground level. The wider frame accentuates the animal's surroundings.

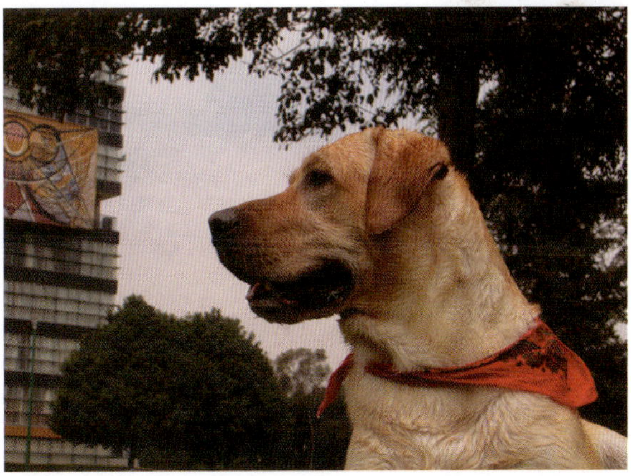

This shot, which was taken from the same position as the previous one, used the zoom to get closer to the dog, and the camera was aimed slightly up. This resulted in a more striking picture in which the dog takes up almost the entire frame. When you take a profile shot it's good to always leave a bit more space in the direction in which the subject is looking.

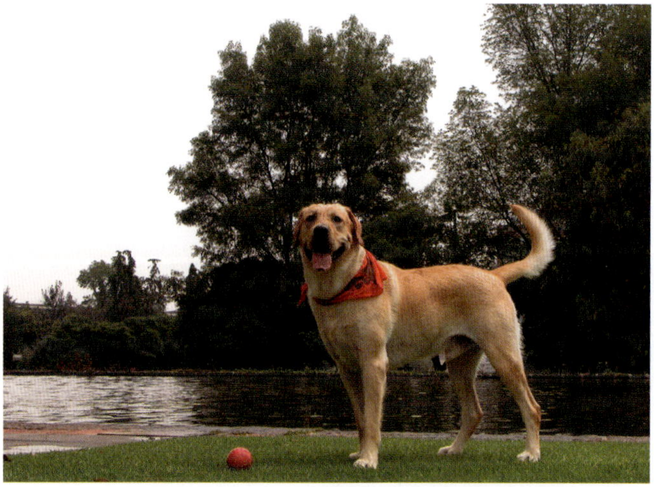

In this picture the dog was standing and it was only necessary to kneel down to get a head-on shot. If this picture had been taken from a standing position the camera would have been aimed down and the animal would have lost its dominance.

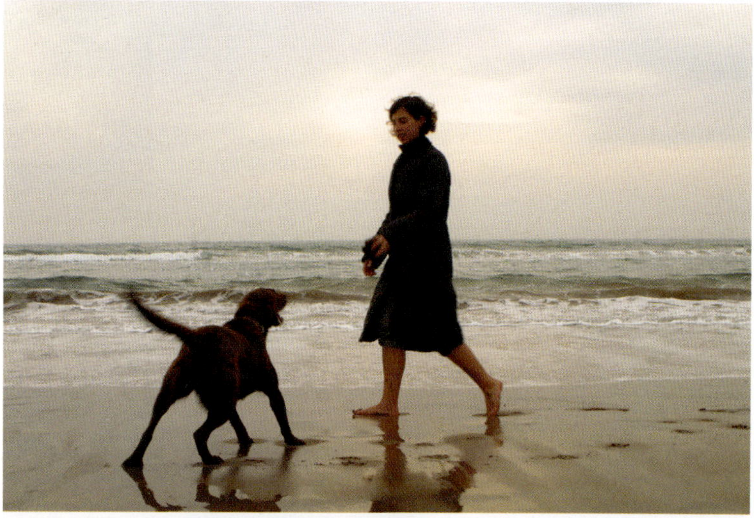

If you want to take a picture of a dog and its master you must find a central angle so that neither subject dominates the other. This picture was taken from a squatting position.

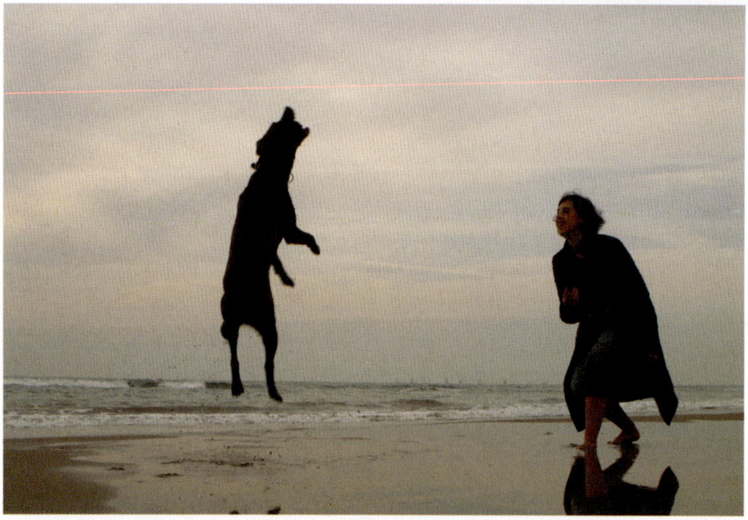

Here the photographer stooped a bit to emphasize the dog's leap. From a higher angle the jump would have been less marked.

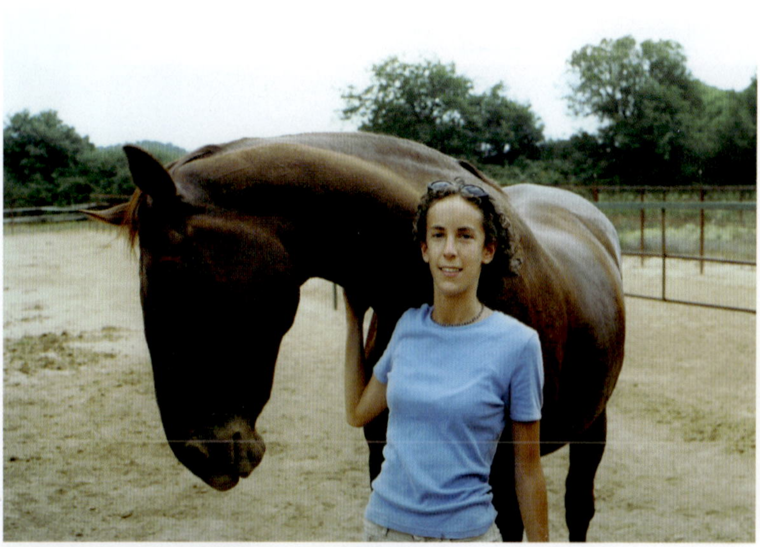

This picture should have been taken from a lower position to make the horse and the young woman look more natural.

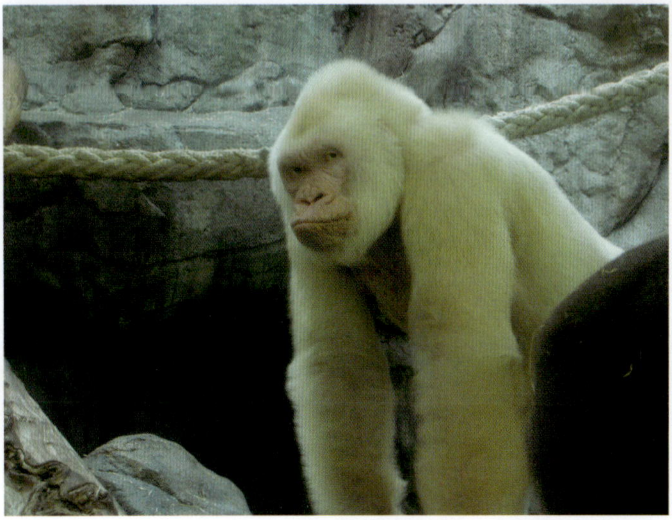

If you want to photograph an animal in captivity, say in a zoo, it's important to find a position from which there will be no glare (or at least as little as possible) from the glass through which you take the picture. Here's a little trick: get as close to the glass as you can and protect against any reflection with your free hand. It goes without saying that you should never use the flash - it would reflect off the glass and affect your entire photograph.

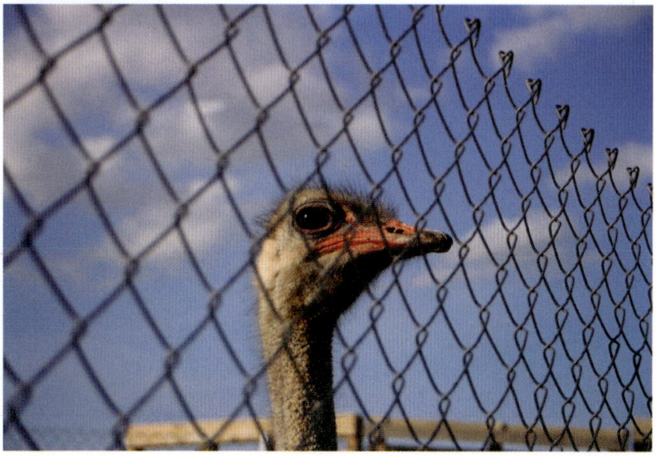

In this picture the ostrich is behind a hurricane fence and because it was so close it was impossible to aim the camera through one of the holes. But we managed to frame the ostrich's eye in a hole in the fence. If a part of the eye were covered by a wire in the fence the picture wouldn't be as interesting.

CITYSCAPES

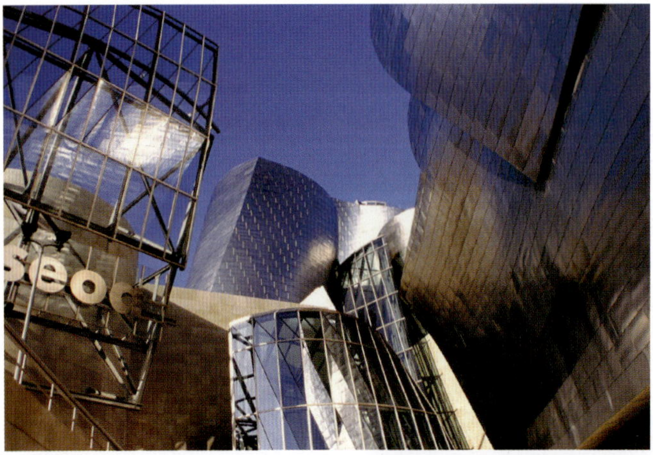

Now we'll see what pictures of a city can look like at various times of the day. We'll add a few pointers to this analysis that will allow you to choose the prettiest parts of the scene that you want to photograph, whether you're in a large metropolis or a little village.

A shot of a town offers a great many possibilities that allow you to experiment with work on details, on parts of scenes, or simply preserving memories.

▲ With any other sort of outdoor photography, it is necessary to keep the time of day in mind. In this picture we see typical white noonday light with little distortion.

▶ In counterpoint to the preceding picture the light is much warmer here, typical of the end of the afternoon. The sun's rays, coming from the side, also emphasize parts of the building much more and create an impression that is warmer overall.

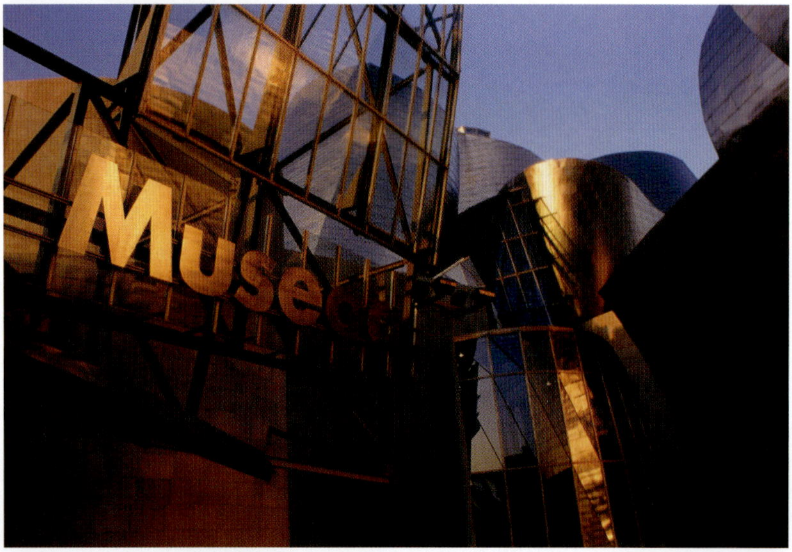

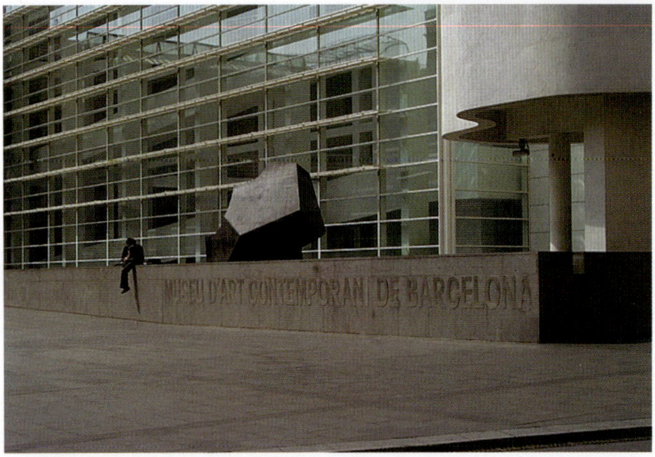

◀ If you're taking a picture of a building it's important to hold the camera as level as possible in order to keep the lines from converging. It's a good idea to include people in such shots to provide a scale so you can more easily imagine the true size of the buildings.

After you've taken the overall, main pictures, you can switch to creative shots by using a more original angle to emphasize buildings' shapes or details.

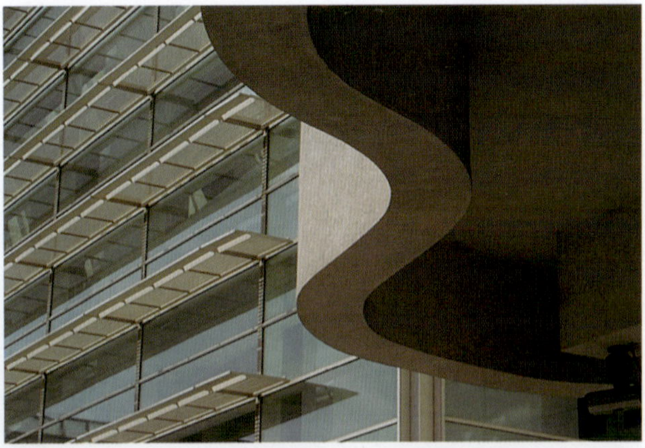

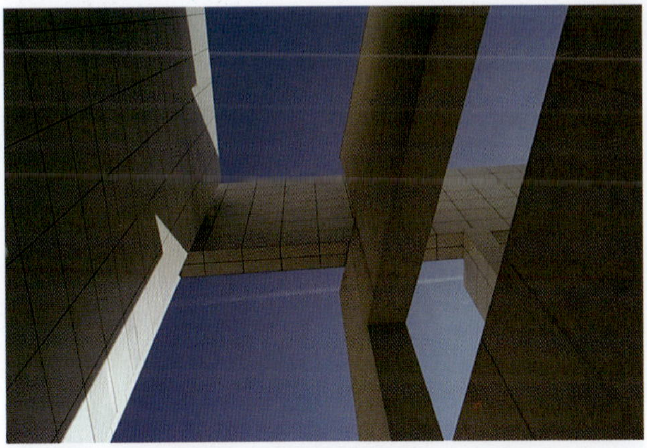

Modern architecture allows you to take interesting, "abstract" pictures. It is then interesting to analyze every angle of view.

When taking pictures of buildings pay attention to shadows. They add space to pictures and give one greater understanding of a building's architecture.

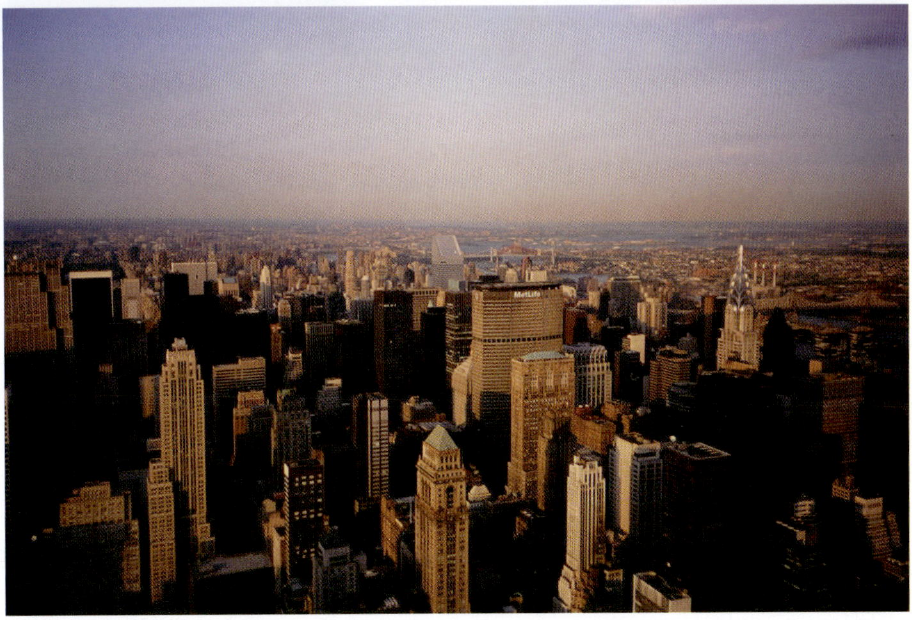

If you want to take panoramic pictures of a city we recommend taking them in the first or last hours of daylight, at moments when the buildings look more corporeal. In every case it's better to avoid the middle of the day.

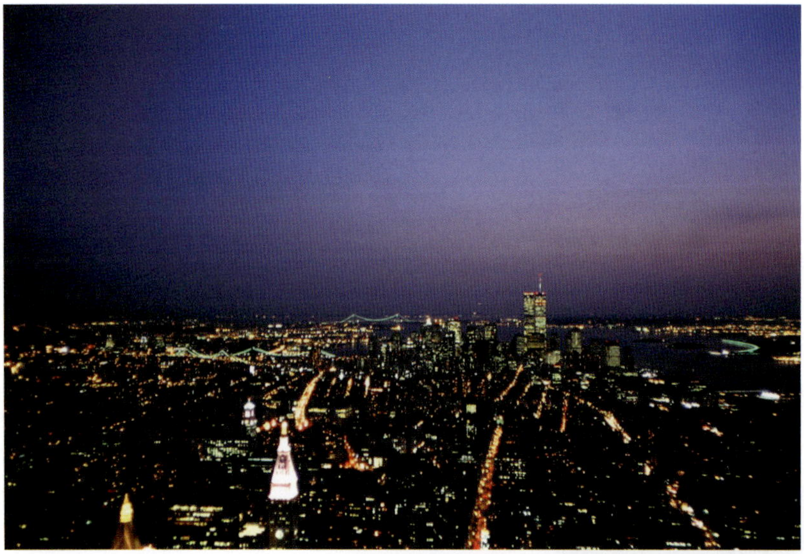

When taking panoramic shots in waning daylight it's good to wait a little while and take another shot after the sun has set and just as the city lights are coming on.
Within a short time you can catch two different temporal phases - sundown and night. This panorama of New York was taken 25 minutes after the preceding picture.

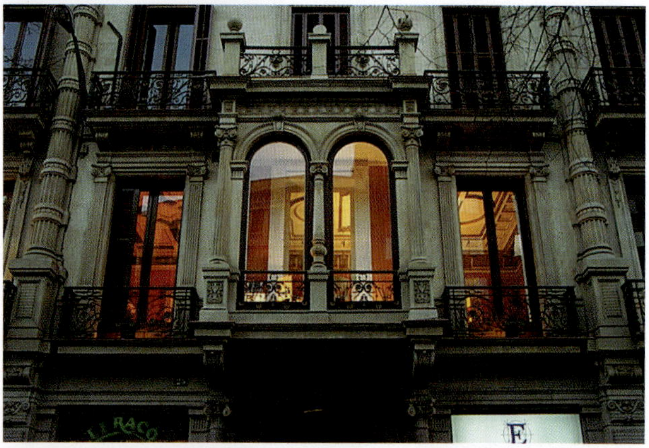

The last hours of the afternoon are ideal for photographing buildings or facades. The outdoor light offers lighting that is similar to indoor lighting. These moments are good for taking balanced pictures without the reflection of the sun off window glass.

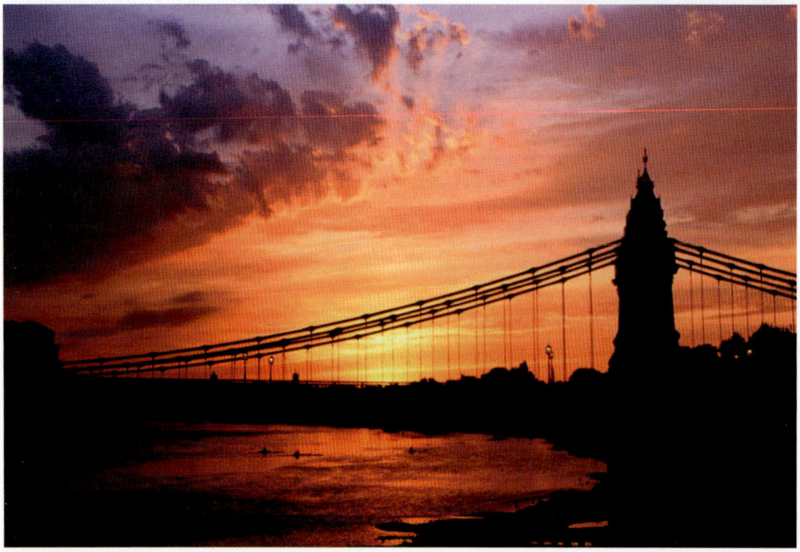

You can only catch contours when taking pictures against the light.
In this case the bridge is entirely without illumination. Nevertheless, its silhouette against the lovely sunset creates a very nice image.

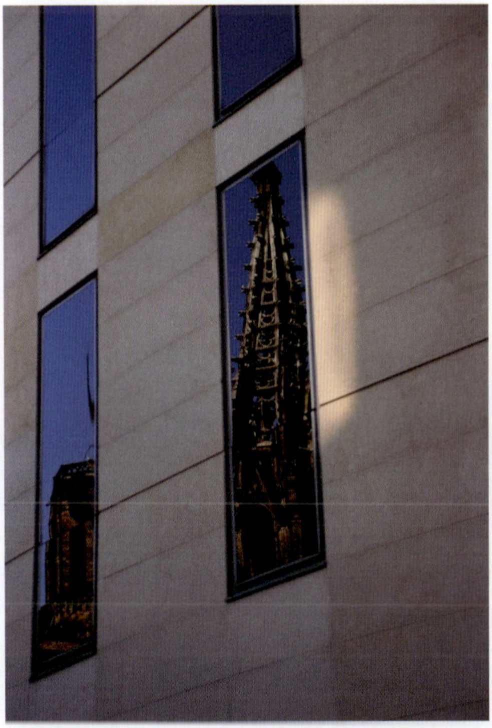

It's common to see various types of architecture separated by only a few meters in large cities. You can get interesting pictures by carefully arranging your shots. In this case a picture was taken of a modern building with reflections of the upper part of an old cathedral in its windows.

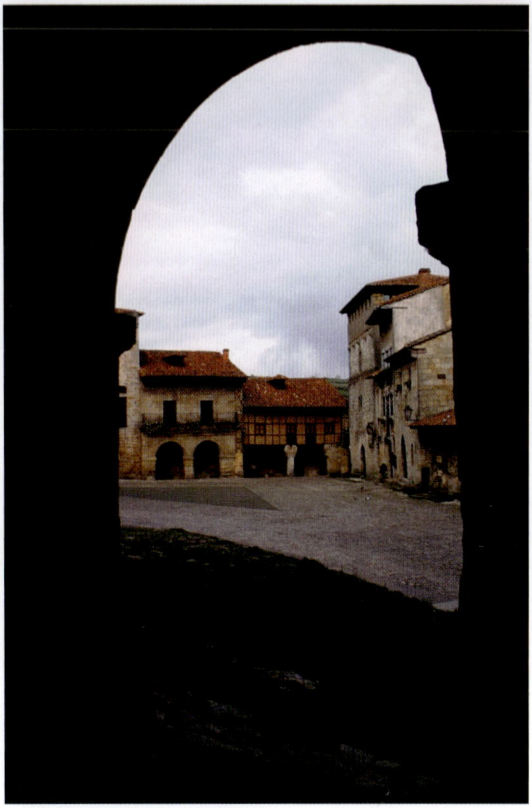

Sometimes it's difficult to "seat" an image in broader contexts, but by selecting a suitable shot it's possible to express it well. This small square was framed by the arch of an arcade on its edge, which indicates that the entire square is made up of buildings of a similar style.

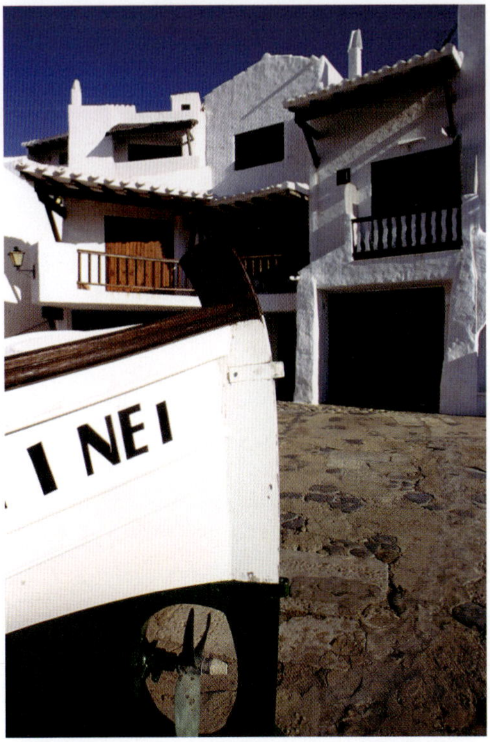

This shot was selected so that in the foreground you can see the stern of a boat, from which you can deduce that it is a fishing village, even though you can't see the ocean.

MOUNTAINSCAPES

Now let's look at various situations we can encounter when taking pictures of mountainscapes, when during the final hours of day the mountains are usually much more pronounced and colorful.

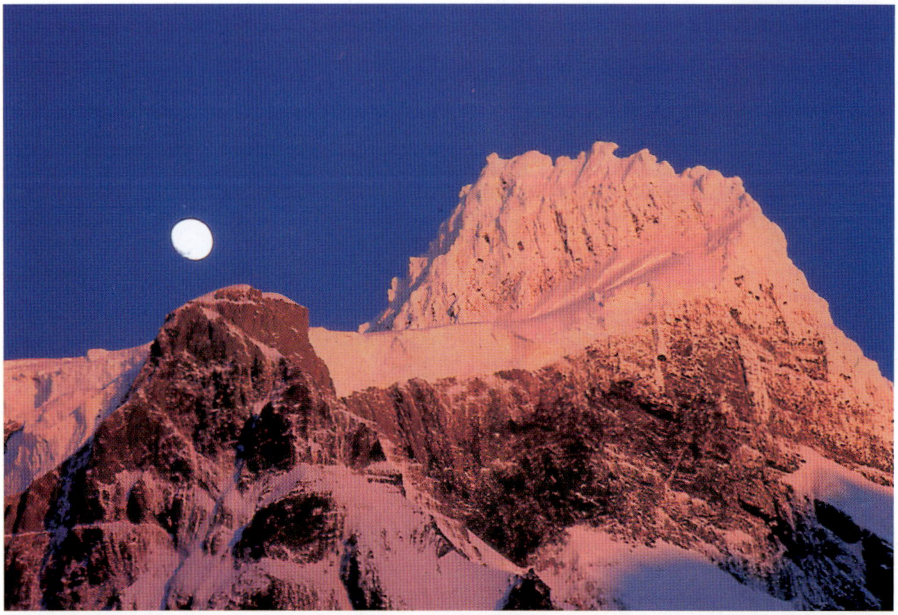

FOTO: JENS BURSELL

We'll start with a situation when the sun is low above the horizon and the light gives everything a reddish hue. That is the case with this picture taken during sunset, which made the snow appear red. The camera was set in daylight mode - three pictures were taken at exposures changed each time by one-half EV in order to find the most correct exposure. The brightest picture was finally selected.

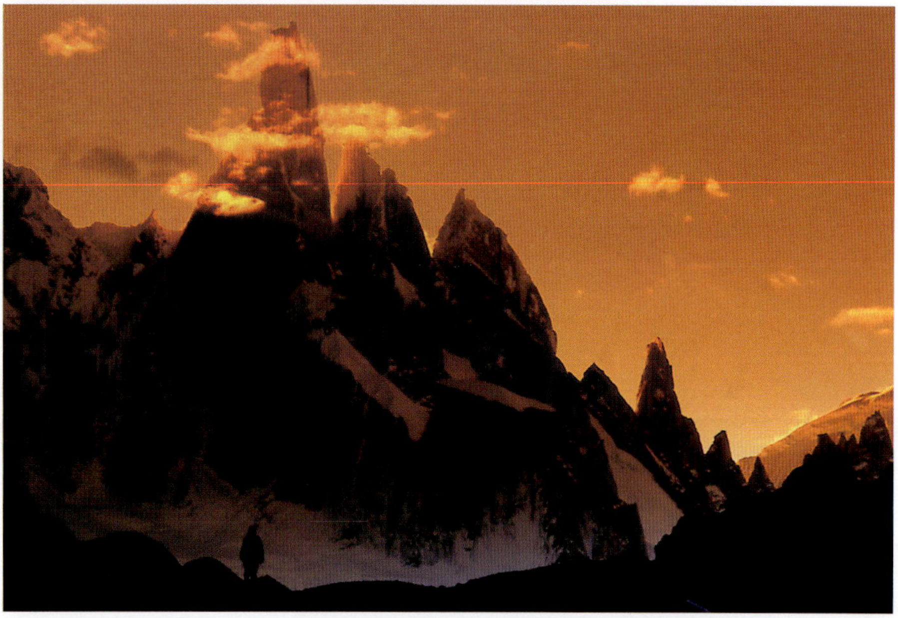

FOTO: JENS BURSELL

The conditions are the same as in the preceding picture. This shot was also taken at the end of the day, but this time without any direct light on the mountains. The light from behind the high peaks gives them a dark, somber appearance.

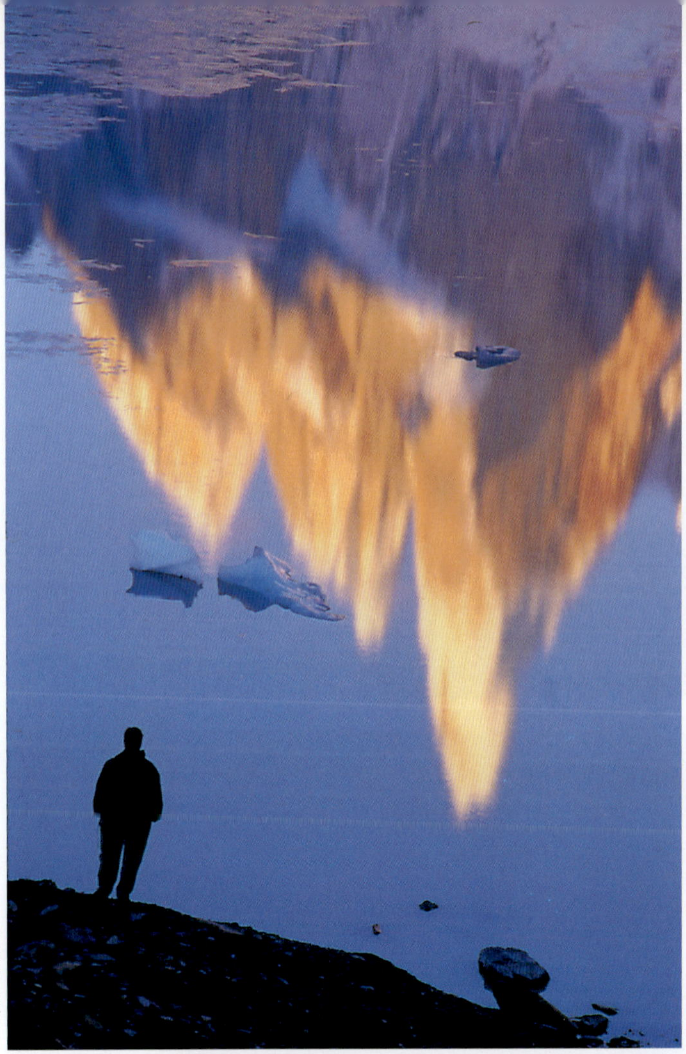

FOTO: JENS BURSELL

◂ Conversely, this picture was taken early in the morning, when the light wasn't striking the lake itself, just the upper reaches of the mountains on the other side.

This allowed the photographer to take a picture of his guide, making partial use of the lake's surface as an interesting mirror for reflecting the background. The exposure was initially focused without the lower part of the scene so that the camera could adjust to the average light reflected from the lake's surface, and then, without releasing the shutter the angle was shifted and the picture was taken with the silhouette of the person.

AWB

▾ Here the lighting of the scene as a whole was even and balanced. Even though the sky was relatively bright, the Cloudy mode was used to make the picture warmer. Then an angle was chosen to allow the little village nestled among the mountains to stand out.

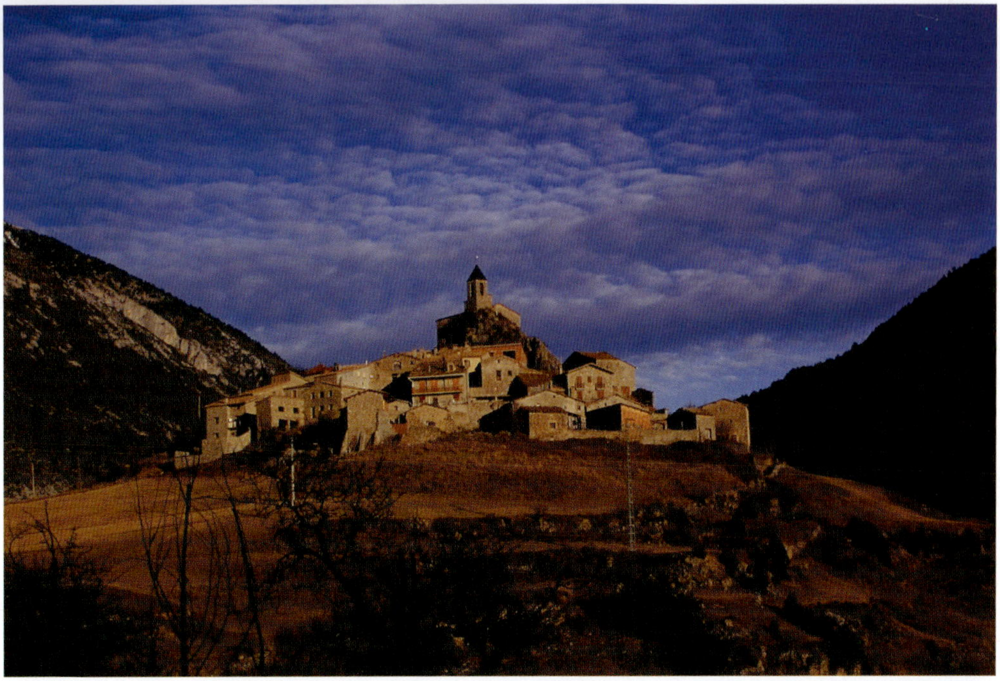

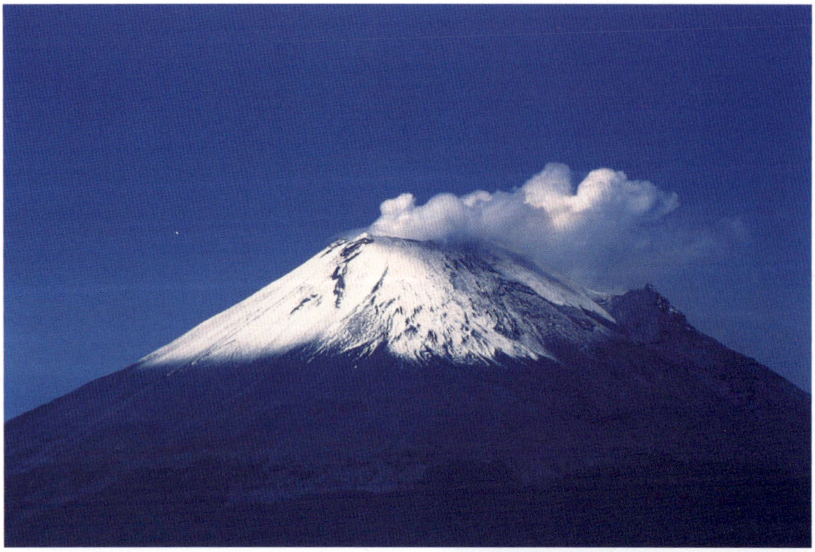

In situations like the one presented in this picture, with an absolutely clear sky, one must pay great attention to the exposure. In fact, the contrast between the whiteness of the snow and the shadow on the side of the mountain (or volcano, depending on the circumstances) presents the danger that the exposure will be set by the camera only according to one of these elements and will thus be incorrect for the other. We recommend that you take several shots with different exposures and then select the one that comes out the best.

The same principle applies with other sharp contrasts. In this case the low clouds are sort of nestled in the valley and illuminated from above. If the shot were underexposed by 2 EV (-2 EV) the valley would be lighter. Conversely, the clouds wouldn't be as detailed and would look like white stains.

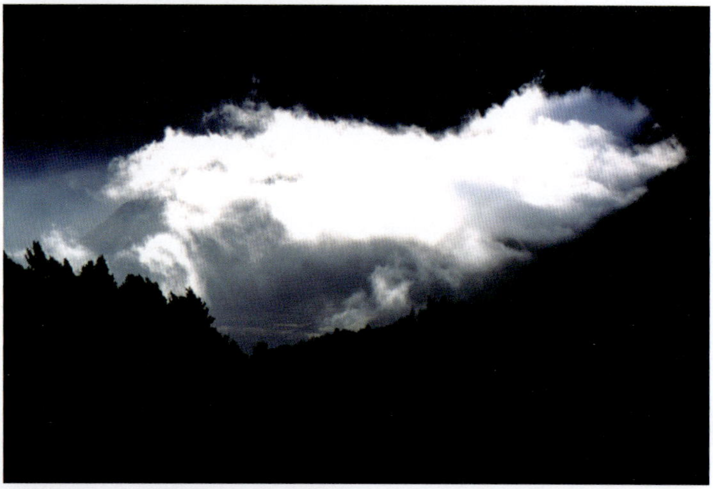

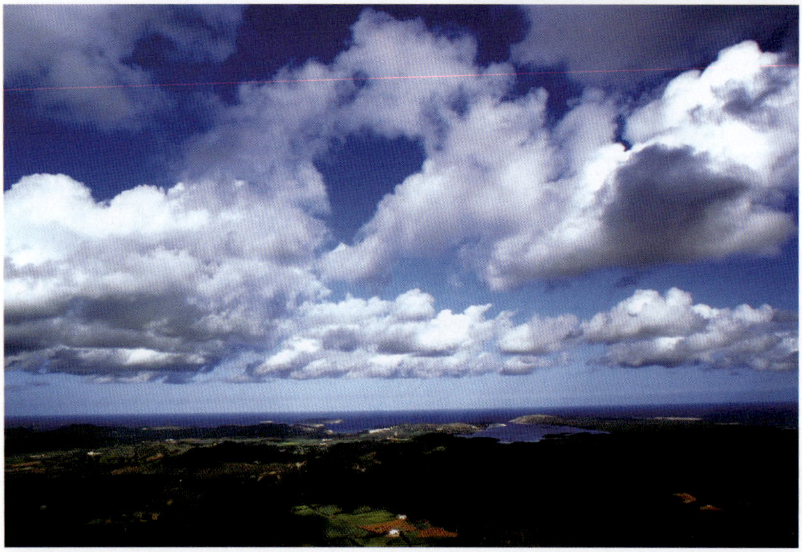

When this picture was taken from an elevated position in the mountains the Cloudy mode was not selected, although it was a relatively cloudy day. The clouds, bright white and very dispersed, let lots of light through. The camera was aimed slightly upwards so that the clouds would stand out a bit (waiting a while ensured that the central part of the land was illuminated). This made it possible to achieve the effect of shadows and light.

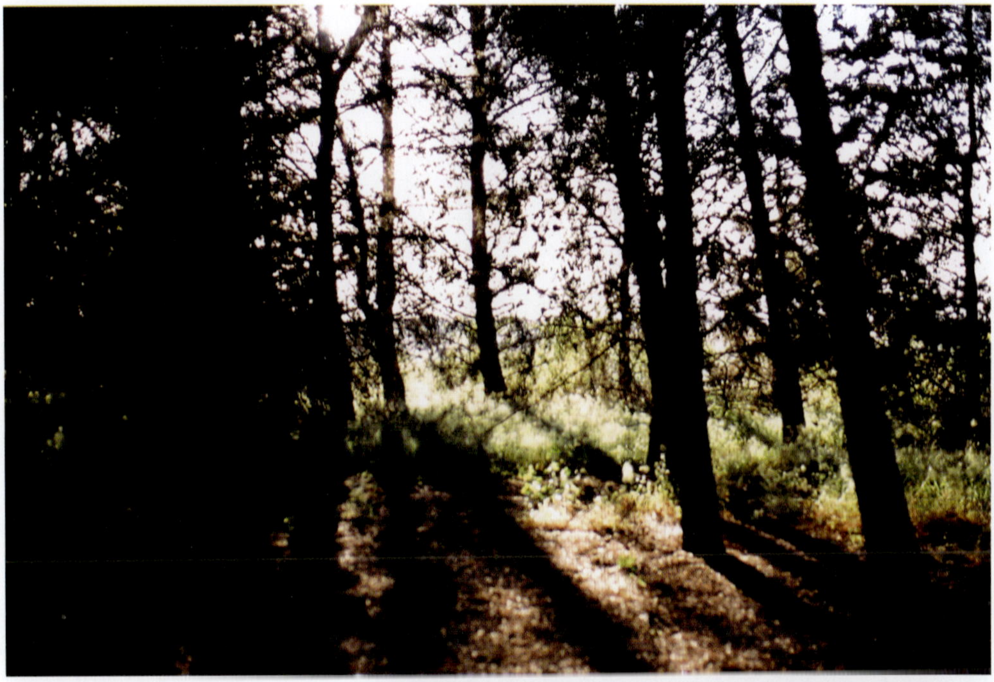

▲ As in the mountainscapes, you can see here the same interesting phenomenon with photographs taken in a forest with tall trees. There is a play of light penetrating among the trunks and a tracing of silhouettes in the bright background. For both of these pictures the Daylight mode was chosen. The first picture was taken against the light, while the second was illuminated from above. ▶

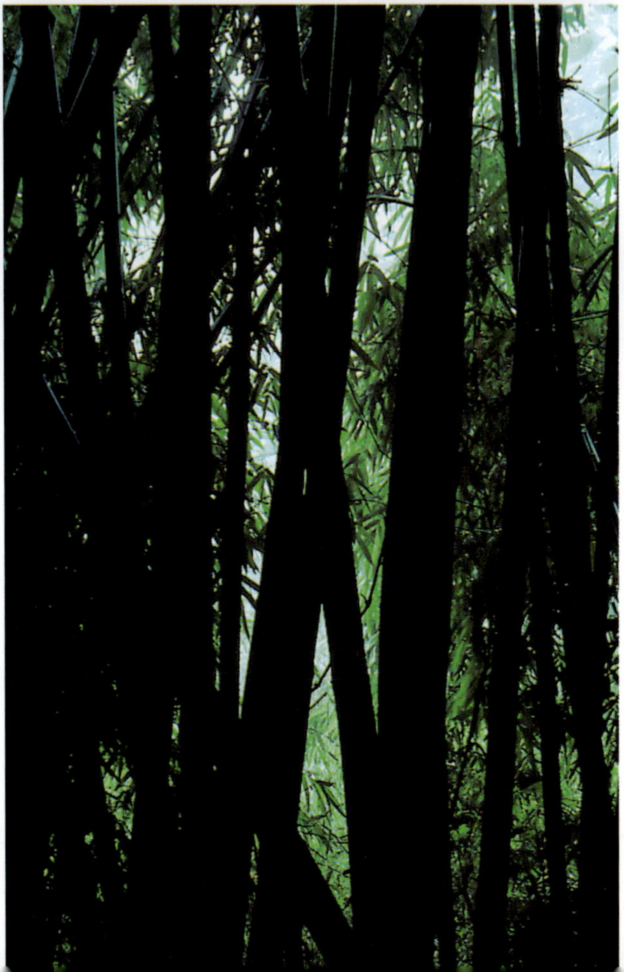

FOTO: JENS BURSELL

Make sure that the rays of the sun don't strike the camera's lens directly. To eliminate this risk take advantage of the long shadows of the trees or shade the lens from the light source with your free hand.

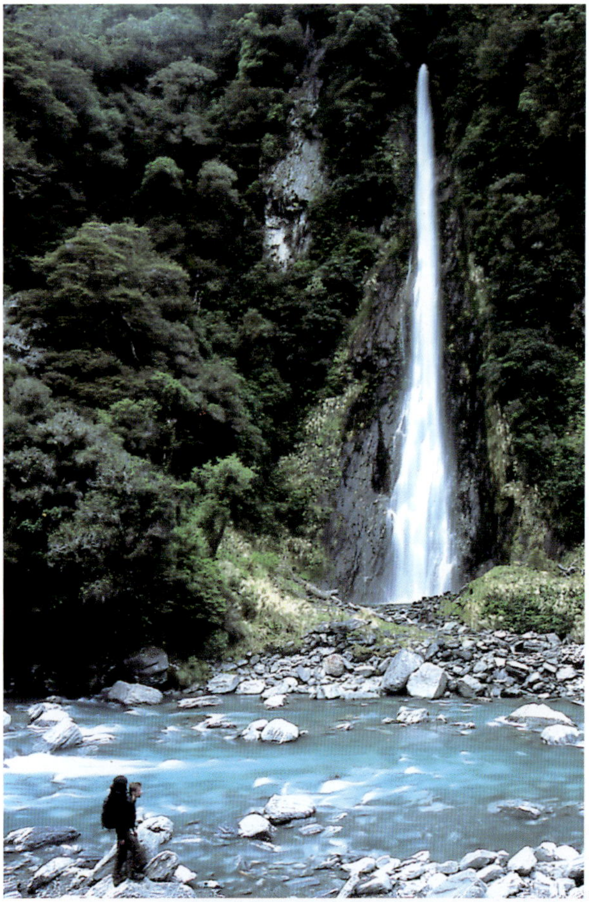
FOTO: JENS BURSELL

In many cases outdoors a photographer encounters flowing water or a waterfall with a strong current, which lends motion to the picture. This picture was taken using the Cloudy mode, because the sky was slightly covered by clouds. The photographed figure was placed opposite the waterfall, which gave the picture balance.

In the case of this intensely blue lake the clouds have the same blue coloring as the water. The light that is reflected off the watery surface gives the entire picture a colorful touch, creates an interesting effect, and adds a cool appearance. This picture was taken using the Daylight mode.

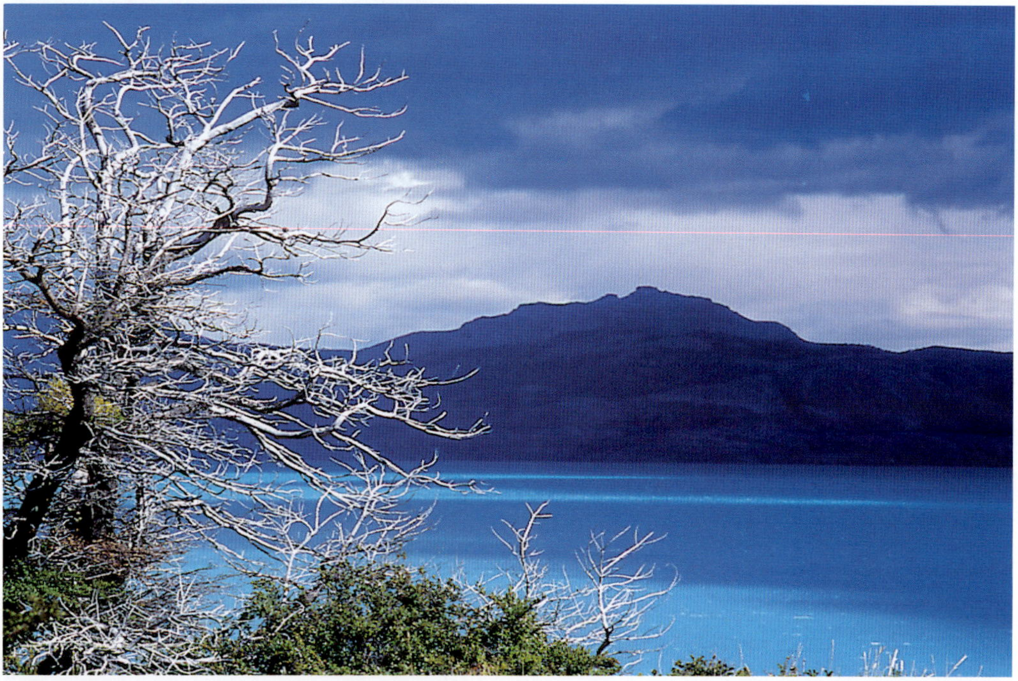
FOTO: JENS BURSELL

Seascapes

In this chapter we will analyze photographs taken in an ocean environment at various times of the day. You will notice that due to reflections in the water, the direction of the sun's rays play a basic role when choosing the shooting angles. You will also recognize the best method for compositions with various elements and subjects. We'll start with examples when the sky was perfectly clear and the sun was at its zenith.

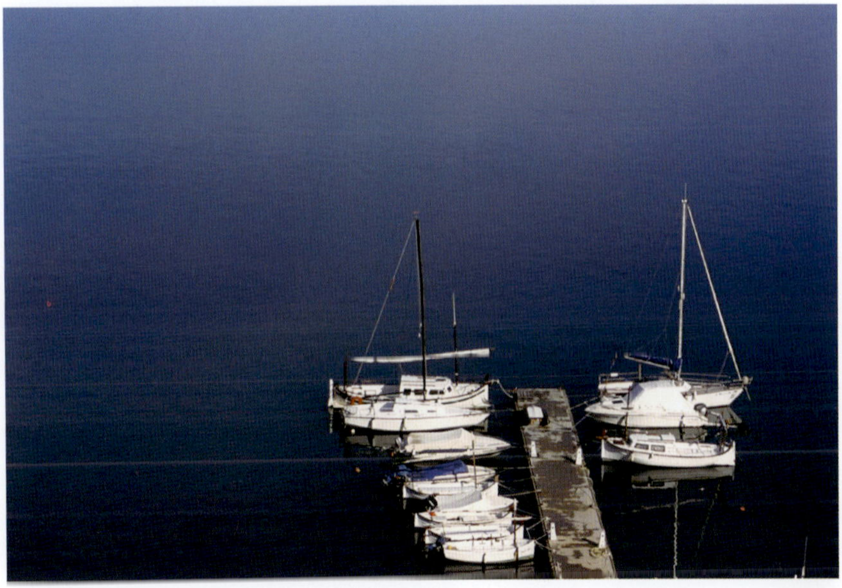

▲ Here we chose the Daylight mode and used two different exposures; the one that the camera selected and the other an underexposure by one-half EV. The underexposed one was finally chosen as the better picture. The main part of the harbor was cut out, as it contained too much information, isolating the pier and the boats and yielding a refined picture.

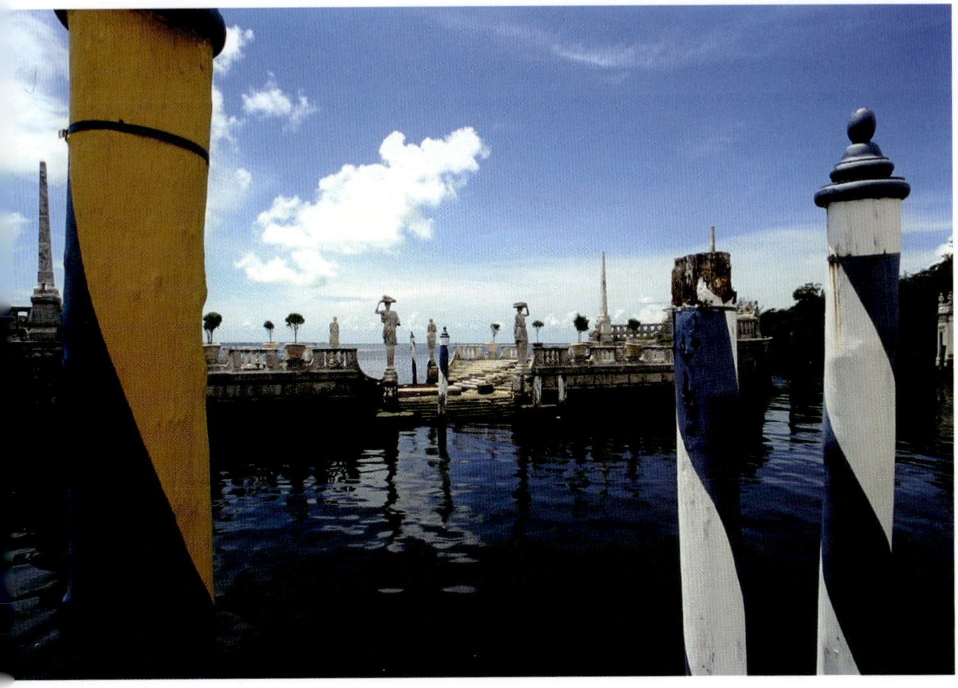

◂ The picture was taken somewhat into the sun, when it was close to its zenith. We chose the Daylight mode and focused the shot on the vicinity of the posts for tying up boats to achieve a more intense image with a sharply defined foreground.

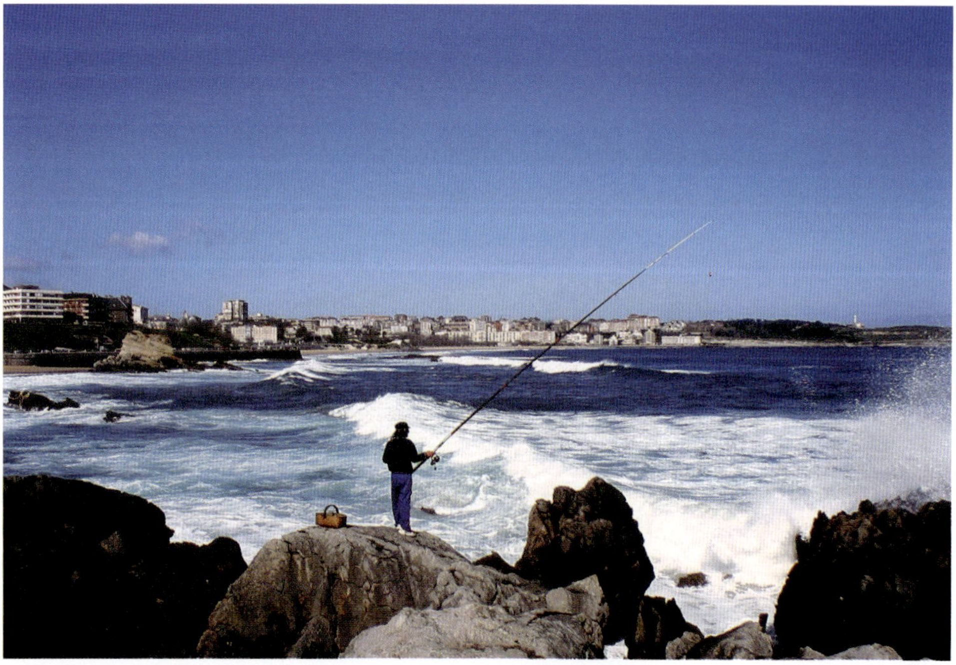

This picture was taken using the Daylight mode. The fisherman is located near the center to lend a certain balance to the rocks on one side and the other of the shot. The photographer waited until a wave started to break against the rocks in order to add a dynamic element to the picture.

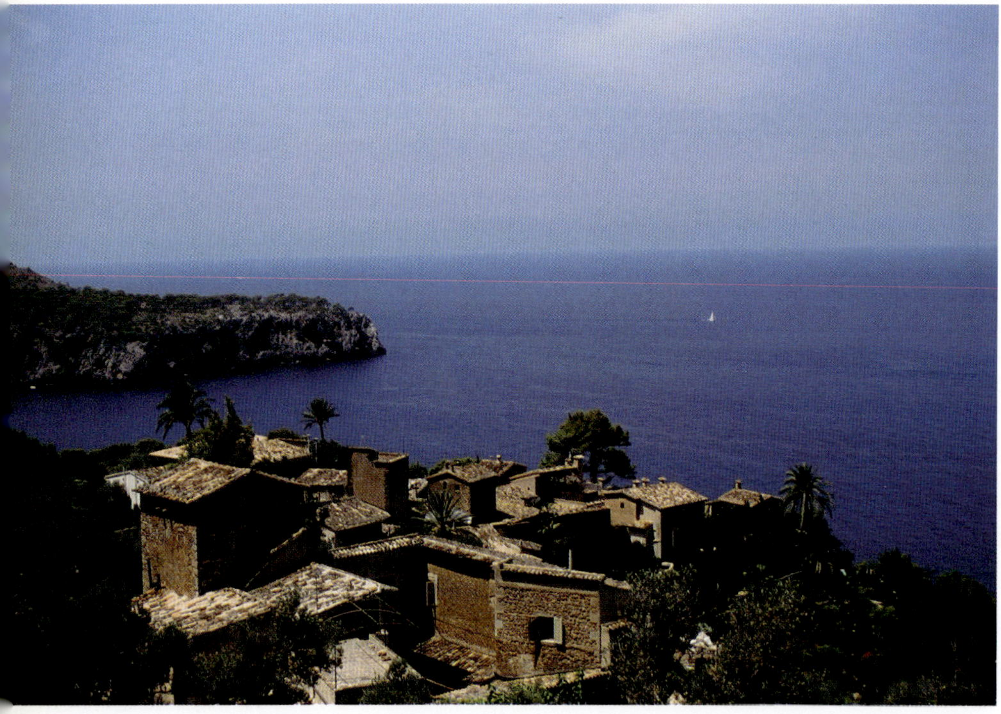

The composition chosen for this shot placed the small Mediterranean village right in the middle. The light was coming from above, so you can't see any long shadows. This picture was taken using the Daylight mode.

In all of the pictures we've analyzed so far the light is coming from above, and the sun's rays provide lighting that is somewhat even. The direction of the sunlight's impact is important for capturing several lighting effects. Here are a few pictures that were taken when the sun was low in the sky or were taken against the light.

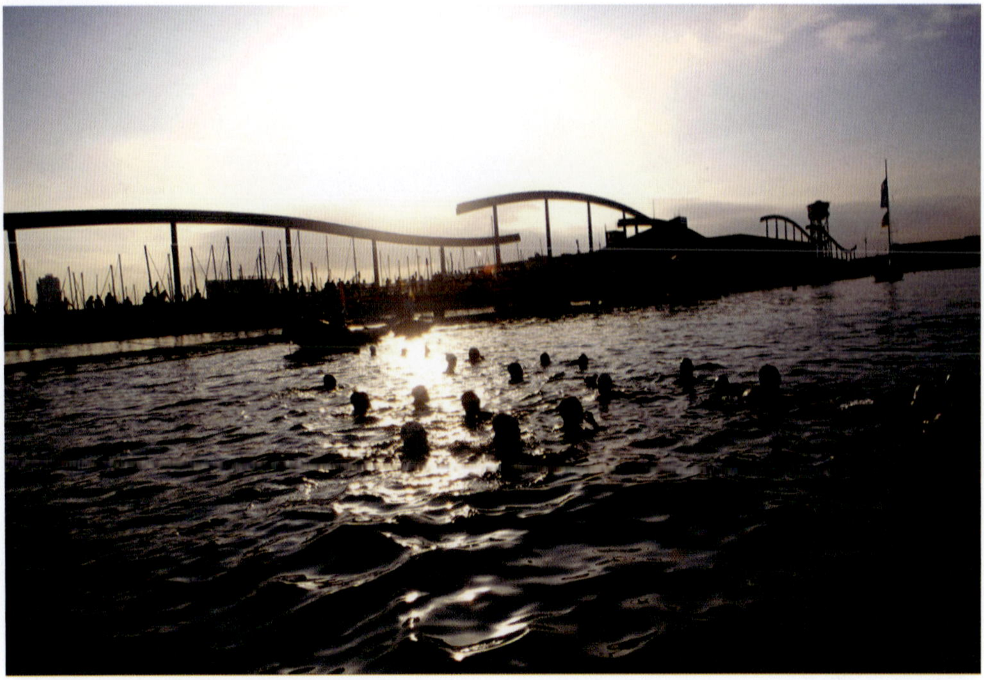

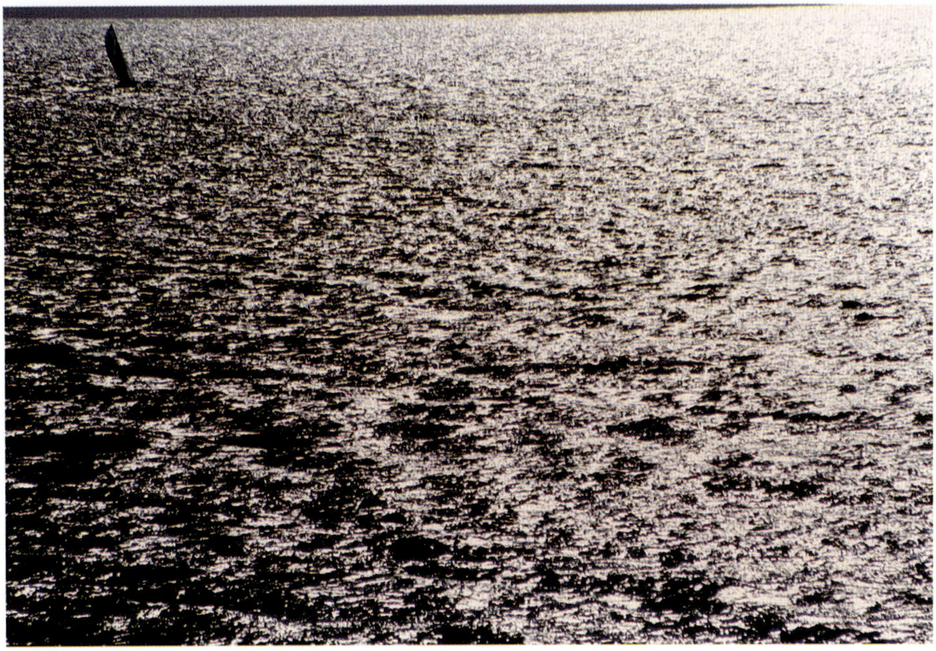

▲ These two pictures were taken early in the day when the sun was low. The slighly overcast sky gives the light a cool shading. ◀

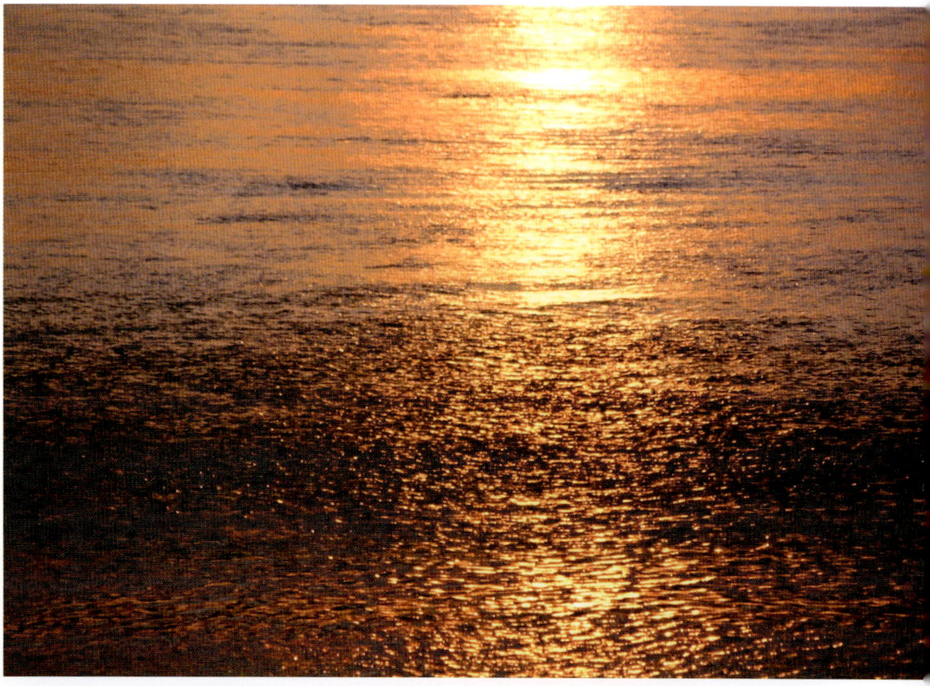

These two pictures were taken at sunset, when the light is warmer. And as you can clearly see, they were taken against the light. Unlike the two preceding shots (taken using the Daylight mode), these pictures were taken using the Cloudy mode in order to emphasize their coloring.

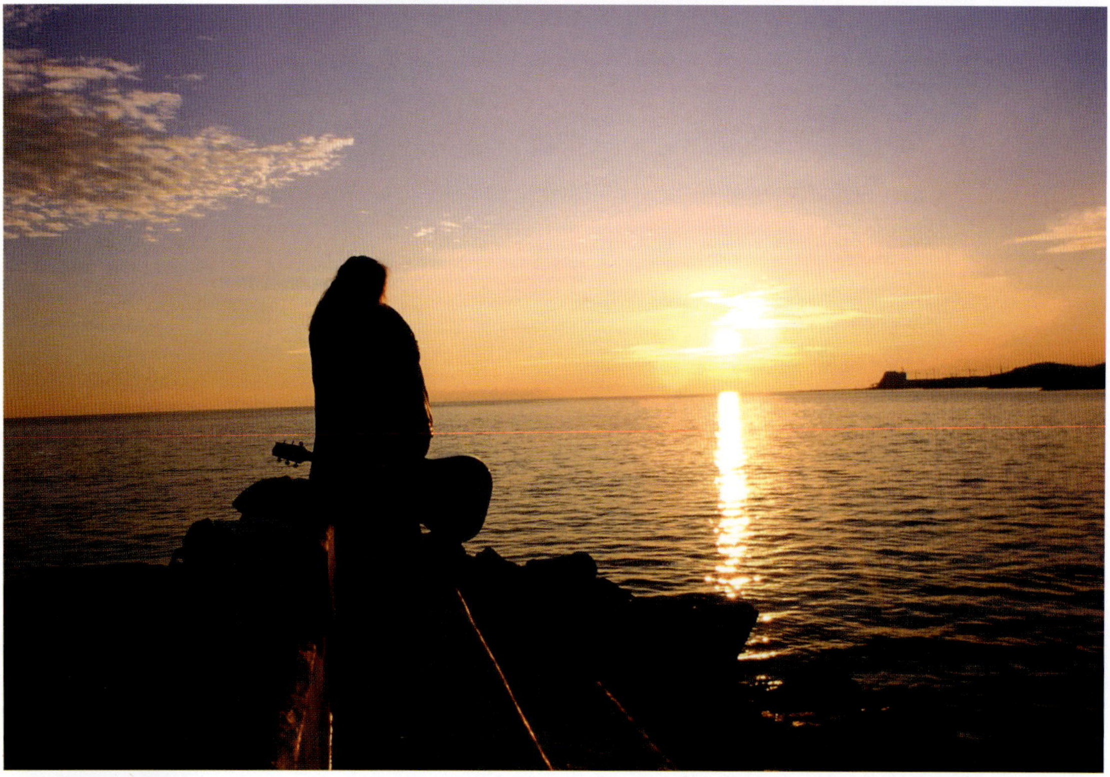

Finally, a few examples of side lighting in the late afternoon

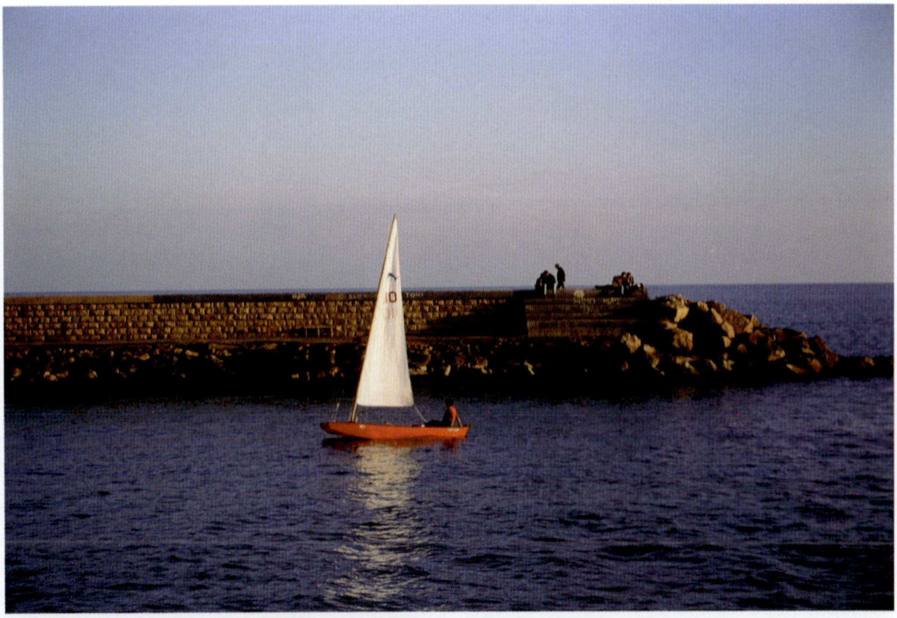

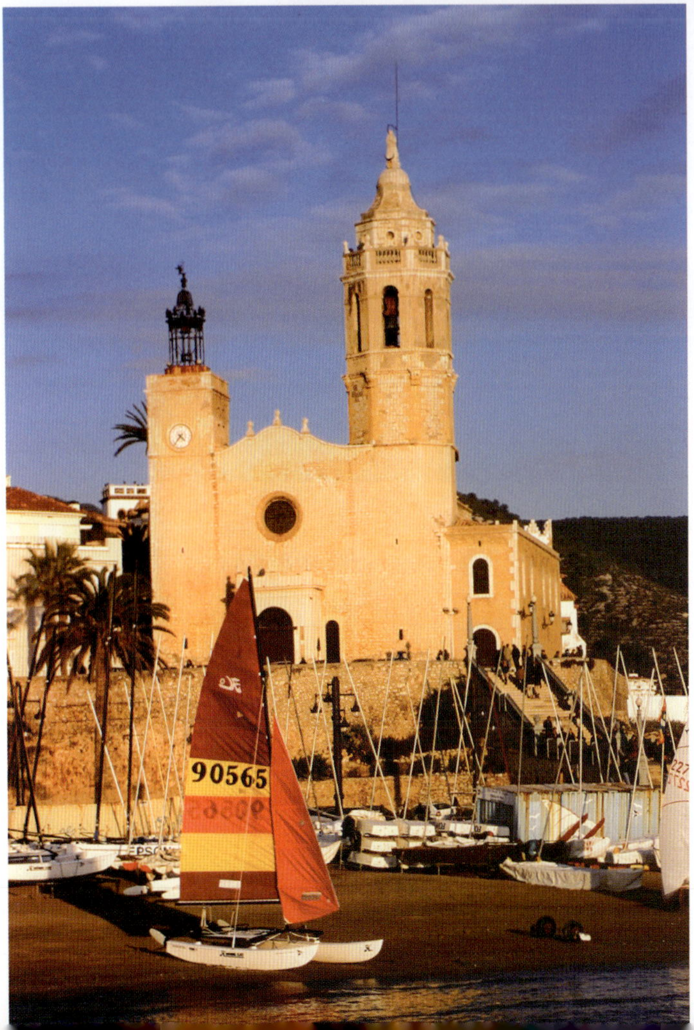

▲ These two examples allow you to appreciate the wave motion of the sea without the excessive reflections that appear when you take pictures towards the light source. The shadows are longer, giving the impression of greater space. In these two pictures the camera was set on Daylight mode. ◄

Pay great attention to shadows. If they are too long they can, instead of providing more space, darken the entire photograph.

MACROPHOTOGRAPHY

Most compact cameras do not have lenses that make it possible to take pictures in the macro mode. But many are equipped with an optical zoom function, which allows you to markedly enlarge a shot and get closer to the subject.

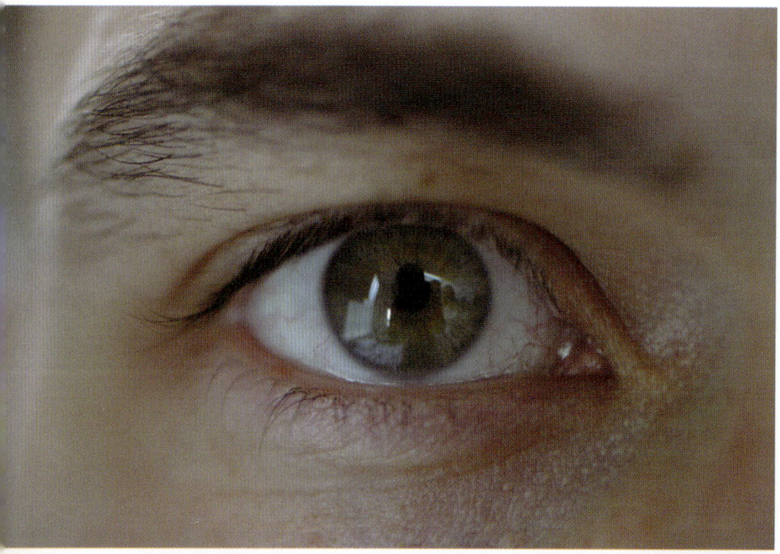

Without optical zoom it wouldn't be possible to catch such a facial detail. The lighting is even, there aren't any shadows in the picture, so it wasn't necessary to use the flash.

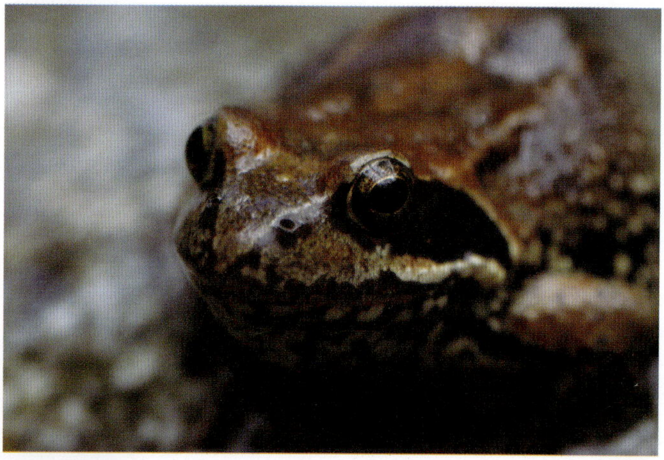

In this picture the frog's entire body glistens - the frog is in a wet environment. The sky was overcast, but the clouds weren't too dense, so they let enough light through. For this type of photograph you have to pay extra attention to focusing. The slightest movement of the camera can lead to an entirely different result. If the camera had moved when the shutter release was pressed the eye wouldn't have been so clear.

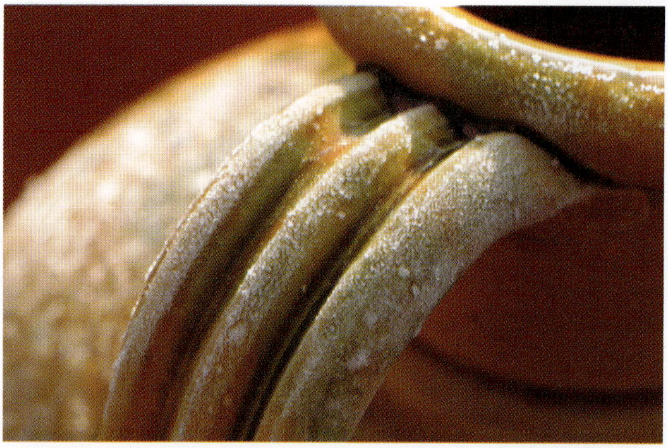

The bright light of the sun's first rays made the articulation of the vessel's handle more striking.

The dragon-fly in the picture was trapped against a window pane of a swimming pool. Because the light was so strong it was necessary to set the camera for underexposure (-1 EV). The picture was taken at a time when there weren't too many waves on the pool and the light wasn't reflected directly into the lens.

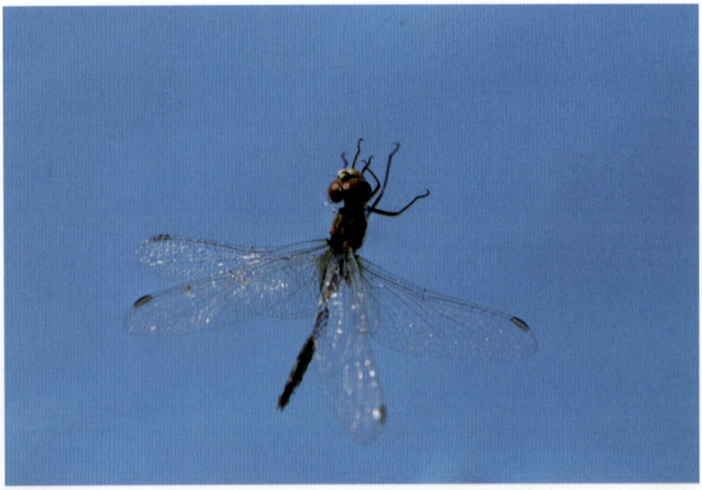

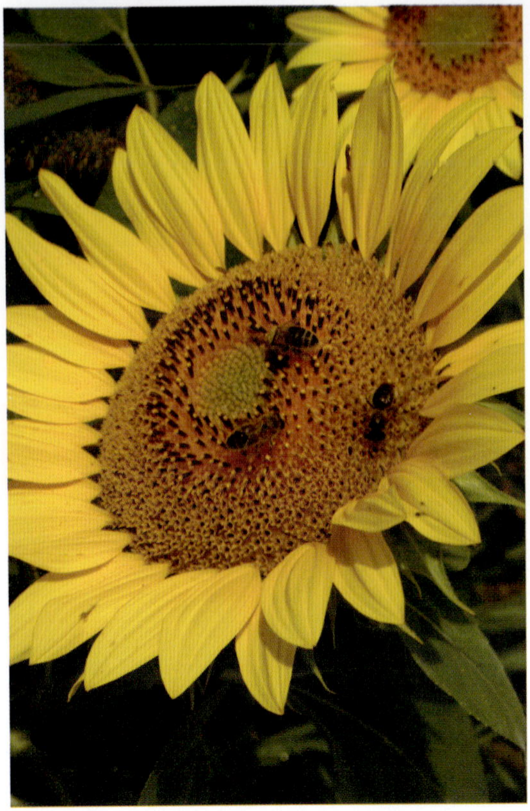

This picture is absolutely flat; the light was falling directly on the sunflower and "took away" all its space. Therefore the bees didn't cast any shadows and it's hard to make them out on the flower.

To get a picture of better quality try to get the lens as close to the subject as possible and then use the optical zoom as well.

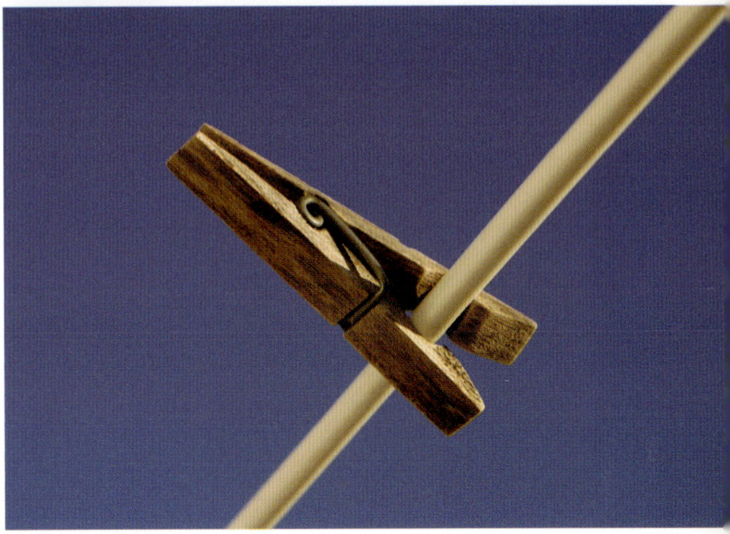

This picture was taken with a short focal distance and the zoom wasn't needed. It was enough to just get the camera as close to the subject as possible and still focus it. The blue background is the sky, and the direct light made it possible to take a bright, clear picture. The shot is lacking space, but that doesn't matter because the subject is very distinct.

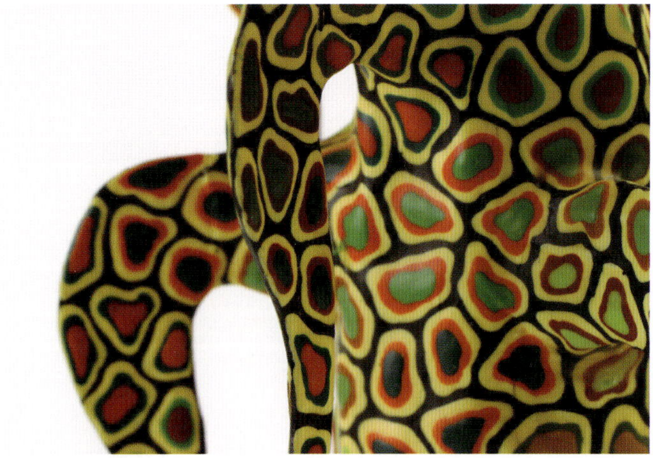

▲ This detail of a hand-painted sculpture is outlined against a rather unclear background. With such a subject you must carefully choose the detail for it to be a clear expression.

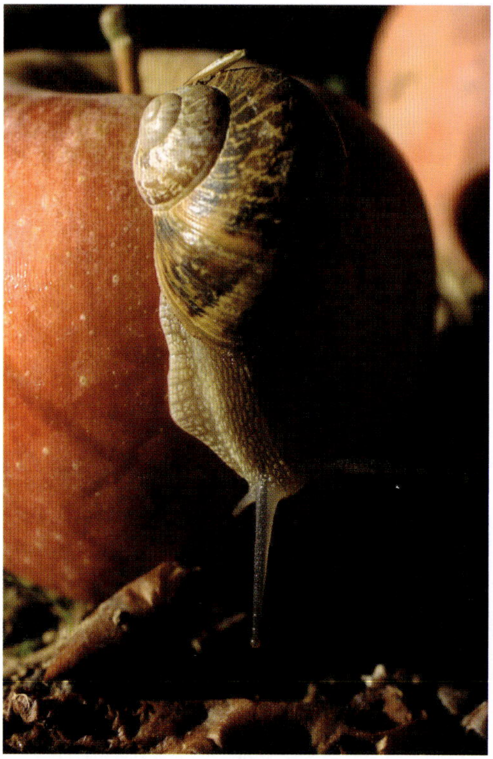

▲ In this case the light of the dawn was falling on the snail from one side, and the spaciousness is very marked.

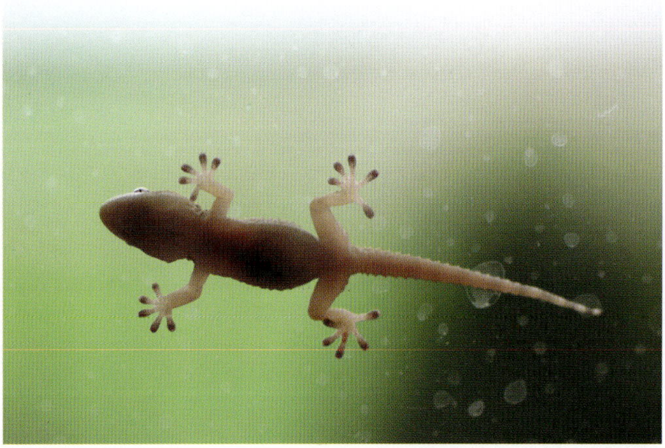

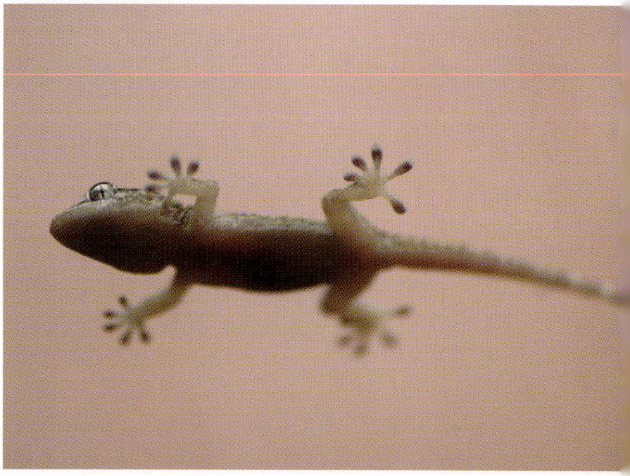

▲ These two pictures perfectly illustrate the fact that with macrophotography a slight change can lead to a completely different result. This gecko was crawling on a window pane. First it was photographed with a green background of trees, then the shooting angle was slightly changed so that the background was the pink of the terrace.

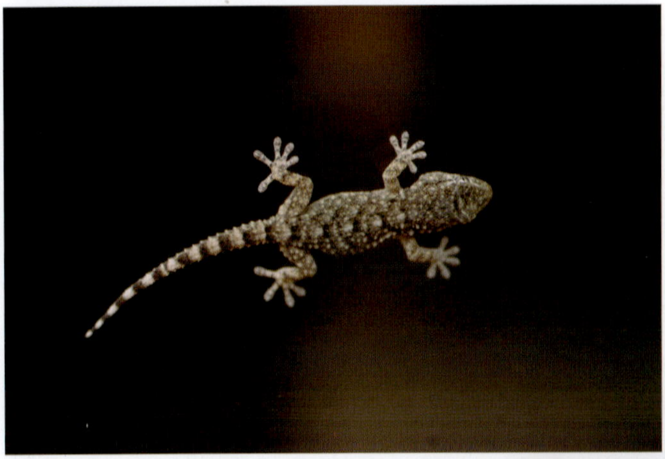

Here is the gecko again, but this time the picture was taken from the other side of the window. This shot allows us to illustrate the differences due to the use of a flash. The first shot was taken with no flash, which explains why the color of the background is the color of the interior.

Unlike the preceding shot, the flash was used this time; the camera was focused on the gecko, and the color of the background can't be recognized. The flash didn't reflect from the window pane because the shot was taken towards the glass but a bit from one side (if it had been taken head on the reflection from the glass would have been visible).

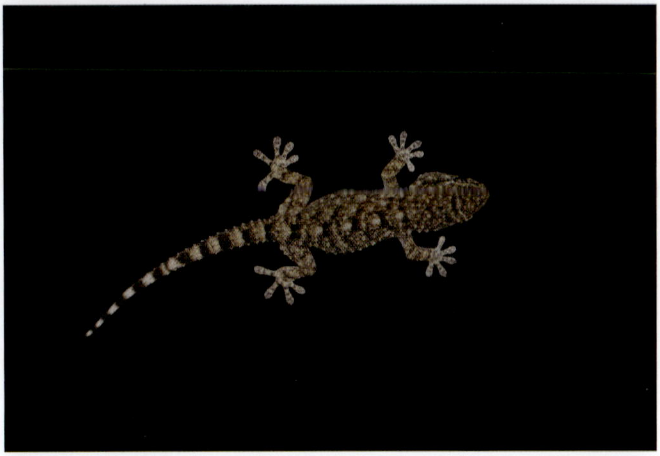

Photographing motion

The subject of a photograph is often in motion. We can see how it is possible to "immobilize" the motion or, conversely, make it visible... and how motion can be simulated if the shot requires it.

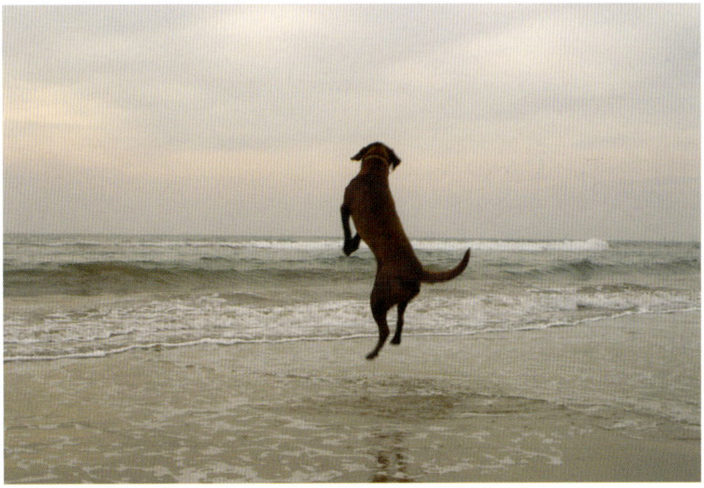

We'll start with an example where the motion was "stopped." In this shot the light was weak, the sky was gray, so the camera was set to a sensitivity of ISO 400; the dog's leap looks as if it's "suspended" in time.

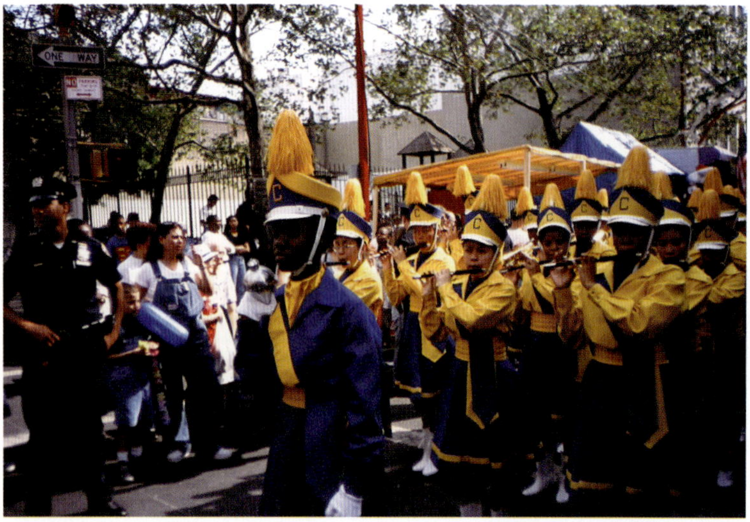

This picture was taken on a sunny day and the passing parade wasn't marching too fast. It was no problem to "immobilize" the motion in the camera's automatic mode without adjusting the sensitivity.

In this shot the person in the foreground is filled with euphoria; his country has won the world swimming championships. The sky was clear, but the subject was moving quickly. In order to freeze the motion the camera was set in the moving subject mode, but it wasn't necessary to adjust the sensitivity.

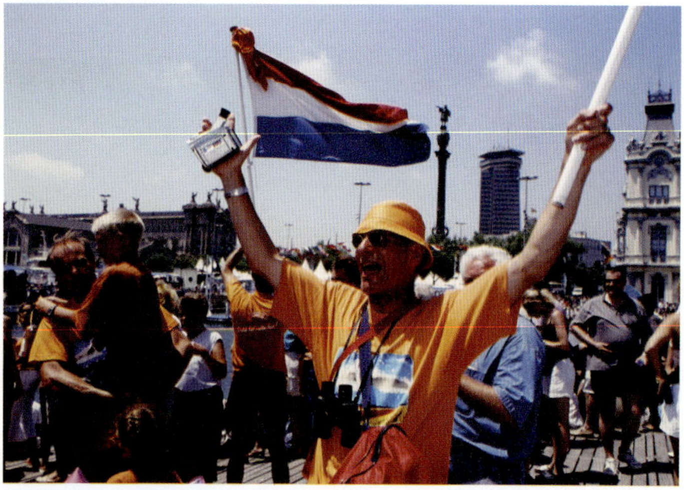

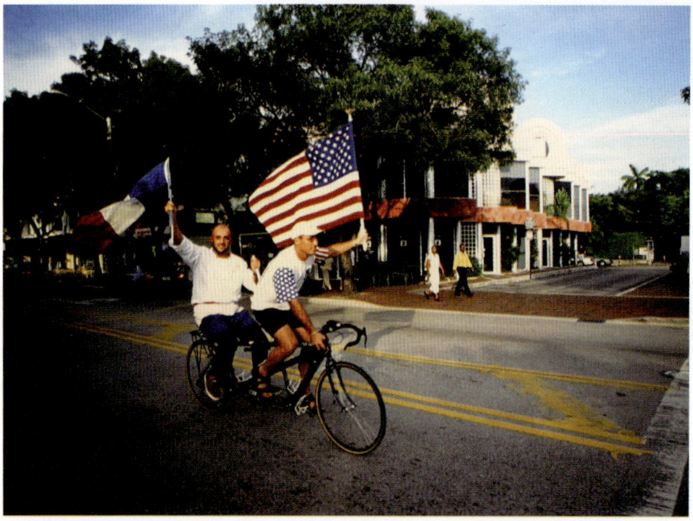

This picture was taken in beautiful weather; the cyclists appeared unexpectedly, so the photographer didn't have time for manual settings and had to rely on the automatic mode. Fortunately, the strong light and the relatively low speed of the tandem made it possible to catch the motion well.

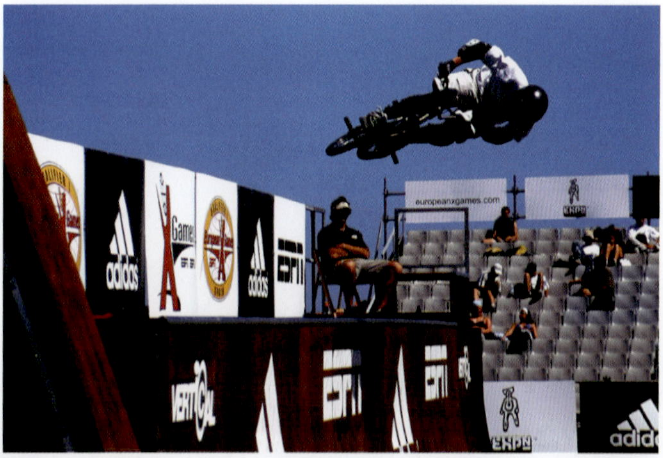

In these two shots it was necessary to set the camera for Photographing motion, as the subjects were moving quickly. The lighting conditions were outstanding, otherwise this mode couldn't be used, and without it it wouldn't be possible to freeze the motion well. But if your camera doesn't have a Photographing motion mode, set the sensitivity on ISO 400 or ISO 800.

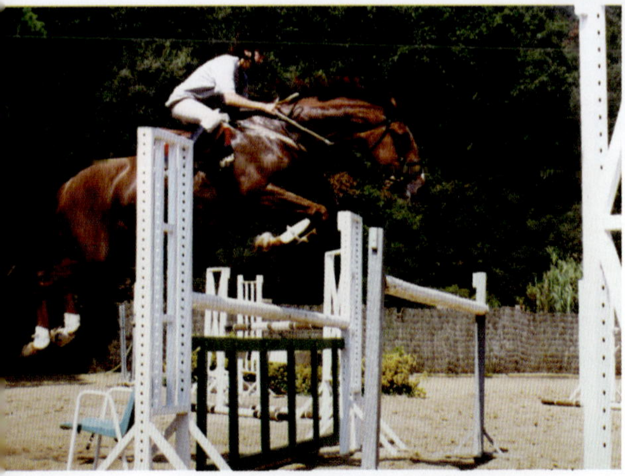

Always remember that it's necessary to adjust the sensitivity (ISO) for the photographed activity. The faster the movement and the less light the scene is shot in, the higher the sensitivity must be set. Unfortunately, the picture will be noisier.

AWB

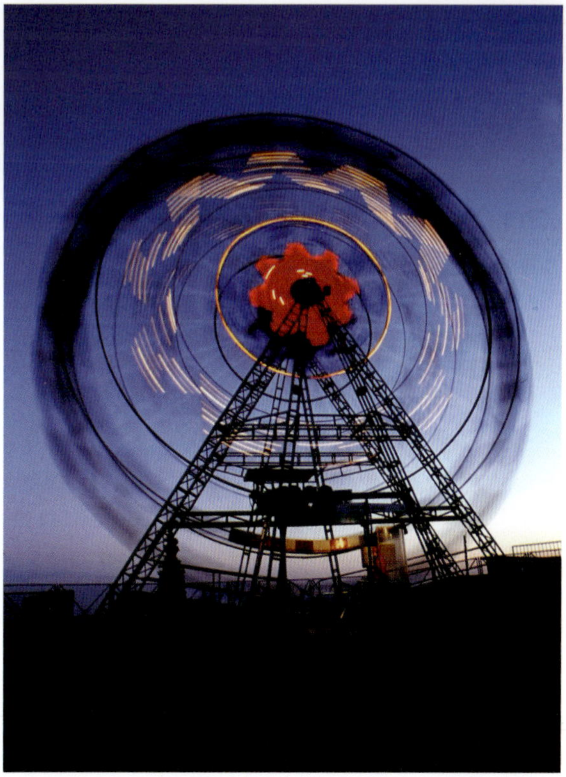

In this case the motion wasn't frozen in the picture, so it looks dynamic. The camera was mounted on a tripod, and because it was twilight, a long exposure was chosen. The result gives the impression that the wheel is turning at high speed.

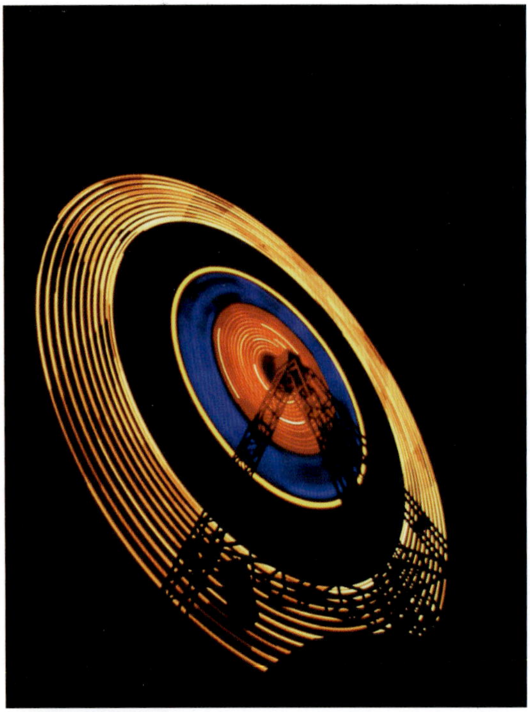

In this picture, taken a few minutes later, the camera was still on the tripod and the exposure was longer. The lights on the wheel stand out more, and the overall impression is of even greater speed than in the preceding shot. In both cases the self timer was used to avoid moving the camera when pushing the shutter release.

AWB

AWB

In another shot of the same wheel we didn't use the tripod so that we could jiggle the camera a little during the exposure, thus achieving an entirely different effect.

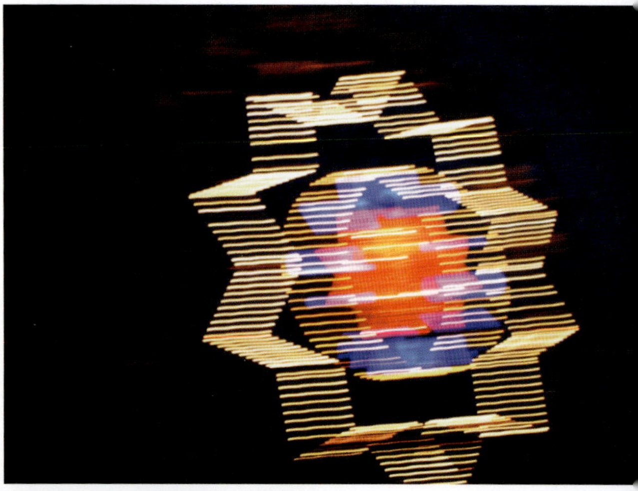

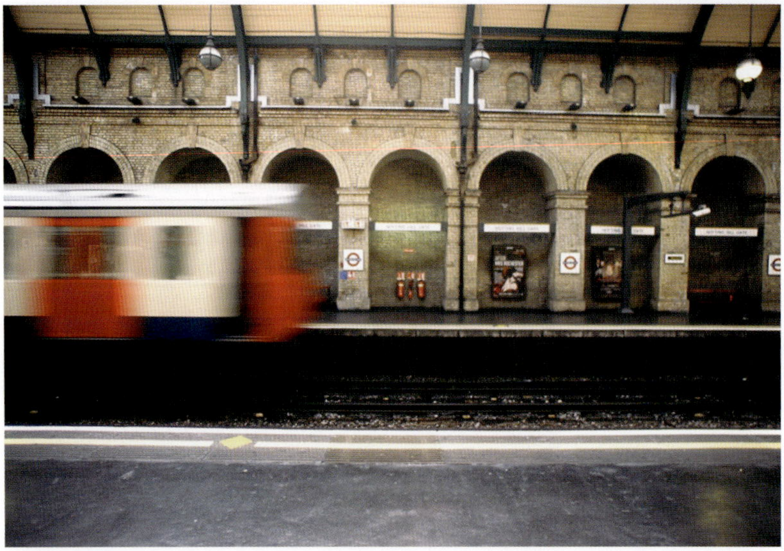

AWB

When taking this London Underground shot we set the camera on a bench at the boarding area and released the shutter as the train arrived. Because the lighting conditions were relatively good (it was outdoors), the camera was set on Auto mode and the flash wasn't activated so that we could make use of only the ambient light to catch the train's motion.

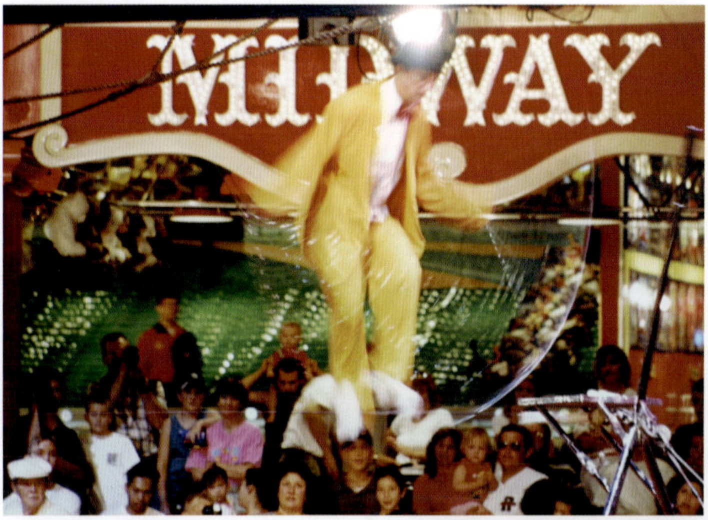

For this circus scene the lighting was close to that in the preceding shot, but it was illuminated by incandescent bulbs. In this case we set the camera for classic incandescent light and held it by hand. The artist, who is moving very quickly on the cable, isn't very sharp in the picture, giving it added dynamism.

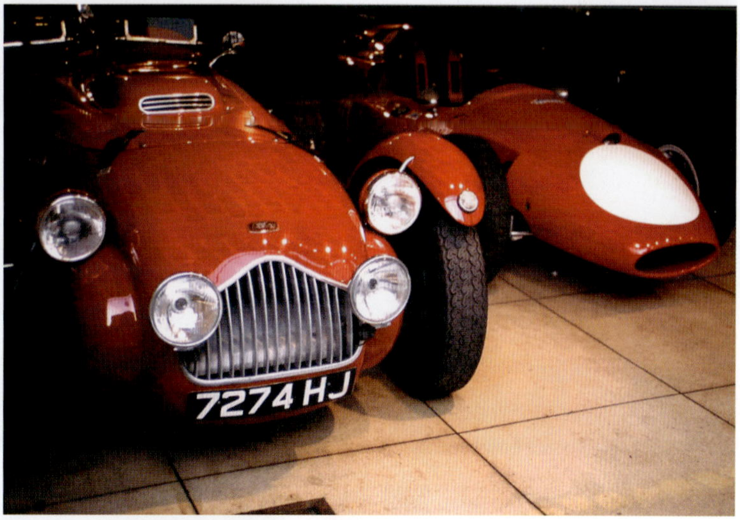

There may be times when you want to simulate speed. For example, in this picture, which we took at a car restorer's showroom, the cars were standing still. By zooming in on the subject and moving the camera during the exposure we got a shot that gives the impression of movement (below).

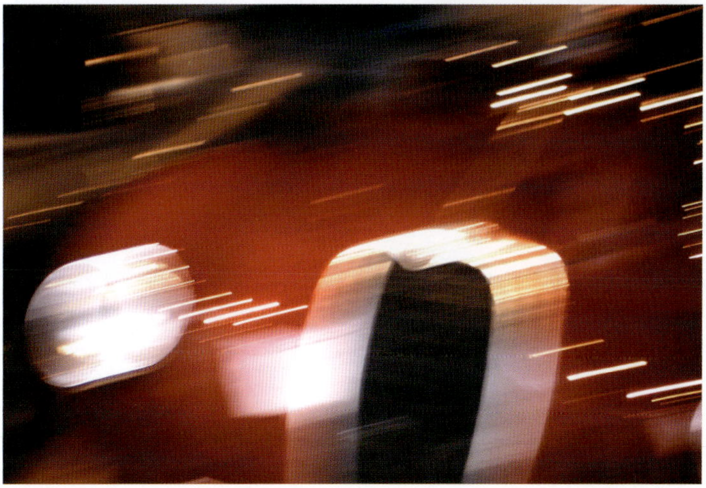

The more light there is, the faster the camera has to be moved during the exposure in order to simulate movement.

NIGHT PHOTOGRAPHY

We can divide night photography into three categories:

• Shots for which the flash would be useless because it couldn't illuminate the entire scene (for example, taking pictures of landscapes or buildings), thus necessitating long exposures.

• Situations where it's possible to completely illuminate the subject, even though by so doing we usually "lose" the background (e.g., taking a picture of a person in a room).

• Shots for which the preceding two options can be combined, that is, using both a long exposure and the flash. We run into this situation at dawn or dusk when photographing a person with countryside in the background.

We'll start out with some examples when long exposures were used.

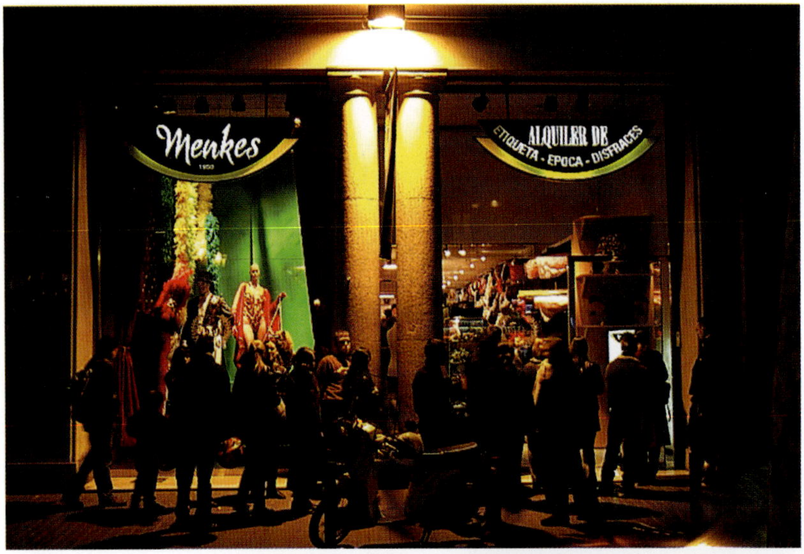

AWB

To create this picture the camera was mounted on a tripod and the flash was not used so that the camera would record the mean ambient light. As you might expect, the people in the line aren't moving too much, even though the exposure was long. Still, in the lower right you can see a blur, which was caused by a car that was passing through the scene just as the picture was taken.

AWB

A concert is another good example of a long exposure. In such cases it's better to turn off the flash and hold the camera as evenly and firmly as possible, and hope that none of the people move. If you used the flash on such an occasion you would probably be removed from the concert (at such occasions taking pictures is usually prohibited), or it could happen that you'll only get a shot of the backs of the heads of the people in front of you.

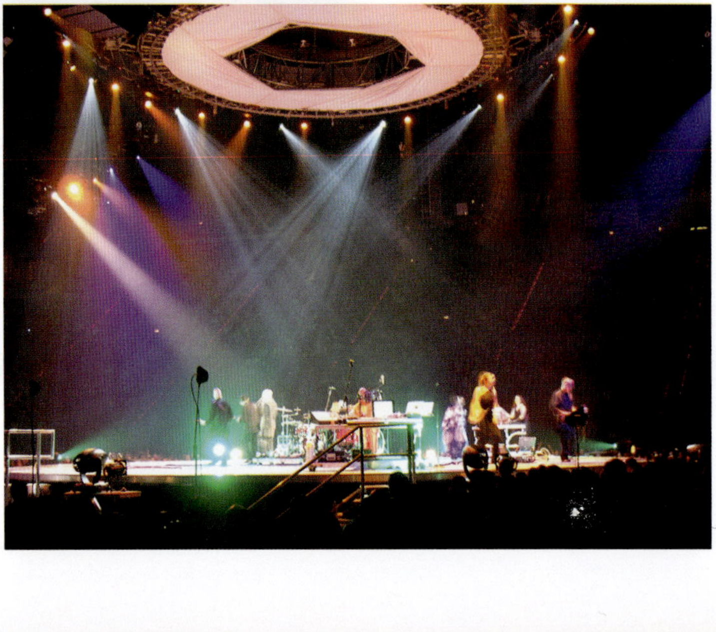

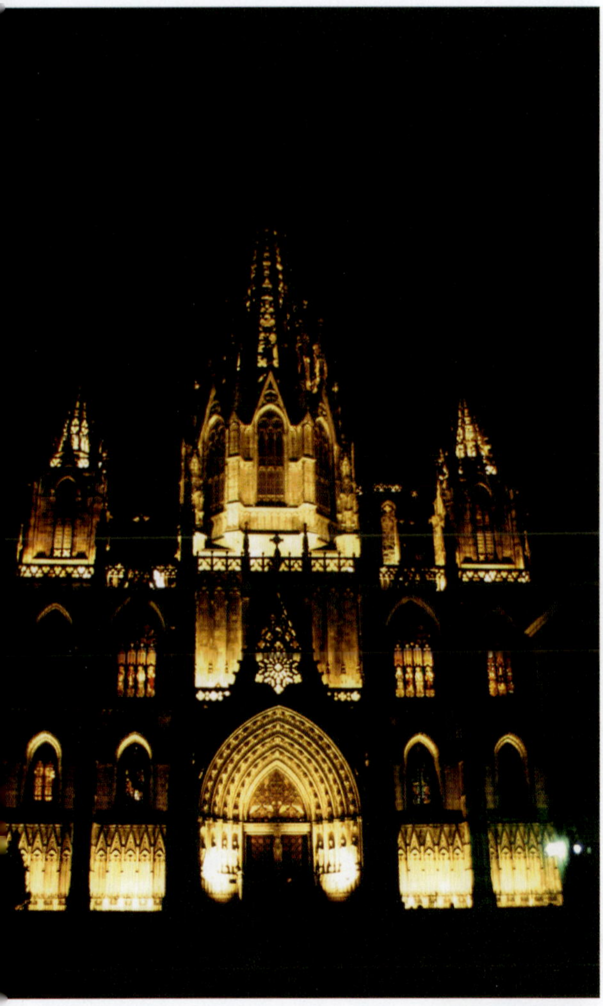

To capture the light on a building's facade you have to mount the camera on a tripod or place it on some other sufficiently solid base to allow you not to use the flash. In such cases the self timer is used. Set the color balance for Daylight, which will emphasize the cathedral's artificial lighting.

At night various types of lighting can provide very different results. Therefore we recommend that you take several shots and then choose the one you like best.

AWB

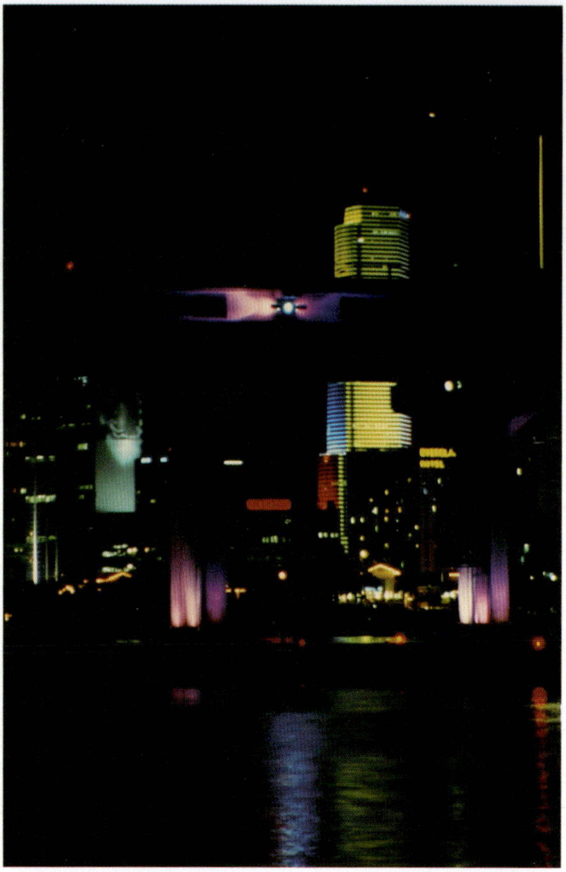

As in the previous shot, the camera was mounted on a tripod but this time it was set for Auto so that the light wouldn't be completely converted (of course under Auto the light is also modified) to achieve a truer image of the colors of the lights as they are actually seen. You could get a similar result if you used the Daylight mode.

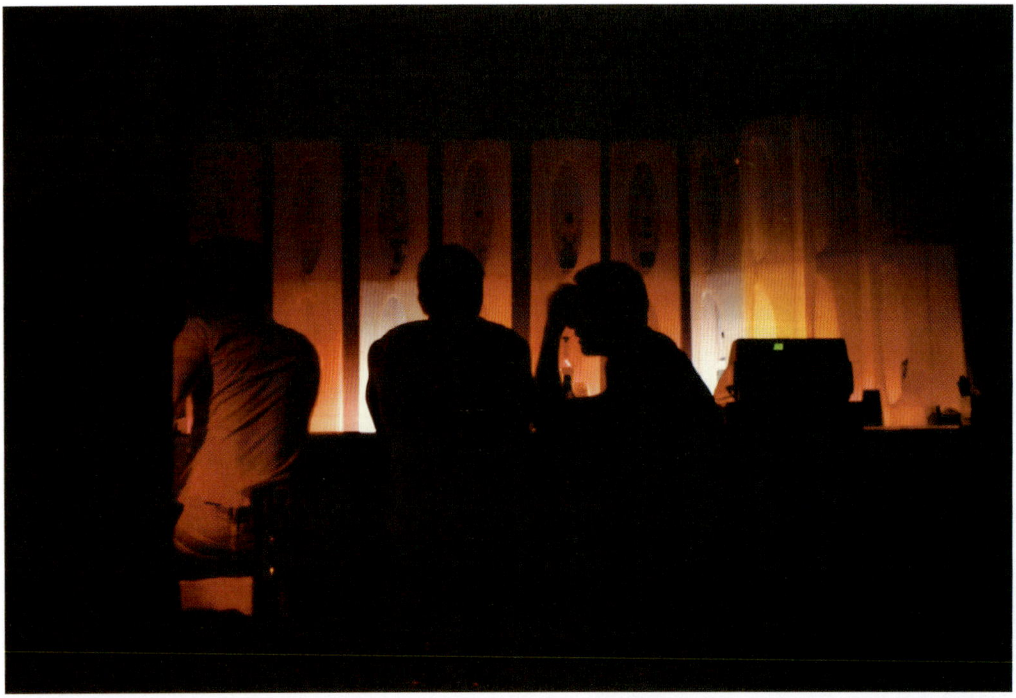

▲ Here we tried to catch a bar-like atmosphere. The camera was set on a table. Without the flash the people appear as silhouettes against the illuminated background.

▼ You've certainly wanted to take pictures of fireworks. It's often difficult to determine the optimal moment to take such a picture.

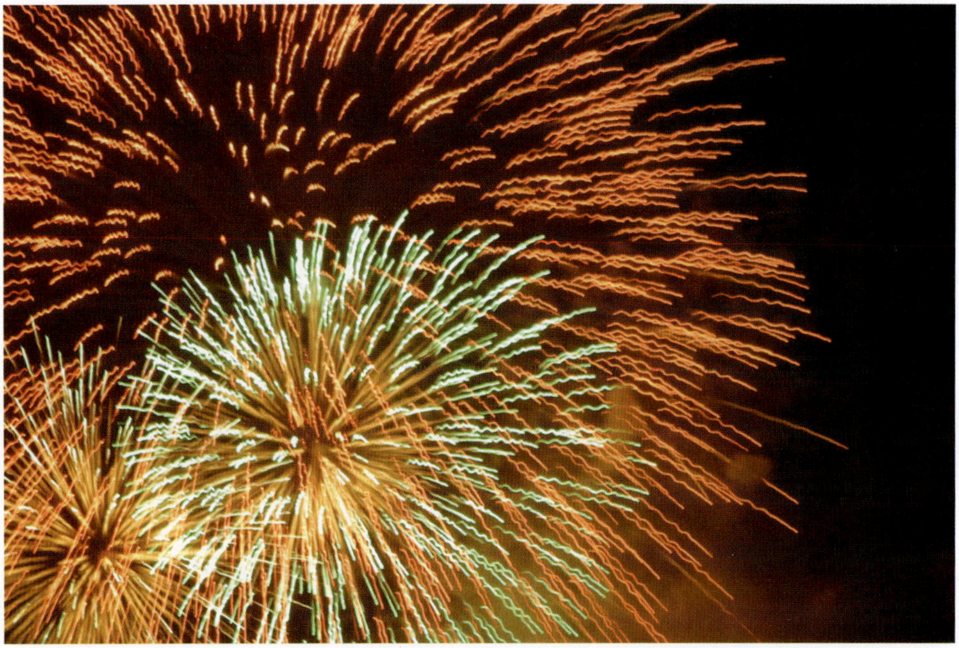

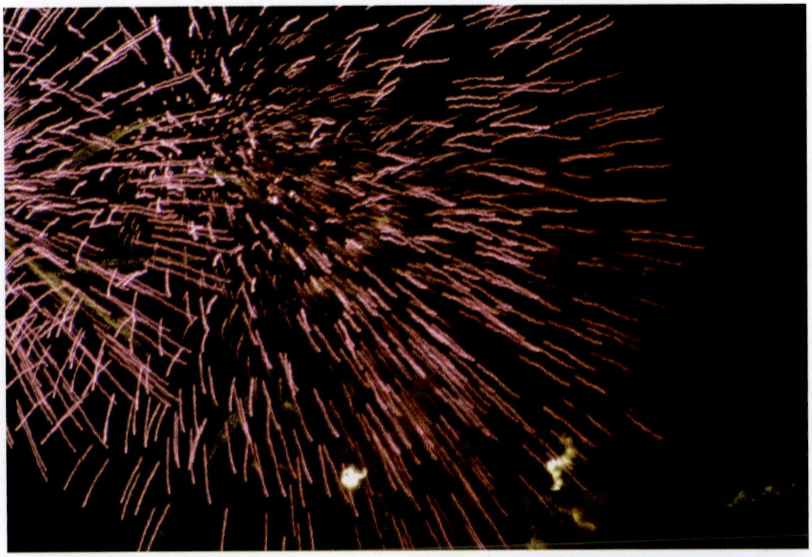

Ideally, you should turn off the flash and start the exposure a few seconds before the rockets explode. This requires a long exposure during which the flashes actually appear. As a result the entire photograph is lit up.

AWB

AWB

During a long exposure you can catch the entire course of a light source. The lights of passing vehicles or fireworks are good examples of this.

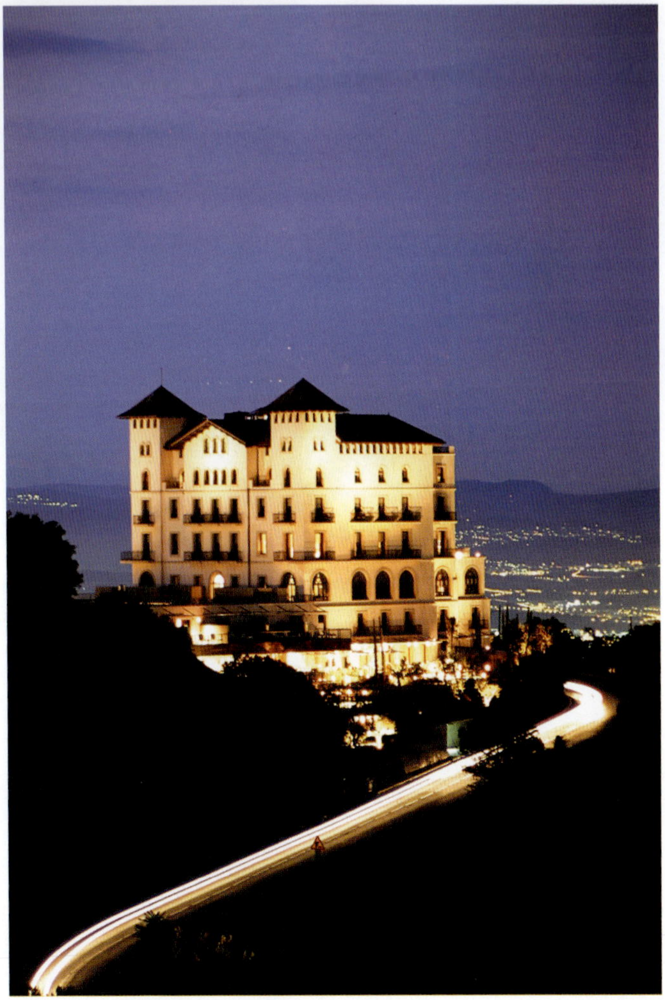

For this shot taken at dusk, the camera was mounted on a tripod and set for Daylight, and the self timer was used. Because it was a long exposure taken right at nightfall, the sky took on a bluish tint (not black, as it would appear to the naked eye). The road that passes near the building is completely illuminated by passing vehicles.

And now a few examples of pictures for which the flash was used.

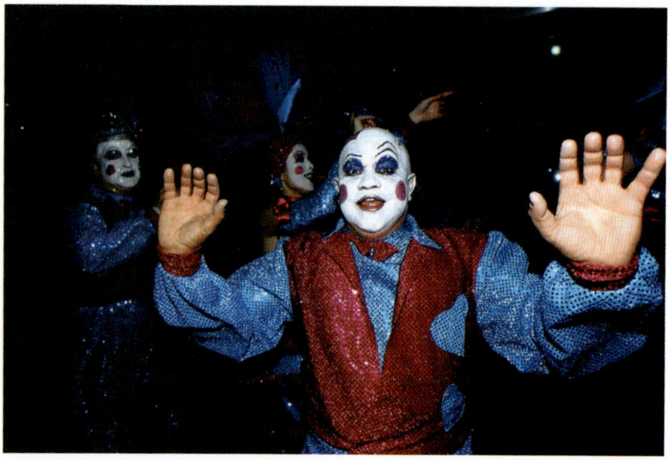

If you want a photograph of a subject but don't want to place emphasis on the background, we recommend that you use the flash. In this shot, taken at a carnival, the photographer was interested mainly in the person with the makeup. The camera was set in automatic mode with automatic flash intensity selection.

Always keep in mind that an ordinary camera has a flash with an optimal reach of no more than three meters.

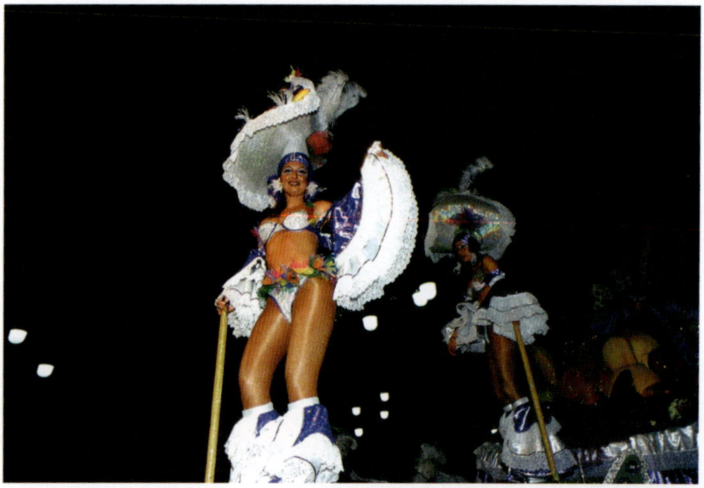

In these two pictures, taken under the same conditions as the previous one, the closest people are illuminated the best because they are not over three meters (ten feet) from the camera. The people in the background are darker because they're too far away and the light of the flash failed to meet them.

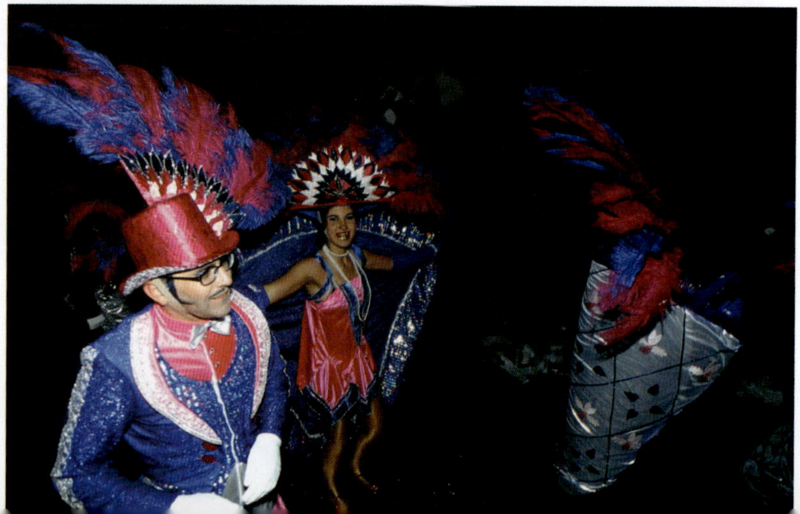

Finally, here are a few examples of long exposure and flash combinations.

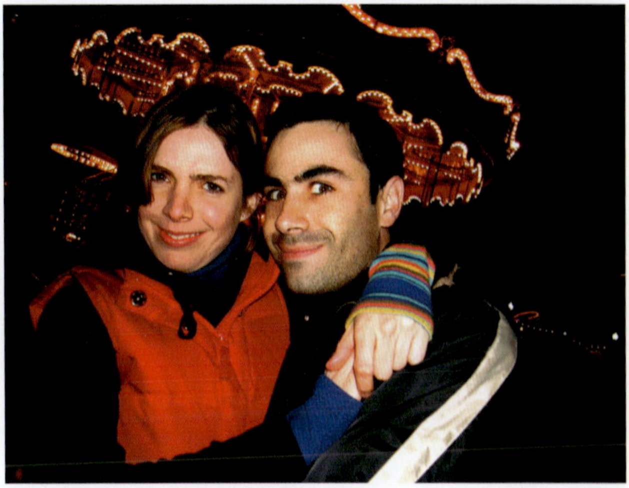

With an active flash but without a long exposure the people are perfectly illuminated but the background details are lost.

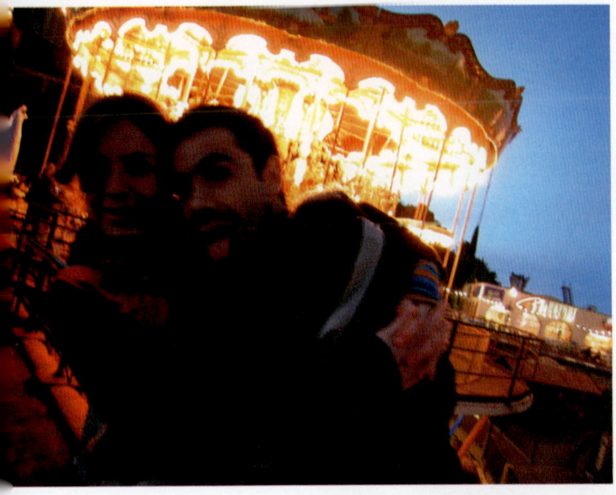

In this shot the flash was turned off so we could have a well illuminated background. This time the people are too dark.

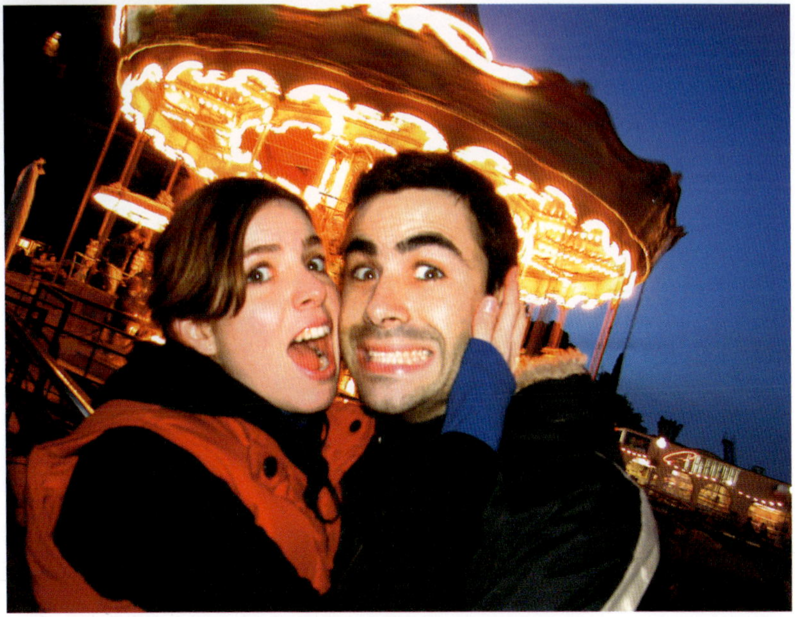

For this shot we used a long exposure and the flash together. The camera was set for Night, and the long exposure allowed an illuminated background while the flash lit up the people in the foreground well.

TOPIC 3 PROCESSING PICTURES

Copying pictures to a computer

Taking pictures and storing them in your camera is far from the end of the story.
The following activities rely on copying pictures to a computer so that they can be displayed, digitally edited, e-mailed, printed, or saved in an archive.

There are two ways to copy pictures to a computer. The first is direct transfer from the camera by means of software that is usually supplied with digital cameras. Because each manufacturer offers its own driver for copying images, there are a considerable number of them. Some are more complicated than others. Nevertheless, all of them try to simplify the process by displaying a file with all of the pictures in the camera right on the screen once the camera has been connected to the computer. You can then resave them wherever you need to.

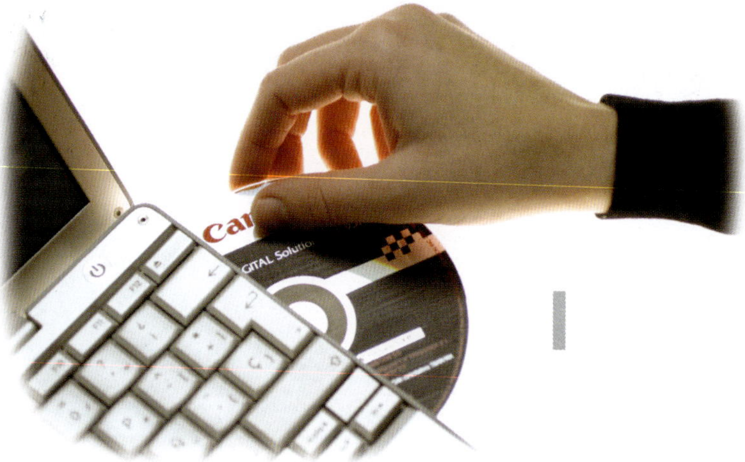

1

The first method for copying pictures to a computer involves three simple steps:

1 Install the software that came with the camera in the computer.
2 Connect the camera to the computer.
3 Copy the pictures to the computer.

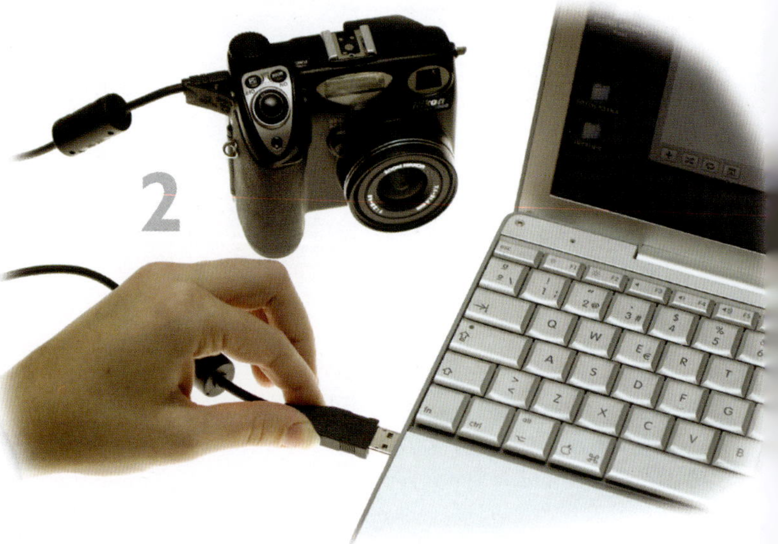

2

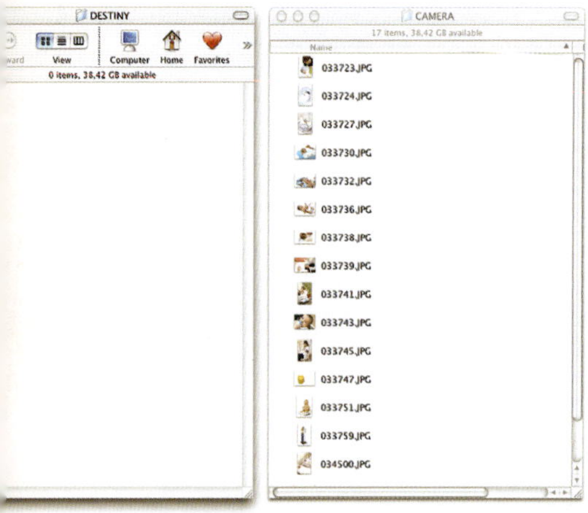

3

The second method relies on the use of a card reader (sold separately) that can be connected to the computer instead of a camera. A good memory card reader has the advantage of being much faster than copying from a digital camera. Another advantage is that no special software is needed. Just copy the file with the pictures from the card reader to the computer.

Copying steps are similar to those for copying directly from a digital camera:

1 Install the card reader software (only for the first use).
2 Connect the card reader to the computer.
3 Insert the memory card.
4 Copy the images (an entire folder or individual shots).

1

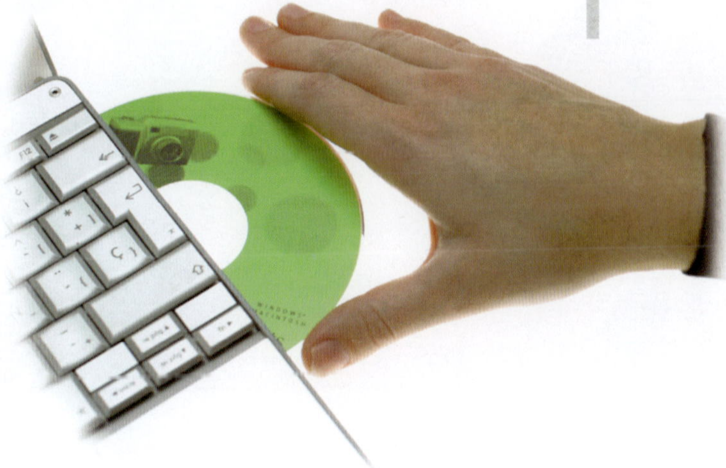

2

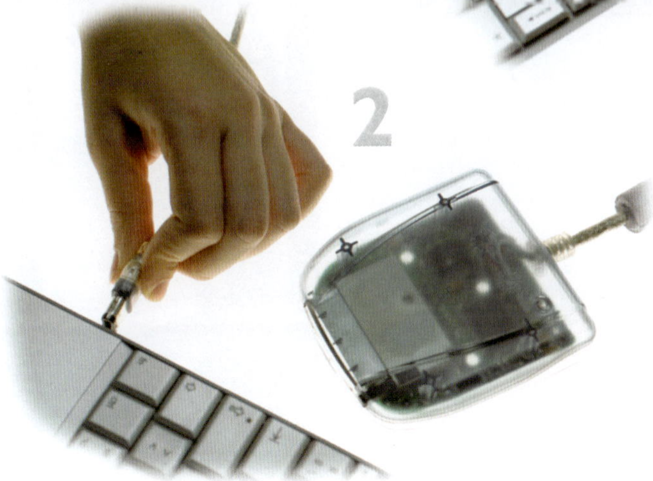

3

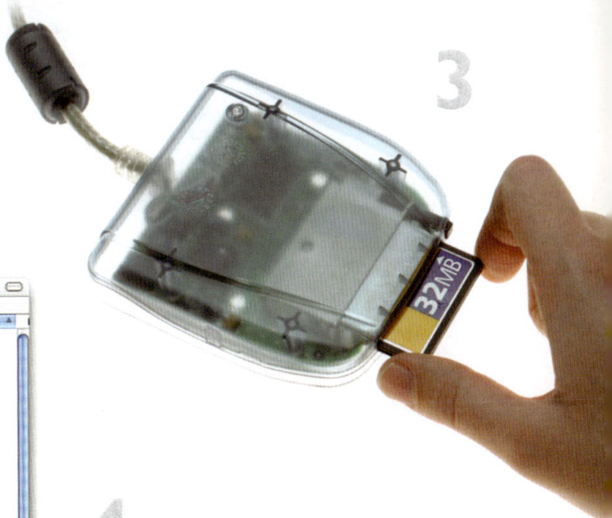

4

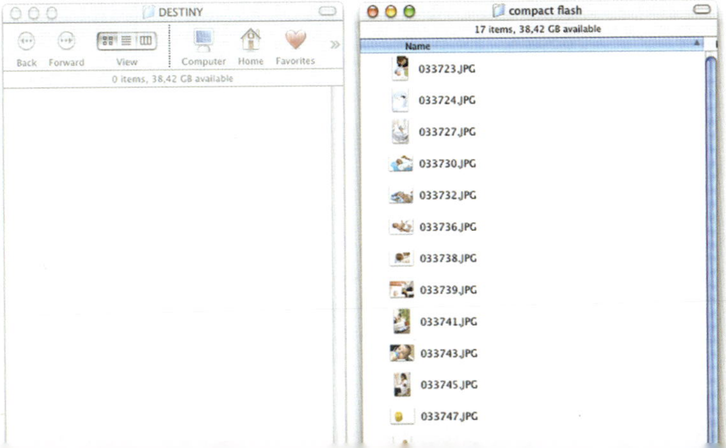

Instructions for digitally editing pictures

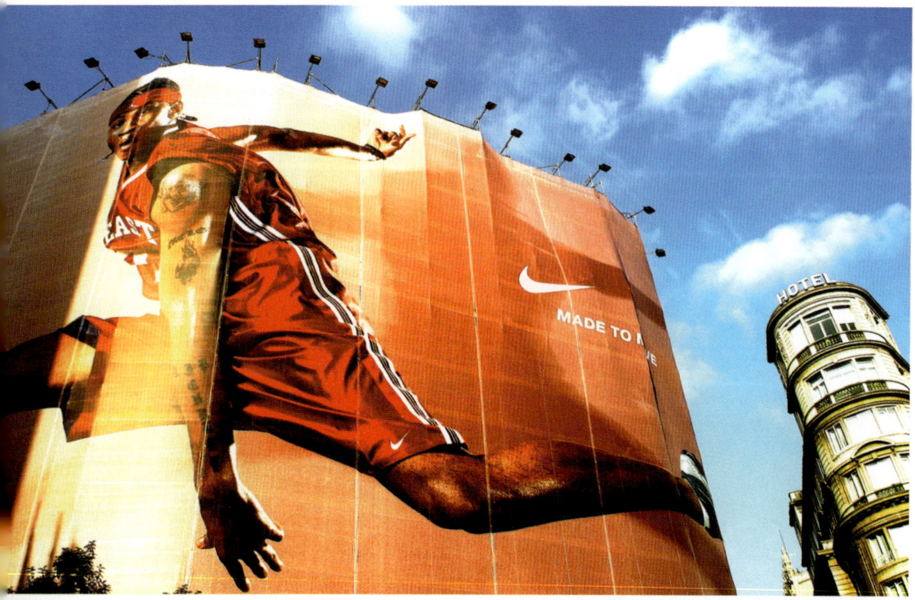

Thanks to new systems for printing, displaying, and sending photographs it's no exaggeration to say that today all the pictures published on the Internet, in magazines, and in the media are digitally edited.

Even before digital photographs became as important and popular as they are pictures were being digitally edited with the use of various software programs. These programs were popular even before the massive digital camera boom. Before pictures could be digitally edited they first had to be digitized. This step was completely eliminated with the development of the use of digital cameras. At one time professional photographers had to be very careful and demanding when they took pictures. Today, thanks to editing software, it's common for the taking of photographs to be nothing but one stage in the process of creating pictures.

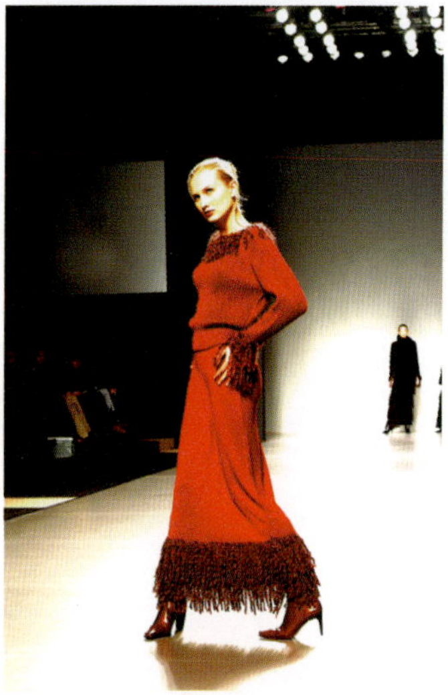

DIGITAAL RETOUCHEREN

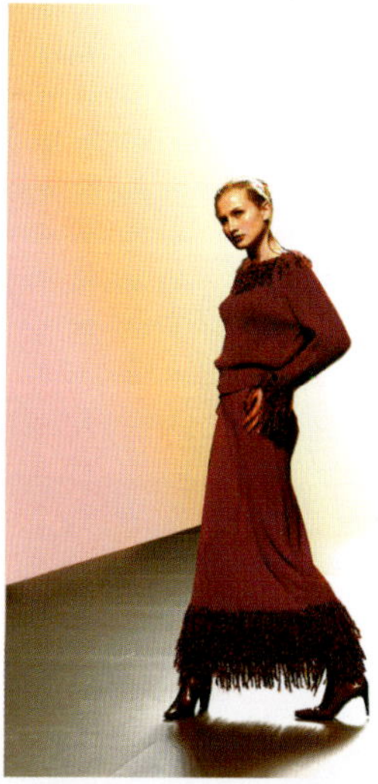

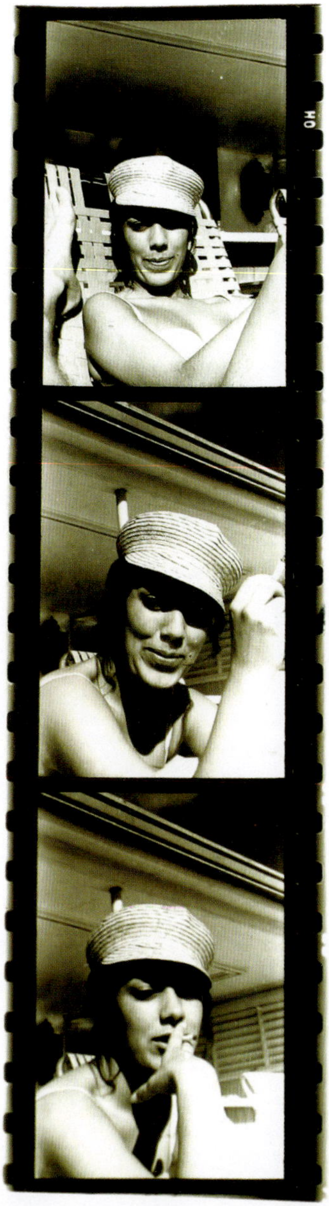

Printing systems evolved in the same way as did digital cameras and personal computers. In order to achieve better results for various types of print formats it is often necessary to convert or alter pictures. Today this is simple when you use image editing software.
We are increasingly more often bombarded with pictures of surprising perfection that far exceed all of the limits that we could have imagined just a few years ago. Picture editing programs do more than just edit pictures, add new elements, or compose surprising pictures. They are also a means for optimizing prints or for digital dissemination.

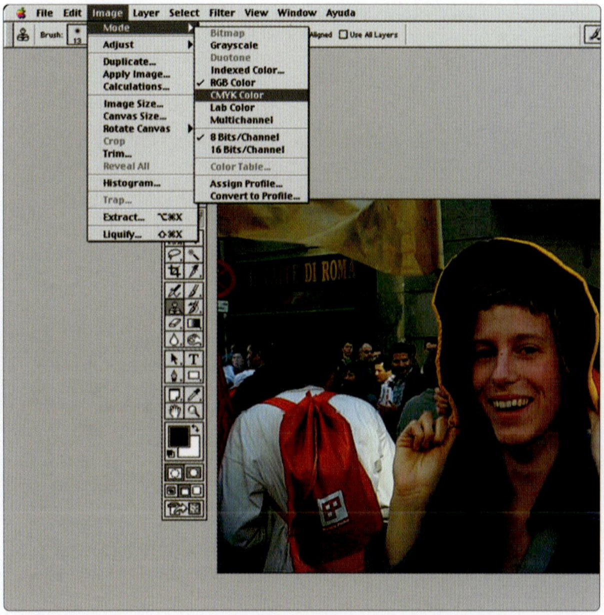

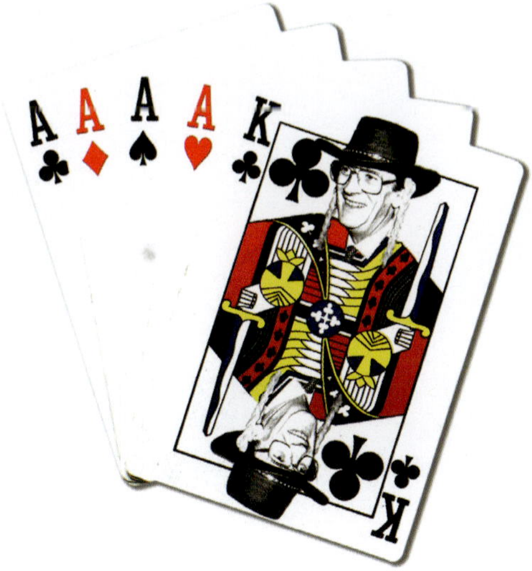

We suggest a few exercises in order to better understand digital modifications. These involve basic modifications. For this purpose we use the most common picture editing software that is popular with both professionals and amateurs - Adobe Photoshop (version 7.0 in our case). Some digital camera manufacturers provide a limited or older version of this software with their cameras. The software includes various tools and commands that are useful for utilizing all editing functions. They are clearly laid out on the screen below, and it's important to know them well and know where they are so that we can make better use of them in the following exercises.

File menu: Contains all the necessary commands for working with the program.

Pull-down menus : Allow you to select the options or tasks you intend to implement.

Toolbox : For selecting the tools you intend to use.

Pallettes: Display the status of pictures and are associated with certain functions accessible through the File menu.

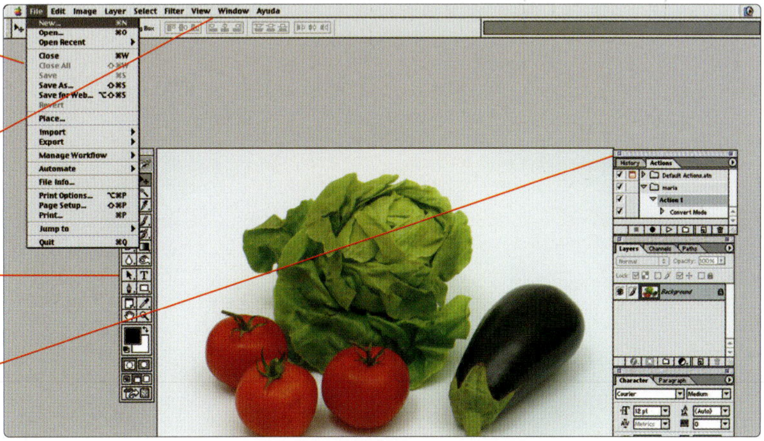

DIGITAL EDITING

Rotating pictures

In general, digital cameras do not correct the orientation of a picture that was taken holding the camera vertically. Also, when you open a file to look at a picture it is displayed horizontally, not vertically as it was taken.

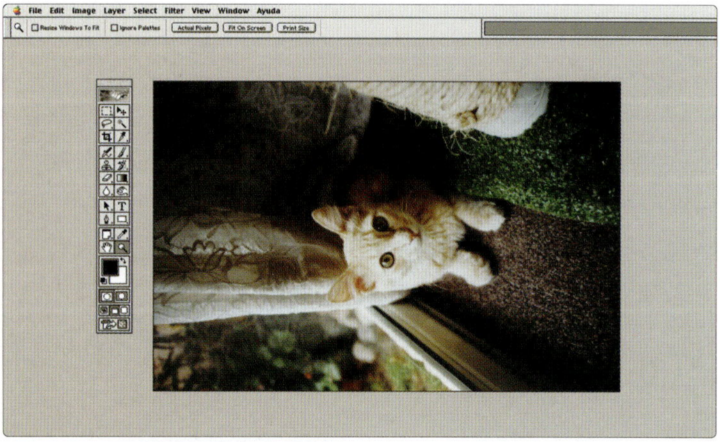

▸ **1** Open the picture in the editing program.

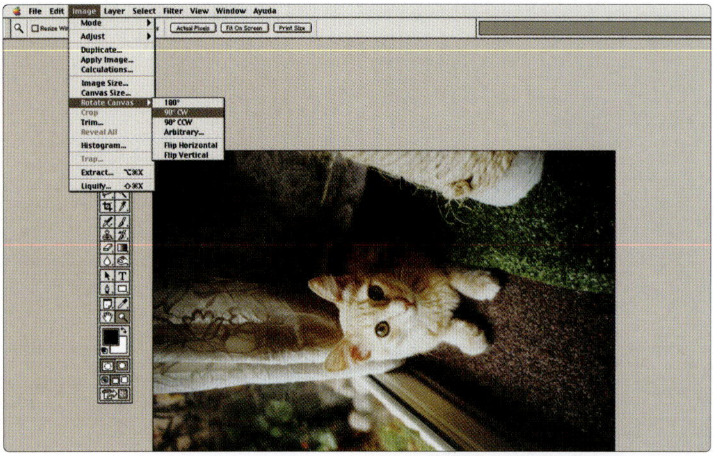

◂ **2** Click on Image and in the pull-down menu find Rotate Canvas, which shows you the various directions in which you can turn the picture (180°, 90° clockwise, 90° counter-clockwise, a different angle, flip horizontal, flip vertical).

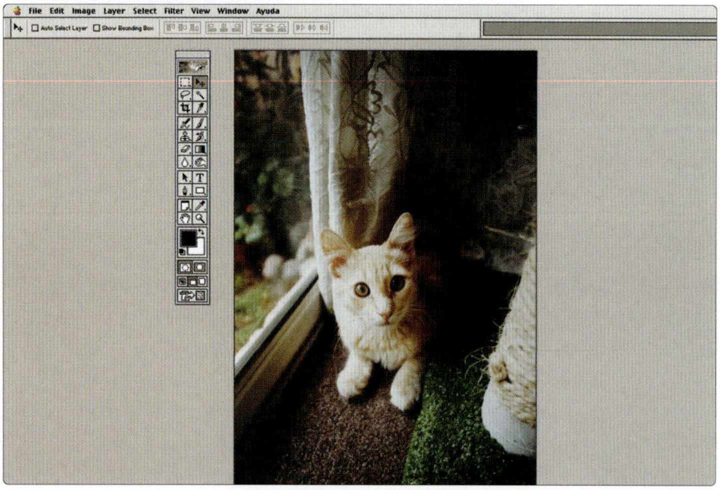

▸ **3** Select the desired tool for modifying the picture.

4 You can reverse any rotation you have made by using the same menu.

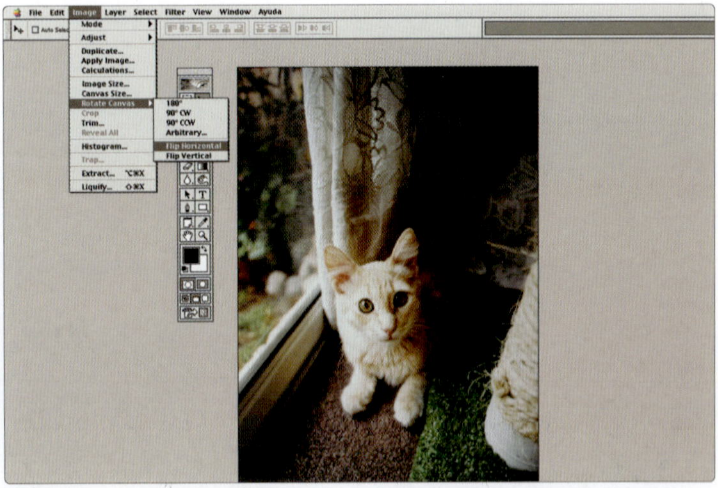

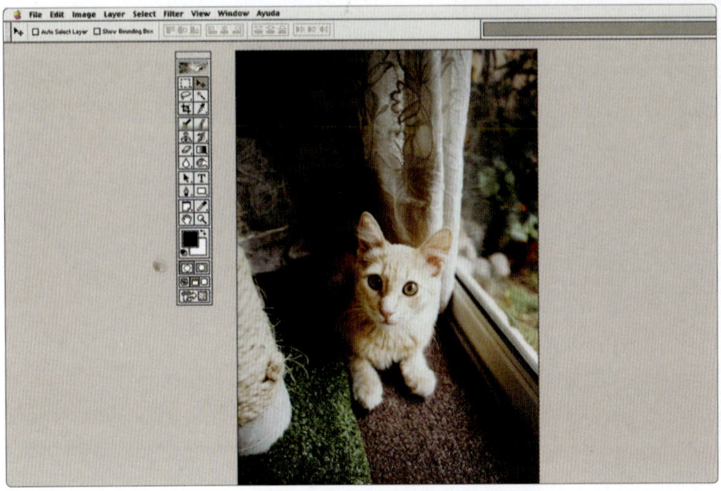

Pay attention to the data that shows you the direction in which the original picture was taken.

5 Thanks to this flip the picture looks like it is a true reflection of the original in a mirror.

So you now have these following pictures:

The original photograph

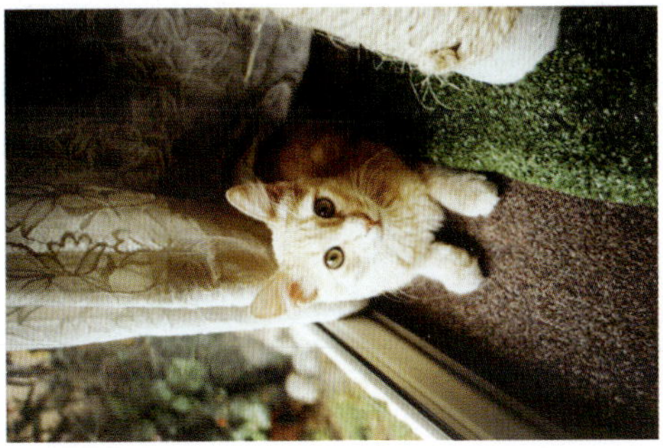

The photograph turned 90° clockwise

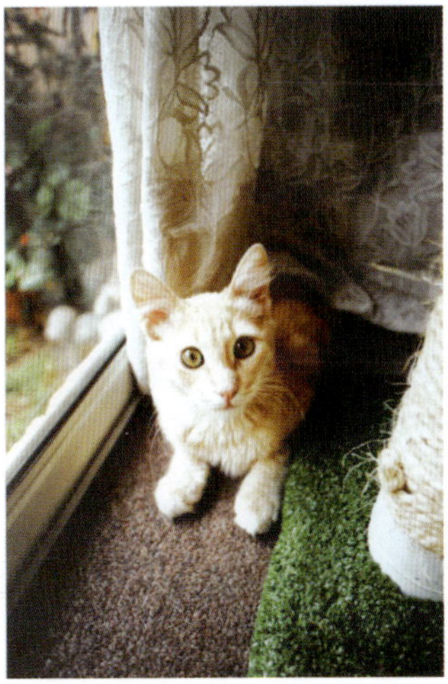

The photograph with horizontal symmetry

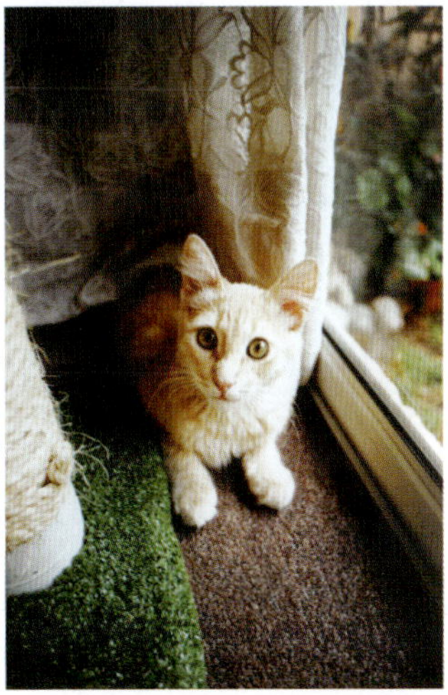

Changing the size of a picture

Knowing how to change the size of a photograph is very useful. It's often necessary to make a picture larger or smaller, depending on whether you want to send it by e-mail or print it.

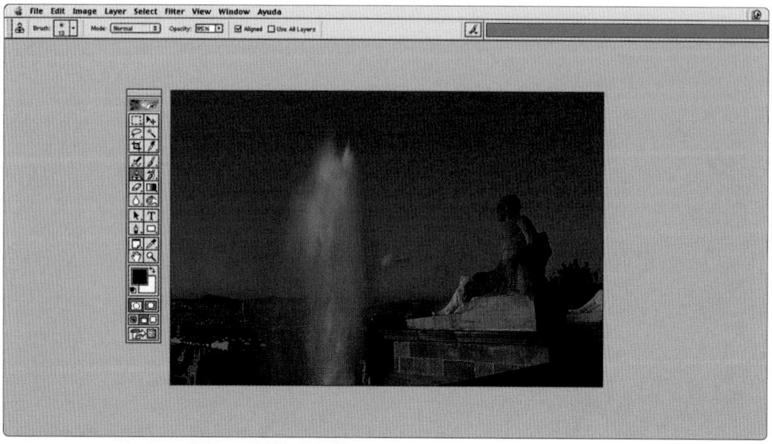

▸ **1** Open the file with the picture in the editing program.

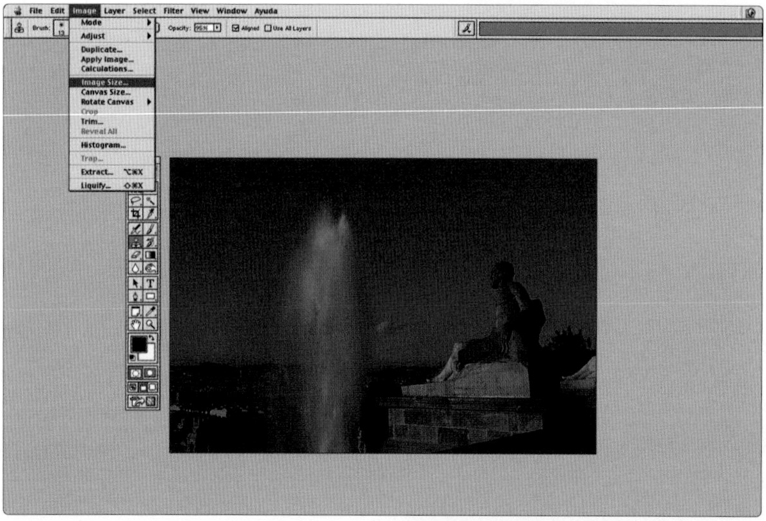

◂ **2** Pull down the Image menu, then click on the Image Size option.

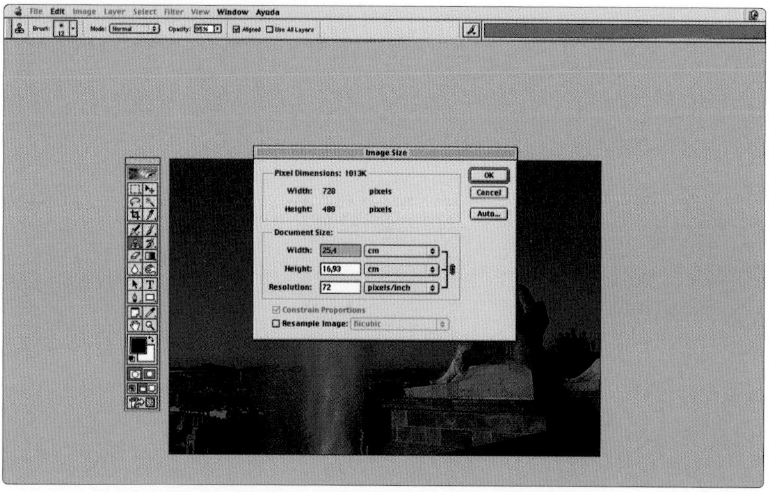

▸ **3** This menu offers several options. First you can change the size by selecting Image size to change the size while preserving the proportions.

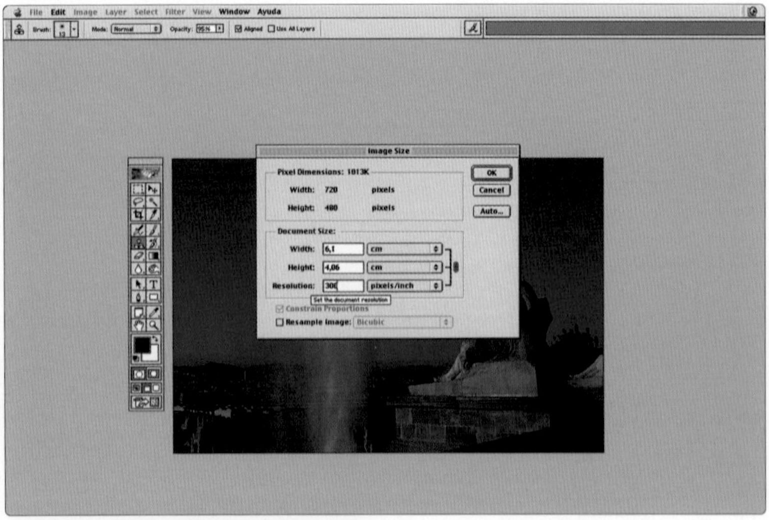

4 After you choose this option, change the picture's resolution. Notice that when you change the resolution the size also changes automatically.

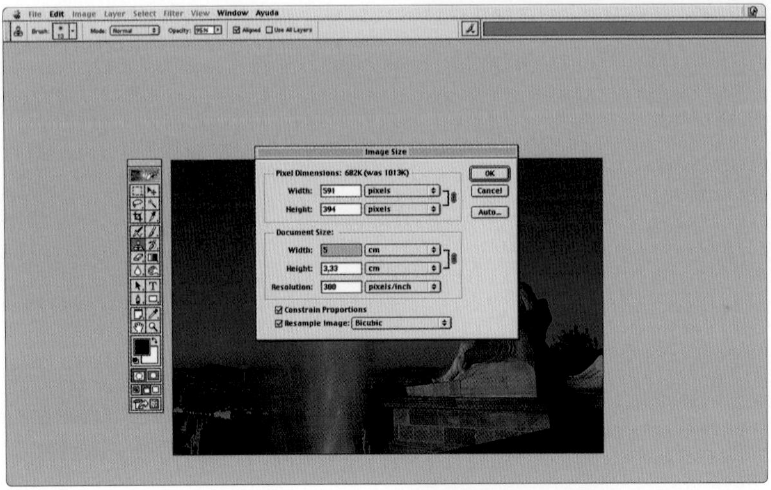

5 You can also change the size of a picture without changing its resolution. To do this you have to select the Preserve proportions command. This allows you to change the picture's size without changing its resolution.

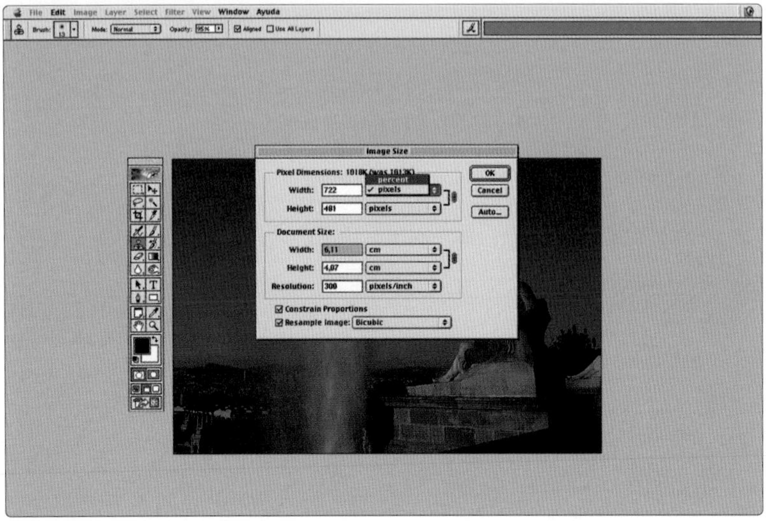

6 The third way to change a picture's size is expressed as a percentage. In the Pixel Dimensions section click on the Percentage (%) option.

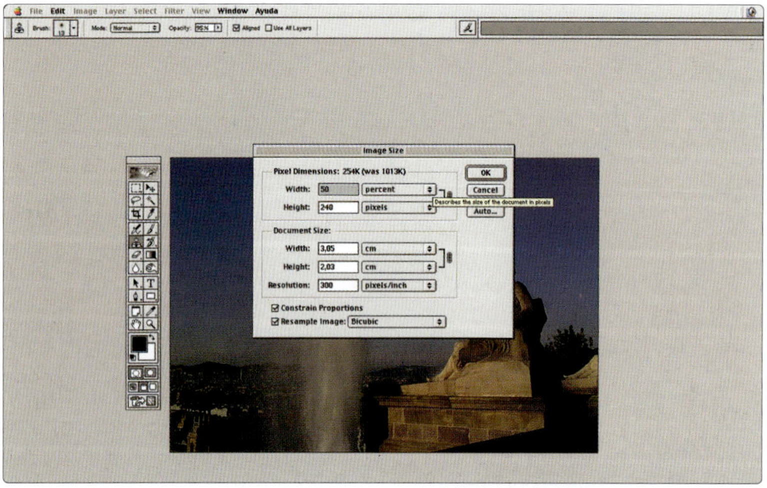

7 When you change the percentage, bear in mind that it's the size that will change, not the resolution.

By combining these options you can change the size of a picture any way you like. But remember that enlarging the size or increasing the resolution of a picture can also affect its quality.

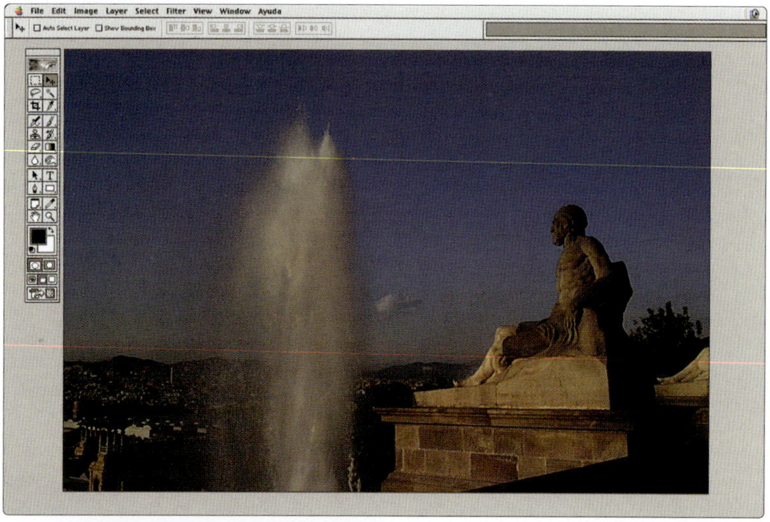

A picture in its original format

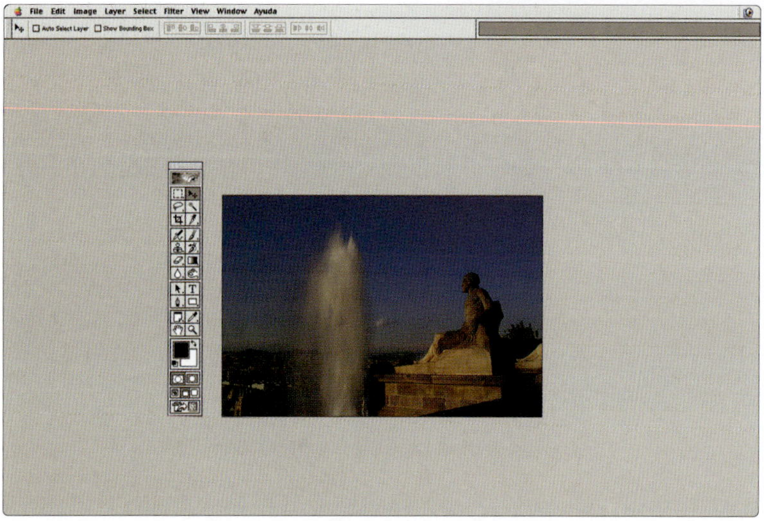

Reduced picture prepared for sending by e-mail

Converting to Gray Scale

Some digital cameras allow you to take black-and-white pictures. Many color pictures can be interesting when converted to black-and-white as well. Now see for yourself how easy this conversion is.

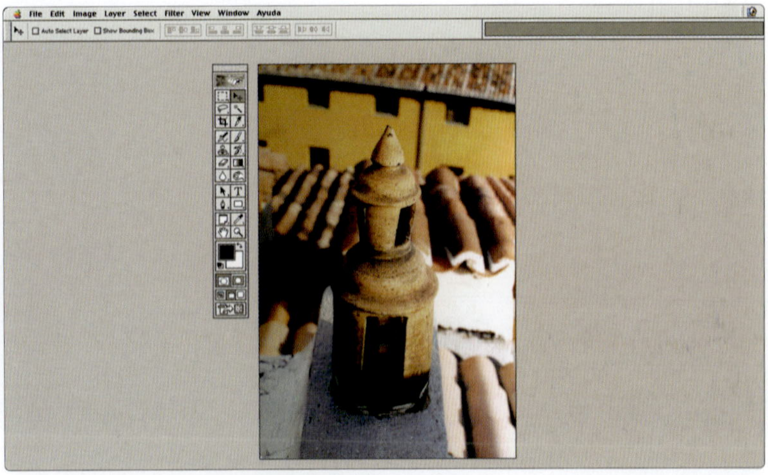

▸ **1** Open the file with the picture in the editing program.

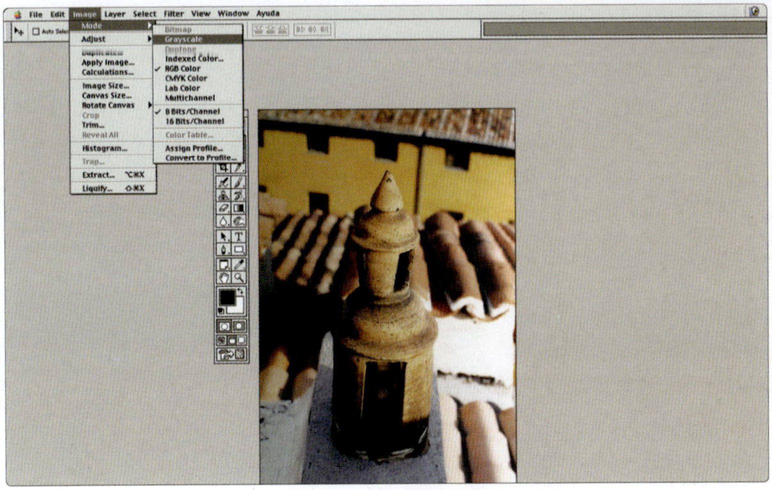

◂ **2** Pull down the Image menu, select Mode, and choose the Gray Scale option.

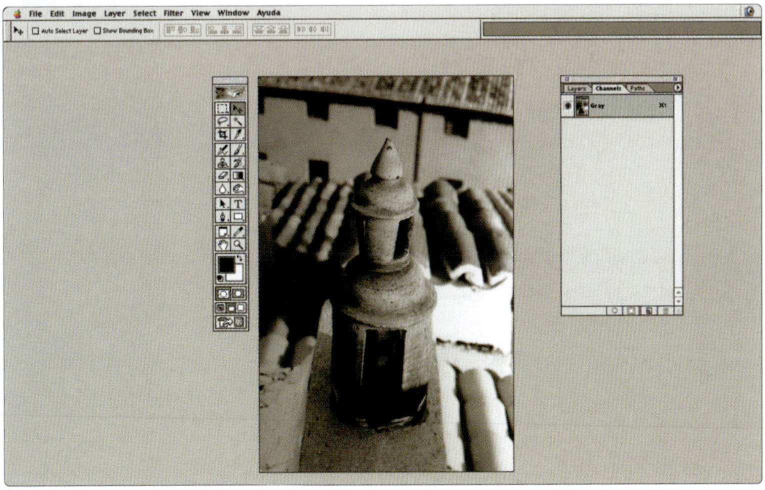

▸ **3** The picture is now changed from color to black-and-white.

▸ **4** Save the image.

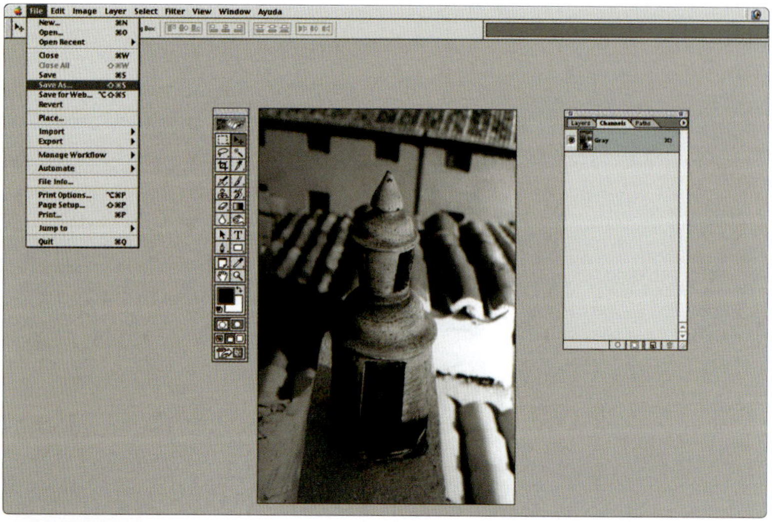

In order to preserve the original shot, you must use the Save As command. Both of these examples are interesting in different ways.

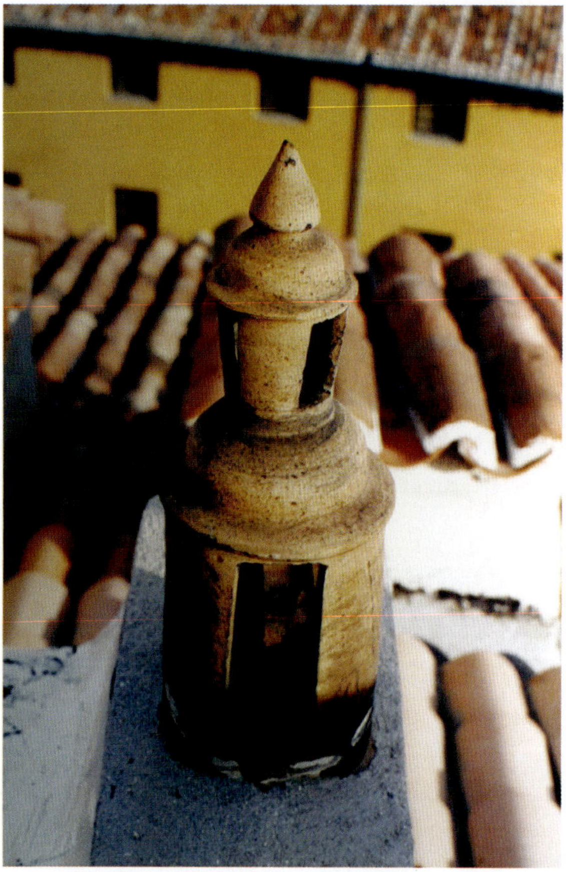

◂ Original color photograph

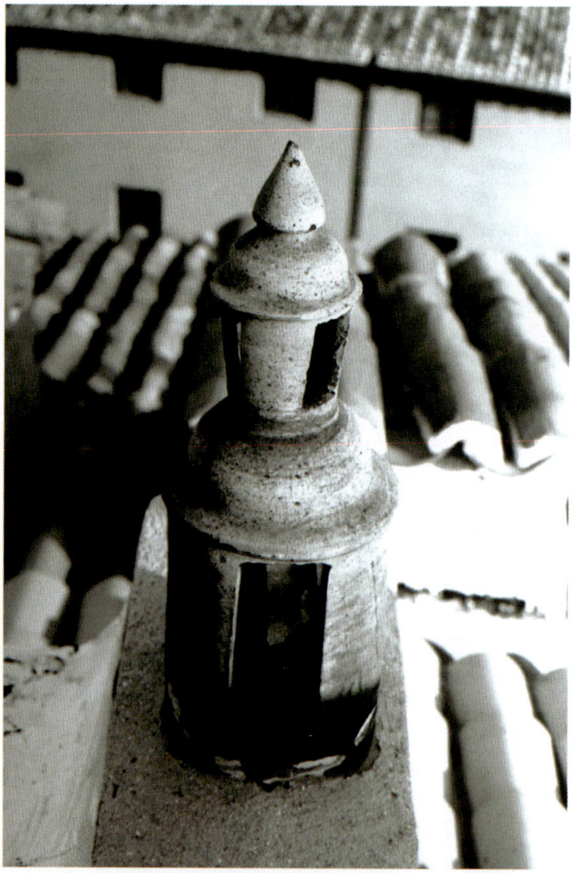

▸ Photograph converted to black-and-white

Adjusting brightness and contrast

It often happens that pictures don't have enough brightness or contrast compared with the photographed scene, which makes them insufficiently expressive. We will show you how to resolve this problem.

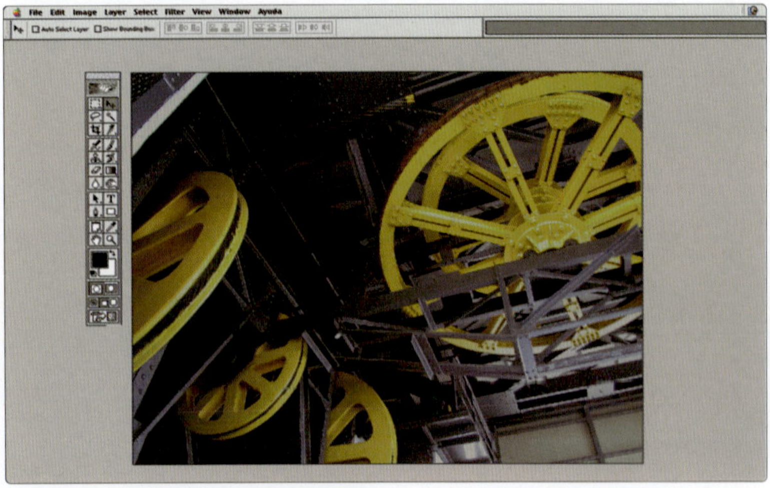

▸ 1 Open the file with the picture in the editing program.

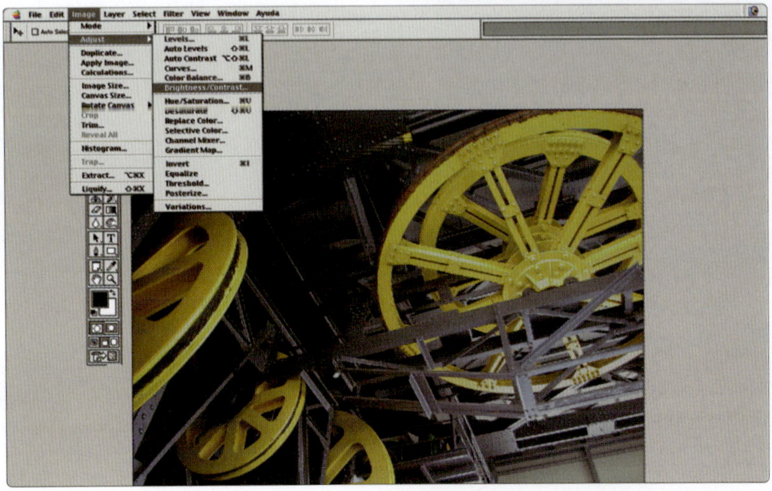

◂ 2 Pull down the Image menu, click on Mode, and then click on Brightness/Contrast.

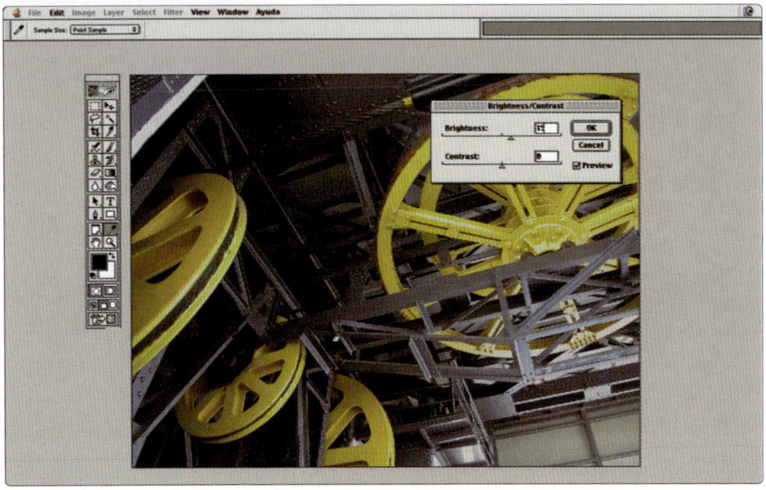

▸ 3 Set the desired brightness.

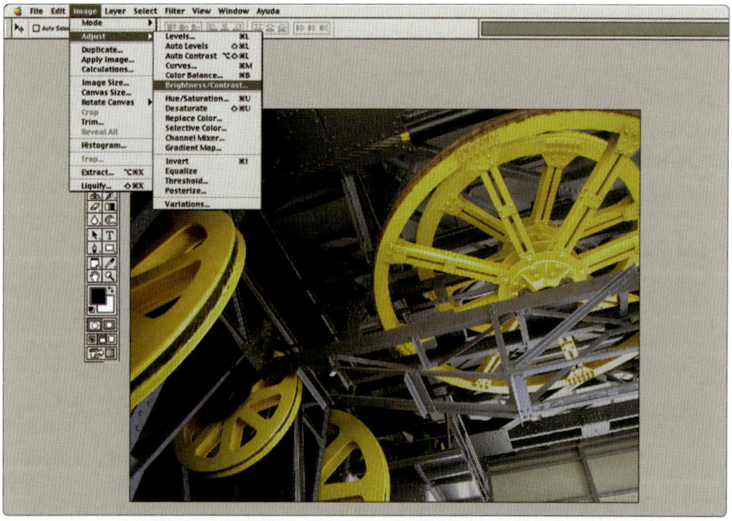

4 If the picture is a little too bright, you can add some contrast to it. Pull down the Image menu, then click on Adjust, and finally Brightness/Contrast.

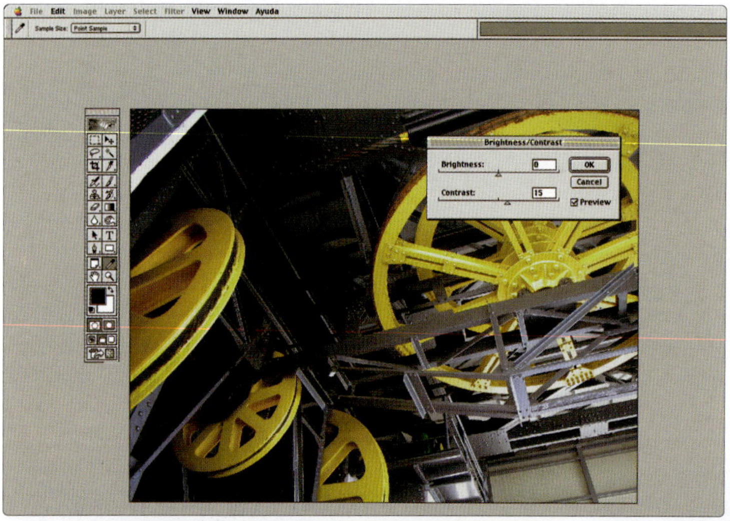

5 Increase the contrast until the colors are sharper.

Pictures with insufficient light or contrast need not be completely lost. The quality of some of these can be improved by editing, as our examples illustrate:

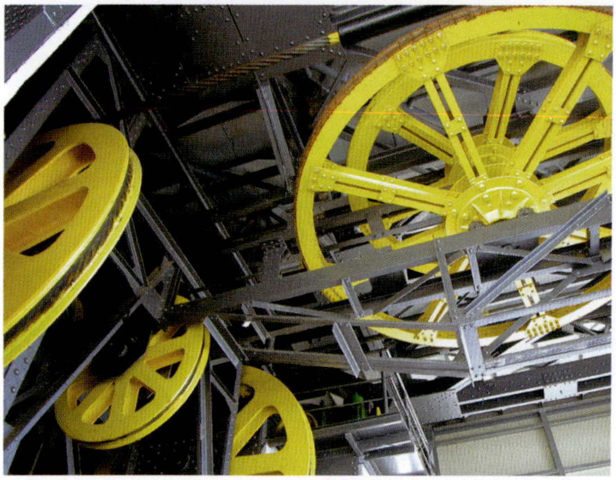

Original photograph

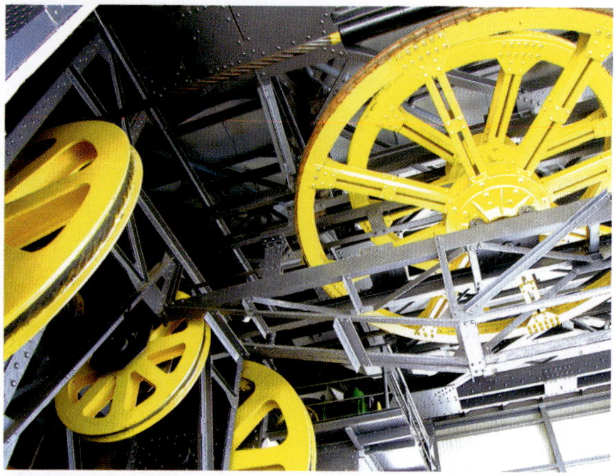

The photograph with modified contrast and brightness

Converting gray scale pictures to color scale (RGB)

Just as pictures can be converted from color to black-and-white, black-and-white pictures can be converted to color. True, your picture won't have the precise colors of the original, but you can make changes within the RGB scale and achieve all sorts of interesting results.

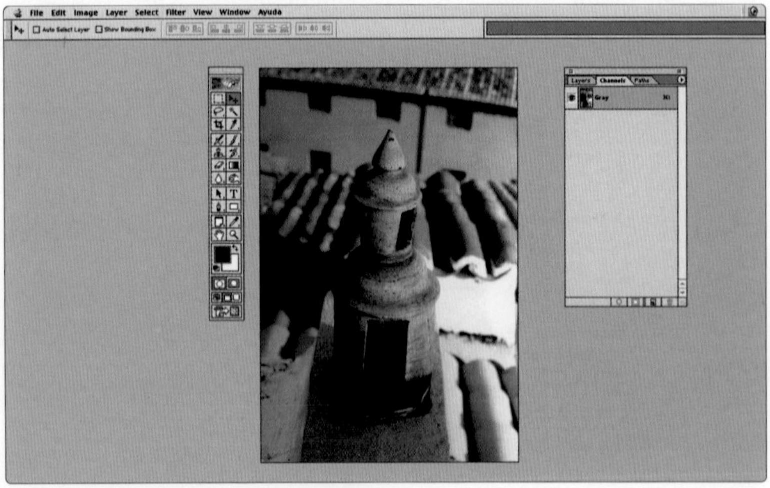

▸ **1** Open the file with the gray-scale image in the image editing program.

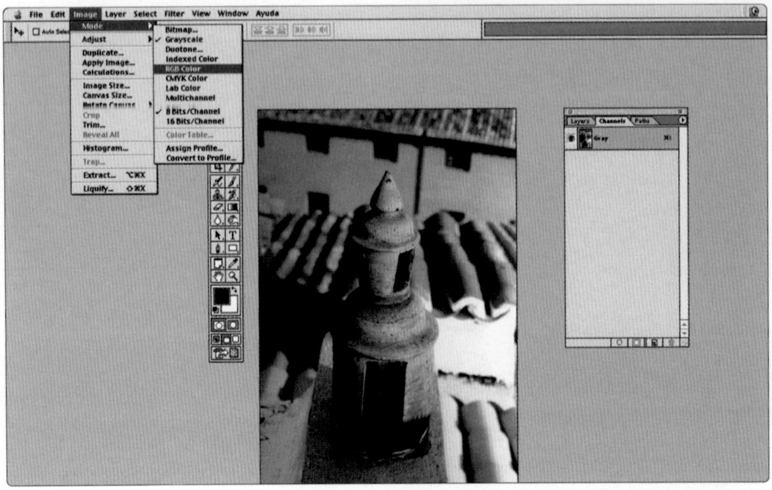

◂ **2** Pull down the Image menu and select Mode, then click on RGB Color.

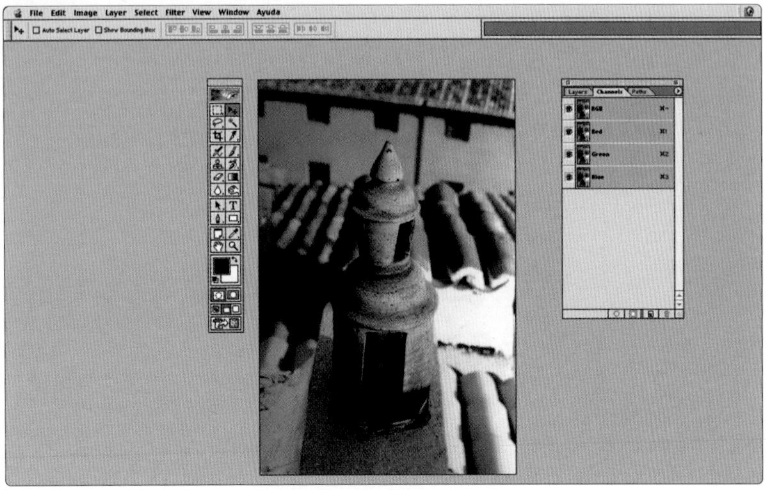

▸ **3** You now have three color layers at your disposal in the pallette.

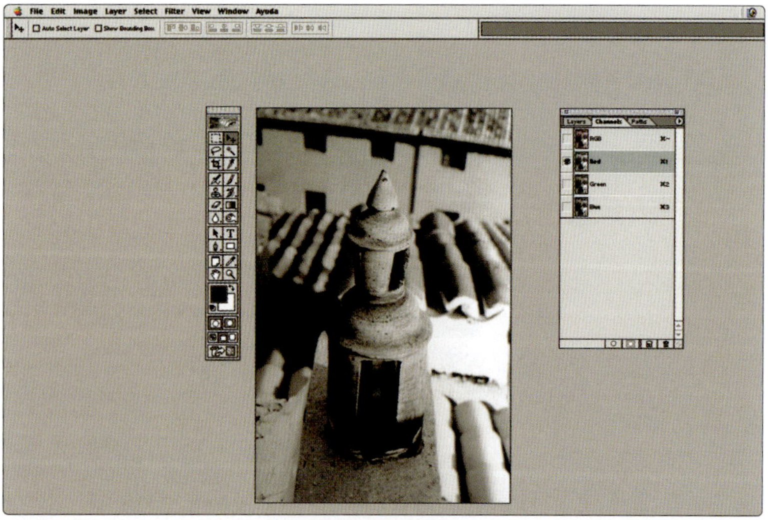

4 If you choose the red layer and make a change in the color balance you'll see that only the color shade scale has been modified.

RGB stands for red, green, and blue. This system is used for computer and television images.

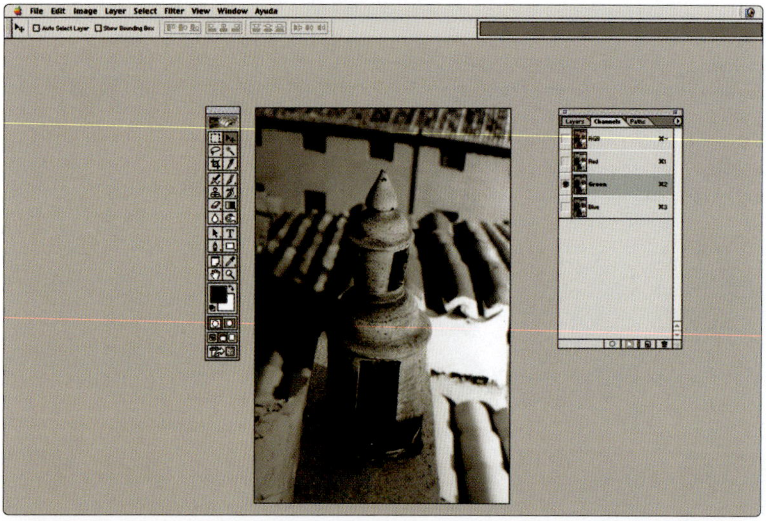

5 You can also choose the green scale...

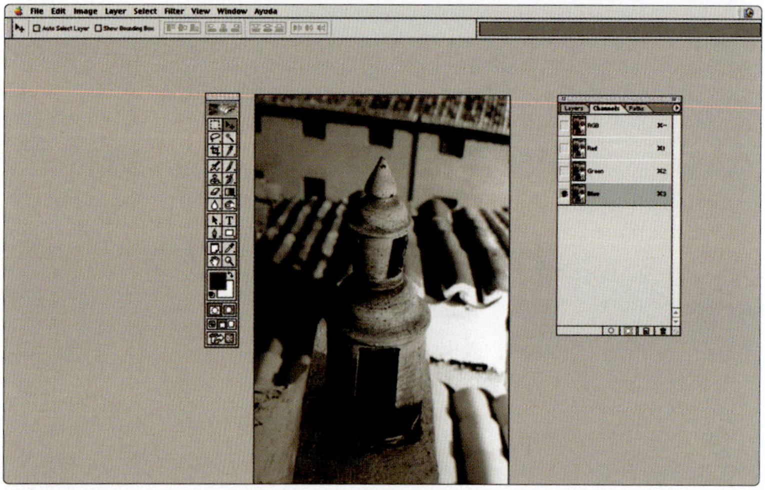

6 ... and shades of blue.

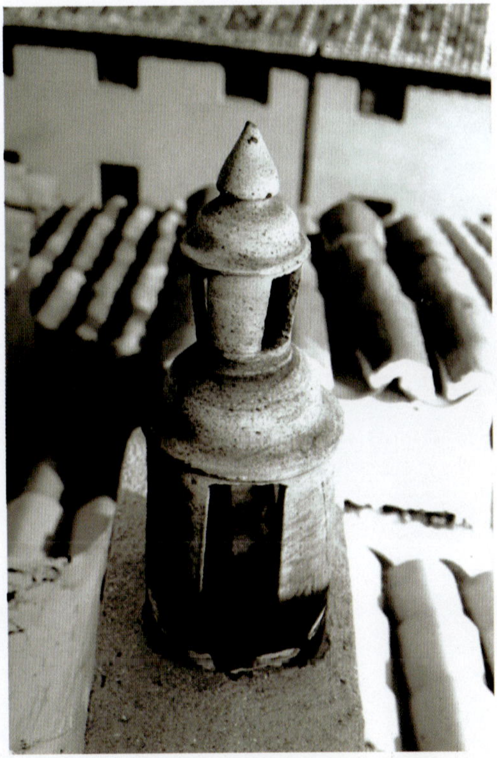

◂ The original photograph in the gray scale

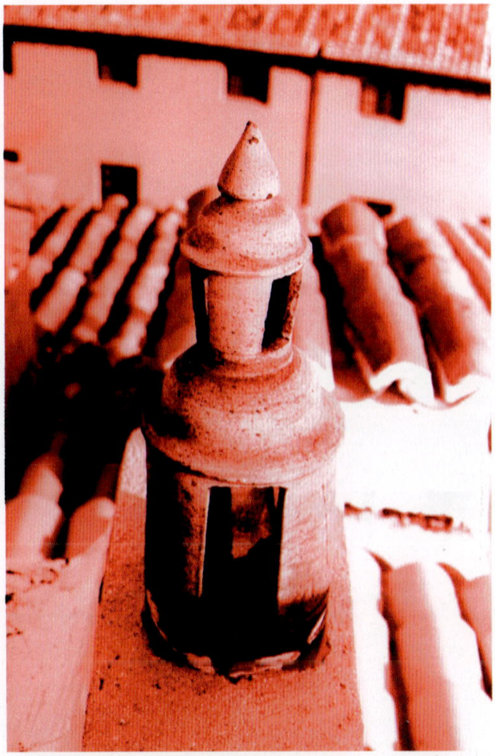

▸ The photograph in the red shade scale

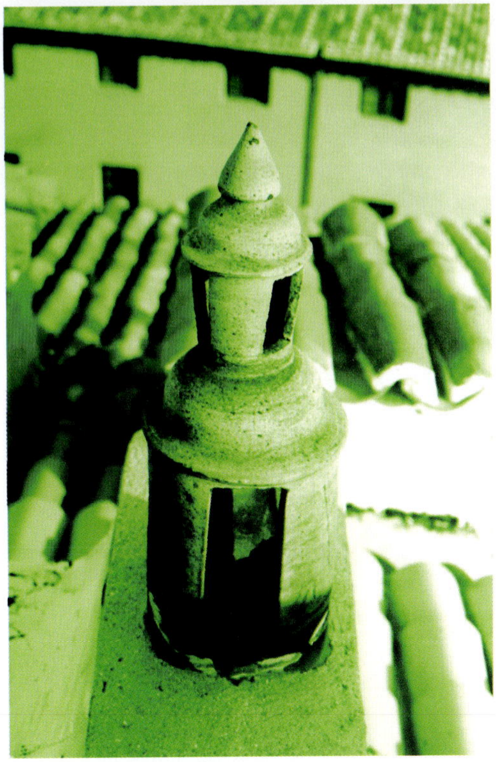

◂ The photograph in the green shade scale

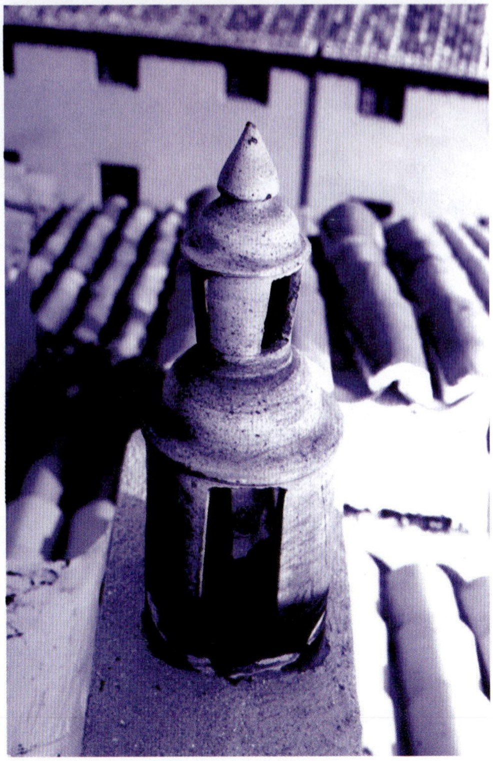

▸ The photograph in the blue shade

Converting a picture to the CMYK system

Since it's possible to convert a picture to RGB or, conversely, to gray scale, it's also possible to convert it to the CMYK (Cyan, Magenta, Yellow, blacK) system.
This can prove useful in some situations, especially if your picture is intended for full-color printing (CMYK).

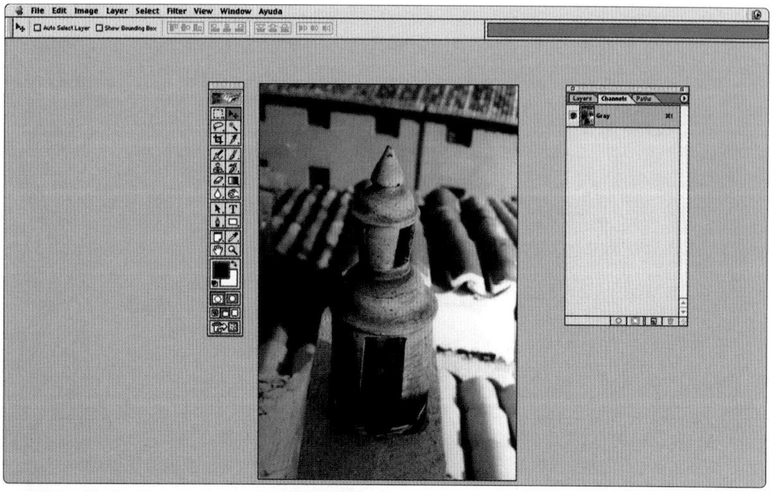

1 Open the file with the gray-scale or RGB picture in your image editing program.

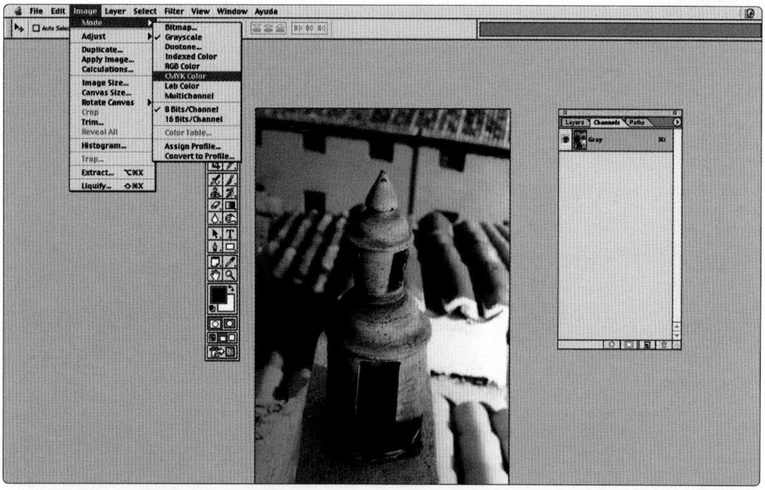

2 Pull down the Image menu, select Mode, and click on CMYK Colors.

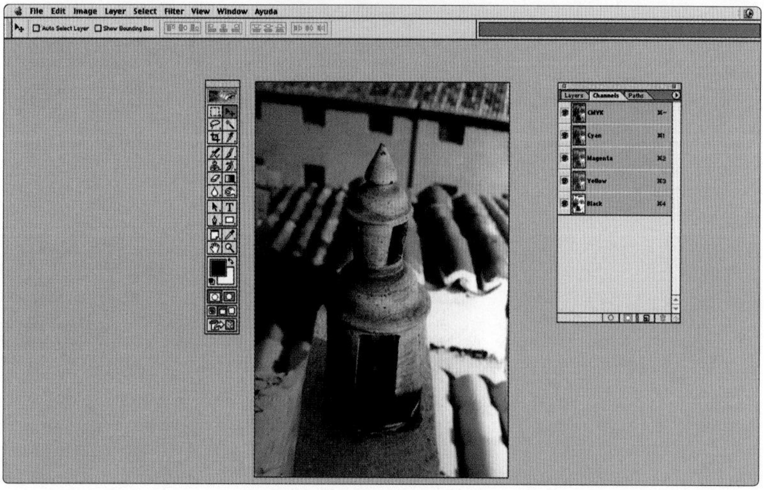

3 You now have four CMYK color layers available on your pallette.

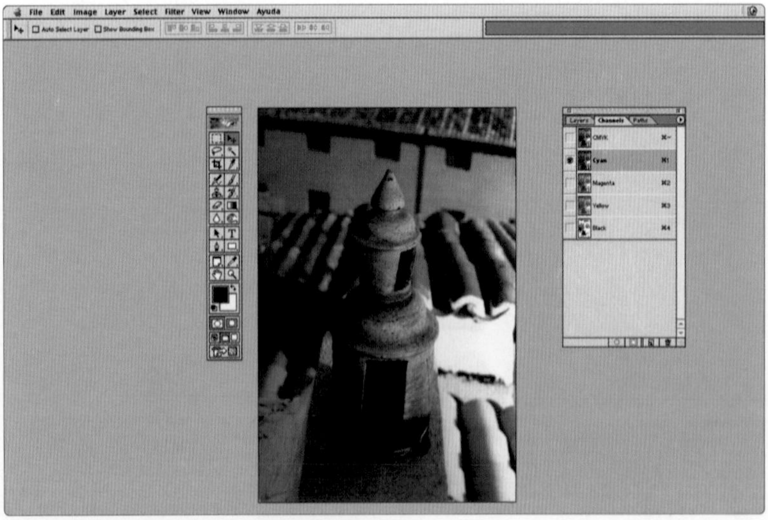

▸ **4** If you select the cyan (azure blue) layer and make any changes in it, e.g., in the color balance, you will modify only the azure shade layer.

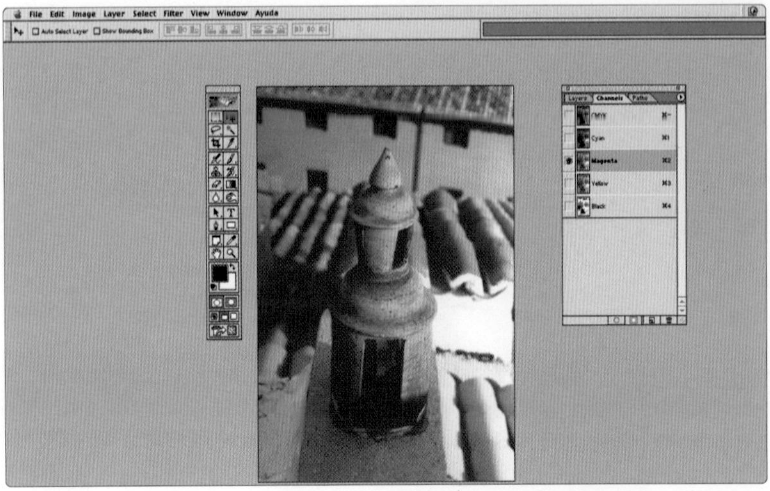

◂ **5** The same thing is possible in the magenta shade layer...

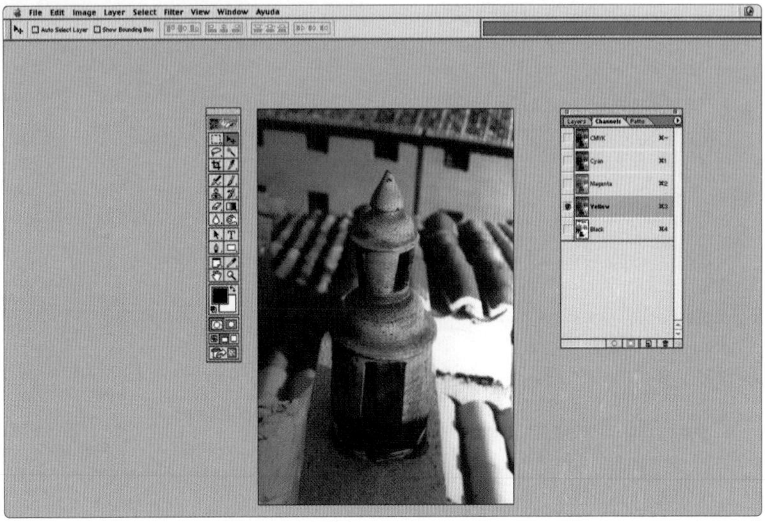

▸ **6** ... in the yellow shade layer...

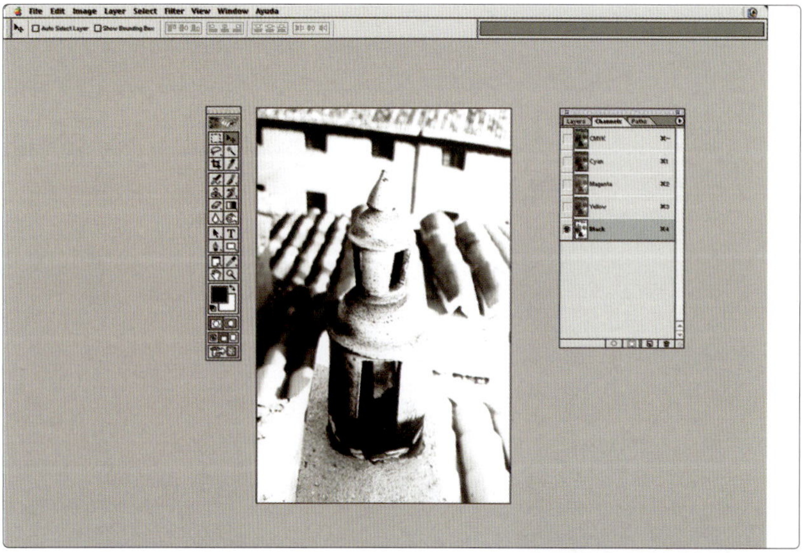

7 ... and finally in the black shade layer.

Don't forget to always save your work after the final modification to an image. Pull down the File menu to save the image to the memory.

The individual color layers that make up the CMYK system can be designated.

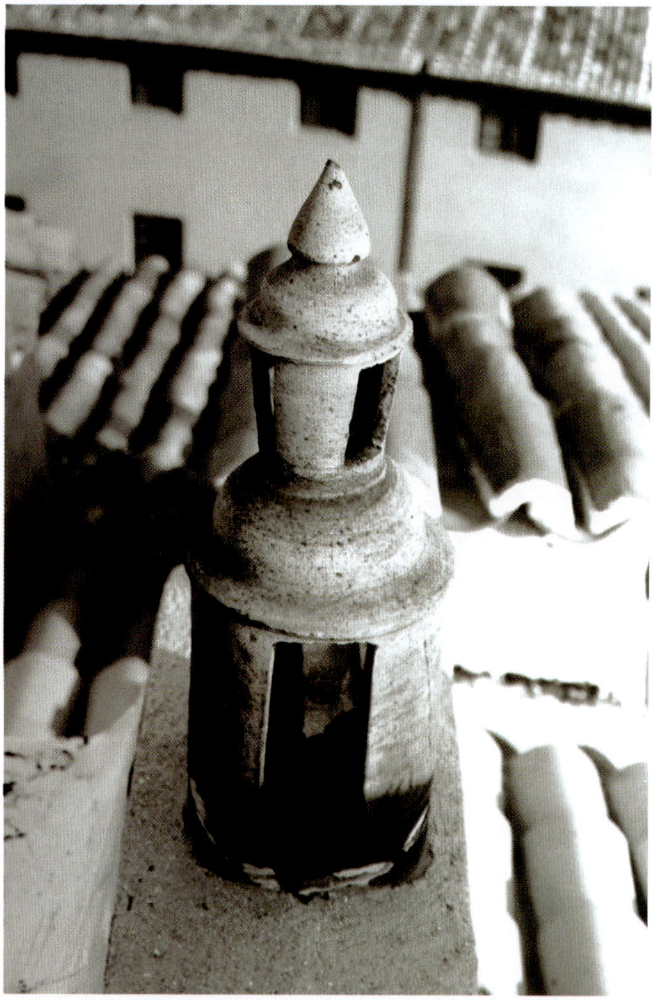

The original gray-scale picture

CMYK stands for Cyan, Magenta, Yellow, and black. This is the set of colors that is used in professional printing.

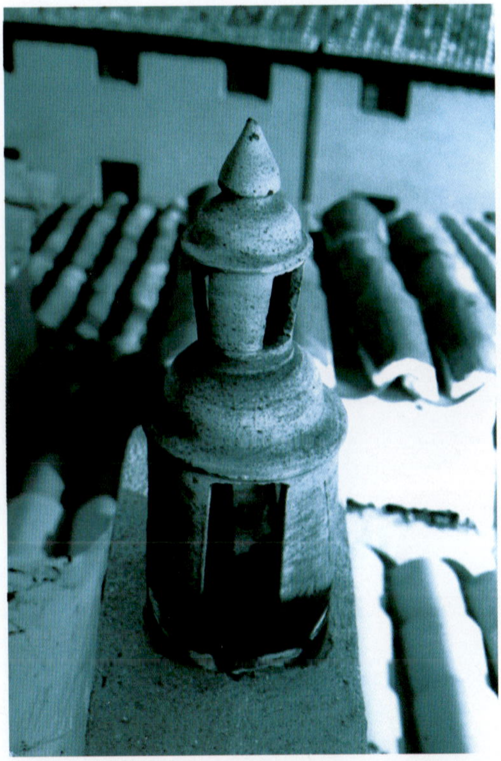

The picture in the azure shade scale

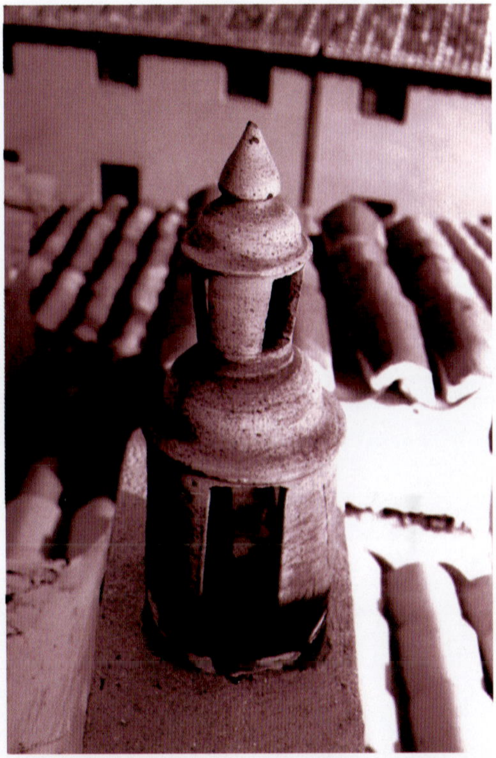

The picture in the magenta shade scale

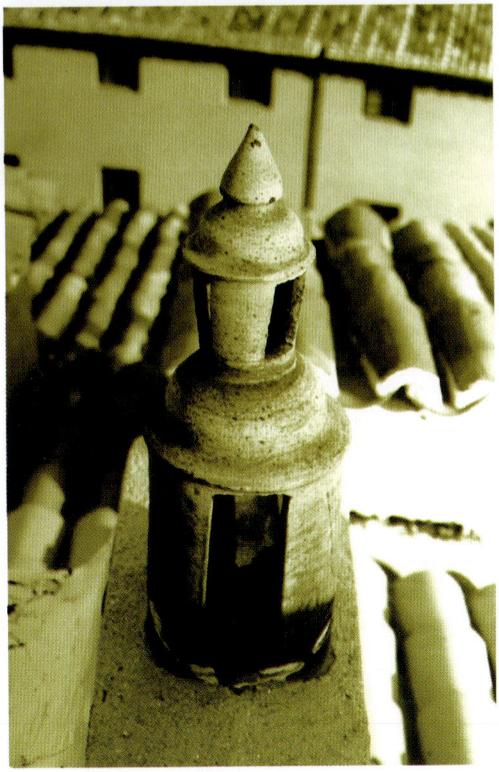

The picture in the yellow shade scale

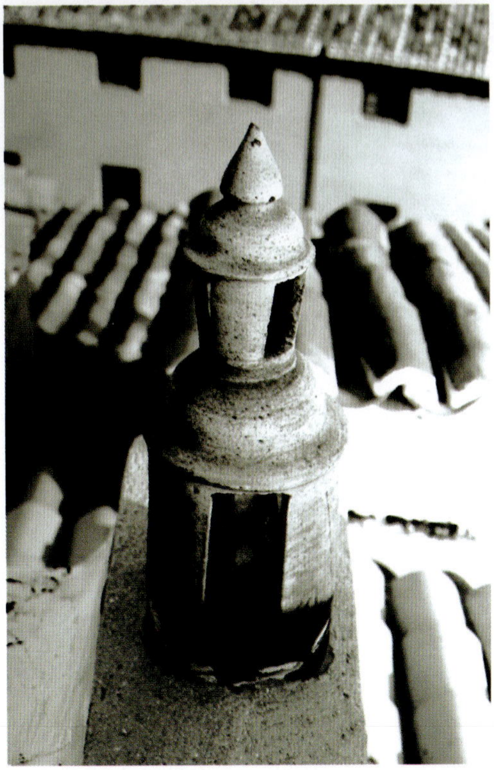

The picture in the black shade scale

Color balance

Sometimes we later realize that we didn't select the correct lighting mode. Or maybe we just want to make creative coloring changes. Here's how to do it:

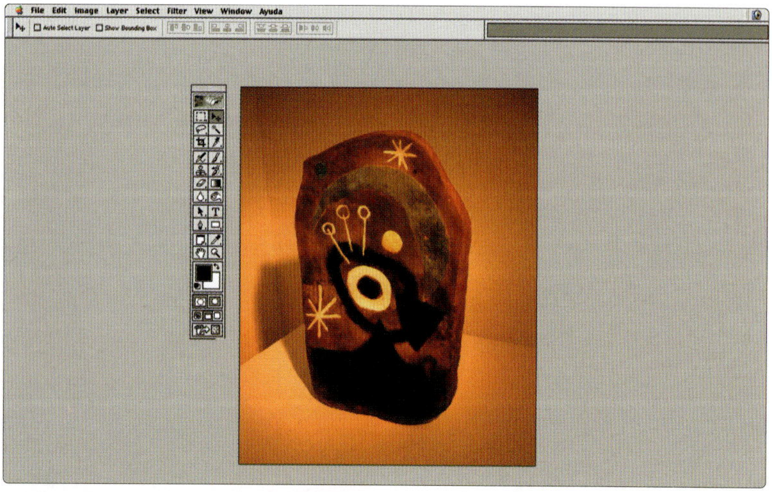

▸ 1 Open the file with the picture in the image editing program.

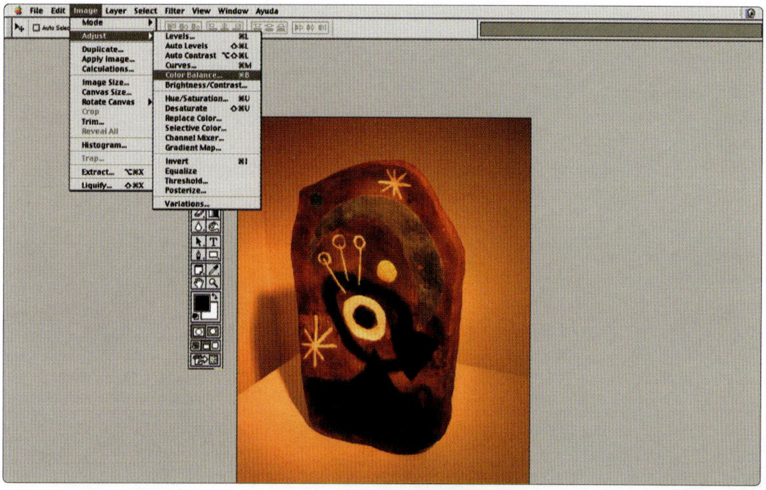

◂ 2 Pull down the Image menu and select Adjust and then Color Balance.

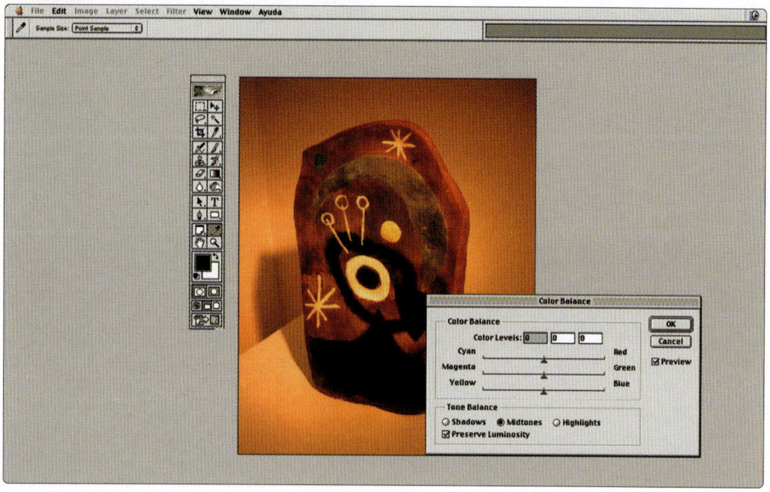

▸ 3 The color balance dialogue will appear.

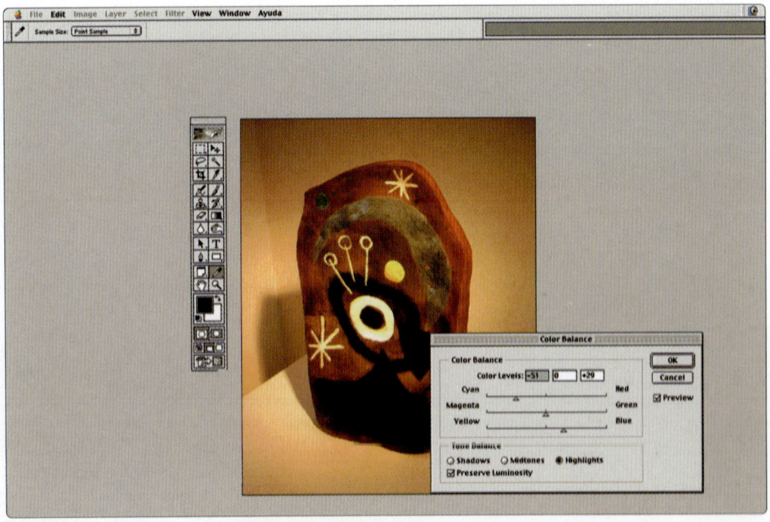

▸ **4** Make the change you had in mind.

In this particular case the classic incandescent lighting mode wasn't used when the picture was taken in a museum. It was therefore necessary to add some blue shades to compensate for the colors in the picture.

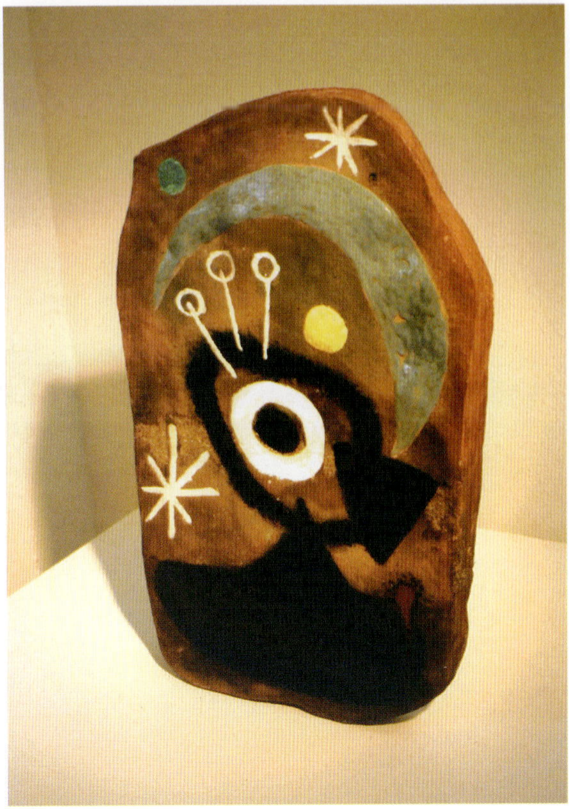

▴ Modified photograph

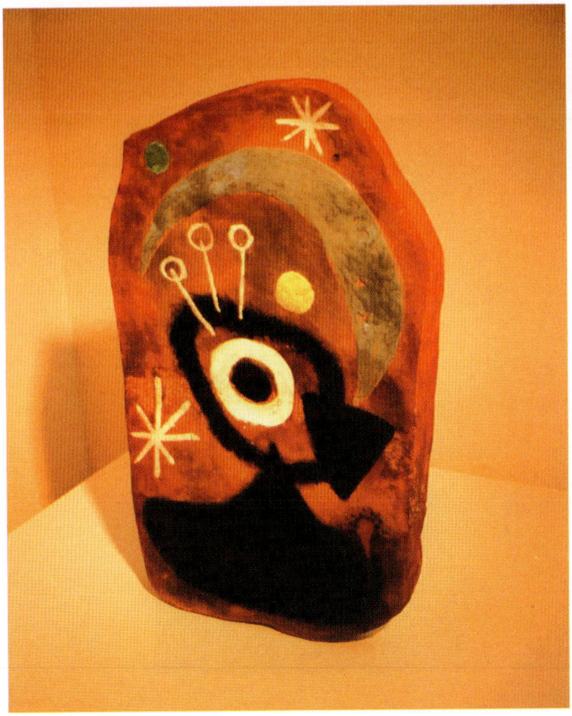

◂ Original photograph

Adding a frame to a picture

If you want to add a frame to a picture to improve its appearance you should proceed according to the following steps:

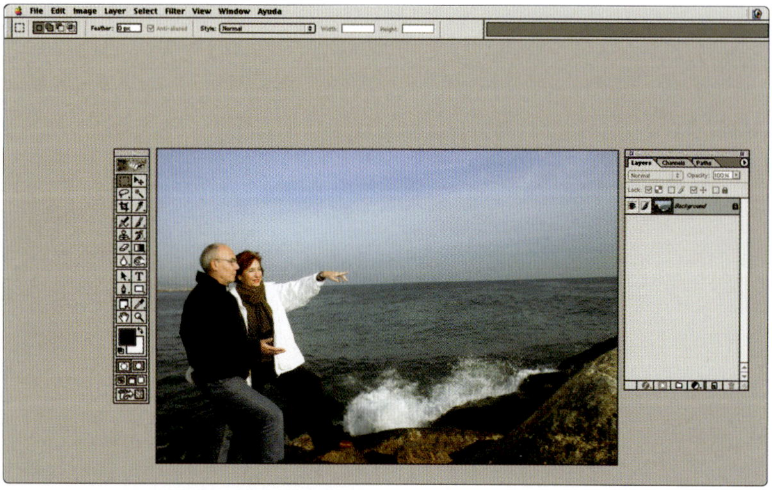

1 Open the file with the picture in the image editing program.

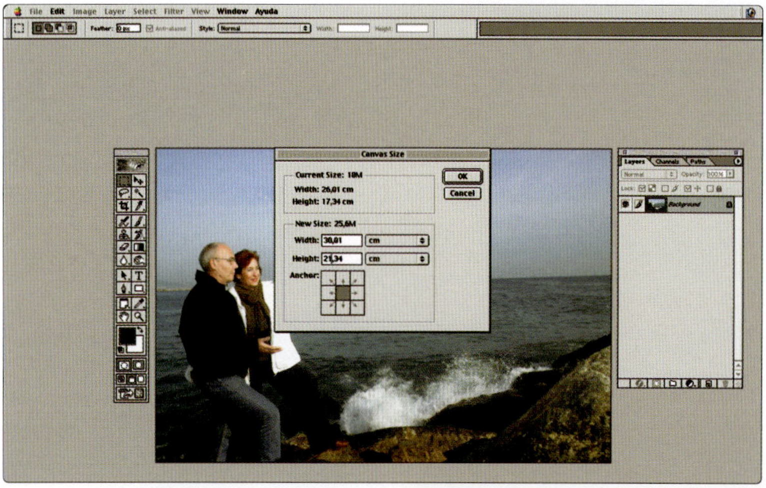

2 Select Canvas Size from the Image menu and increase the dimensions to select the desired frame width. This doesn't change the size of the picture, it just affects the size of the work zone.

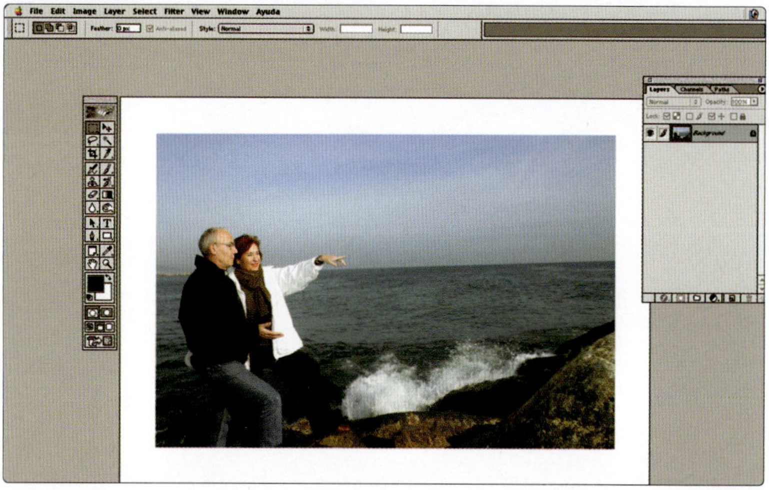

3 A white background will appear around the picture, representing the selected size and width of the frame.

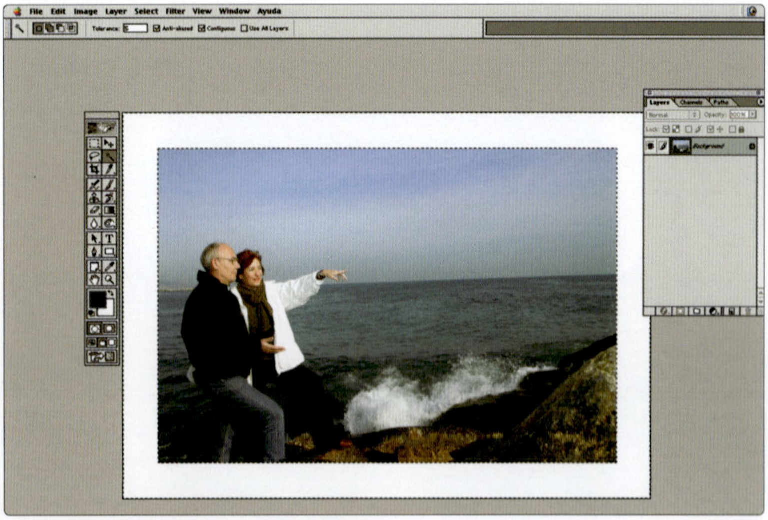

4 If you want a more interesting frame, find the Magic Wand and click on the white frame.

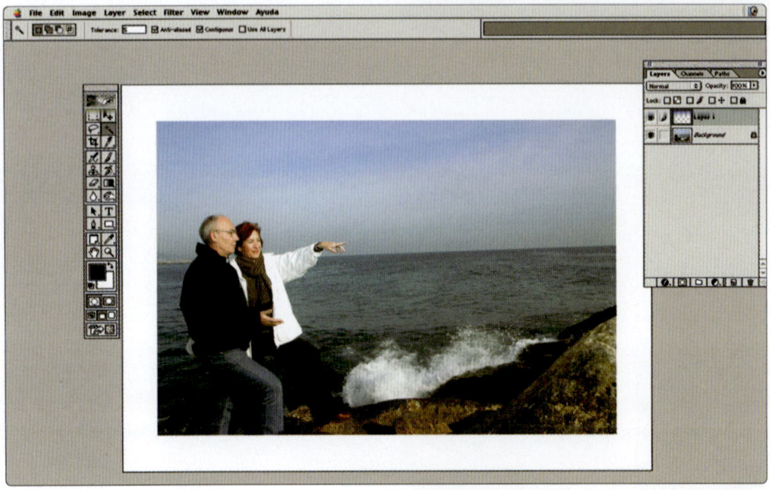

5 After making this selection enter Copy and Save, so that the frame appears as a separate layer.

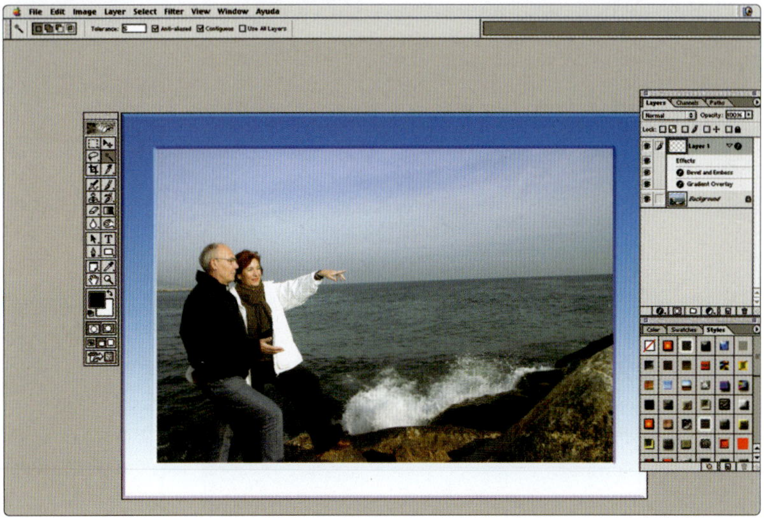

6 Then select Styles from the Window menu, select the one that suits you best, and drag it to the layer of the frame. Then go to the Layer menu, select To One Layer, and confirm.

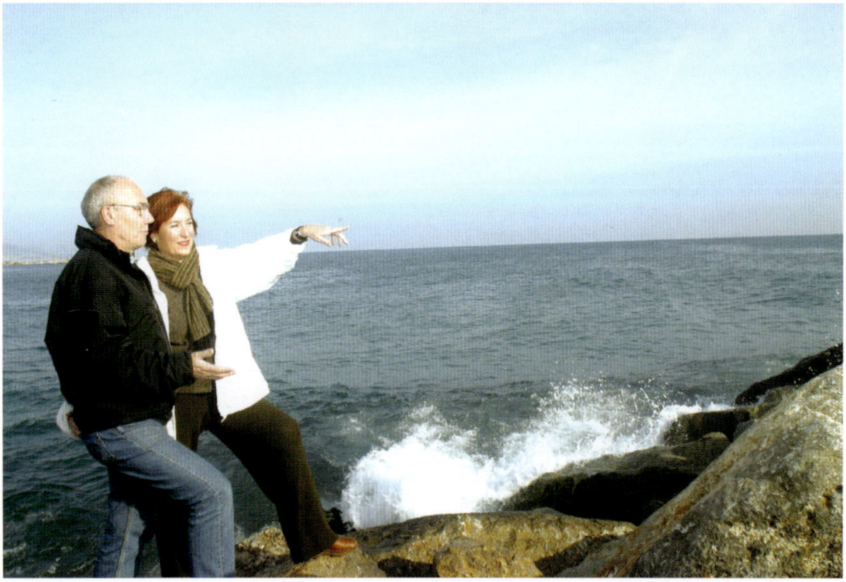

It's very easy to create endless possibilities involving various frames that improve the appearance of pictures, especially when they are intended for commercial purposes.

Original photograph without any frame

Here are a few suggestions meant to inspire you.

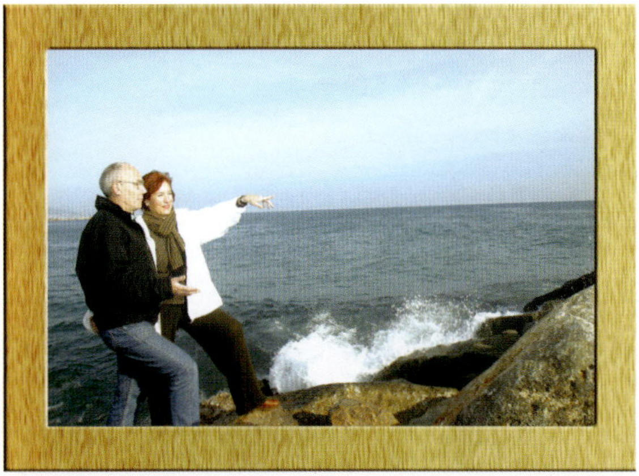

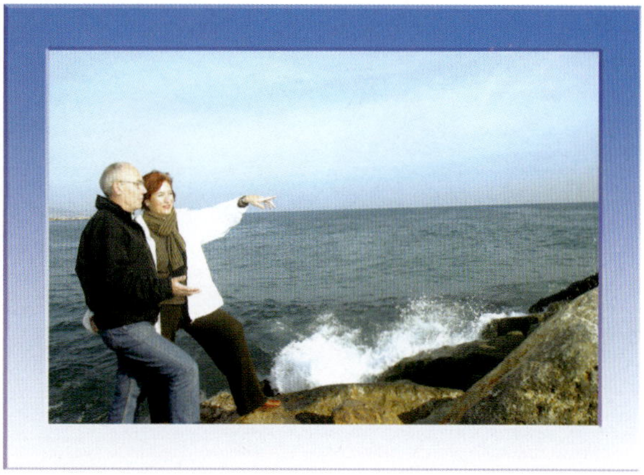

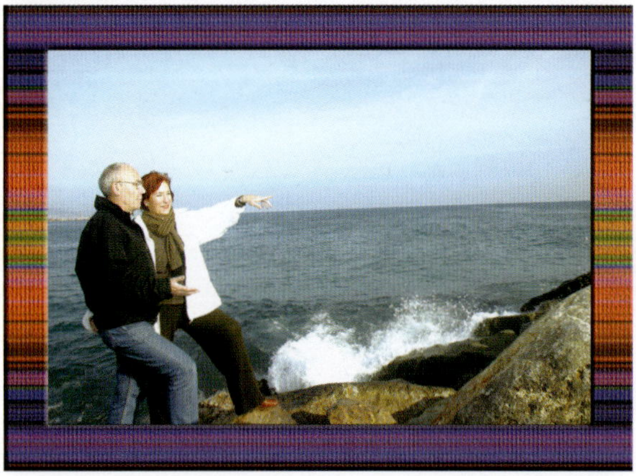

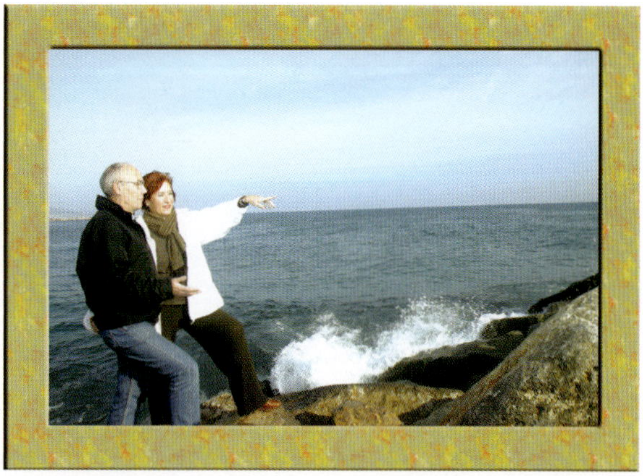

Underexposed and overexposed pictures

You will often find there are areas in pictures that have overly intense lighting or, conversely, areas with overly dark shading. In such situations you can modify pictures by either lightening or darkening them as needed.

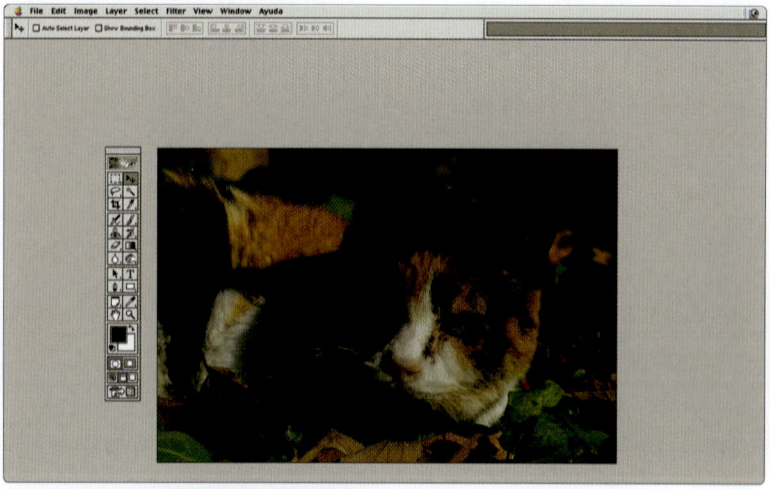

▸ 1 Open the file with the picture in the image editing program.

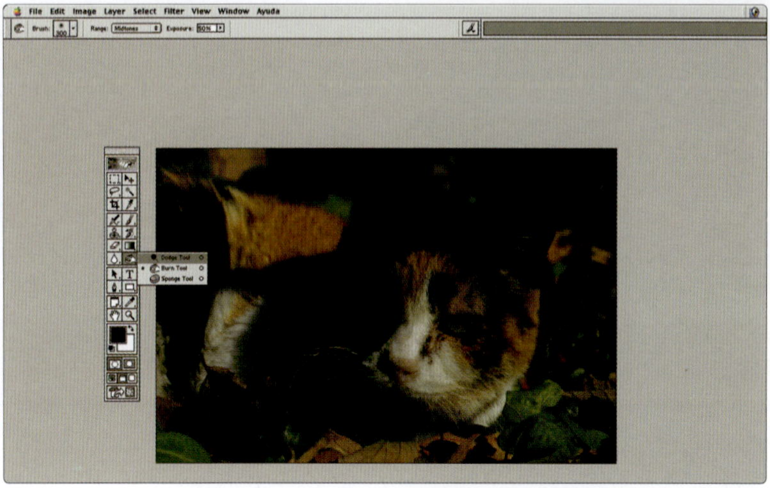

◂ 2 Select Lightening from the Toolbox, then click on Trace in the Exposure menu.

▸ 3 Go to the area that you want to lighten and modify it as needed.

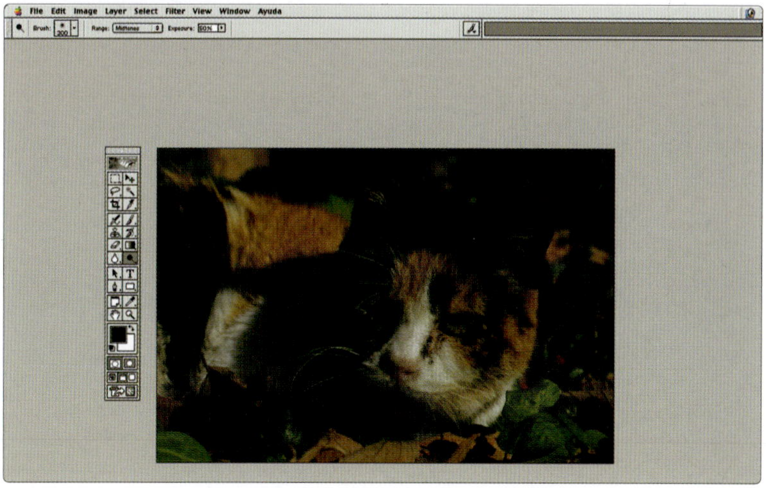

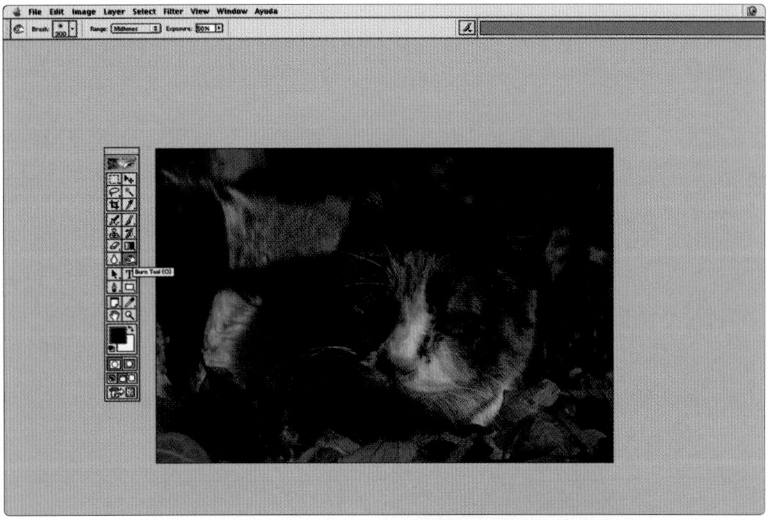

4 In the Toolbox, click on Density.

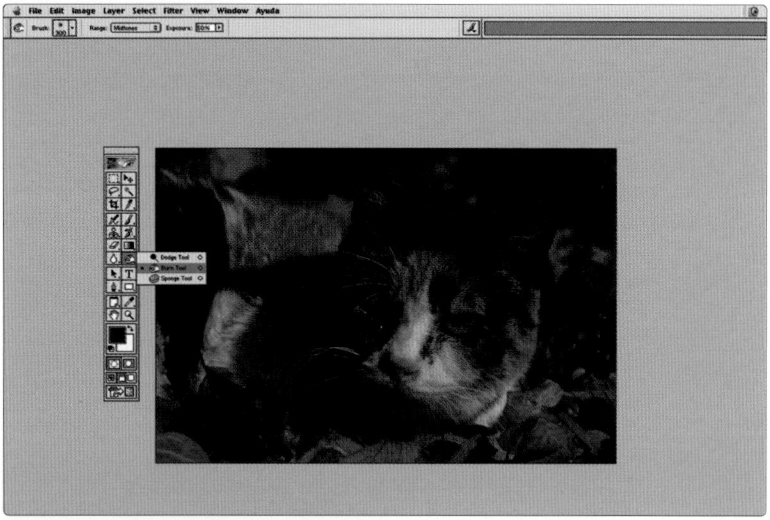

5 Select the Darkening Tool, then Trace and Exposure.

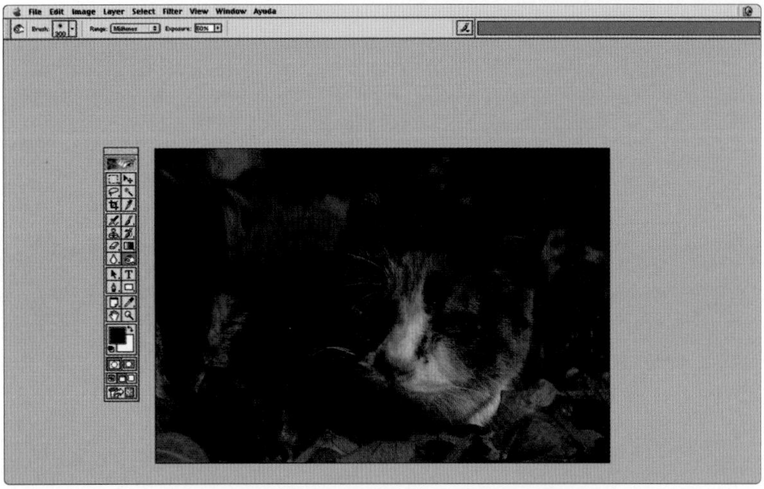

6 Modify the area you are interested in.

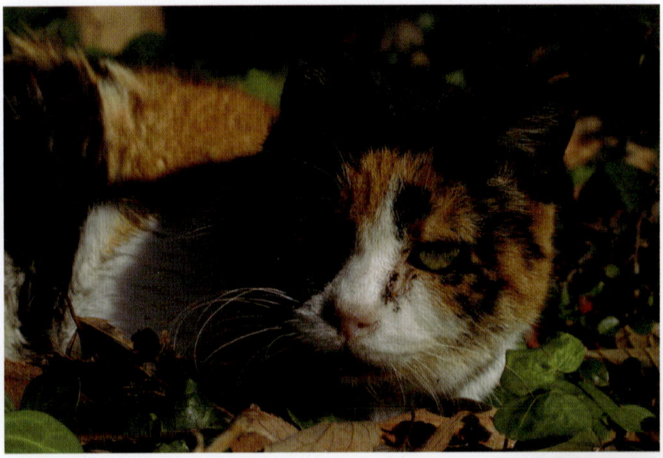

◀ Original photograph

Make sure you don't overdo underexposure and overexposure modifications, because it could give the picture a boring appearance without contrast, or it could turn it into a reverse image.

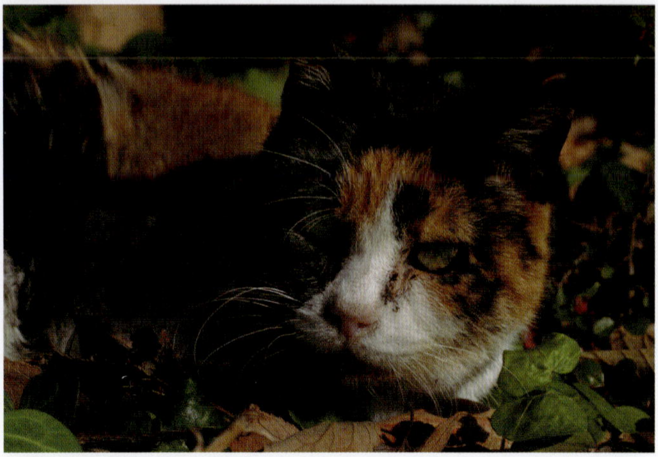

▶ Photograph with modified overexposed and underexposed places.

Hue and saturation

All color photographs have predetermined color modes - e.g., RGB or CMYK. In some cases you may want to change some colors in a picture.

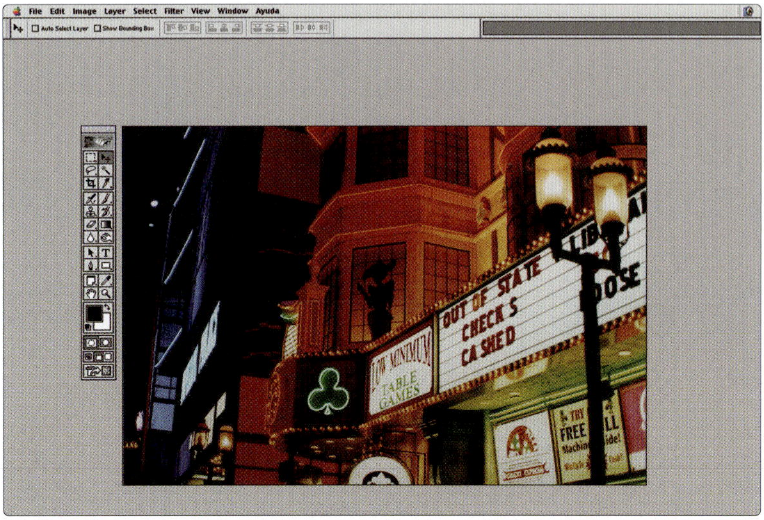

▶ 1 Open the file with the picture in the image editing program.

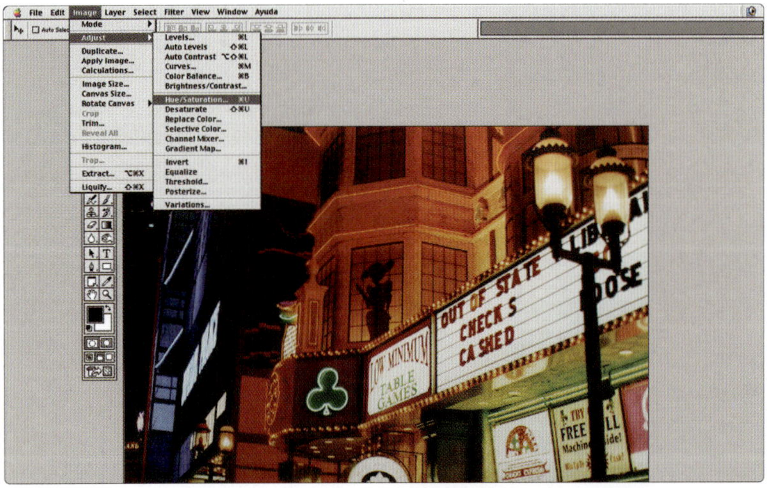

2 Pull down the Image menu, click on Adjust, and then on Hue/Saturation.

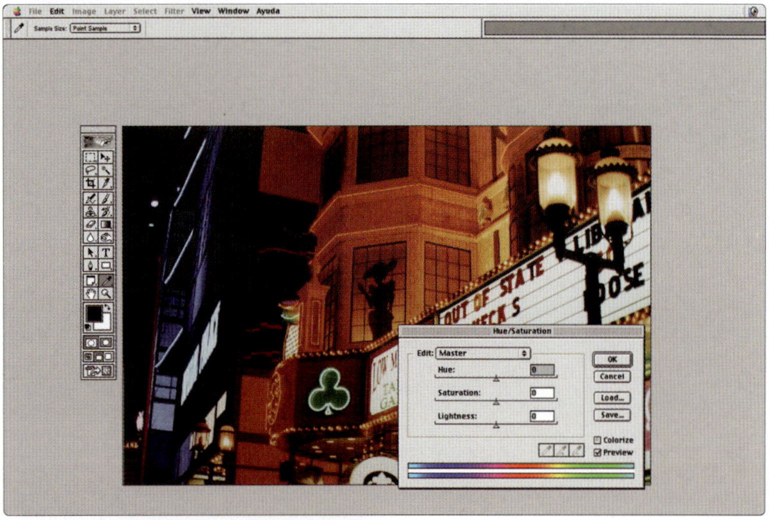

3 An options menu will appear.

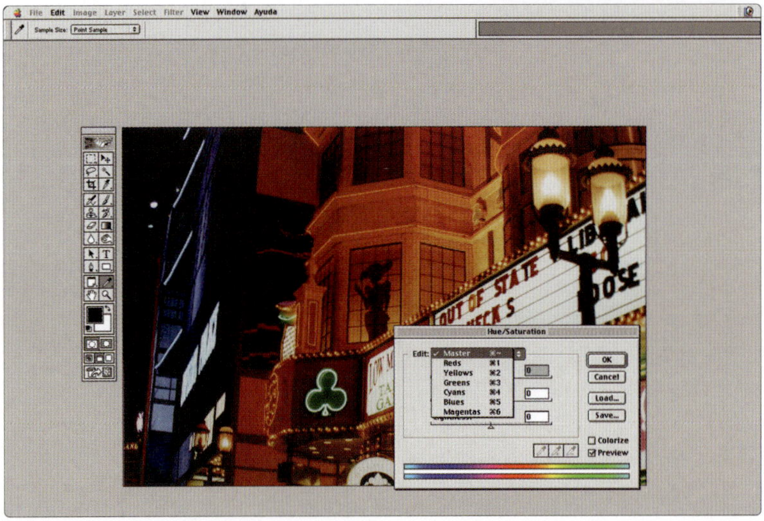

4 Go to Edit at the top of the box and select Master.

This option can also help give a cooler atmosphere to a "warm" picture. The only thing you have to do is lower the saturation of yellow and red shades.

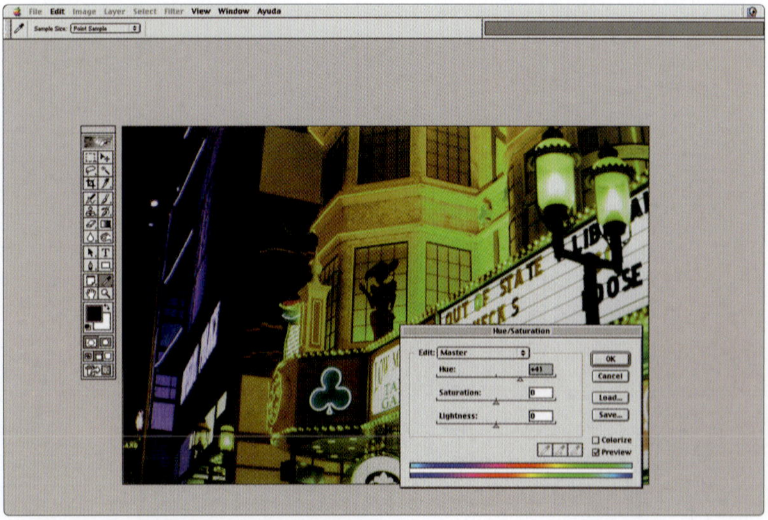

▸ **5** After you make a change you can see that all the colors in the picture have changed.

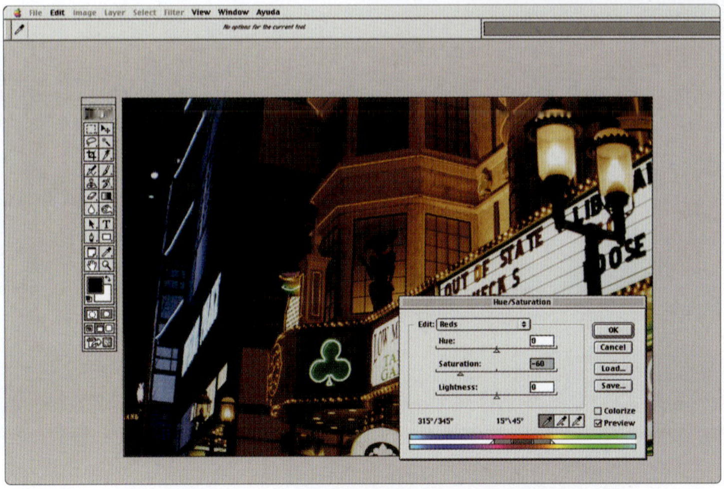

◂ **6** Repeat this operation, but when making the change select Reds instead of Master. You will see that only the red shades are changed.

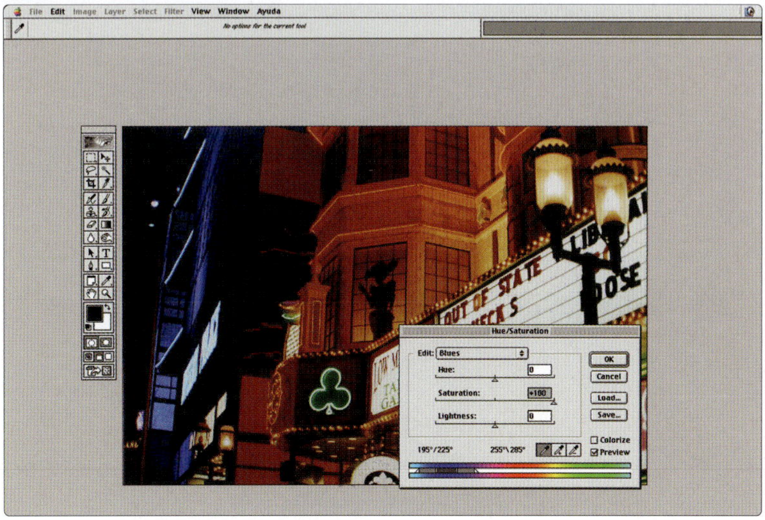

▸ **7** Repeat the operation one more time, but this time select Blues. The change affects only the blue shades.

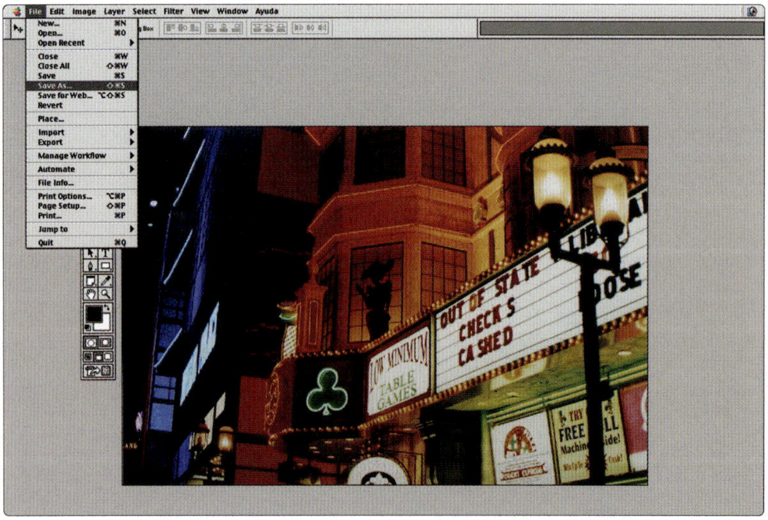

8 Save the changes you have made.

It's also possible to make an individual color stand out by increasing its saturation: for example, if you want to emphasize the blue of the sky.

Notice that in this way you have intervened only in the colors that you are interested in.

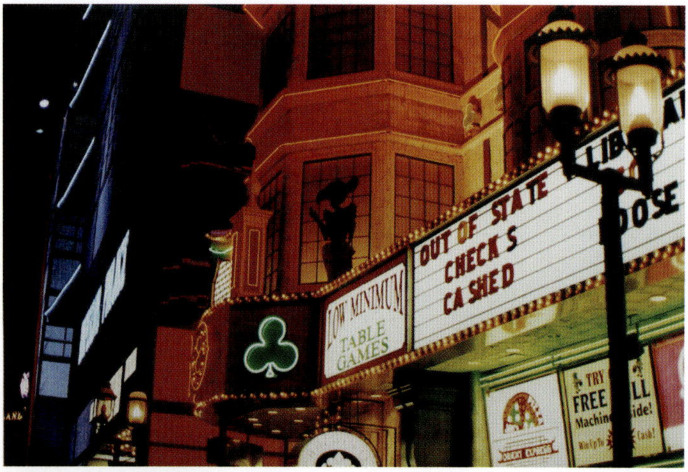

Original photograph

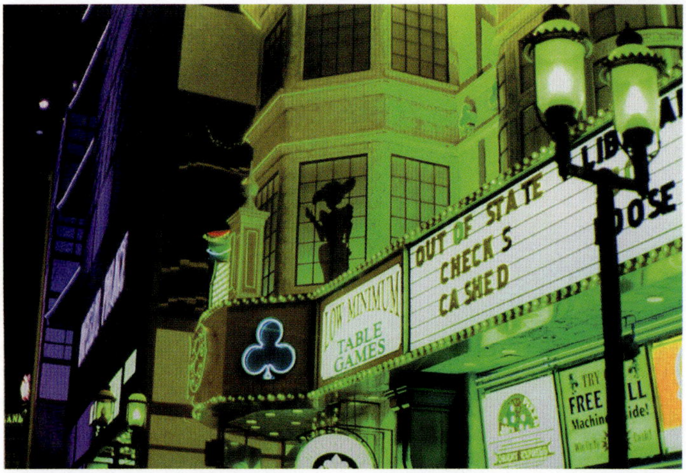

Changes in all colors

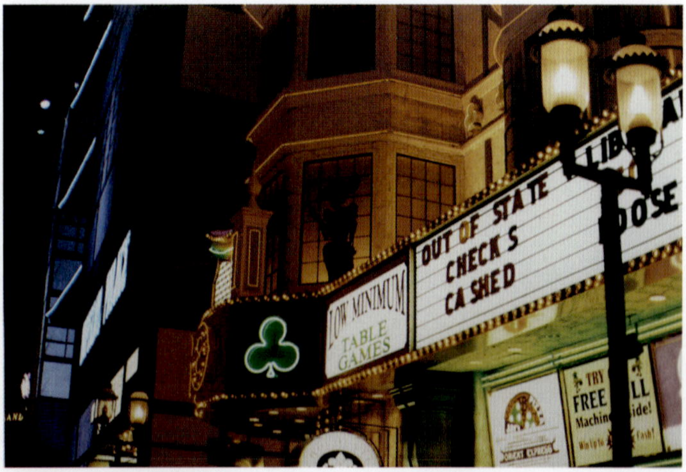

▸ Changes in red shades

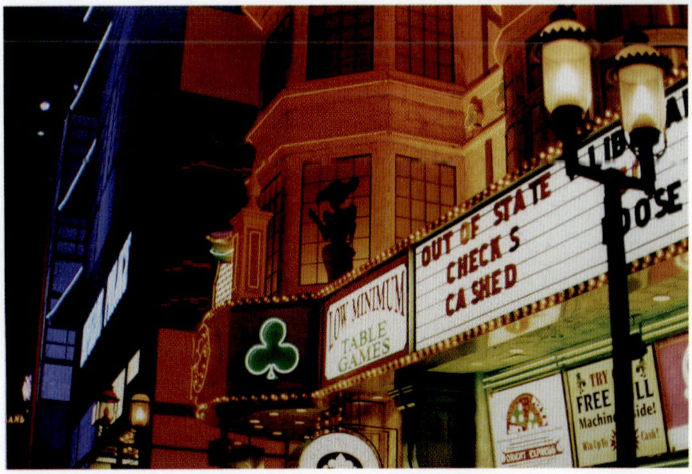

◂ Changes in blue shades

Variations

Besides the selection method for changing colors in a photograph you can also make variations in a single color on the entire image. Proceed according to the following steps:

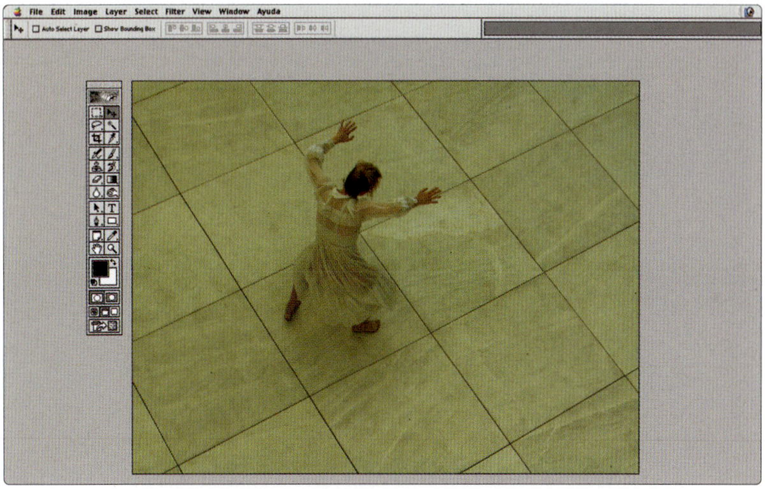

▸ 1 Open the file with the photograph in the image editing program.

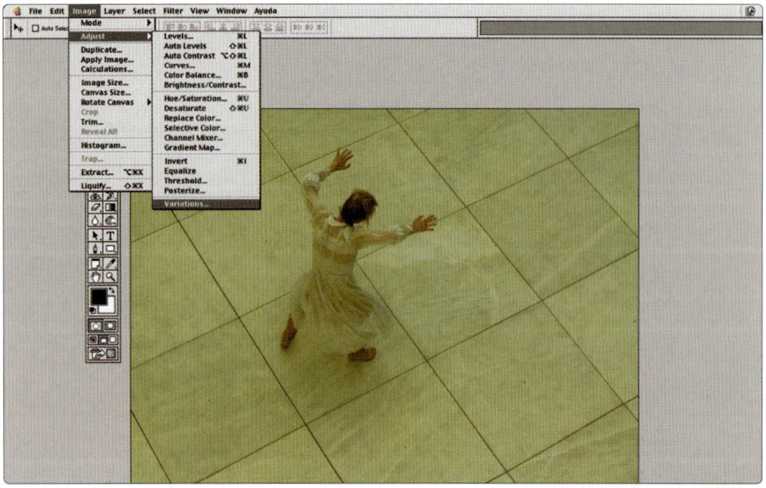

2 Pull down the Image menu and select Adjust and then Variations.

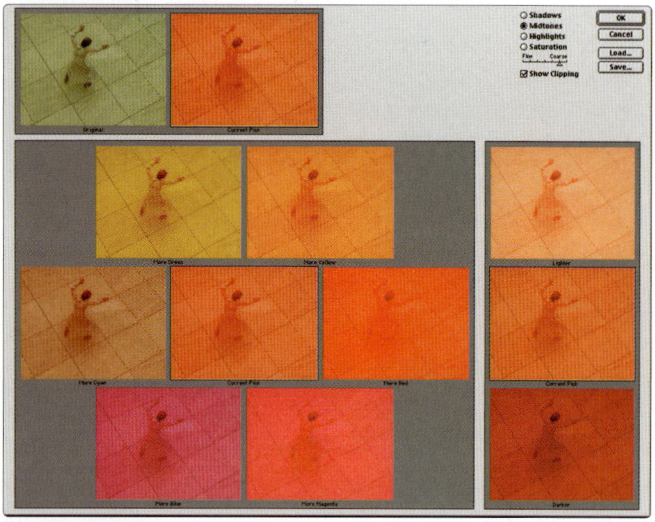

3 A graphics pallette appears in which you need only click on the color that you would like to impose on the photograph. Here we first chose one of the red shades.

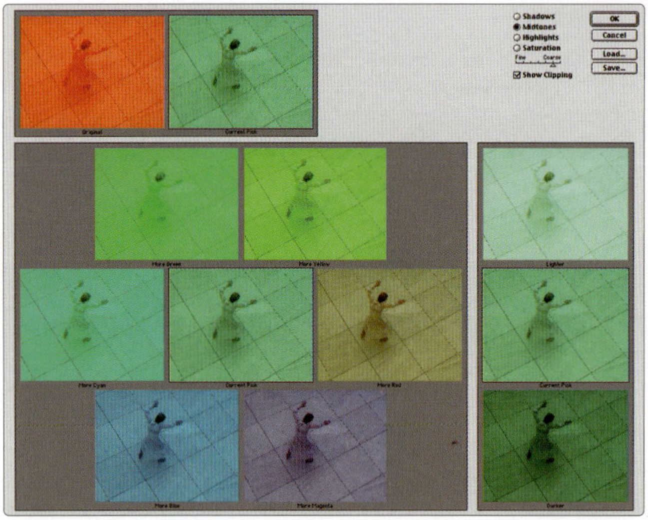

4 After tinting the picture red this way, try an azure shade.

▸ **5** When the picture appears in the desired colors you can either lighten or darken it. We decided to darken it.

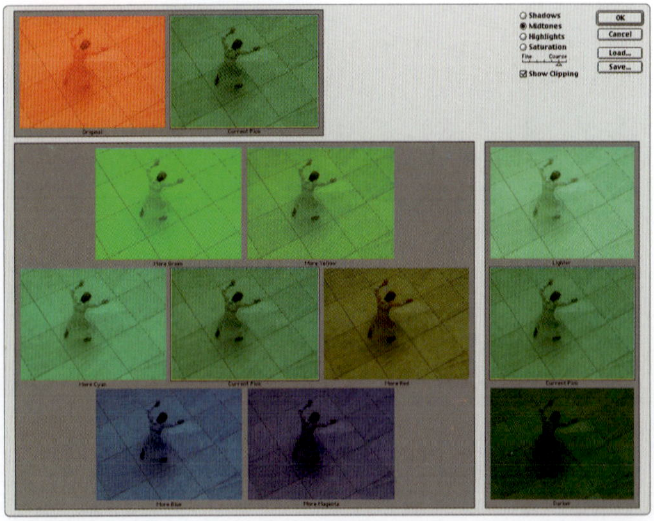

Thanks to this option you can produce pictures with great variation of color shades. For this purpose it's good to acquaint yourself not only with possible combinations of different variations but also with the ways you can lighten or darken a picture.

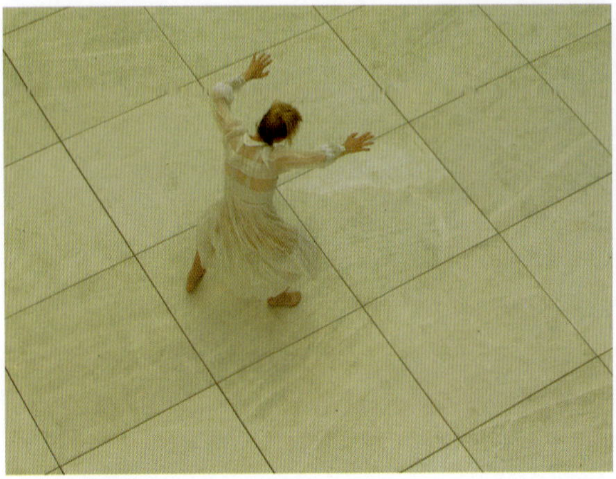

▲ Original image

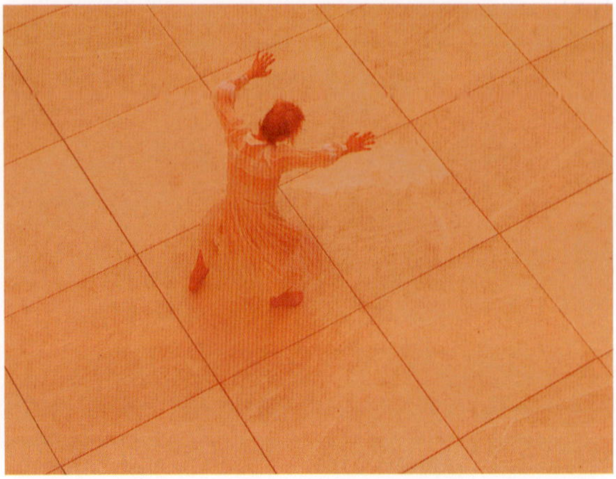

▲ Variation in the direction of red

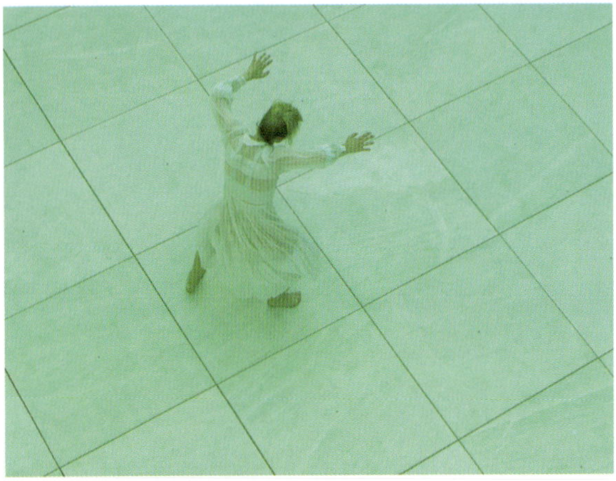

▲ Variation from red to azure

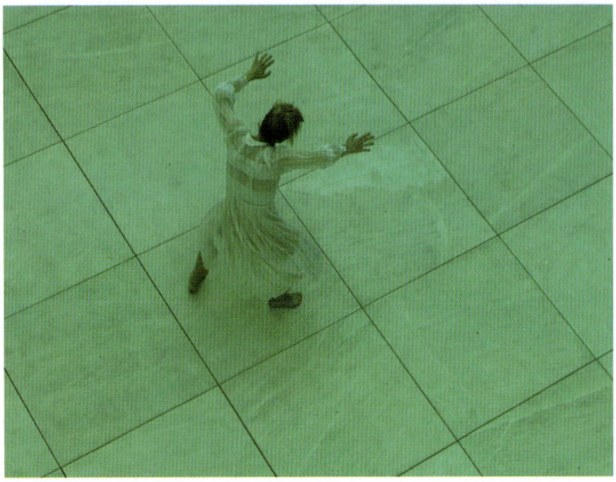

▲ The same variation towards azure, but this time darkened

Coloring

Digital image editing also allows you to color black-and-white pictures, thus achieving entertaining results. Just proceed according to the following steps:

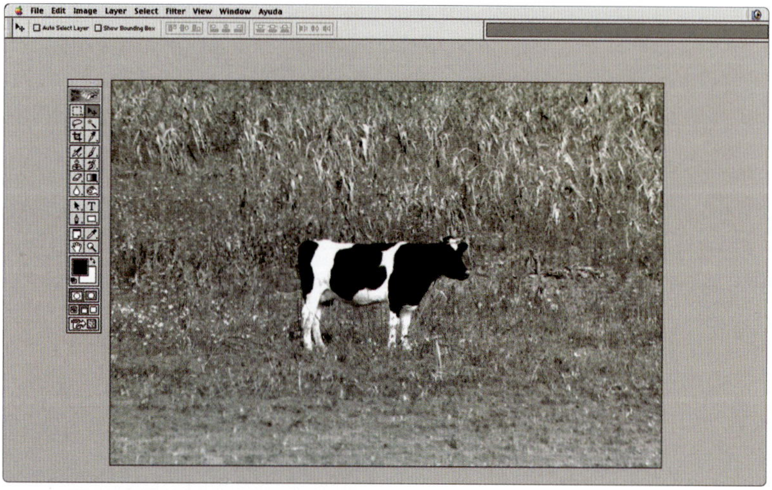

1 Open the gray scale photograph (or convert it to gray scale) in the imaging editing program.

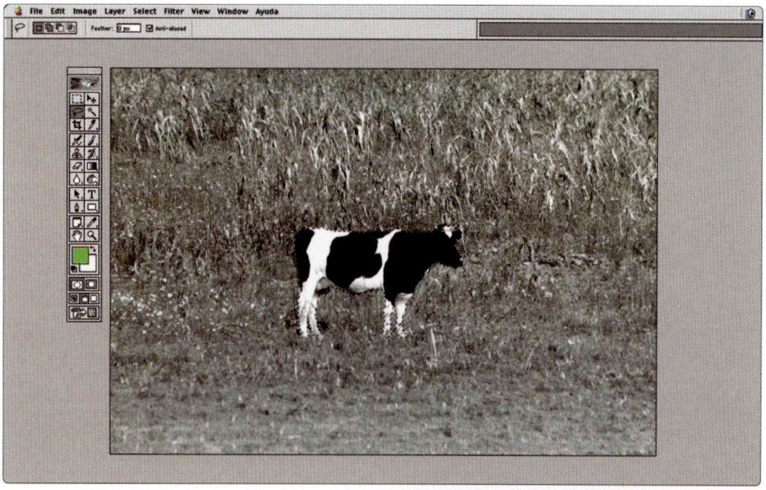

2 Separate the subject from the picture using the Lasso tool that you find in the Toolbox.

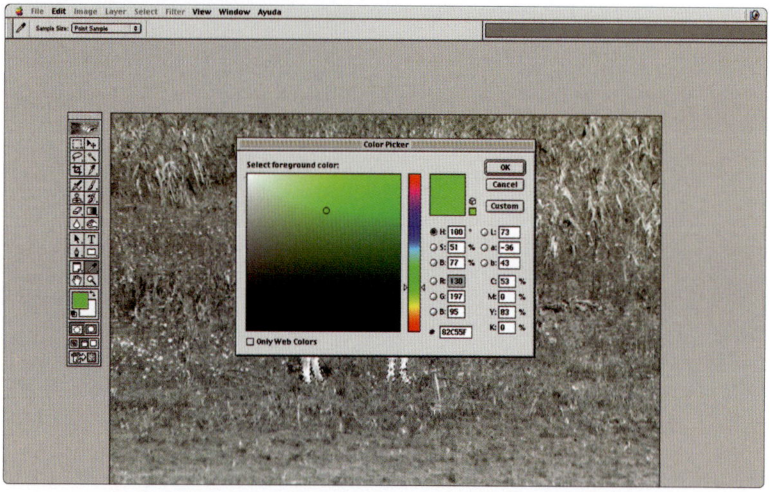

3 Also from the Toolbox use the Color Picker and then Foreground Color to select the color you want to use.

Always keep in mind that you have various tools for drawing or coloring a picture. All you need to do is choose the one that best meets your needs.

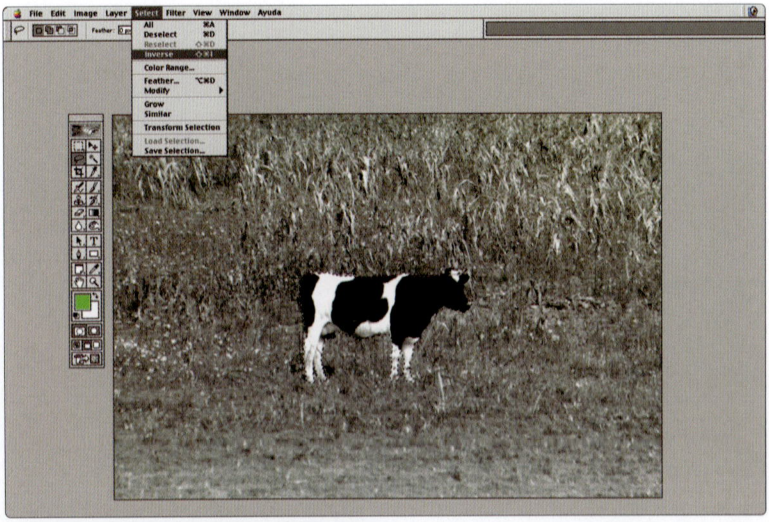

4 Before you can color the background you must invert the image. Pull down the Select menu and click on Inverse.

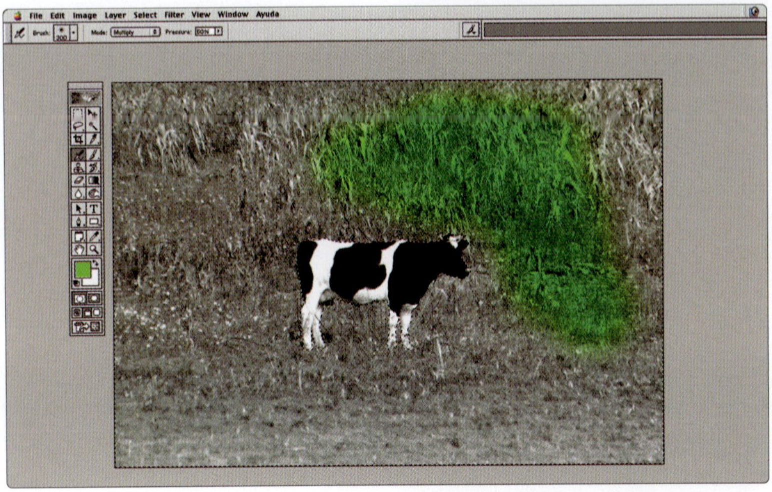

5 Now that the background has been selected and saved it can be colored in any way without you having to worry about affecting the subject - the cow.

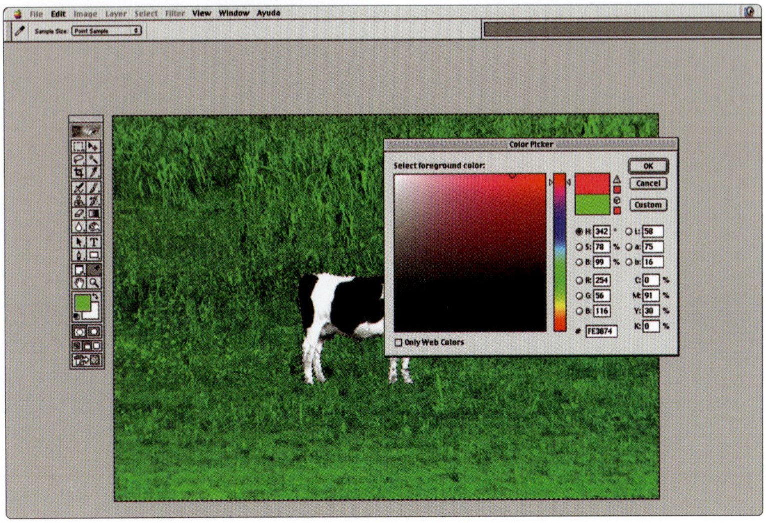

6 When you have finished coloring the background use Foreground Color to choose the cow's color.

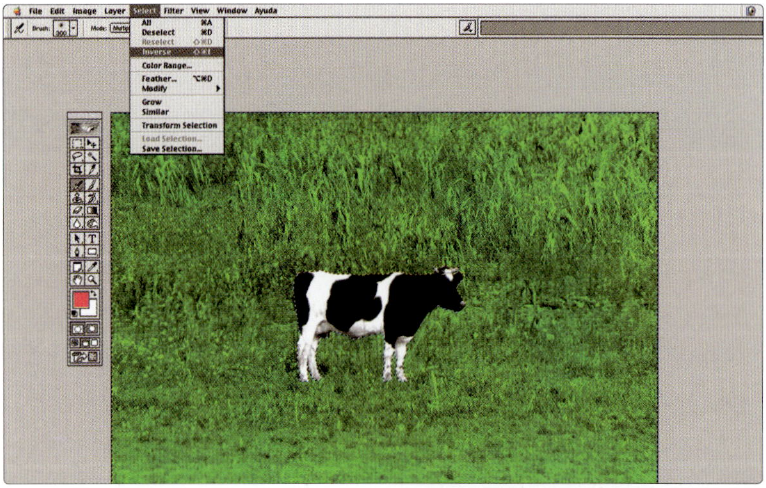

7 Once again you have to invert the selection in order to isolate the subject - the cow. Pull down the Select menu and click on Inverse.

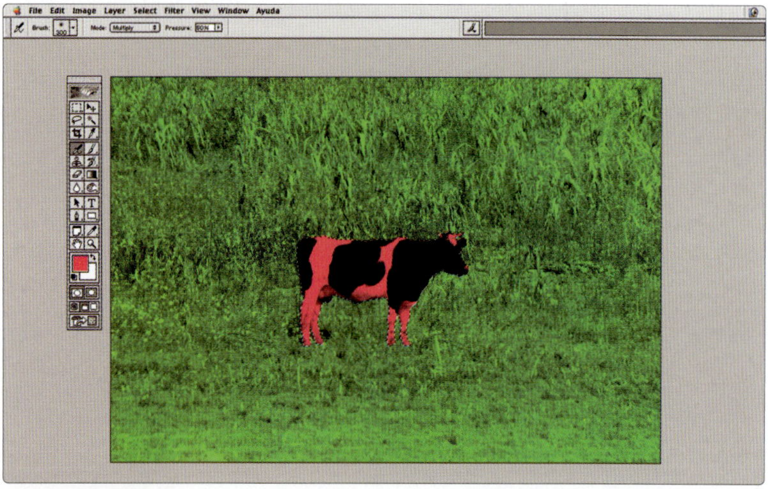

8 Color the cow with whatever shade you wish.

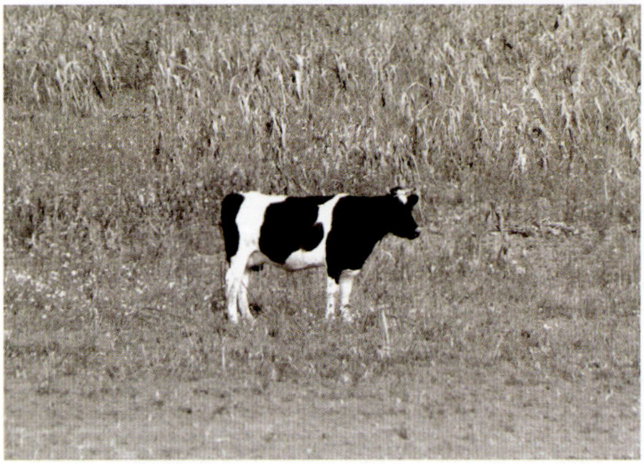

Original photograph

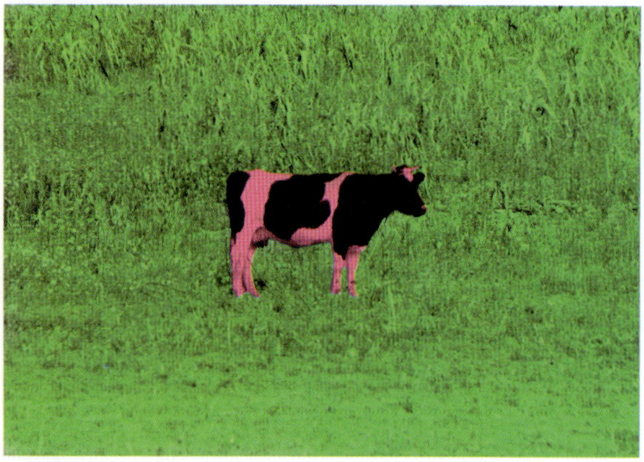

Colored photograph

Changing a color

Now let's look at how to replace one color with another. In this way you can take pictures in certain colors and then easily replace them with other colors to achieve much more interesting pictures.

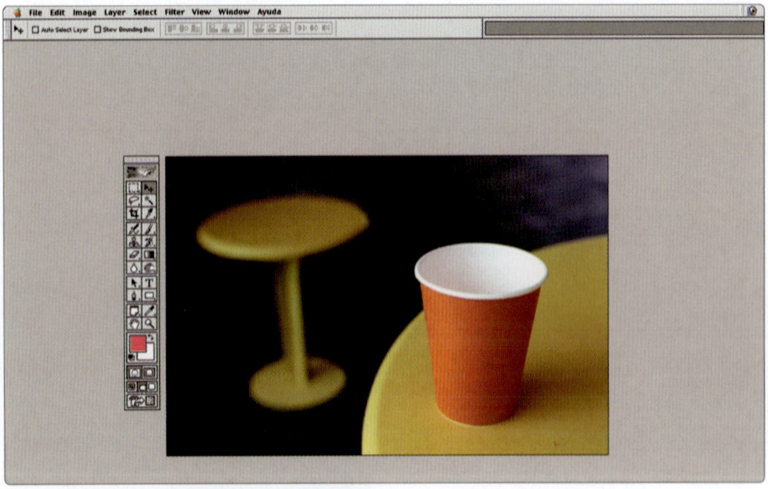

▸ 1 Open the file with the photograph in the image editing program.

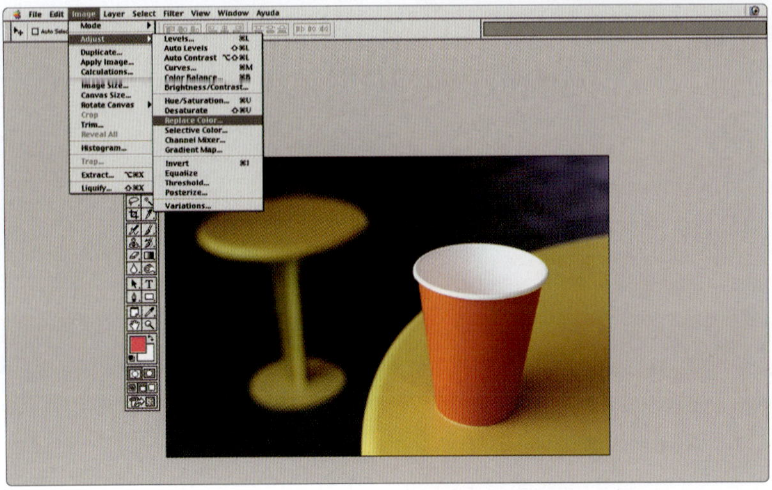

◂ 2 Pull down the Image menu and select Adjust/Replace Color.

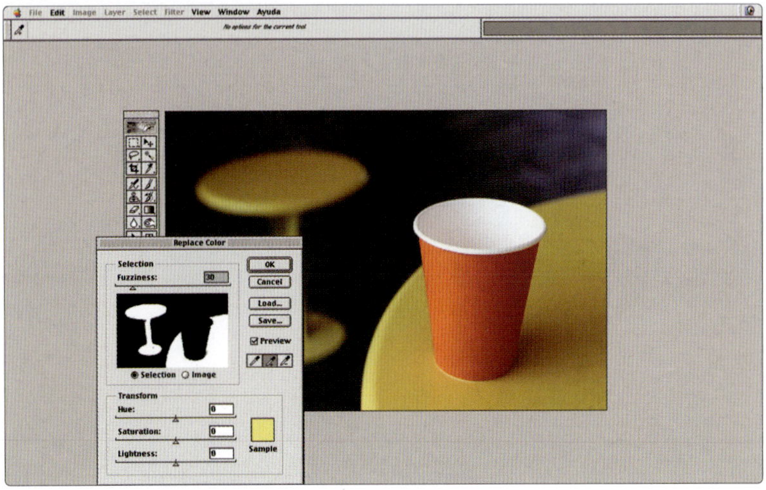

▸ 3 A dialogue appears that allows you to select the color that you want to change. In this case we used the cursor and a left click of the mouse to select the yellow color of the table.

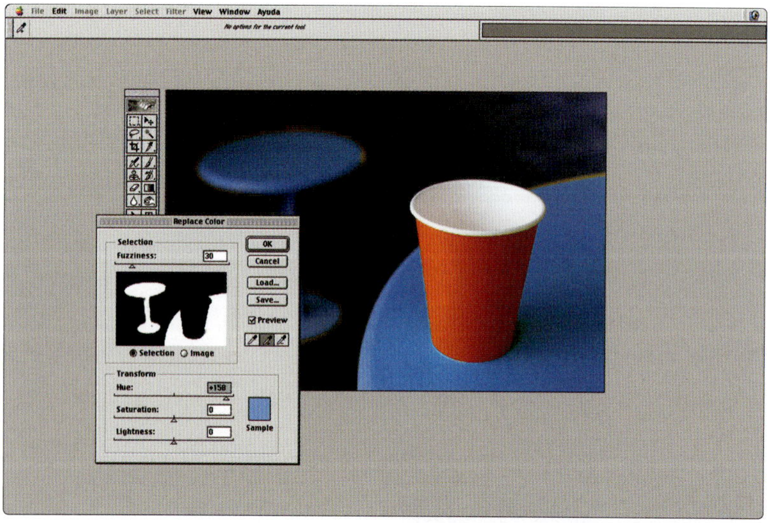

4 In the pallette, change the selected color by changing the Hue, Saturation, and Lightness. In this case the yellow color of the table was changed to blue.

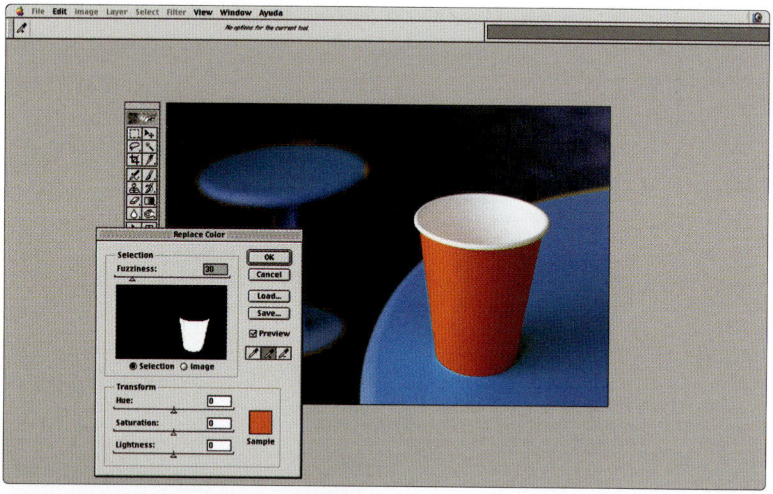

5 We used the same process to change the color of the cup.

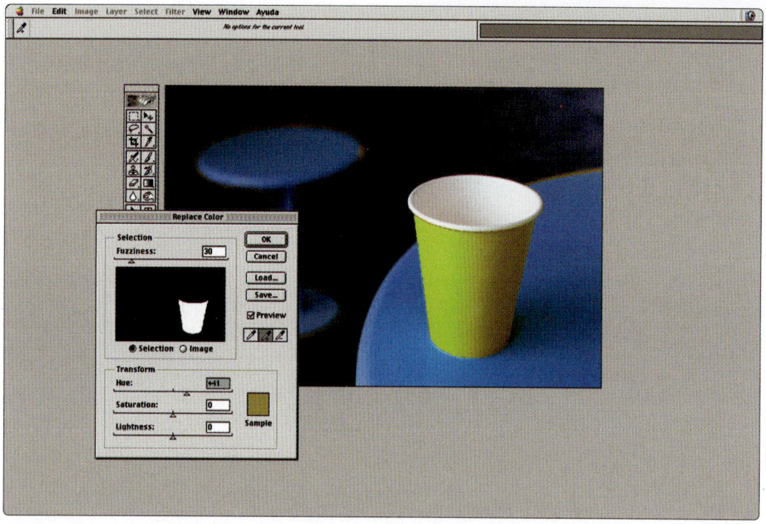

6 The change was recorded.

Notice that this is the same photograph, but the result is entirely different.

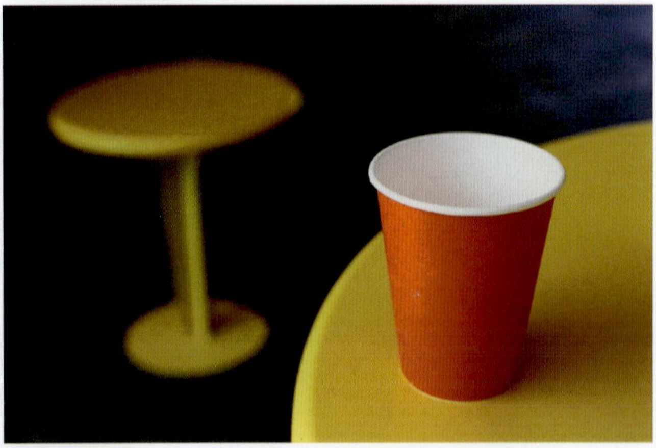

Original photograph

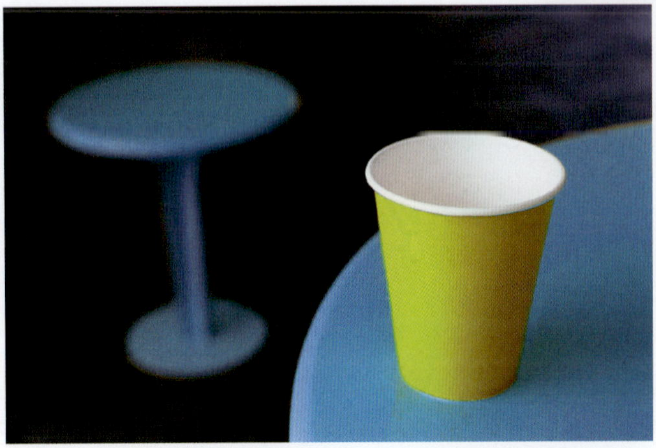

The photograph in changed colors

Choose the very best colors and make sure they really go well together.

Composite imaging

One of the great virtues of digital editing is the possibility of combining multiple photographs together.

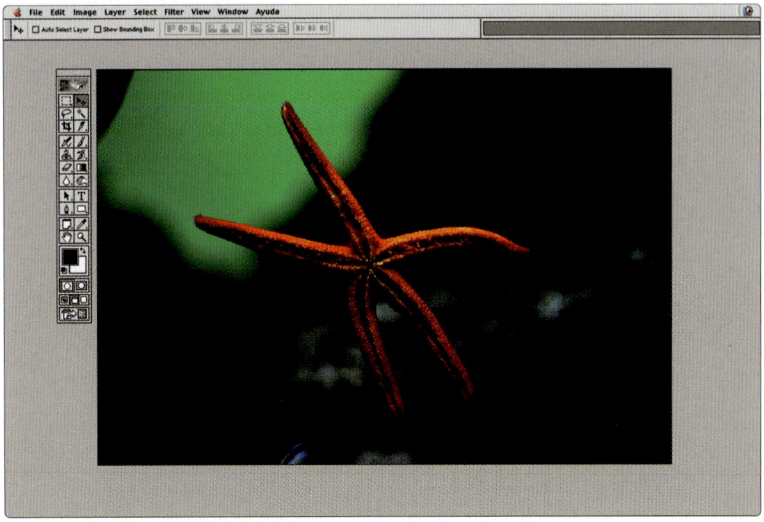

1 Open the file with the first picture in the image editing program.

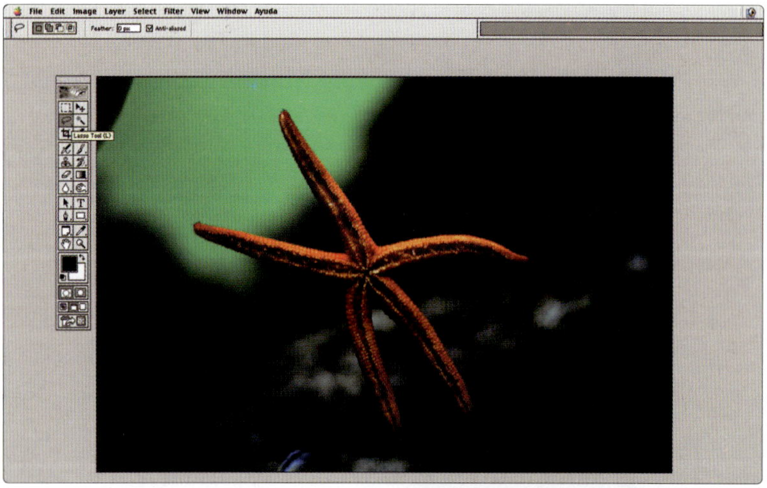

It's important to demarcate selected subjects well in order to facilitate their selection.

2 Select the Lasso from the Toolbox.

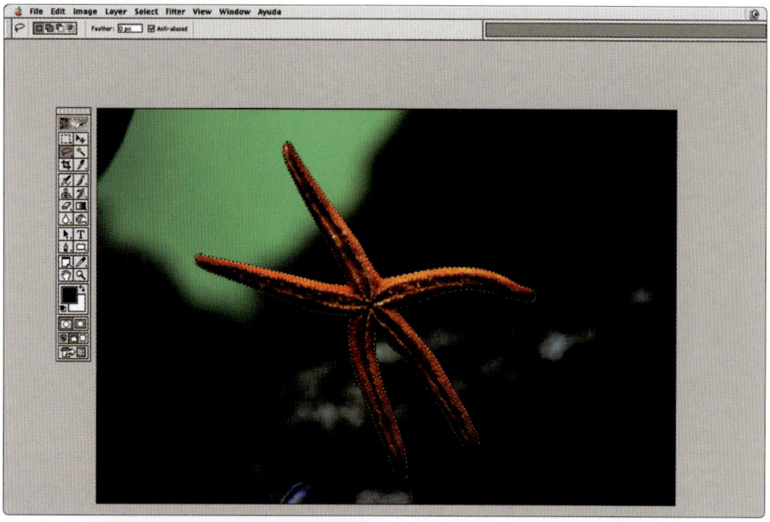

3 Carefully trace the entire starfish.

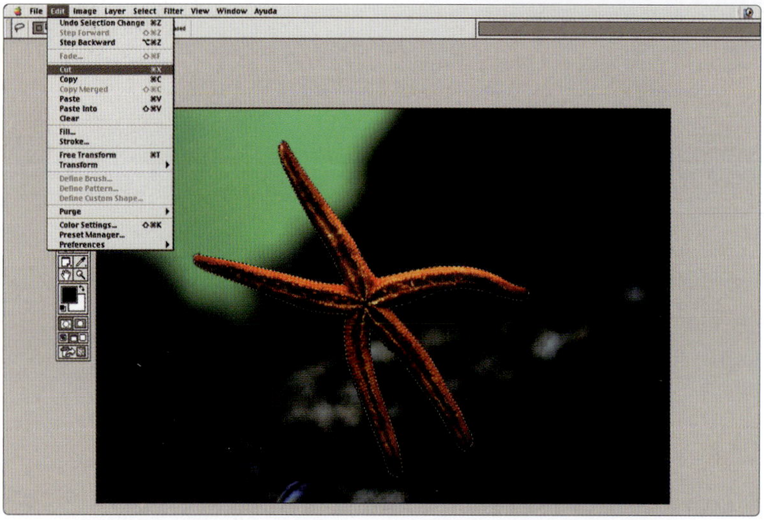

4 Pull down the Edit menu and click on Cut.

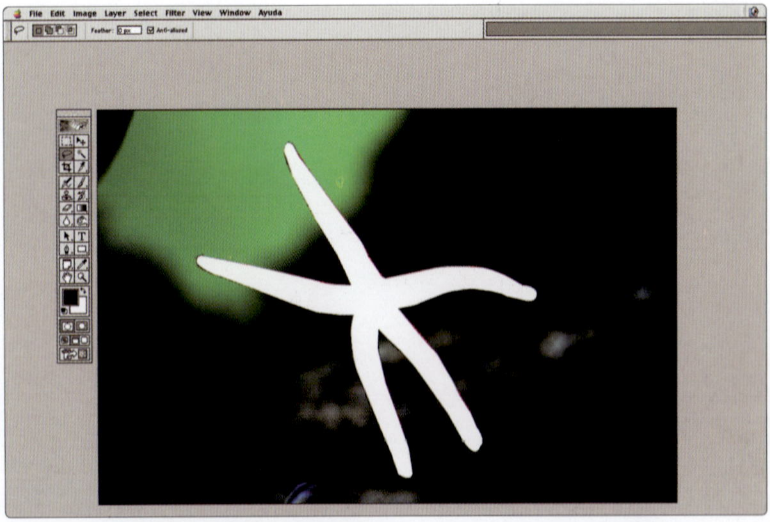

▸ **5** The subject disappears, but it remains saved in the computer's memory so that it can be pasted in somewhere else at any time.

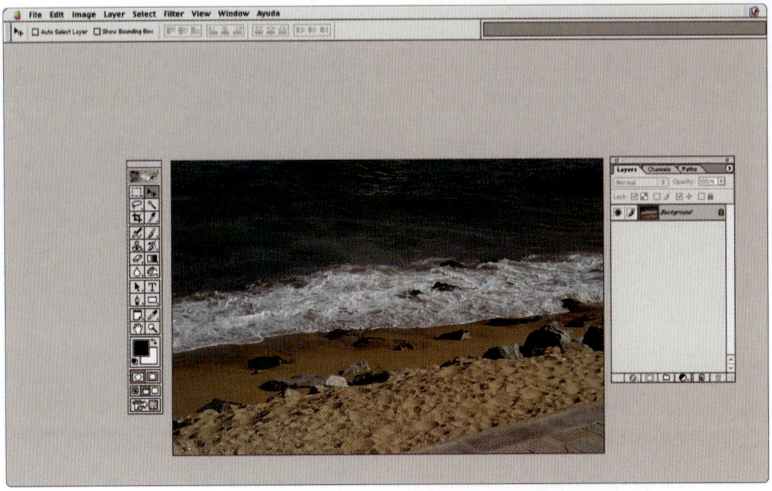

◂ **6** Now open the other photograph in the image editing program.

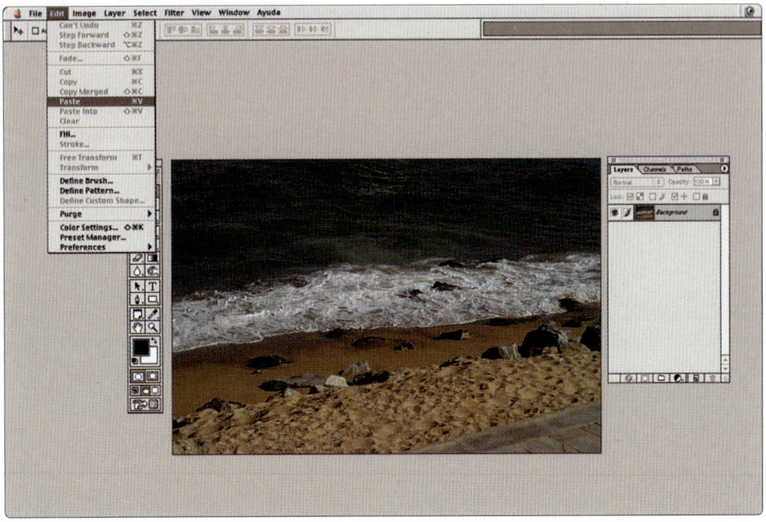

▸ **7** Pull down the Edit menu and click on Paste.

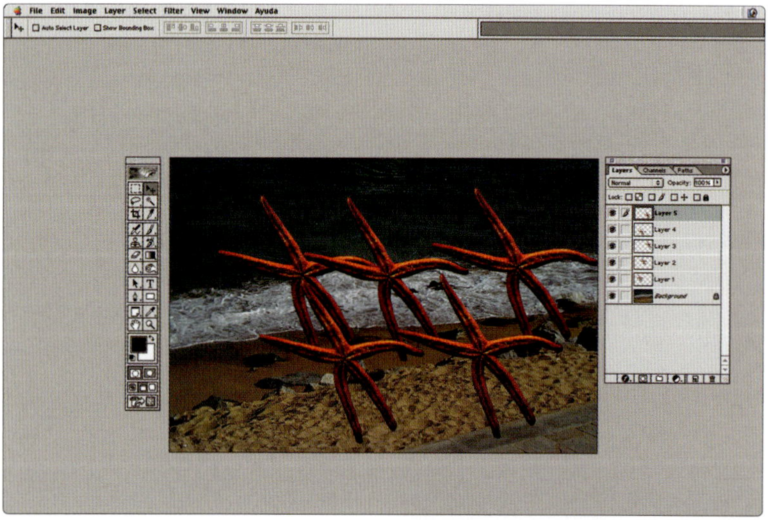

8 You can repeat the Paste operation until you have the number of starfish that you want in the picture. The editing program will create a new layer for each pasted starfish.

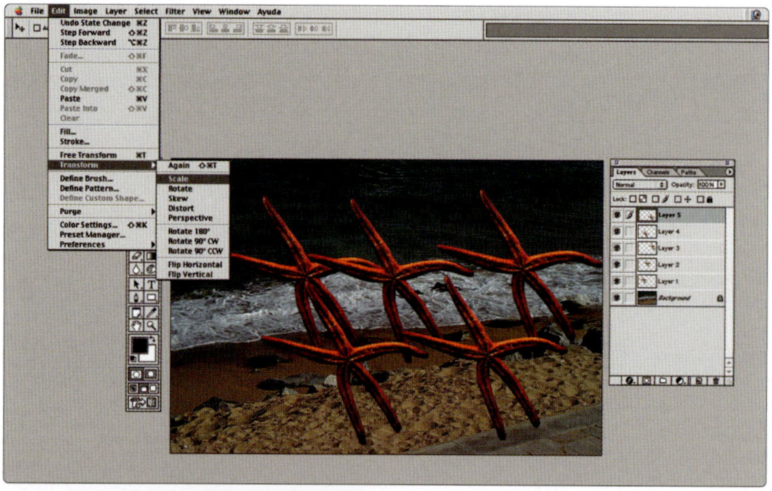

9 In the first picture the starfish covered nearly all of the surface. So for the intended use in the second picture it is necessary to reduce its size. Pull down the Edit menu, select Transform, and click on Scale. Repeat this operation for each starfish or copy thereof.

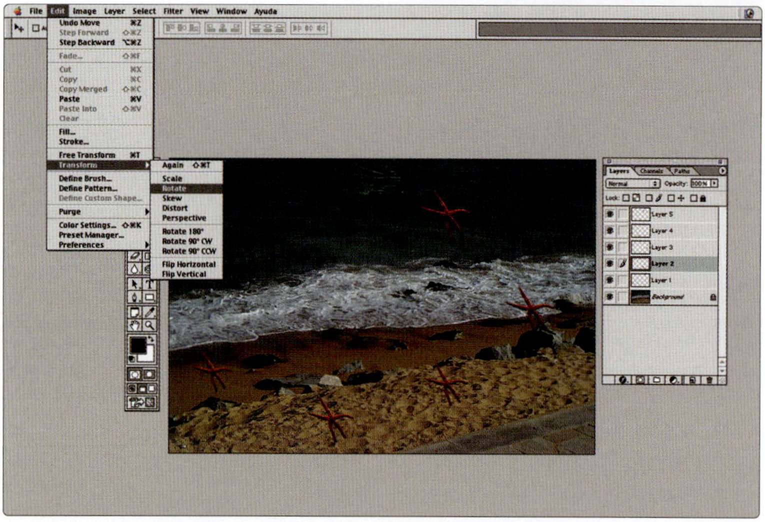

10 In order for all the starfish to not be aligned in the same direction, you can rotate or slant some of them. Just pull down the Edit menu, select Transform, and click on Rotate.

▸ **11** Place the starfish along the beach using the Shift tool from the Toolbox. If you want, you can also do a few retouches with the Clone Stamp as we did here on the starfish that touches the water. When you are moving multiple copied subjects around in the Layers dialogue box, you have to make sure that you have correctly selected the one you want to relocate.

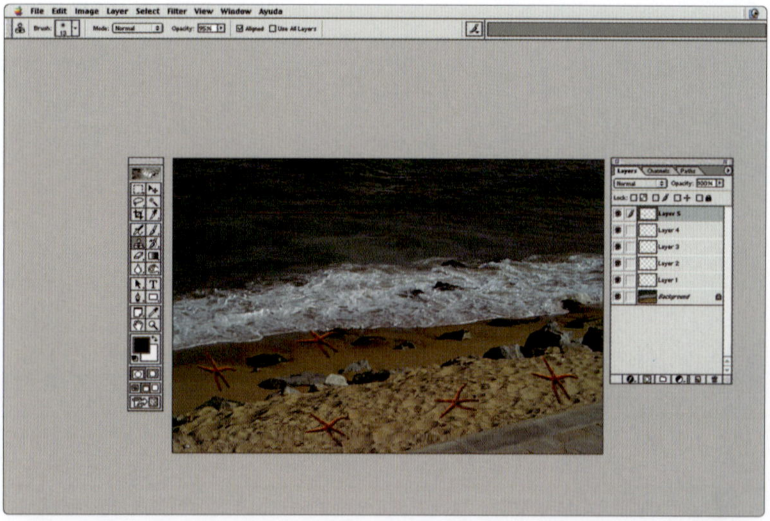

▸ **12** When all the starfish are finally in the right places you have to put them all together by using the Flatten Image command in the Layer menu.

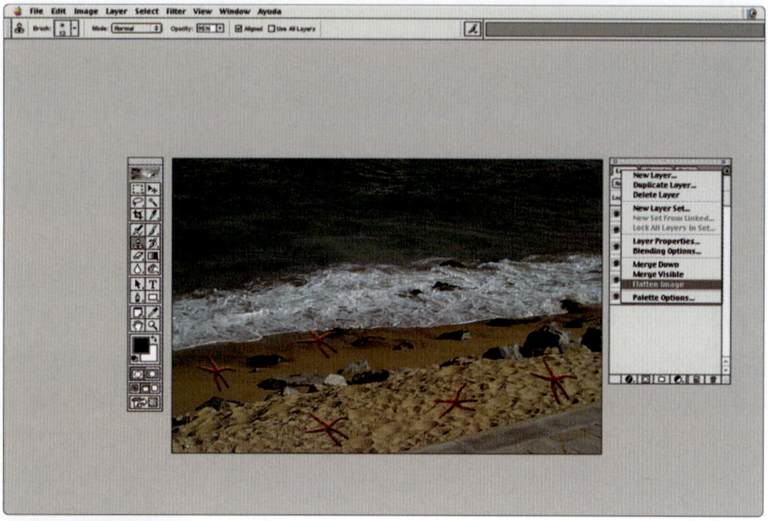

This is a simple example of combining two photographs.

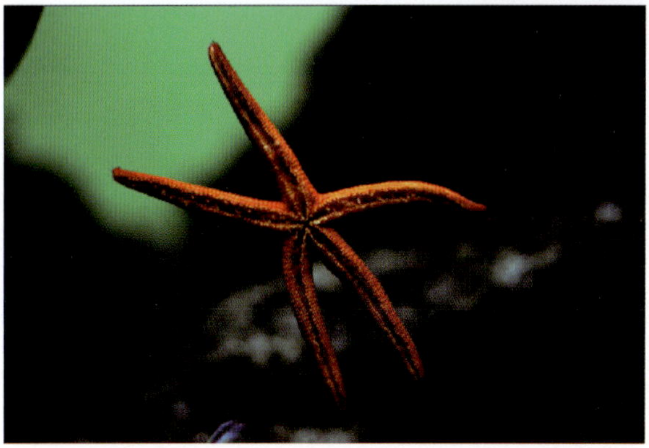

◂ First picture

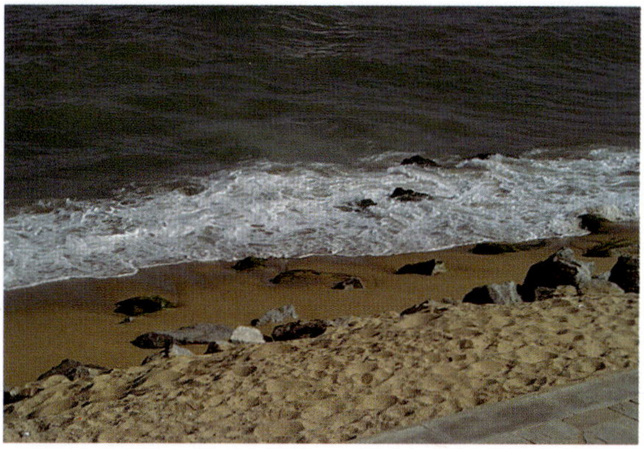

▸ Second photograph

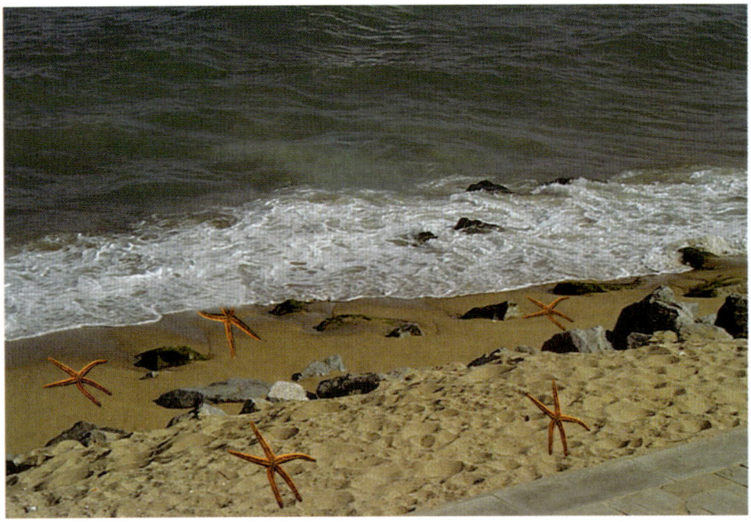

Modified photograph

Important!
Don't combine pictures until you've made sure that all the elements are in their intended places.

Retouching pictures

It often happens that in a photographed scene or landscape there are elements that are disruptive. There is a solution for such cases:

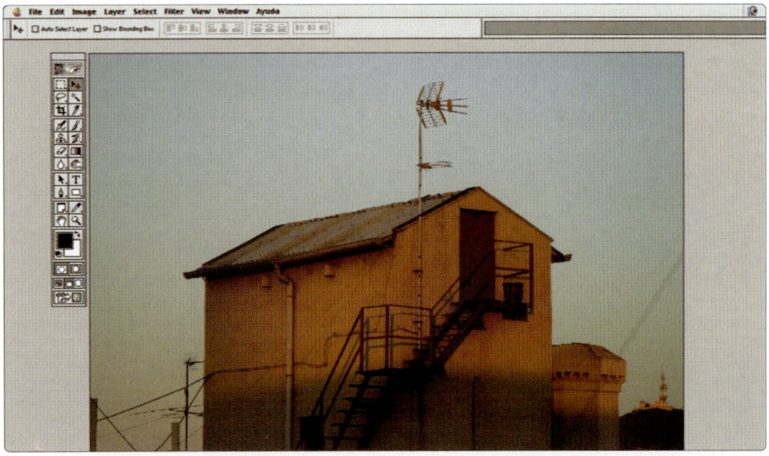

1 Open the file with the photograph in the image editing program.

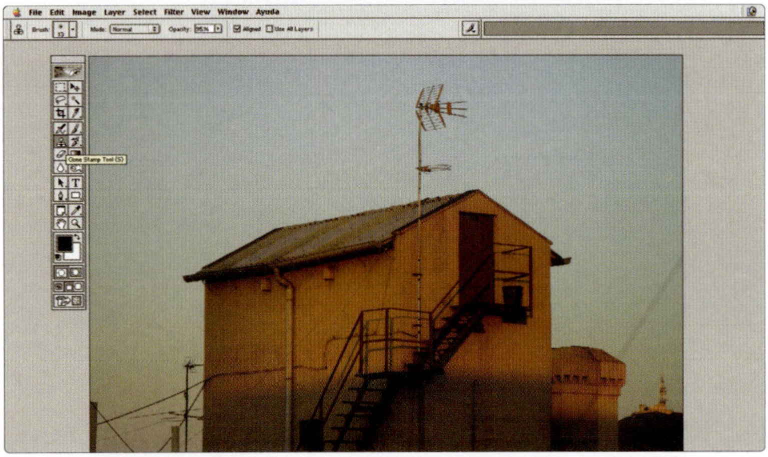

2 Select the Clone Stamp from the Toolbox.

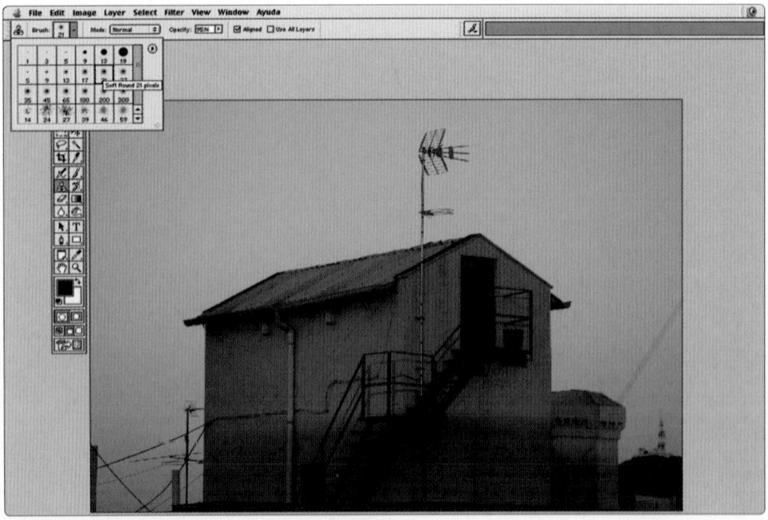

▸ **3** We'll start by retouching the upper part of the antenna. Because you don't want to deal with details, use a soft round brush.

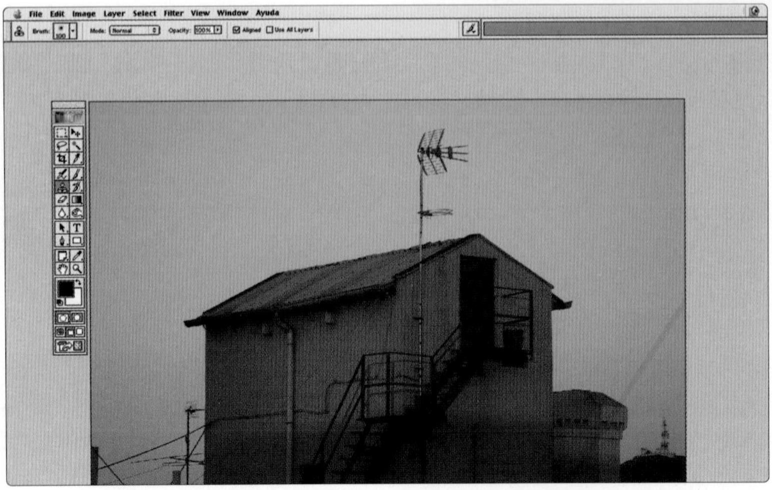

◂ **4** Use the stamp to mark (Alt + left mouse button) the part of the sky closest to the antennas as the source area that you want to remove.

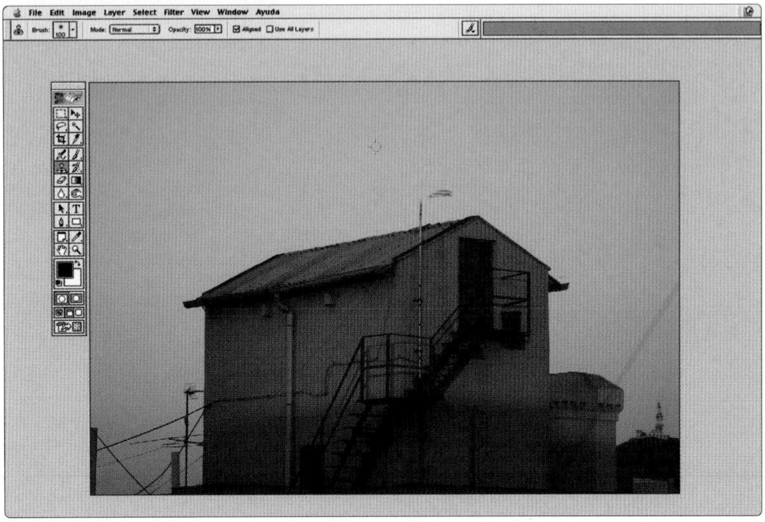

▸ **5** Go across the antenna that should be removed with the stamp of the cursor.

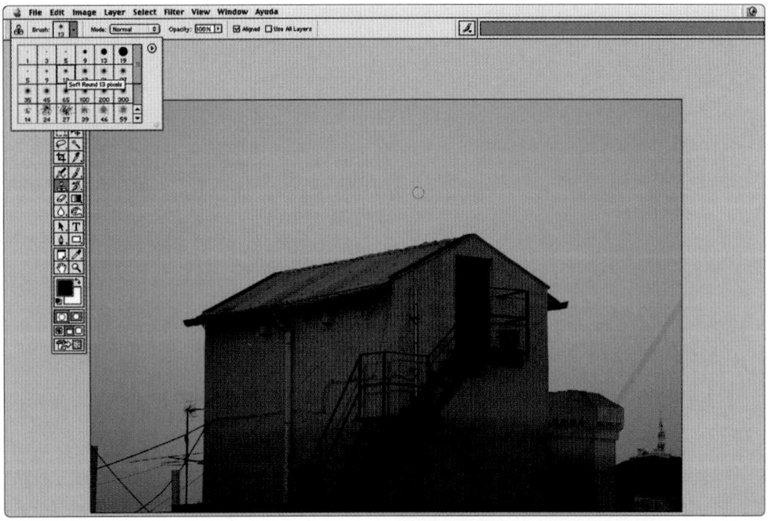

6 Select the finest brush for retouching the lower part of the antenna. Essentially, you must remove a few small elements.

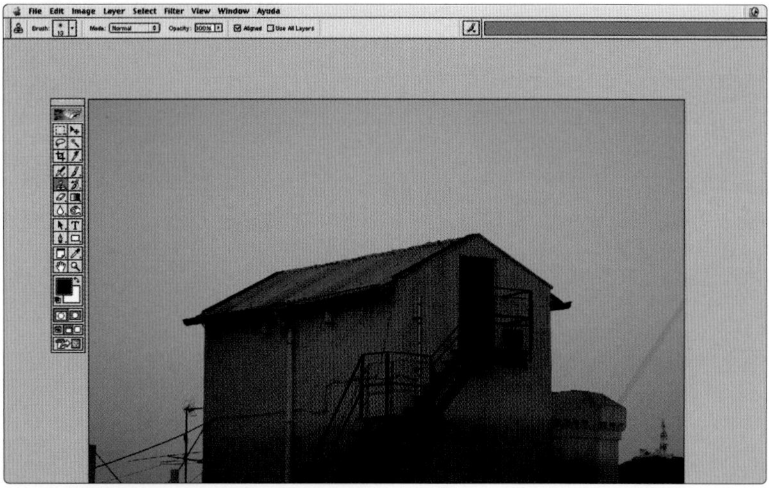

7 In the same way, carefully transfer the parts of the roof and wall that you want to use in the places that need retouching.

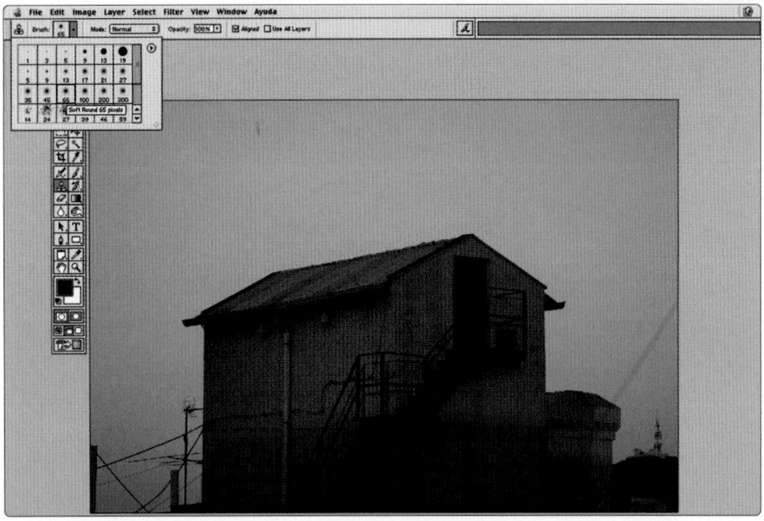

8 Again select a wide brush to remove the electrical wires in the background of the picture.

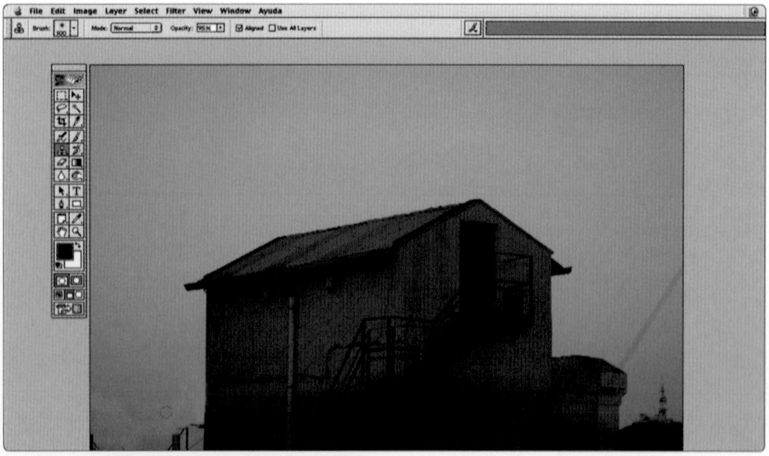

9 Mark the part of the sky closest to the electrical wires as the source area and then use it to erase the wires.

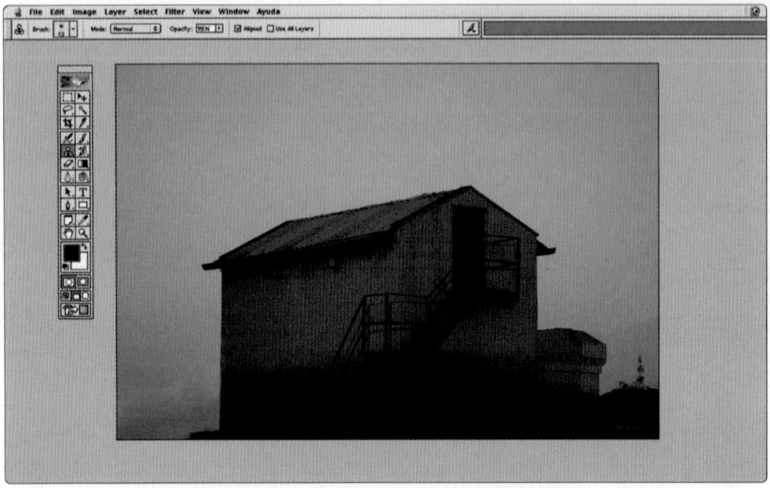

10 Carefully touch out the shadow to the right of the stairs, the bucket on the top landing, and the downspout in the left part of the picture.

After its retouching the picture is much more effective. The electrical wires, the antenna, and the other elements cluttered up the picture.

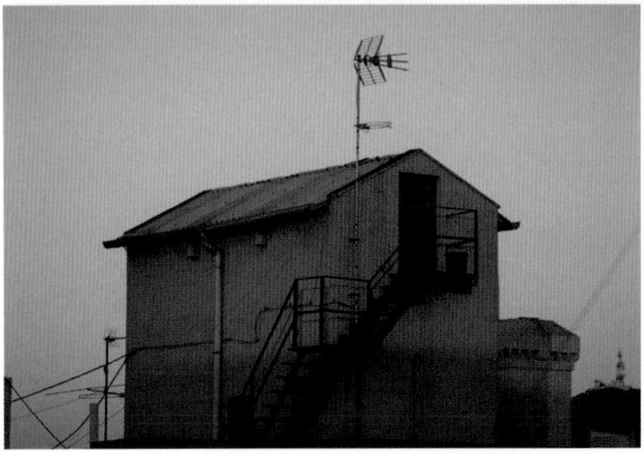

Original photograph

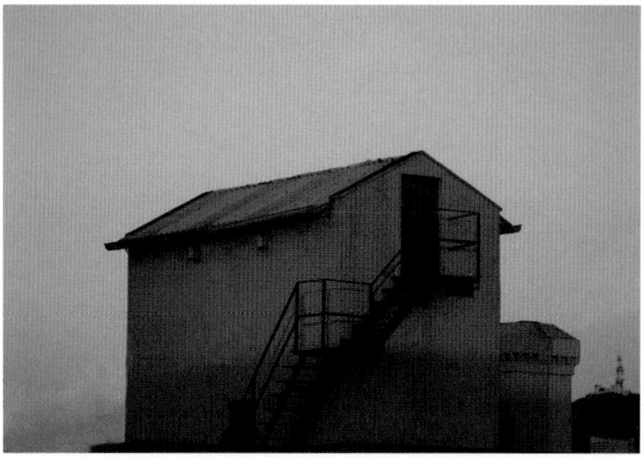

Retouched photograph

Distortions

Image editing programs offer ever more effective tools that allow you to create effects that are sometimes startling.
Here are a few humorous modifications of a portrait:

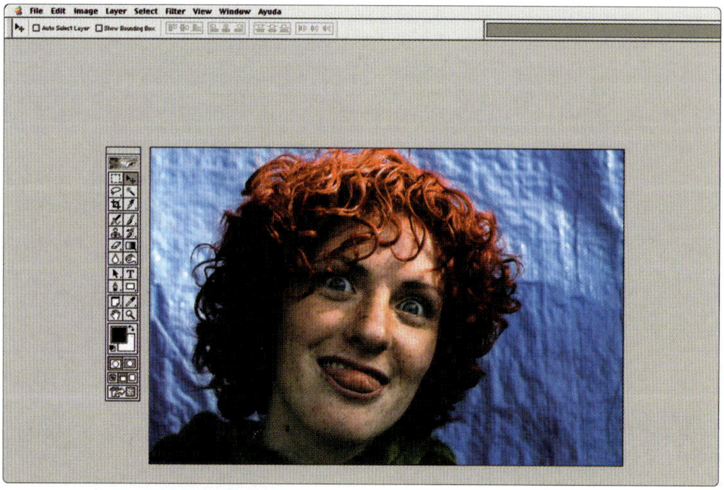

1 Open the picture in the image editing program.

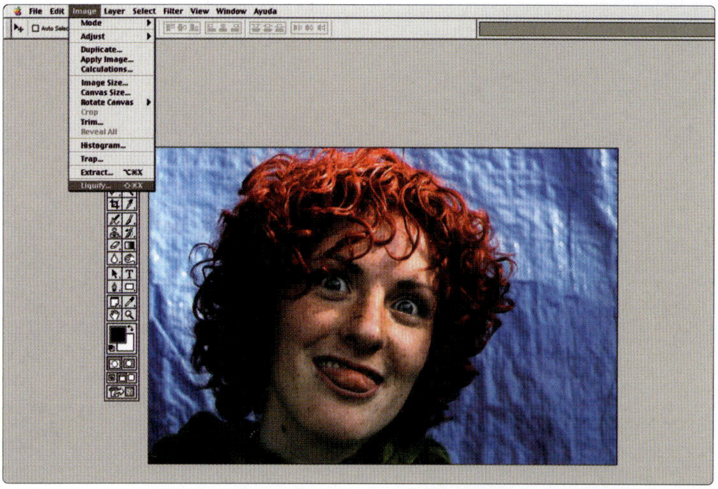

2 Pull down the Filter menu and click on Liquify.

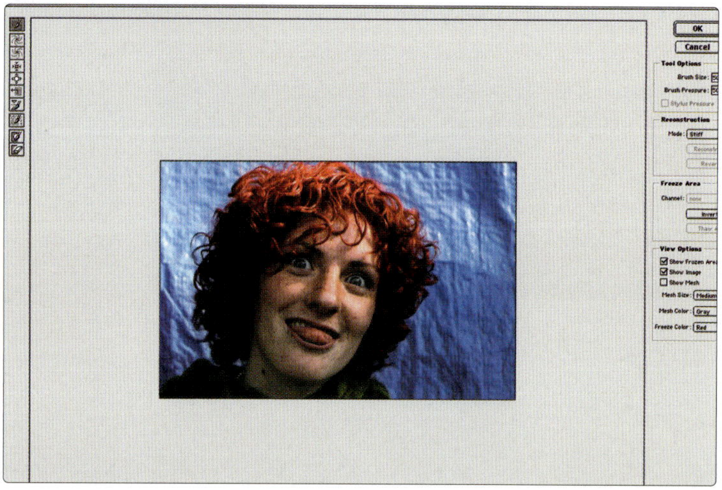

3 The image will appear in a new window with a new list of tools.

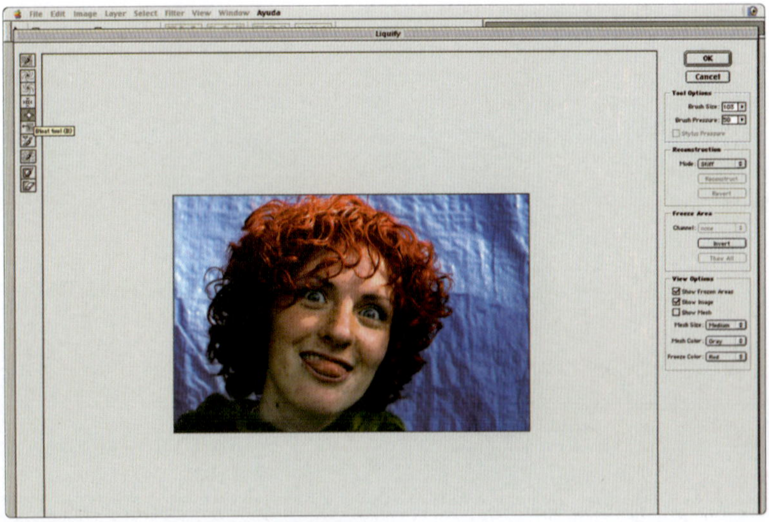

4 From this new list of tools (on the left side of the screen), select the Bloat tool.

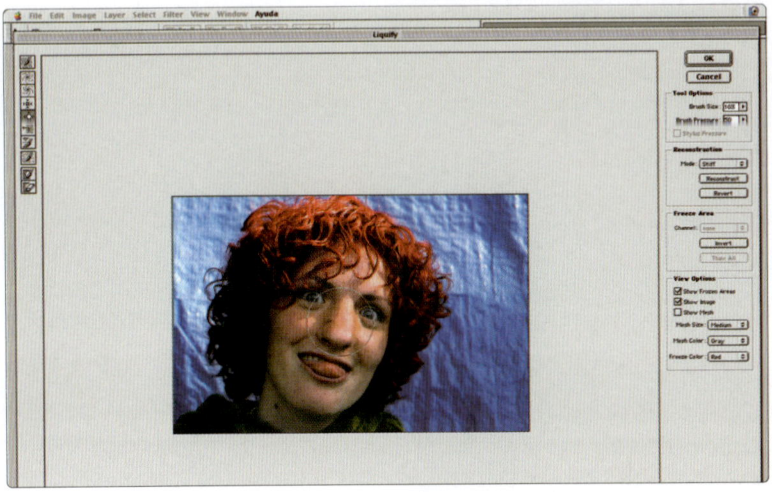

5 After you choose this tool move it onto the girl's nose and click it until you get the desired effect.

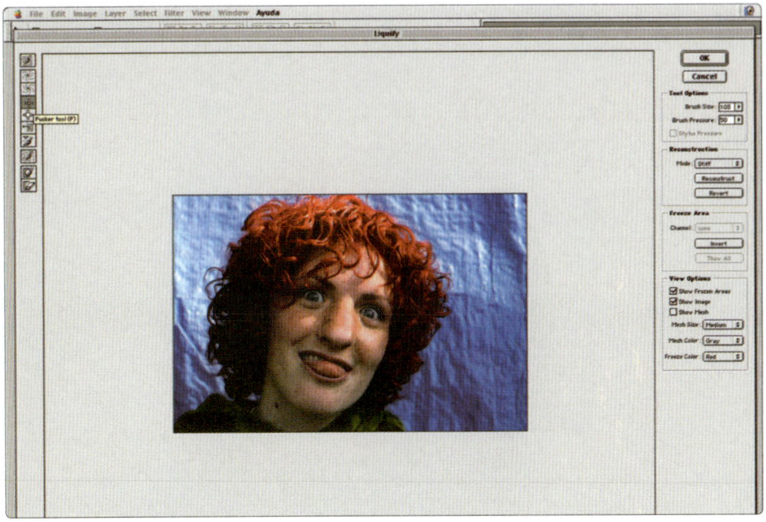

6 Now select the Pucker tool.

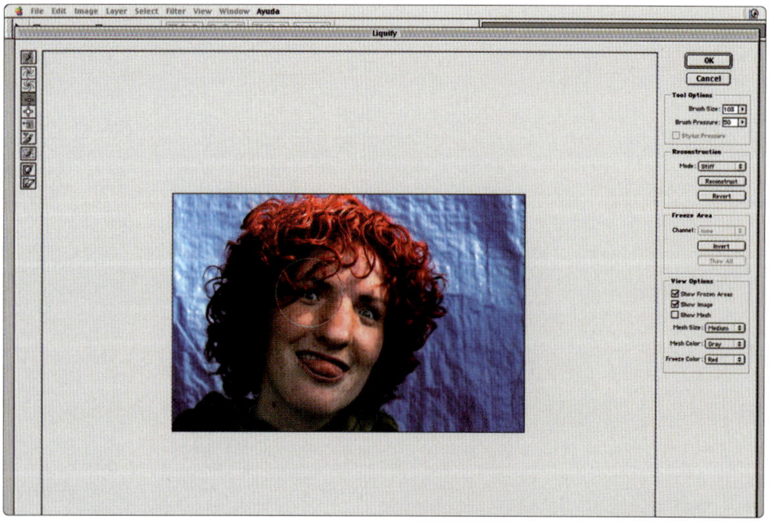

7 Use it on her eyes.

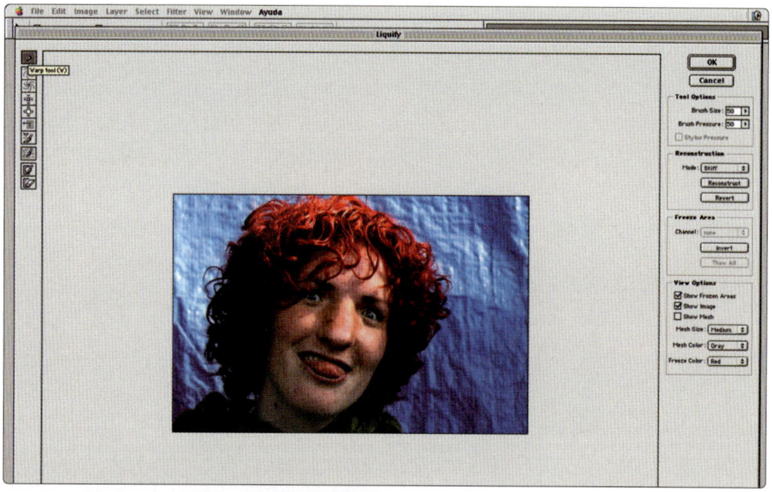

8 Select the Warp tool.

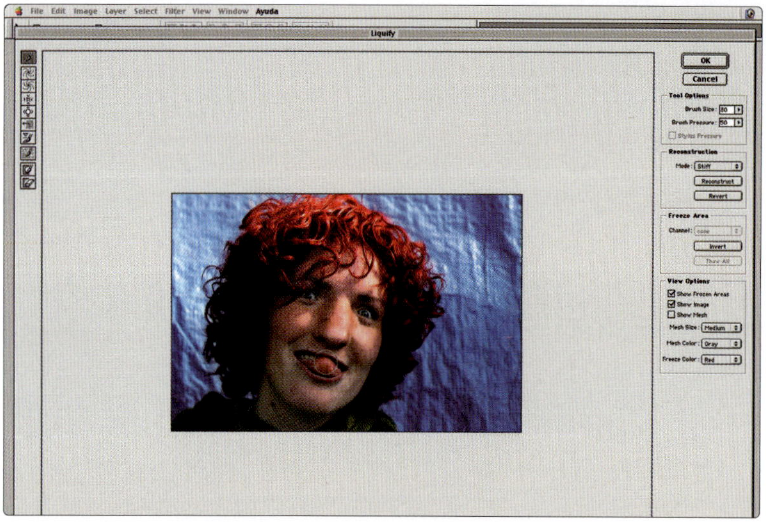

9 Use it on her mouth and click until you get the desired effect.

The results are definitely surprising. If you get really good at using these tools you'll be able to use them on all your pictures and on any photographed subject.

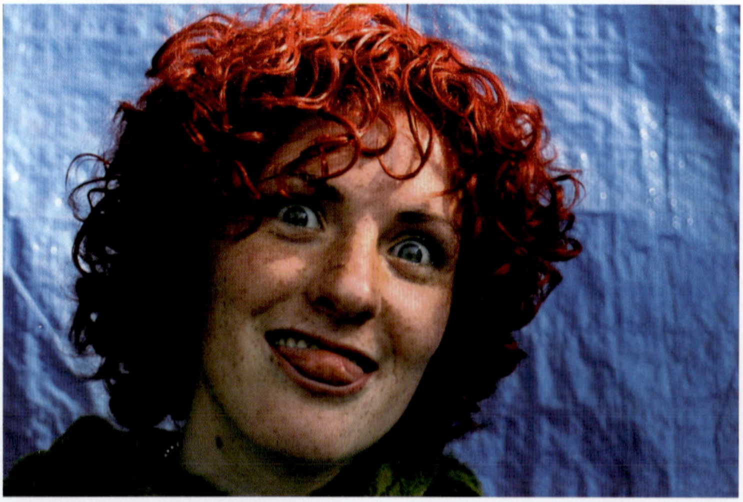

Original photograph

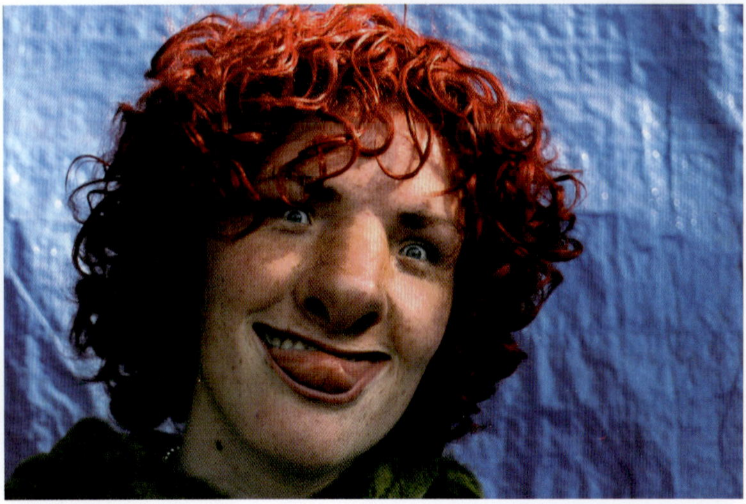

Distorted photograph

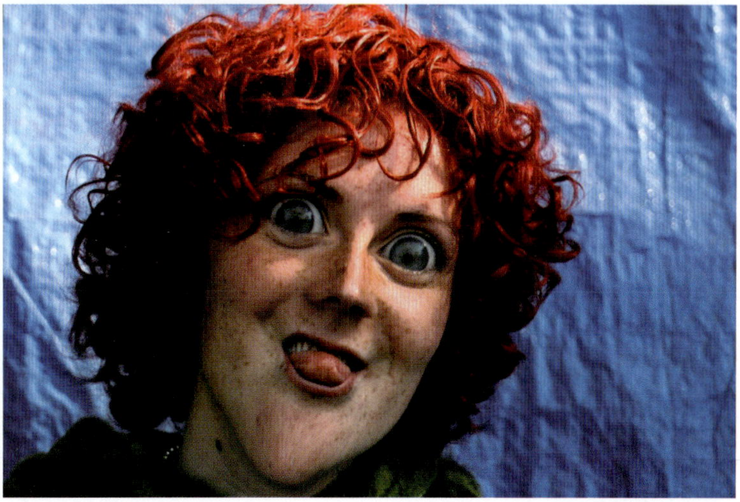

The photograph, distorted by operations that are the reverse of the operations used on the preceding example; the eyes are "bloated" and the nose and mouth are narrowed.

TOPIC 4 HOW TO ARCHIVE DIGITAL PHOTOGRAPHS

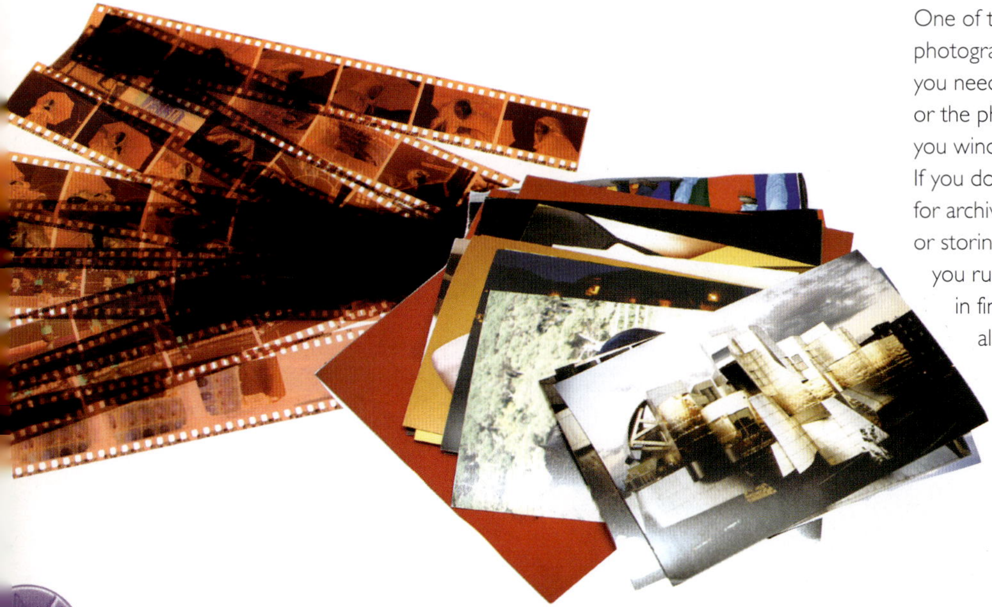

One of the great drawbacks of classic photography is that as a photographer you need space to store negatives, slides, or the photographs themselves. Usually you wind up with a jumble of pictures. If you don't have the time and patience for archiving or sorting your pictures, or storing them under suitable conditions, you run the risk of problems later in finding negatives; they are often all mixed up, or even damaged.

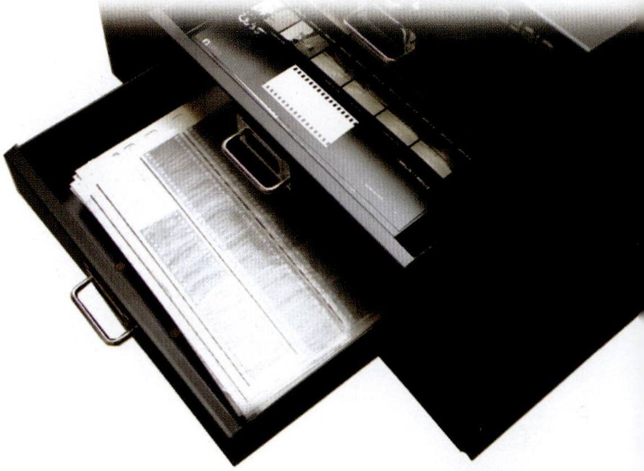

Besides the time factor you also have to keep in mind the amount of space you need for well organized documents. If you take pictures regularly you'll soon find that you need huge amounts of space, even if you don't have it at your disposal...

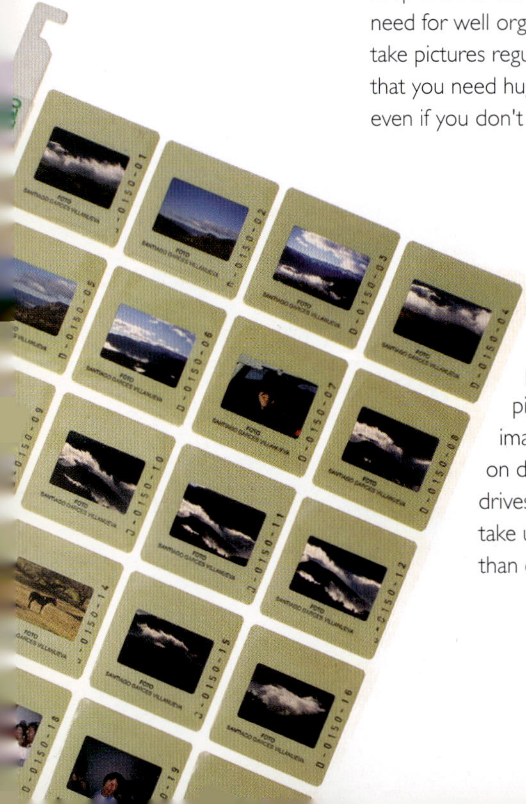

...and you won't need it for digital photographs, even if you take pictures constantly! Digital images are stored and preserved on data carriers such as hard drives, CDs, or DVDs, so they take up incomparably less space than classic photographs.

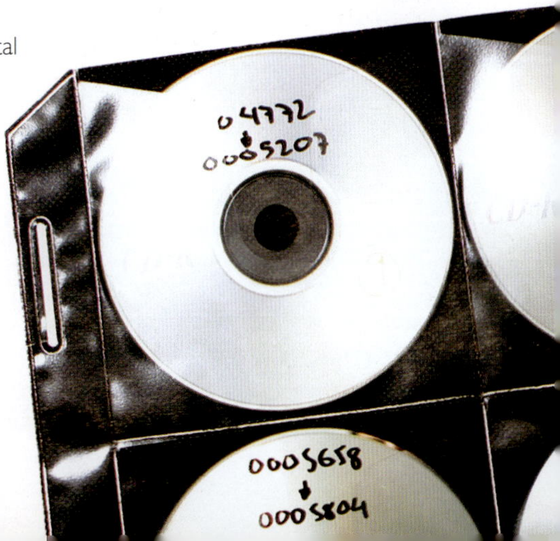

There are currently a great many programs that guarantee fast, simple, and effective sorting and management of digital pictures. You always have an ideal overview of your pictures, the dates they were taken, and the properties of the files that make them up.

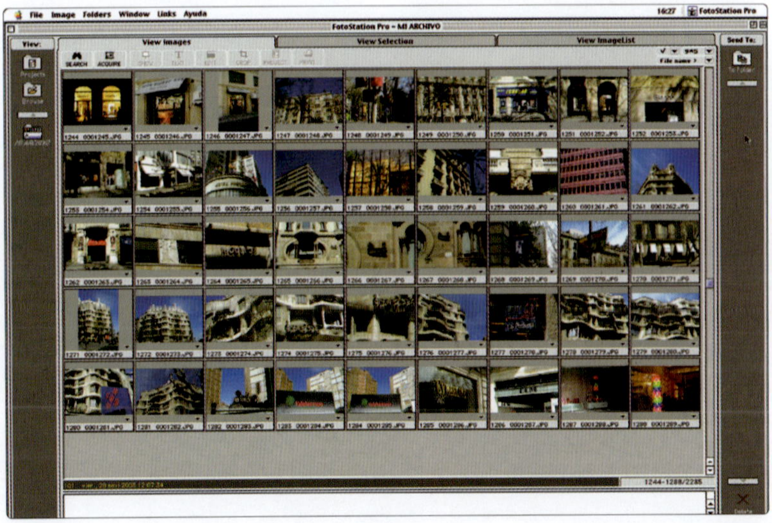

In this chapter you will learn how to create a digital album that is suitable for sorting and effectively storing photographs. You will also learn how to share images over the Internet by using services offered by several large websites.

PROGRAMS FOR MANAGING PHOTOGRAPHS

First let's look at how to create a new album for archiving digital photographs. "Photostation" was specially created for archiving and managing digital images, but there are also lots of other high-quality programs, e.g., Zoner Media Explorer. Also, many digital cameras are sold with their own software for managing images which meet at least the minimal requirements for effective sorting. See for yourself whether your program offers the functions used in the following exercise:

▼ 1 Open the image management program in your computer.

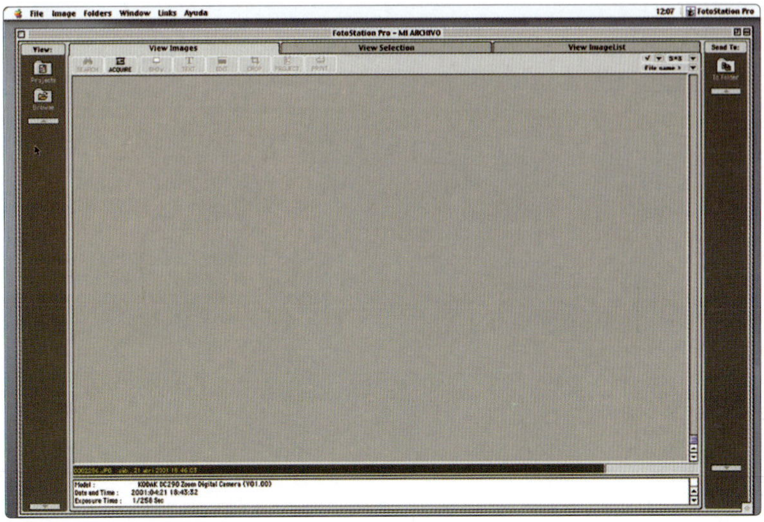

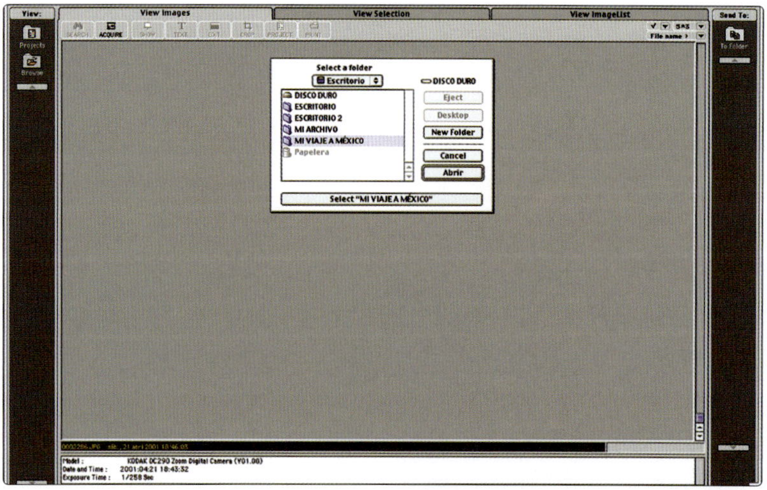

2 After you've opened the program, select the folder that contains the pictures you want to archive. In our case we selected Mexico.

3 Notice the pictures were stored in the original folder, the additional information is on the left end of the bottom strip, and the numbers are automatically attached to each picture as they are taken.

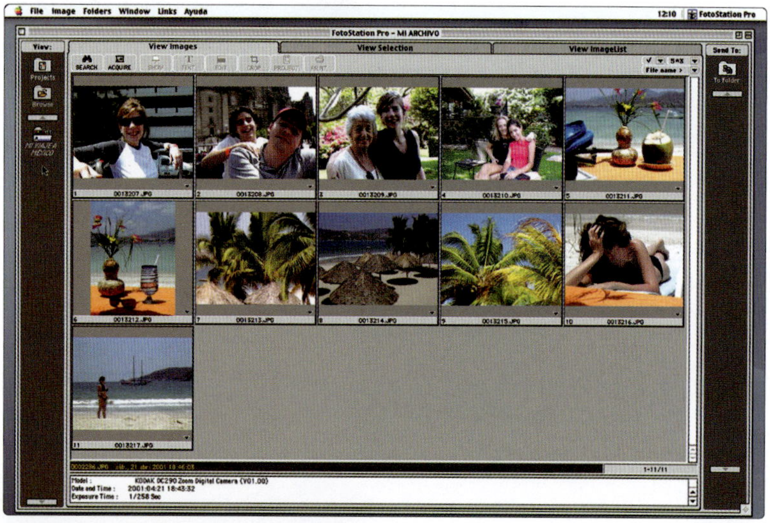

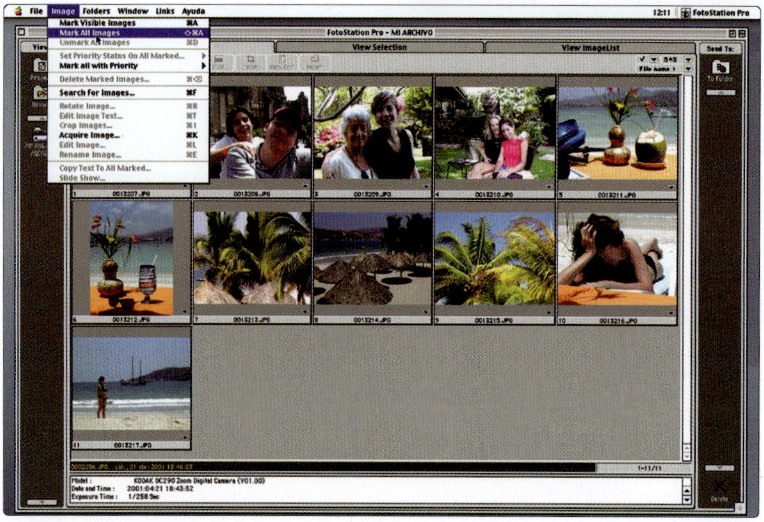

4 You can renumber the pictures according to a special sequence to facilitate future searches. For this purpose pull down the Image menu and select Mark All Images.

5 The arranged pictures appear.

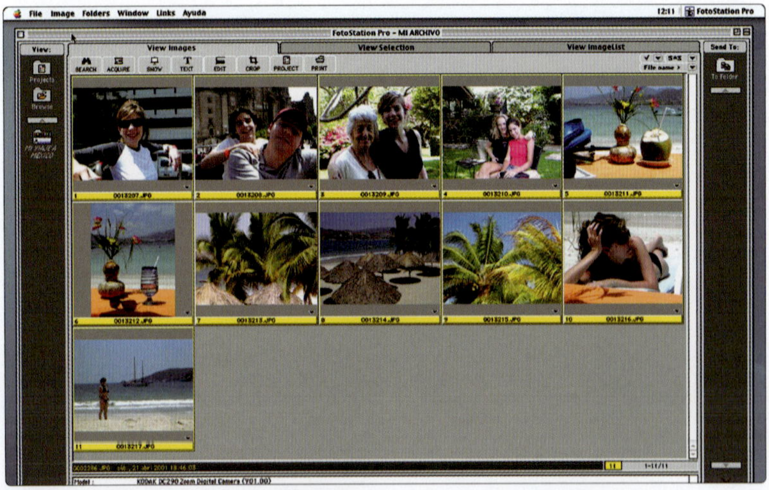

6 In order to rename them, pull down the Image menu and click on Rename Image. Select all the pictures that you want to archive.

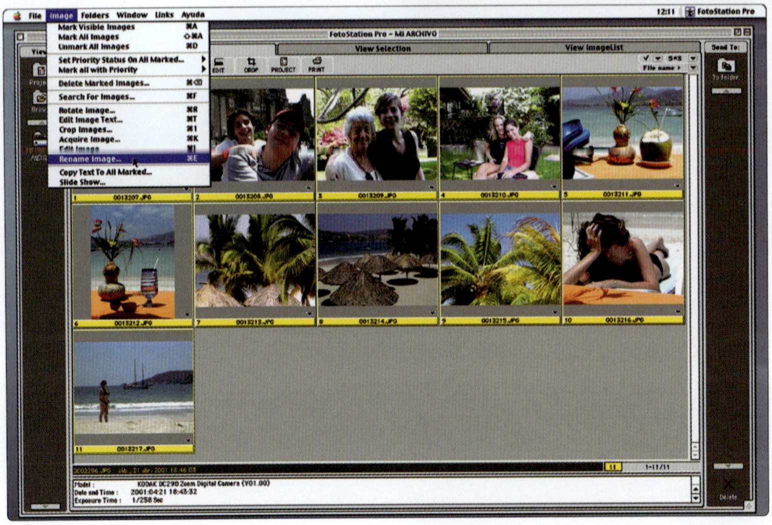

7 The Rename window opens. Enter the number from which you want to start numbering. In the program you must activate the option that allows you to attach a new number to each renumbered picture. We chose to start with 0002287, the last number in an already archived file. The three zeroes in the prefix guarantee that the the computer will always work with the same number of places so that the numbers won't get mixed as the archives grow. Confirm the numbering system you have set up by clicking on OK All.

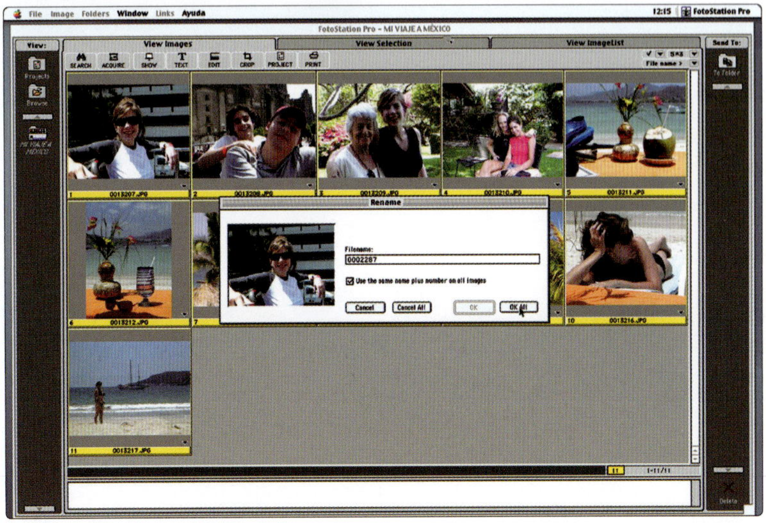

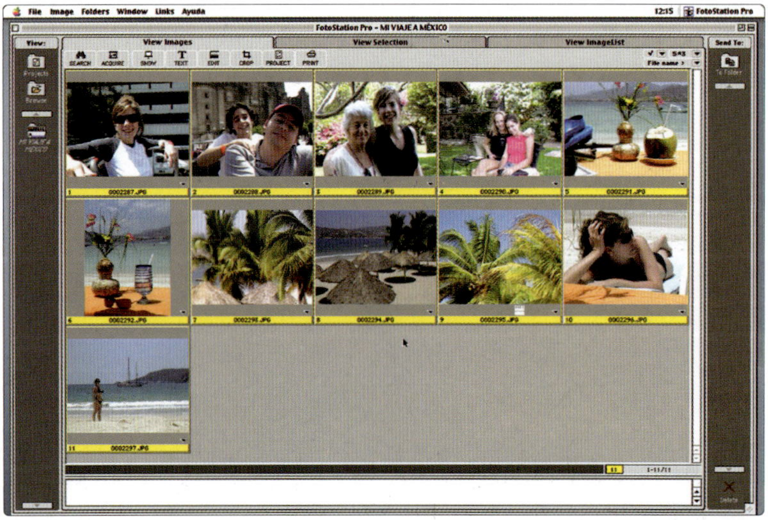

8 For further use, all of the pictures are renumbered according to the desired archiving.

9 Now you just need to fill in the text field for sorting pictures taken on different occasions. When all of the images have been selected, pull down the Image menu and go to Copy Text to All Marked.

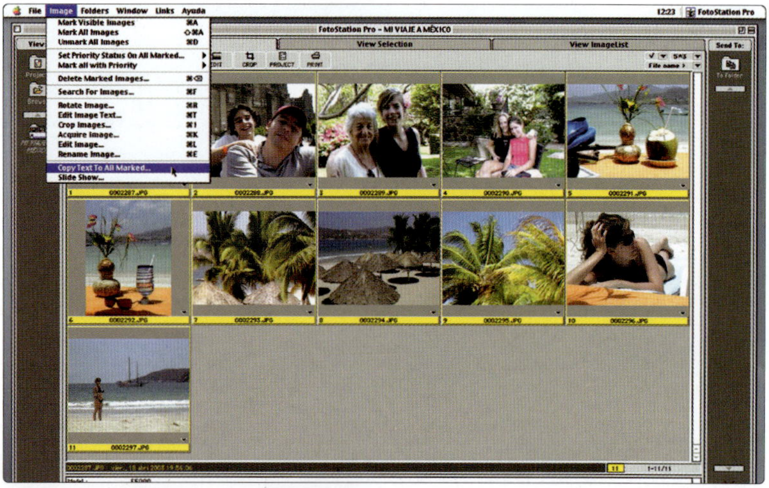

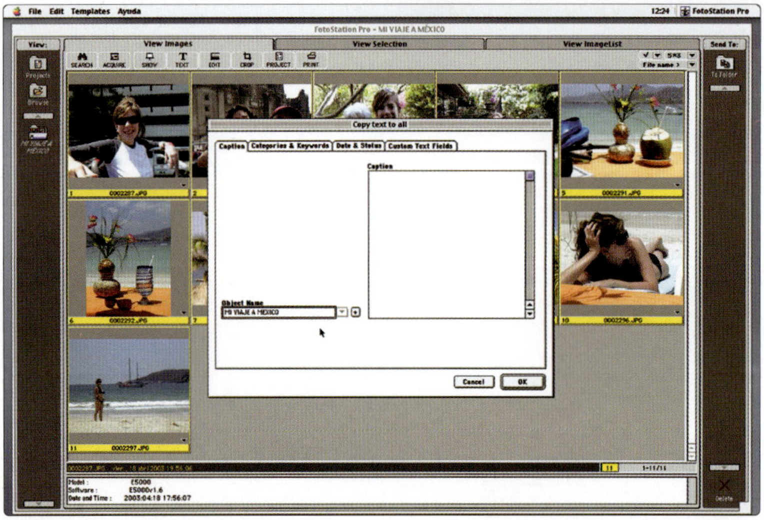

10 The Copy Text to All window will open. In the Object Name field enter the name that you want to give to all the images in this file – we used Mexico.

11 To make sure that it has been done properly, select any image in the file and click on Caption. The appropriate name appears. So far only the first level of sorting has been created, allowing you to find pictures from the Mexico series.

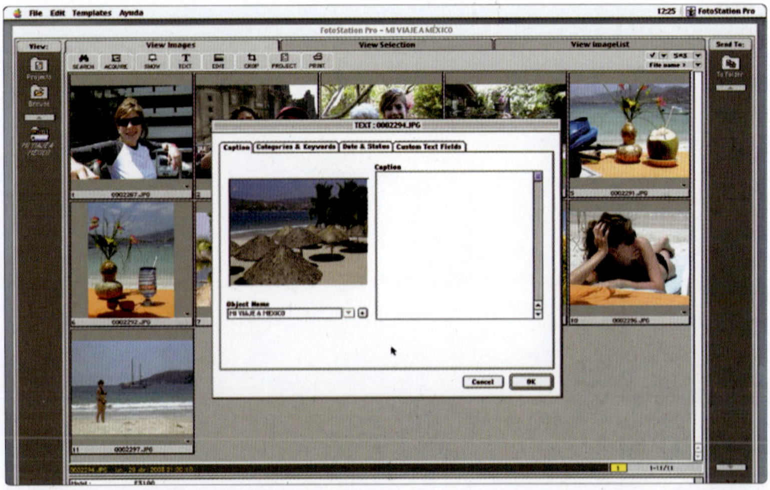

If you want to achieve more complete sorting and more detailed searching, it is possible to create a second level of sorting.

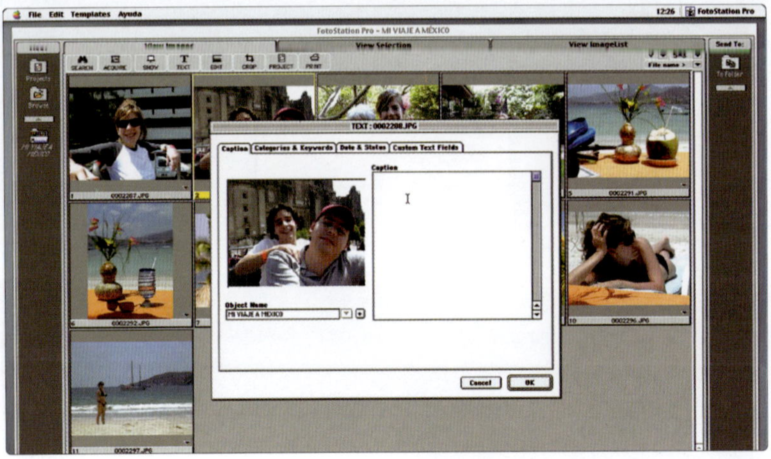

12 Select an image or group of images to which you want to add a name for the next level. Open the Caption window by clicking on the appropriate tab. Here the Object Name field is already filled in.

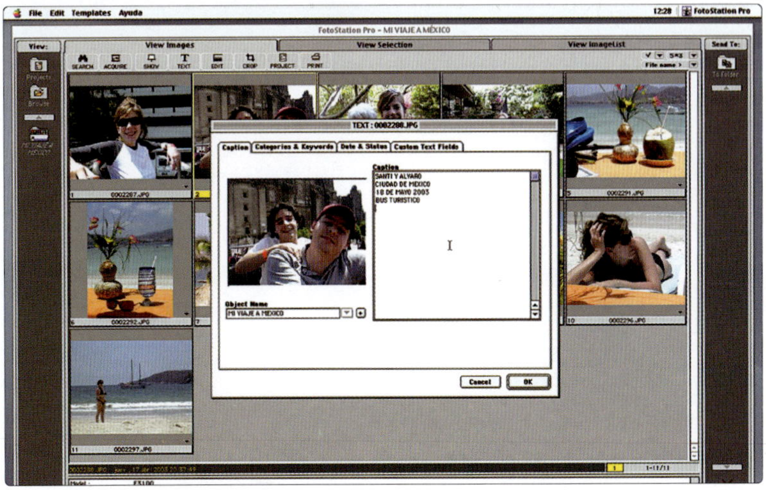

13 In the Caption field enter all the information you want to attach: date, name, place, and designate a key word for easy searching later on.

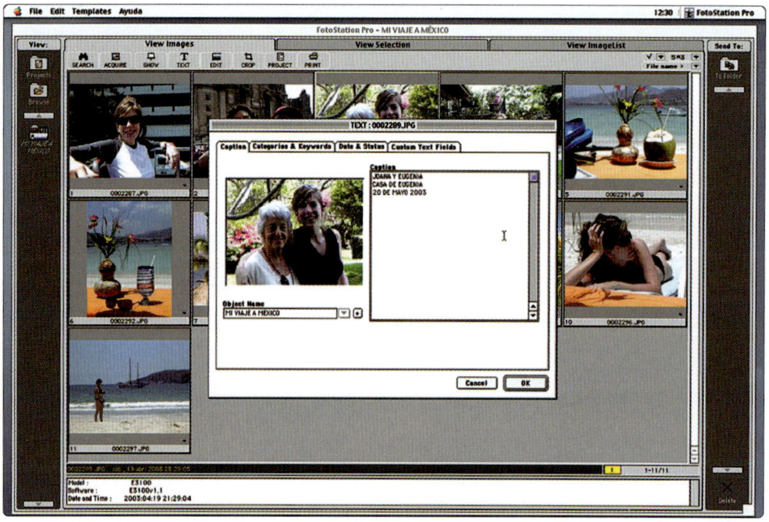

14 Continue by repeating the same operation for all the saved pictures.

Don't forget to designate the key word that will facilitate later searches. Archiving programs usually allow you to use any word you wish.

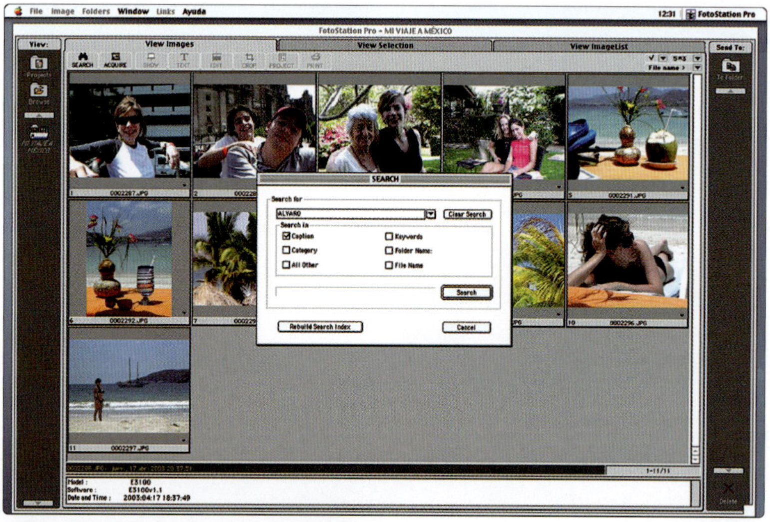

15 This way you can search for a photograph by using any word entered into the Caption field. To make sure it really works, go to Search and enter the term assigned to a picture. In our case we are searching by using the word Alvaro. Click on Search.

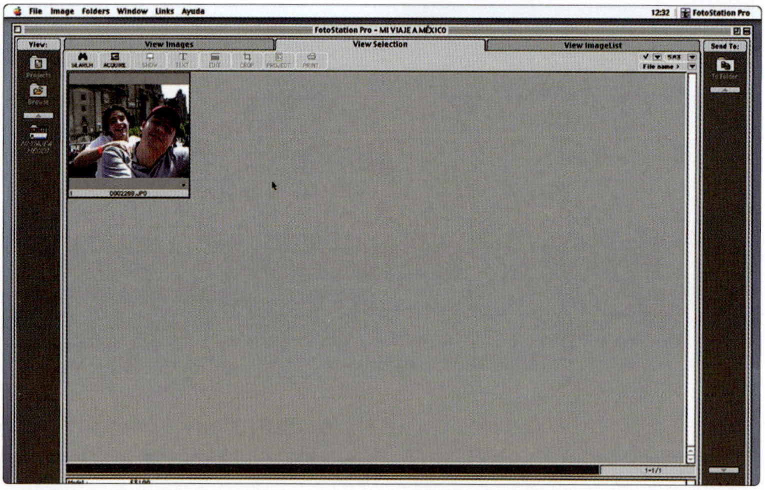

16 The search engine offers the one picture with the name Alvaro added to it.

▸ **17** When you have entered all the data in the file that contains the most recently taken pictures (in this case, Mexico), you can connect them to all the pictures you have taken in the past. Don't be afraid of their getting mixed up. They are as of now distinguished by their numbering (starting with 0002287), the name Mexico, and their captions (Alvaro, etc). To carry out this operation you have to open a file that contains all your earlier photographs. In the case of this program you have to click on the View Image List tab at the upper right of the screen. The Copy File window will open in which you select the object file.

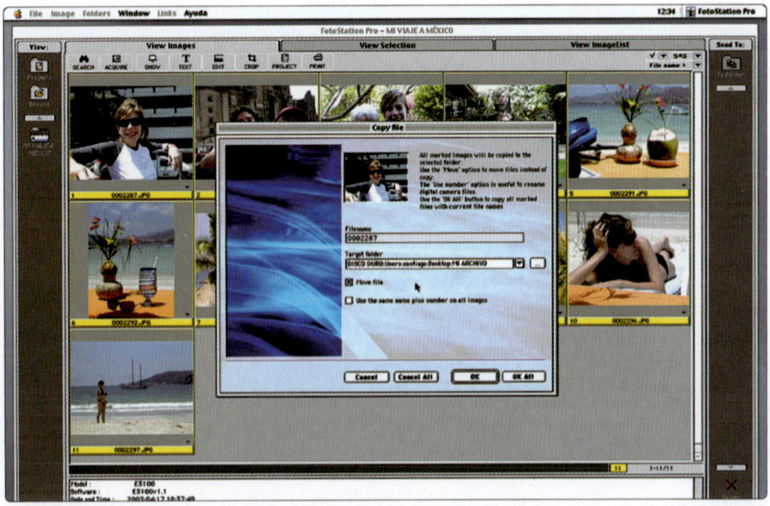

Here we selected the My Archive file, which contains all the pictures taken before those from Mexico. Before confirming with OK, you have to make sure that all the pictures from the Mexico file have really been selected.

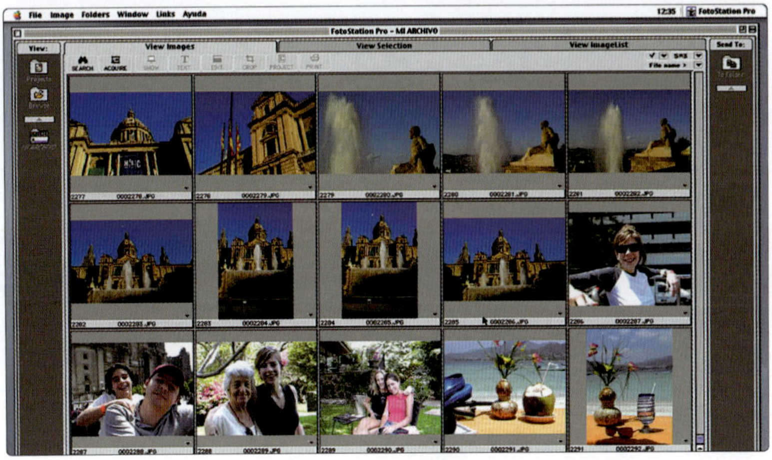

◂ **18** As you will notice after opening the file with the copied pictures – in this case My Archive – the newly included pictures appeared right after the previous ones thanks to the sequential numbering that we assigned.

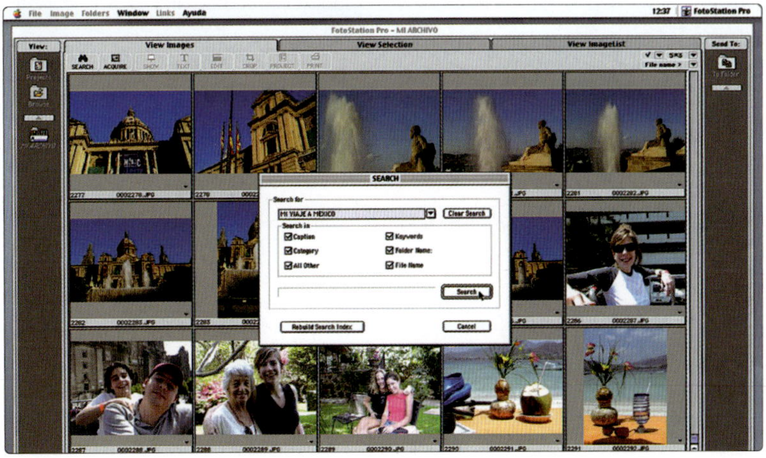

▸ **19** To search for these pictures all you need to do is use the Search option in the Mexico file.

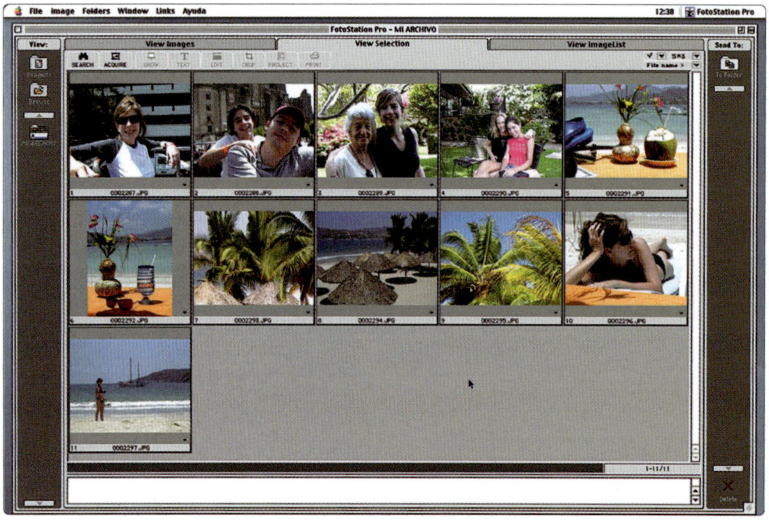

20 Note that the program searched only the photographs in this series.

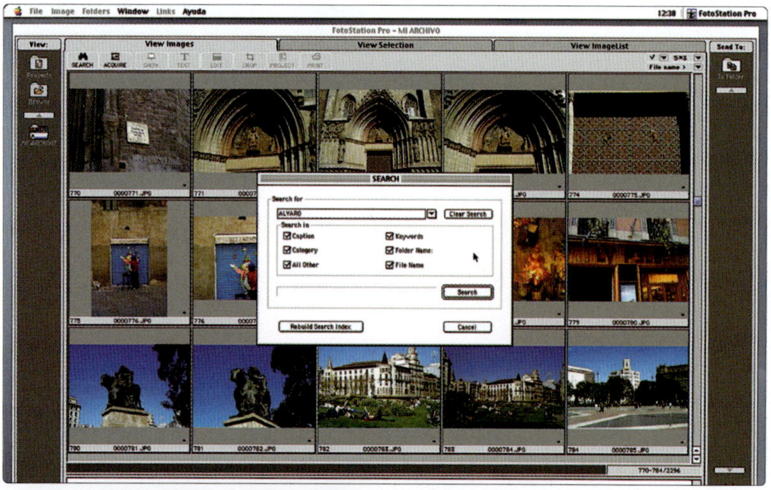

21 If you want to search the My Archive file for an individual picture, like the one marked Alvaro...

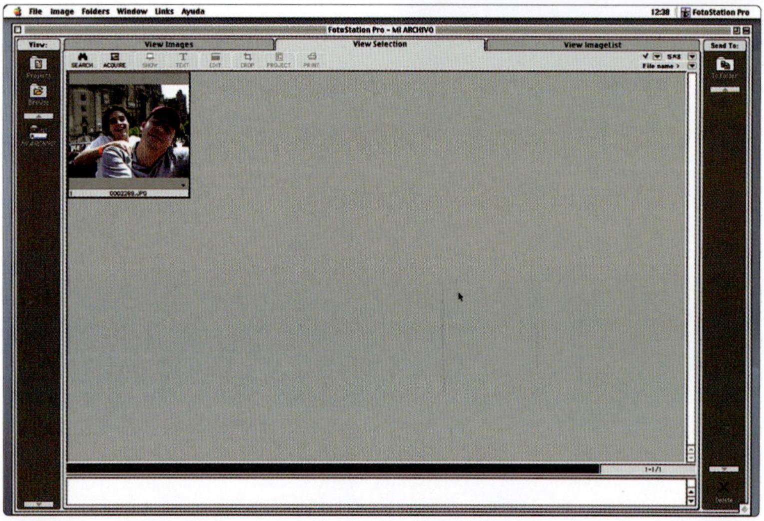

22 ...the program will show you only the picture that is marked that way.

Now let's look at the free services for archiving and sharing photographs that are offered by some large websites. They allow you to present selected photographs. As an example we explain the service offered by Yahoo (www.yahoo.com). It's necessary to have an open e-mail account at this website.

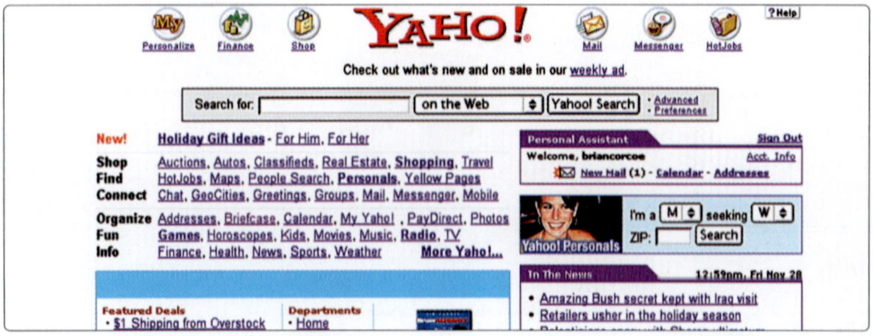

▸ **1** On the home page select the Briefcase service.

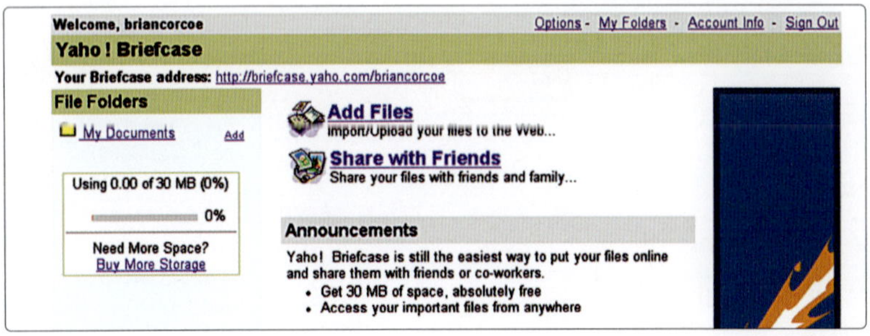

◂ **2** In the new window click on Add Files.

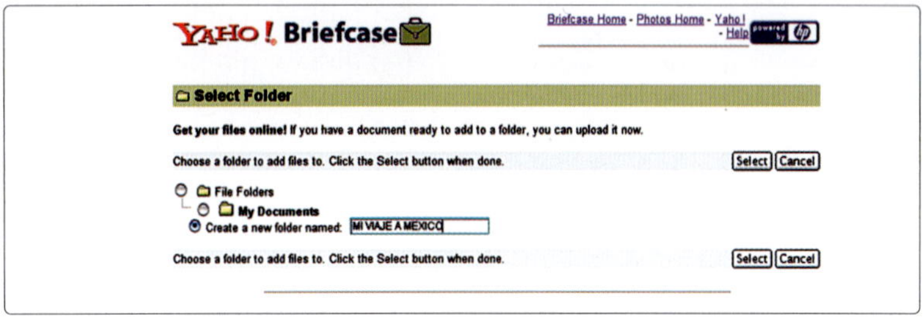

▸ **3** In the next window create a new folder for the pictures you want to share - here, for example, we chose the folder named Mexico. To continue, click on Select.

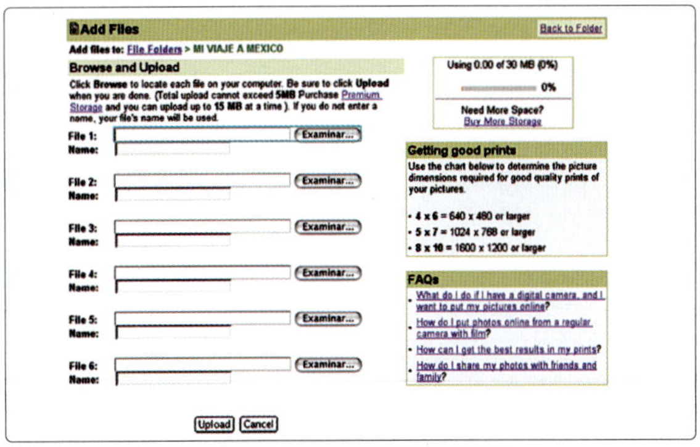

◂ **4** A menu will appear in which you have to choose one picture after another for sharing. You do this by clicking on Browse.

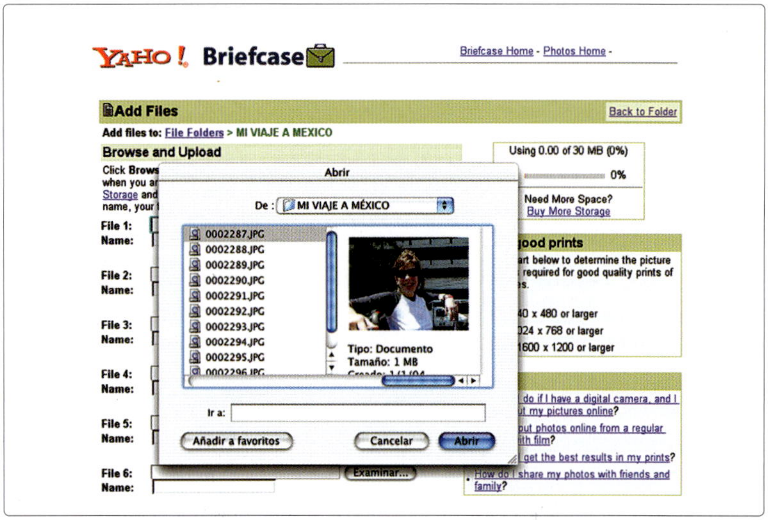

5 Select the first picture you want to present. Then repeat the same operation for all the pictures.

6 After selecting all the pictures click on Upload.

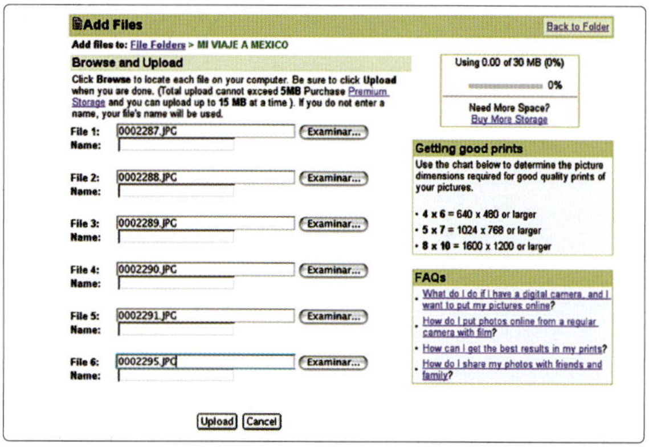

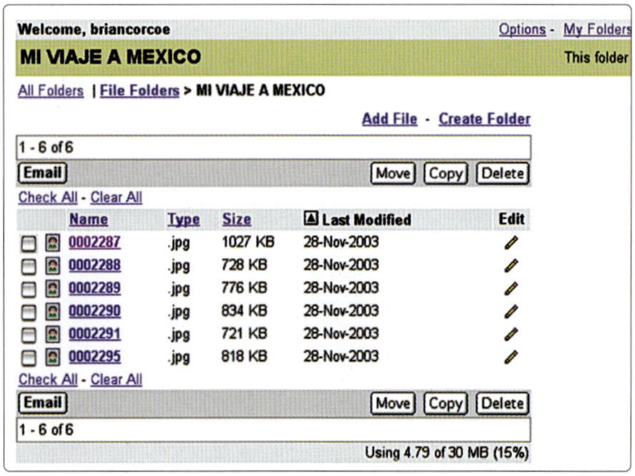

7 All of the photographs you selected appear on the website. The site has only limited space at its disposal. In the bottom right corner there is an indicator of remaining free space. In our case we needed 4.79 MB of the available 30 MB.

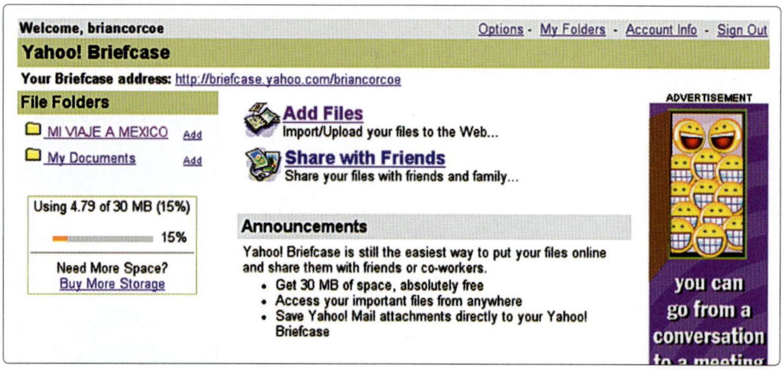

8 After uploading all your pictures you have to designate with whom you intend to share them. Return to the main Briefcase menu, which now contains the Mexico folder. Click on Share with Friends.

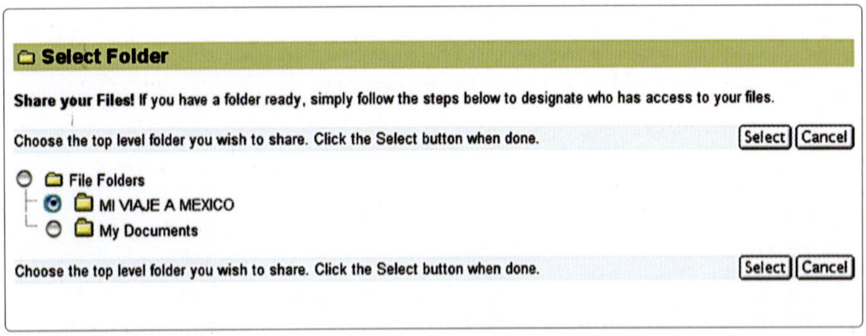

▸ **9** Select the folder you want to share – in this case Mexico – and click on Select.

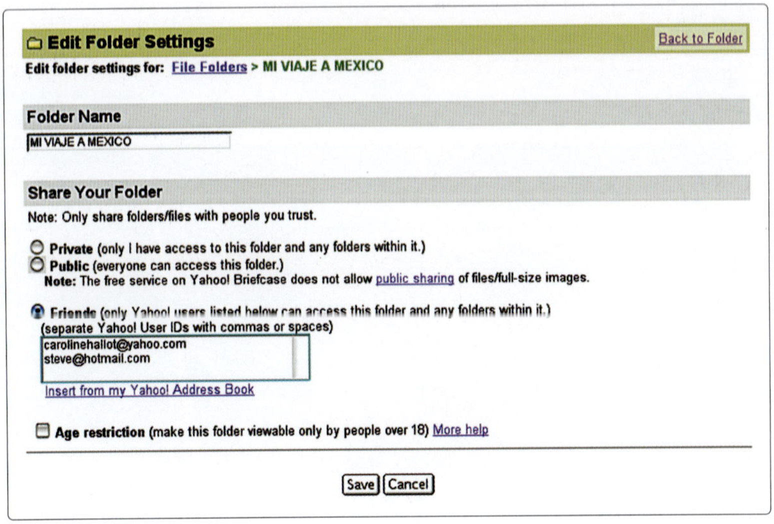

◂ **10** A new page with the Mexico folder will appear. Now select the people you want to share the pictures with. (This website allows you to share pictures only with people who have open e-mail accounts with Yahoo). Then click on Save.

▸ **11** When the people you have designated have been authorized to look at your photographs they can visit Briefcase in the main menu, where they can click on Share with Friends.

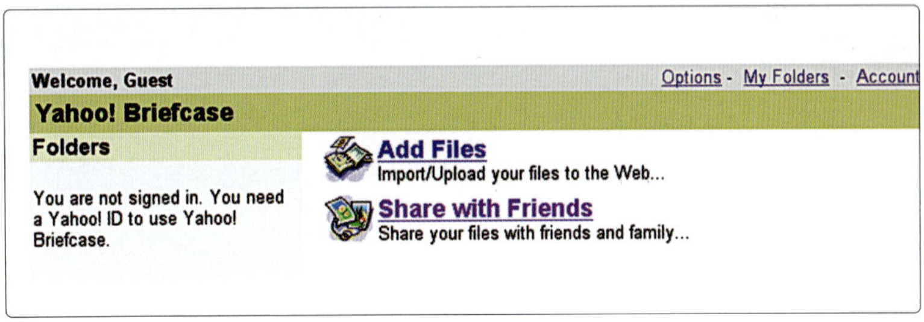

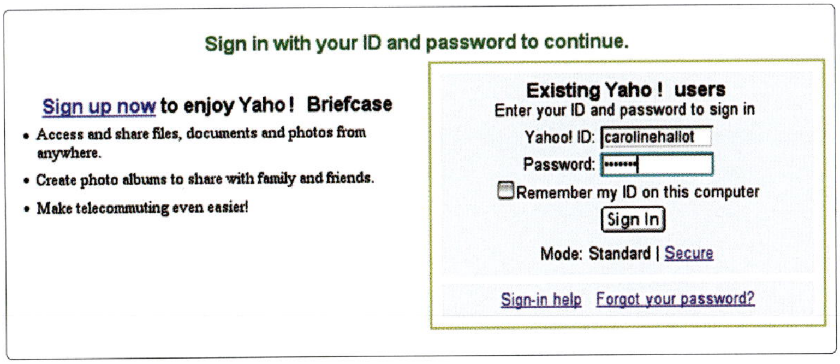

◂ **12** After the window for access to your account appears, enter your password and then click on Briefcase and Mexico.

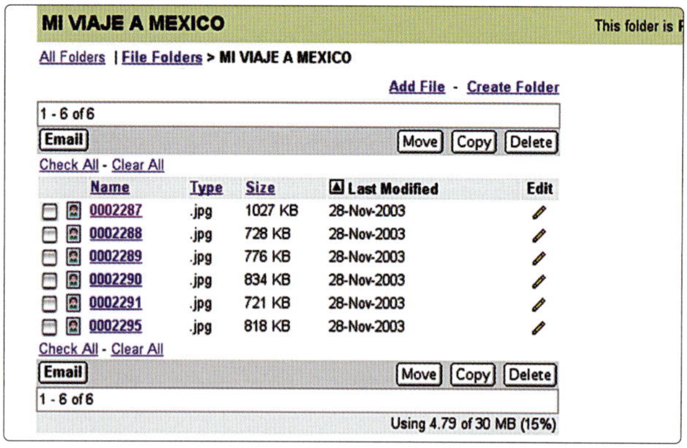

13 A list of the pictures in your briefcase will appear. Just click on the name of the picture you wish to view.

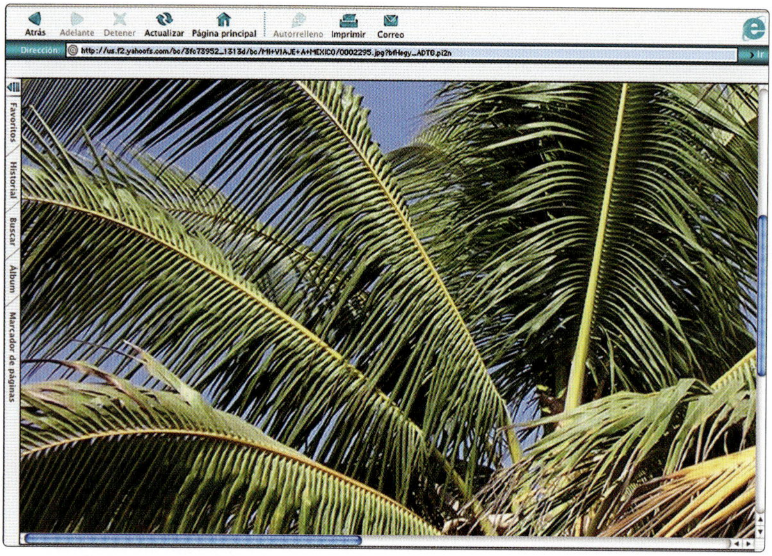

14 The selected picture will appear.

How to preserve digital photographs

It's good to save sorted and archived pictures on an external medium other than your computer's hard drive.
There are two reasons this is a good idea: it saves space in your computer's memory and you have your photographs securely stored.
Pictures create large files that take up lots of memory, but the capacity of computer hard drives is constantly increasing. Still, if you have saved all your pictures in your computer there may come a time when you have to delete some pictures to free up hard drive space.
As far as security goes, computers can have technical problems or come under virus attack, possibly resulting in the loss of your pictures.
To rule out this risk it's a good idea to save copies of pictures to CDs, DVDs, or external hard drives as soon as you can. Here we will briefly describe them to help you choose the best of the three types for your needs:

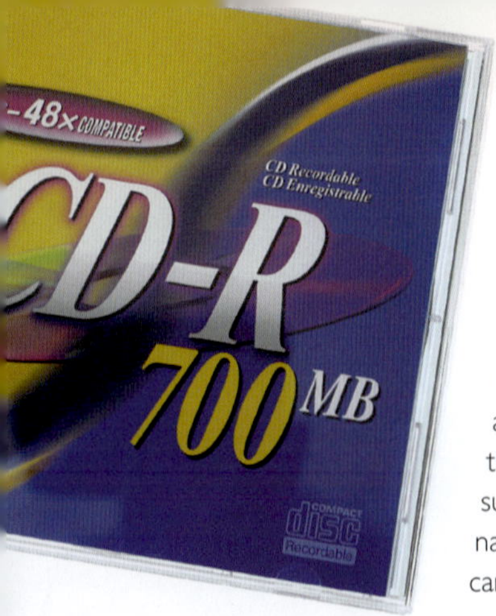

◂ CD (Compact Disc)

These discs are very reliable and are distinguished by their long lives. They generally have 700 MB of storage capacity and they're affordable. Today nearly every computer comes with a CD burner. There are a great many CD manufacturers, but the quality of their products isn't always equal. In order to be sure you're buying a high-quality product look for a brand name of a firm that you know also manufactures digital cameras or accessories.

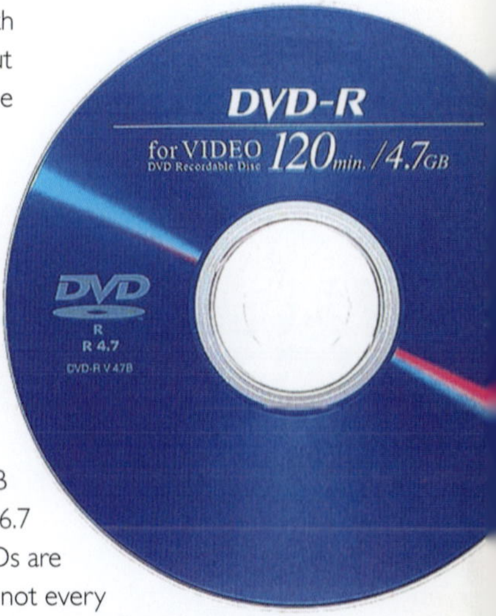

▸ DVD (Digital Versatile Disc)

Like CDs, DVDs are reliable media. But their great advantage over CDs is their substantially larger memory. While you can't store over 700 MB on a CD, you can store 4.7 GB on a DVD, about 6.7 times as much data as on a CD. However, DVDs are more expensive than CDs. One drawback is that not every computer comes with a built-in DVD burner, but you can buy peripheral devices. When shopping for DVDs we also recommend brands that are associated with digital photography products.

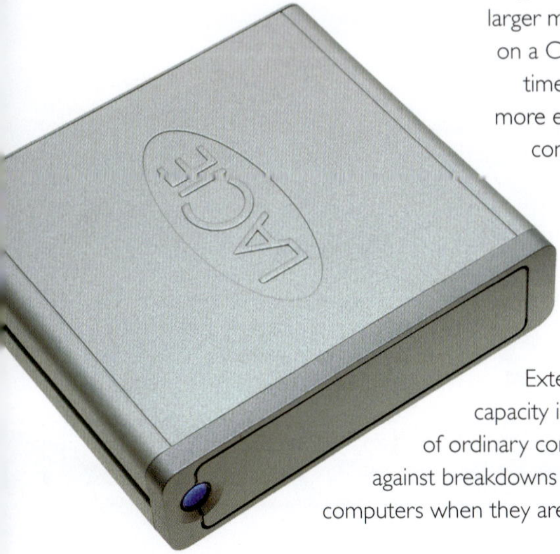

◂ External disc

External hard drives are attached to computers, and their storage capacity is enormous (some of them have several times the capacity of ordinary computers). Their disadvantage is that they are not protected against breakdowns or viruses because they are in direct contact with computers when they are hooked up.

How to use CDs and DVDs correctly

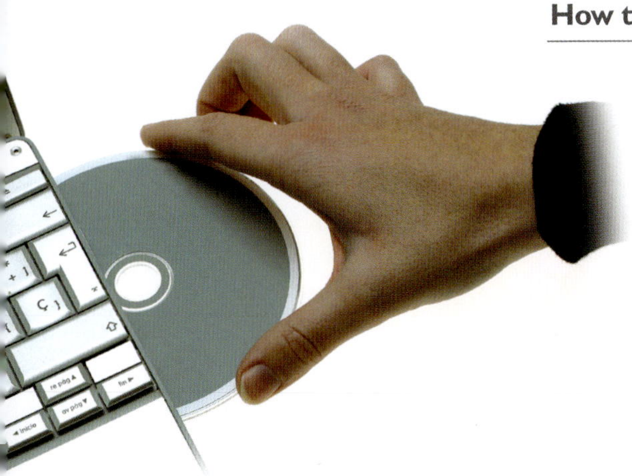

◂ **1** Burn the pictures saved in a folder onto a CD or a DVD. Depending on the type of disc – CD or DVD – you can record varying numbers of pictures. In order to avoid wasting disc space needlessly, wait to do the burning when you have enough pictures to fill the disc.

▸ **2** Once your pictures are saved to a disc, mark the disc with the numbers of the pictures for easy searching later on. Use an alcohol-based indelible marker to describe the contents. Don't use a marker with a hard, sharp tip!

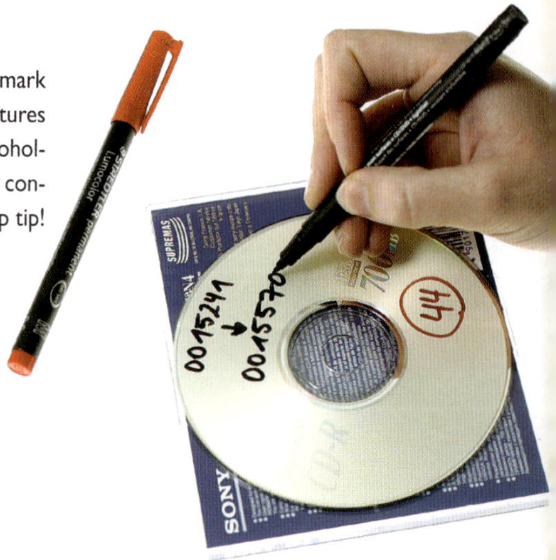

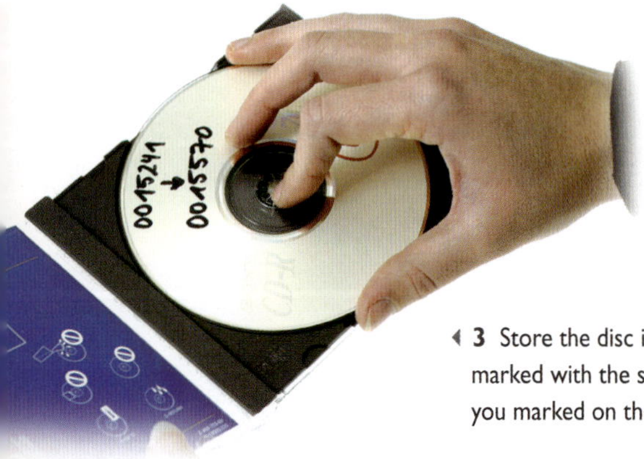

◂ **3** Store the disc in a sleeve marked with the same numbers you marked on the disc.

▸ **4** Or in a case in which you keep all the discs that constitute your archive of pictures.

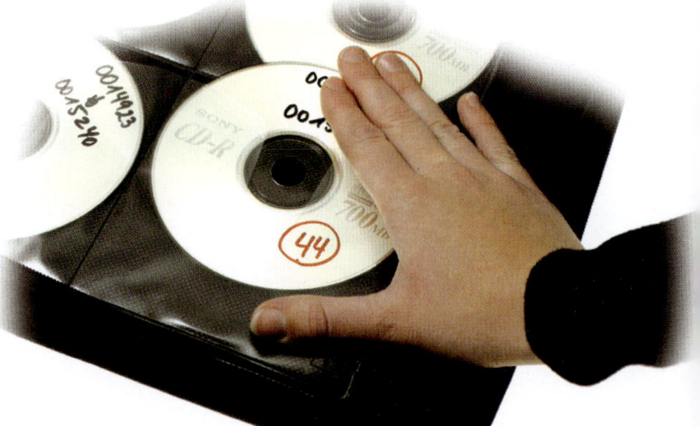

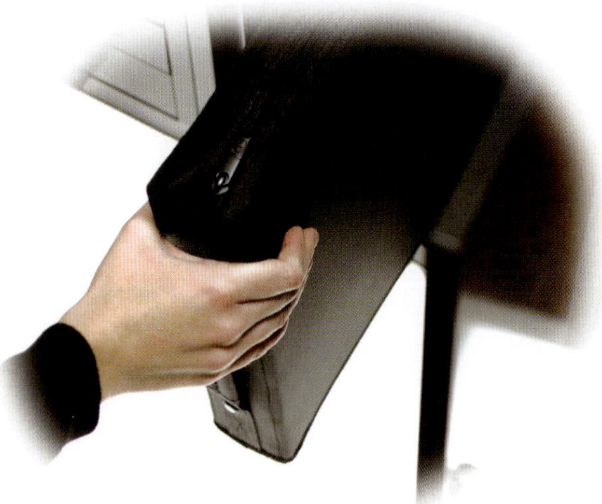

◂ **5** Finally, make sure your discs are stored in a place that is protected from direct sunlight and dust.

TOPIC 5 PRINTING POSSIBILITIES

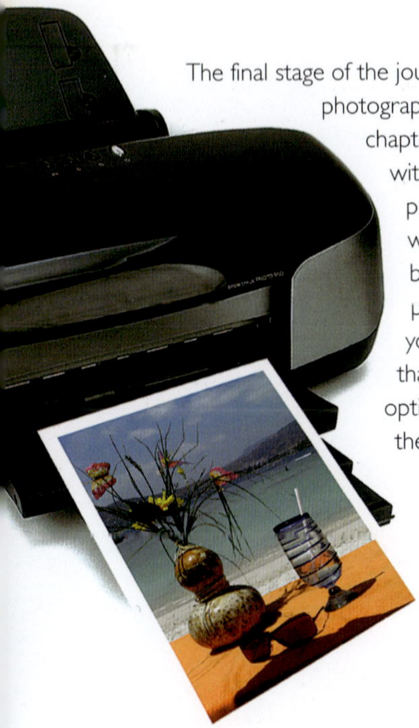

The final stage of the journey into the world of digital photography is printing pictures. In this chapter you'll become acquainted with various methods for printing digital photographs, with emphasis on the very best quality. Learn about the processes that lead to getting your own printed photographs, that is, the processes for optimizing pictures according to the type of printing selected.

To start, let's look at various types of existing printers. Ink-jet printers are the simplest and most widespread, and they are without a doubt the best adapted for most users. They can be simple office printers, but there are also much more complicated machines. Even though the prices of ink cartridges and special photographic paper are relatively high, the printers are often priced affordably, and if we use paper of desirable quality we can get very good pictures from these printers. Another virtue of these printers is the wide selection of all sorts of paper and ink.

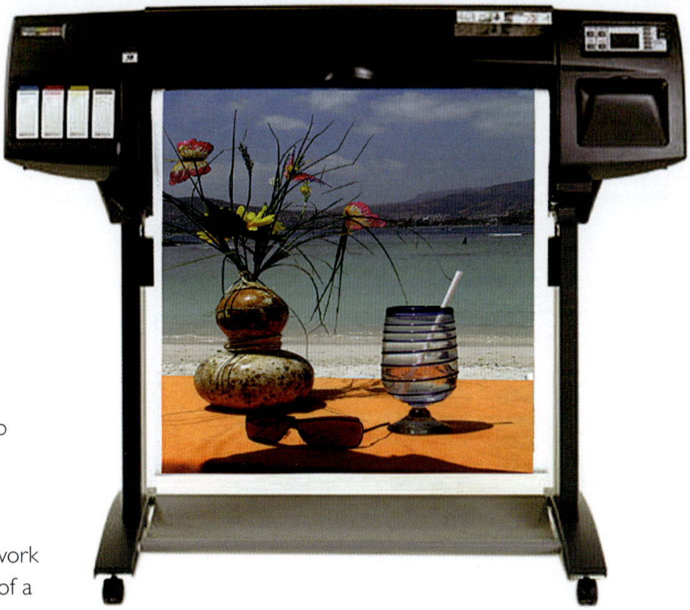

There are a great many printers designed to print up to A3 format. There are also printers for A4 format in which you can use rolls of paper, and this allows uninterrupted printing or prints of panoramas. Another type of ink-jet printer is a plotter. Plotters work just like office printers, but they have the advantage of a more extensive choice of colors in their ink cartridges – unlike office printers, which usually have three colors plus black in their cartridges. Plotter-generated prints are most often offered at photo labs. The equipment is too expensive for individuals to own, so it's more economical to take CDs to a photo lab for printing.

Don't forget that not all pictures are taken with resolution that is suitable for large-format printing. So it's a good idea to always ask what the ideal resolution is for a large-dimension photograph.

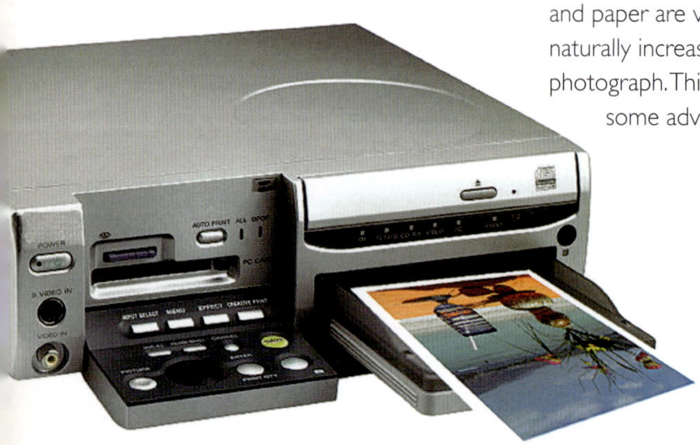

Although heat sublimation printers make outstanding prints possible, their drawback is that their maximum format size is 10 x 15 cm. Additionally, the inks and paper are very expensive, which naturally increases the final cost of each photograph. This type of printer also has some advantages: easy handling of pictures, and a port for the memory card of a camera. It can also download the needed data from a CD. Most of these printers can be connected to a camera and make prints directly from it.

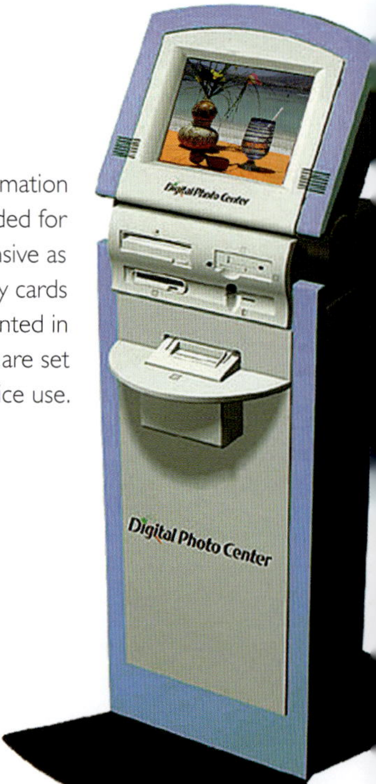

It's also worth noting that there are heat sublimation printers for larger pictures, but they aren't intended for home use. These printers are extremely expensive as they are built for professional laboratories; memory cards or CDs are inserted and photographs can be printed in various formats in a few minutes. Some of them are set up for self-service use.

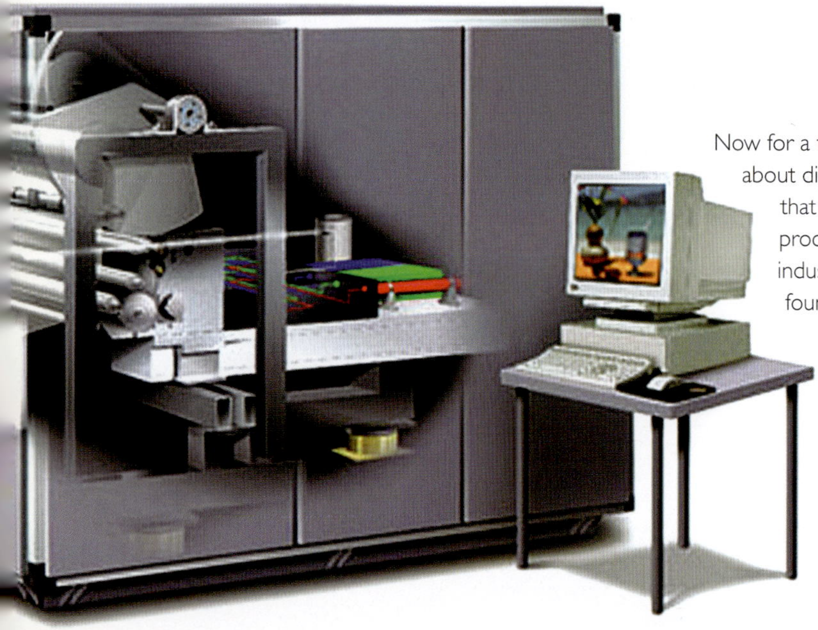

Now for a few words about digital printers that use chemical processes. These are industrial printers and are usually found in professional laboratories. Pictures are processed digitally on them too, but they use paper with a photosensitive layer, as in classic photography. With these printers you can print large-dimension pictures on photographic paper. The prices of such prints are constantly dropping, and there are now laboratories that accept pictures or files over the Internet and then send the printed pictures by regular mail.

Some advice in closing. Usually, a high-quality ink-jet printer is suitable for normal picture printing. Otherwise, many professional photographers have printers of this type in their studios, and their prices are affordable. For higher quality it's always possible to have your pictures printed in professional laboratories which offer higher quality prints.
It's essential that you use special paper for printing photographs in your printer. There are such papers of all sizes and qualities. To be sure you're choosing the right paper, read all the information on the package carefully. Always give precedence to paper made by the same company that made your printer – the results will be better, because brand-name papers are always the best adapted for printers of the same brand.

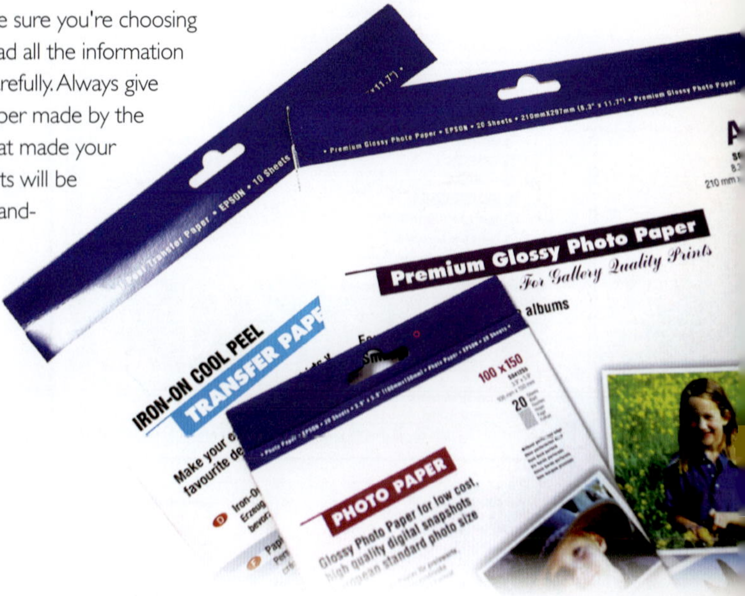

HOW TO PRINT PHOTOGRAPHS

There are two methods for printing on an ink-jet printer. The first method consists of simply using the program that is usually sold with the printer. The drawback is that the possibilities for adjusting brightness or contrast are limited. Everything is preset to make the procedure as simple and easily understood as possible. Just follow this procedure:

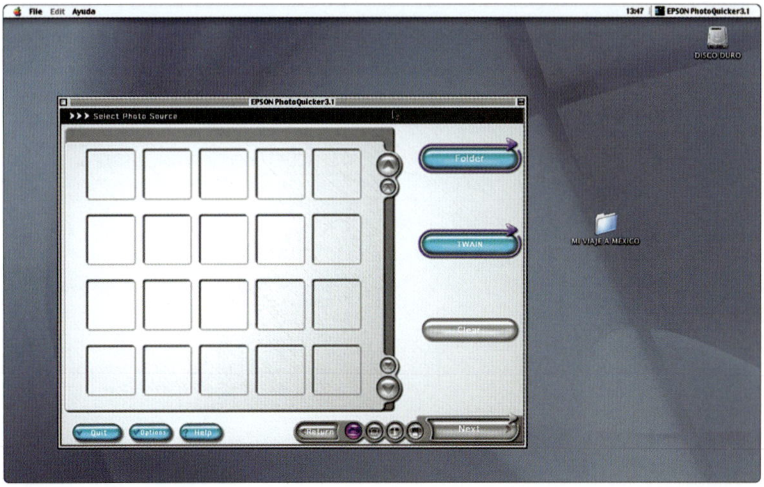

▸ **1** Turn on the program that came with the printer. Click on the Folder button at the top right.

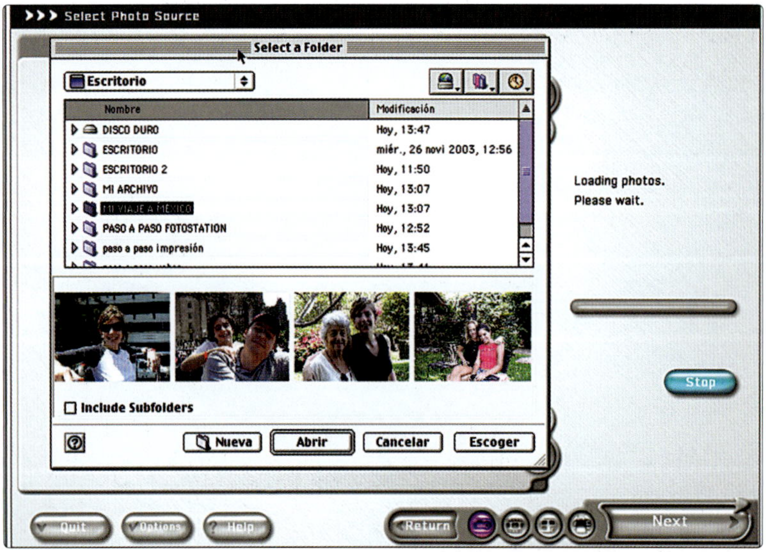

◂ **2** A window with the pictures you intend to print appears. Here, for example, they are in the Mexico folder.

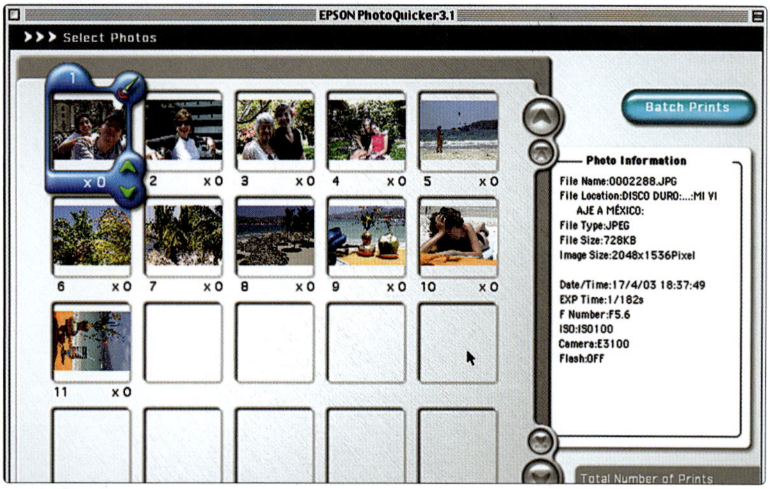

▸ **3** The program "pulls out" pictures from the selected folder.

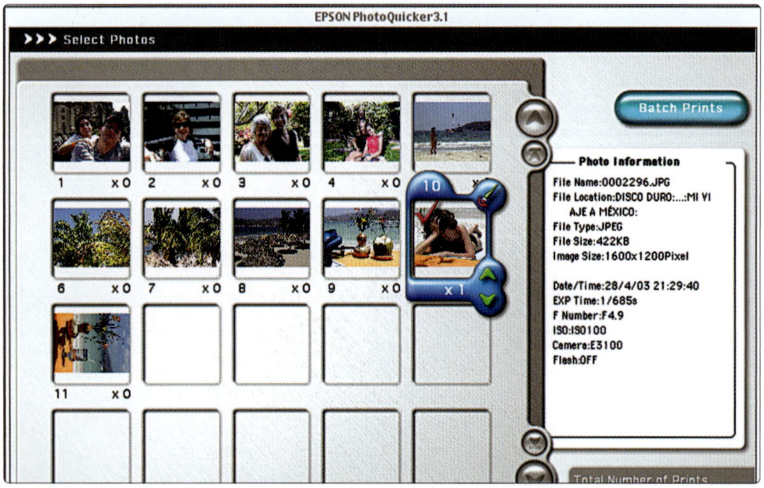

◂ **4** Click on the selected picture. Use the little blue borders that appear to set the number of copies. In our case we want only one print. Click on the Next button at the bottom right.

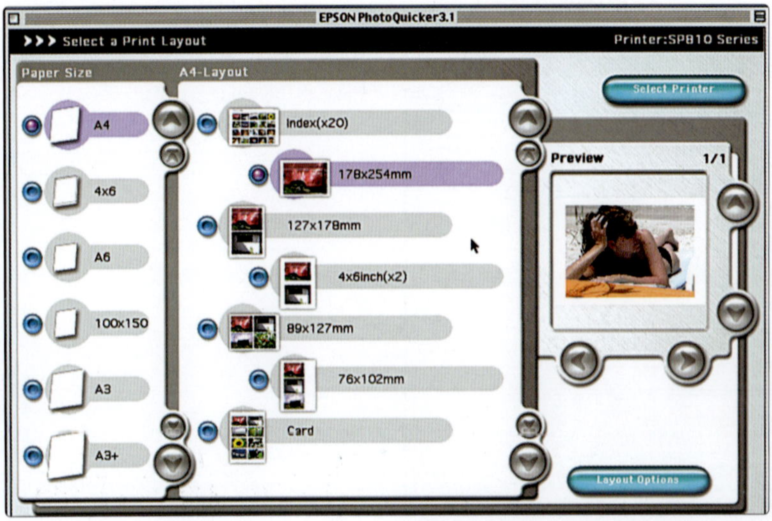

5 A new window appears in which you have to select the paper size and photograph format. Here we chose A4 paper and a photograph whose format corresponds to the paper size plus a white border. Click on the Print button at the bottom right.

Another method allows you to print directly from the image editing program. When the image has already been edited, before printing the picture you have to set a few parameters, like size. Proceed as follows to print from the image editing program:

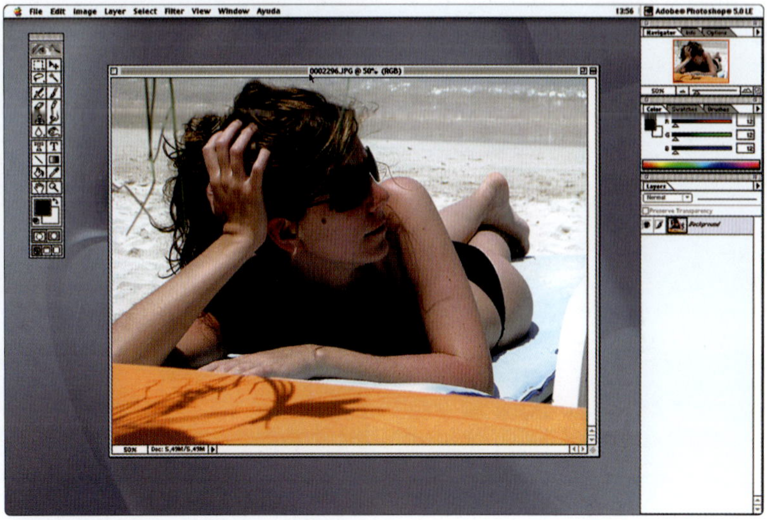

1 Open the photograph in the image editing program.

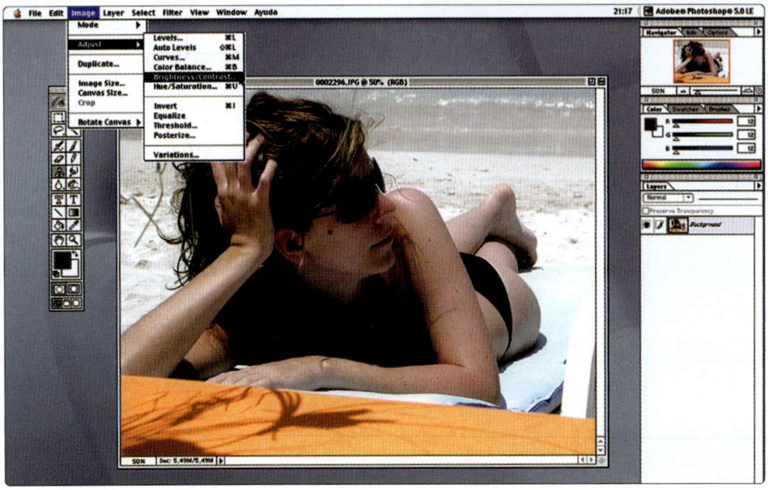

2 If necessary, adjust the contrast or brightness. To do this pull down the Image menu and click on Adjust and then Brightness/Contrast.

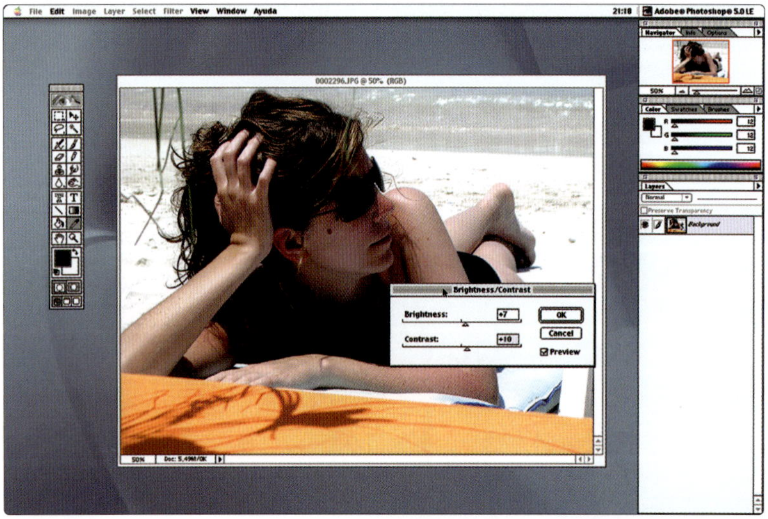

3 A dialogue box for image modifications will appear. Make all the modifications you consider useful.

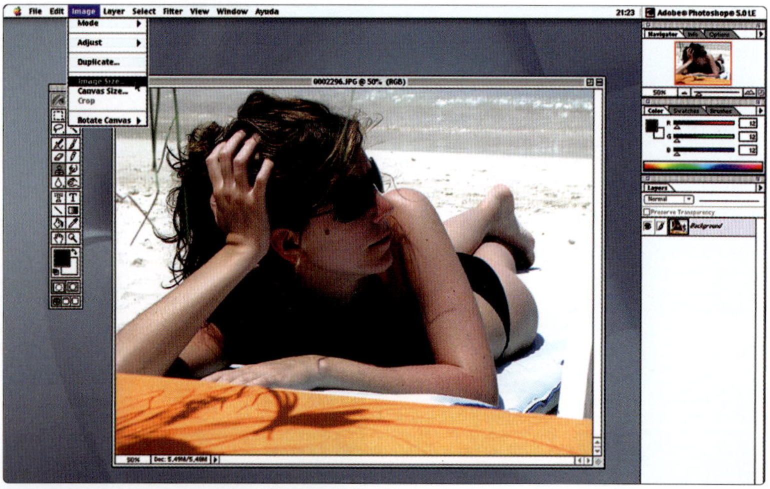

4 To set the desired size of the print, pull down the Image menu and click on Image Size.

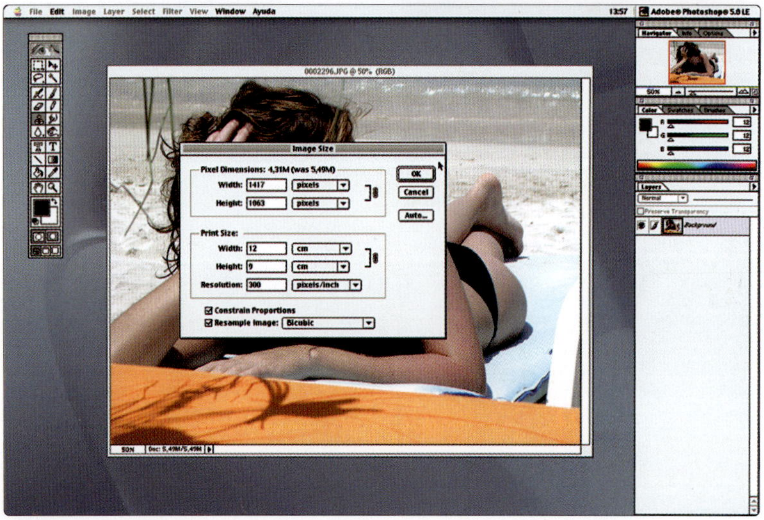

5 The Image Size dialogue box will appear. Select the desired size and resolution for the printed image. The resolution will depend on which printer you use.

▸ **6** Now save one copy of the document, but make sure the original isn't replaced by the modified picture. Pull down the File menu and click on Save As Always. Save the original, too, so that at any time in the future you can make new modifications.

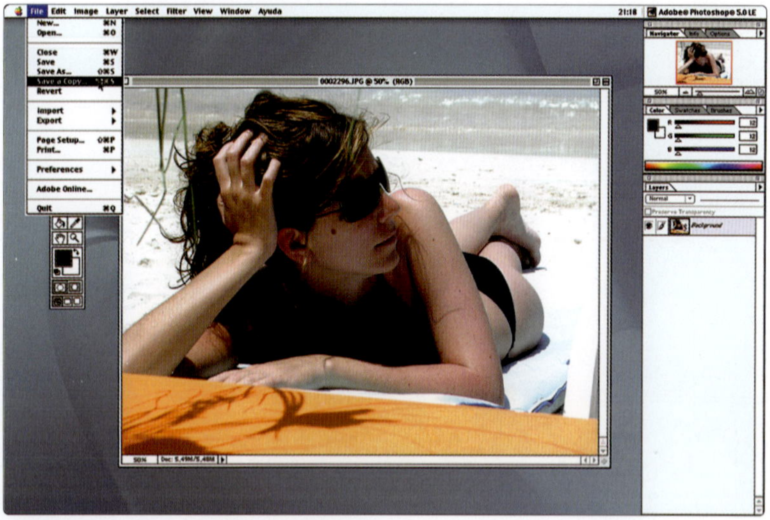

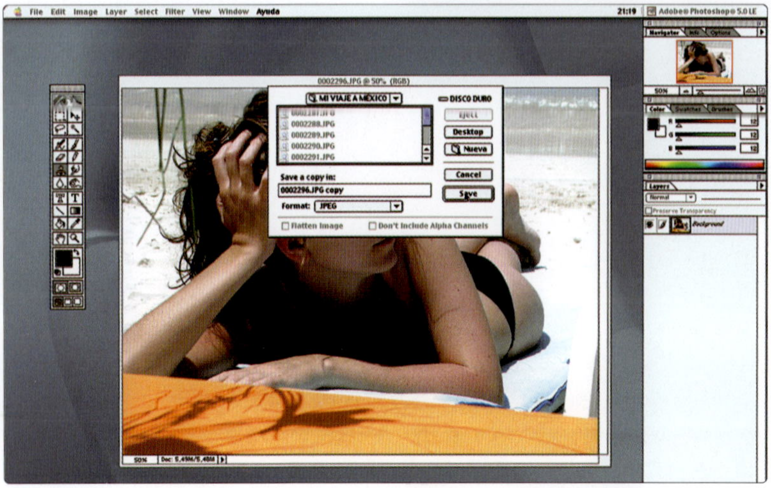

◂ **7** Select a folder to save the image in.

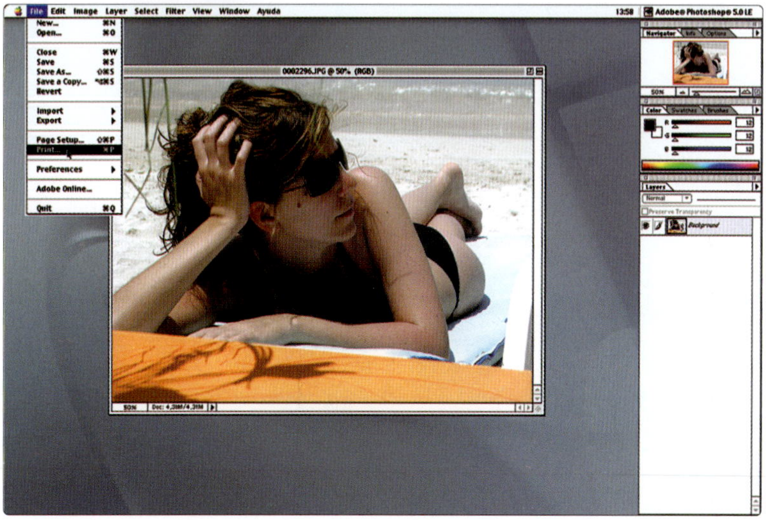

▸ **8** Print by clicking on Print in the File menu.